# EPICS AND MAHĀPURĀṆAS ON THE VEDIC SACRIFICE

# EPICS AND MAHĀPURĀṆAS ON THE VEDIC SACRIFICE

Madhavi R. Narsalay

Aryan Books International
New Delhi

Epics and Mahāpurāṇas on the Vedic Sacrifice

ISBN: 978-81-7305-527-0



Published in **2015** by

Aryan Books International

Pooja Apartments, 4B, Ansari Road, New Delhi-110 002 (India)

Tel.: 23287589, 23255799; Fax: 91-11-23270385

E-mail: aryanbooks@gmail.com

**www.aryanbooks.co.in**

Designed and Printed in India by

ABI Prints & Publishing Co., New Delhi

Dedicated to Dr. S.A. Dange and
Dr. (Mrs.) S.S. Dange
My Parvati-parmeshvarau.

सिन्धुसदाशिवौ नत्वा शिवाविव शिवप्रदौ ।
तदाशिषा फलितं ग्रन्थं ताभ्यामेव समर्पये ॥

# Preface

Literary works reflect the ideals, customs and practices prevalent during their times. This is evident in the case of Vedic sacrifices which was an integral part of Vedic religion in Ancient India. Rules and regulations of performing the Vedic sacrifice have been documented in the Saṁhitā-s, Brāhmaṇa-s and the Śrautasūtra-s. But, it is interesting to observe and then analyse the references to the Vedic sacrifice in texts other than specialized texts on Vedic sacrifice.

Ritual is a concrete expression of the principles of any religion. It is the institution of Vedic sacrifice through which the Vedic religion is expressed. In due course of time the sacrifice underwent modifications. Literary works can serve as tools in tracking the changes faced by this institution. Hinduism, which owes its roots to the Vedic religion, is also an outcome of various changes which the Vedic religion underwent. The reflections of Vedic sacrifice in Ancient India, observed in the Sanskrit texts, viz. the Epics, Mahāpurāṇa-s, Classical Sanskrit Mahākāvya-s and dramas, help in understanding the changes which have contributed to the development of Hinduism.

As a student of Sanskrit, I had studied some passages from the Brāhmaṇa-s which described some sacrificial procedures. I had wondered as to how Vedic religion has modified itself into Hinduism. To answer these questions the study of Vedic sacrifice was inevitable. Therefore, when this topic was suggested to me for the doctorate degree by Dr. S.A. Dange, it touched my heart and stimulated my intellect.

I express my indebtedness to Dr. S.A. Dange, the eminent Indologist (former R.G. Bhandarkar Professor and Head, Department of Sanskrit, University of Mumbai), who took active interest in this topic and gave me an insight in handling this subject. I still cherish the memories of prolonged discussions on different aspects of this topic and the valuable points which he suggested for my work, before he left for the heavenly abode. He was always concerned about my work and had looked forward for its completion. This is a debt which can never be repaid! Had Dr. S.A. Dange not suggested the topic and given insights, I would not have indulged into this subject. Words fall short to express gratitude and indebtedness to Dr. S.A. Dange, I dedicate this book to him.

I acknowledge my deepest gratitude to Dr. (Smt.) S.S. Dange, reputed Indologist (former R.G. Bhandarkar Professor and Head, Department of Sanskrit, University of Mumbai), who has been my teacher and guiding light. She has been with me right from the inception of this book. After the sad demise of Dr. S.A. Dange, she took keen interest in my research work and provided me different dimensions for this subject. This book is an outcome of her continuous encouragement and support in times of difficulty and anguish. She has several times gone through the chapters and given valuable suggestions. She spent her invaluable time and energy and also set aside her personal project for the book to be in proper form. I recall long hours of discussion at her place and on telephone on different issues pertaining to Vedic sacrificial rituals as well as Epics and Mahapuranas, which were like *upa+ni+sad*. I dedicate my book to her.

I take this opportunity to express my thanks to my guide Dr. (Smt.) A.B. Bakre (former R.G. Bhandarkar Professor and Head, Department of Sanskrit, University of Mumbai), who has encouraged me in this endeavour. Dr. (Smt.) A.B. Bakre initiated me in the field of research on 10th March 1990, when she introduced the library of Ramnarain Ruia College to me. This actually crafted the course of my academic career. As a guide, she stressed the importance of systematic reference work.

I express sincere thanks to the University of Mumbai for permitting me to publish the thesis titled "Reflections of Vedic Sacrifice in India (as seen from Epics, Mahapuranas, Classical Sanskrit Dramas and Mahakavyas)" in this book form.

I am thankful to Dr. (Smt.) Gauri Mahulikar (Head, Department of Sanskrit, University of Mumbai), who has been my teacher and is my senior colleague at present. She has always been very cooperative and motivating.

I thank the Library staff of the Jawaharlal Nehru Library and Rajabai Tower Library of the University of Mumbai as well as the Library staff of the Asiatic Society of Mumbai.

I owe my thanks to Dr. Laurie Patton (Professor, Emory University, Atlanta, U.S.A.), who promptly sent photocopies of books as well as Dr. Urmila Patil for sending me articles, which I required for my study.

I express gratitude to the scholastic works of Mm. P.V. Kane, Dr. S.A. Dange, Dr. (Smt.) S.S. Dange, Dr. T.N. Dharmadhikari, Prof. Alex Heesterman, Dr. Fredrick Smith, Rev. Israel Selvanayagam and all those, whose names and titles have been incorporated by me in the bibliography. The photographs of the sacrificial implements from the book 'Yajnayudhani' ed. by Dr. Dharmadhikari has helped clear many concepts of Vedic sacrifice. I am indebted to the unknown seers of Vedic literature and the composers of the Śrautasūtra-s, who documented the rituals in a systematic way for a researcher of the 21st century to study.

I convey my indebtedness to Shri Girish Jani (Deputy Director, Bharatiya Vidya Bhavan's Post-graduate & Research Department), for his help in composing the title verse. I am grateful to Dr. Prachi Moghe for the valuable help she rendered in the course of this work.

I am thankful to my husband Raghav Narsalay for his continuous encouragement in this work and for acting like a task-master to correct errors in the work. I am also thankful to my parents and in-laws for being extremely helpful to me. Last, but not the least, I am thankful to Maitreyi, my daughter, for being so patient.

Shri Vikas Arya of Aryan Books International agreed to publish this work. I am grateful to him. I am thankful to Shalaka Patil for designing the cover of this volume.

I will consider myself to be fortunate, if this study is a help in understanding the change and continuity of Hinduism, through the changes faced over a period of time by the VEDIC SACRIFICE.

Devabodhini Ekadashi **Madhavi R. Narsalay**

# Contents

# List of Abbreviations

| | | |
|---|---|---|
| *AIRSC* | : | *Ancient Indian Rituals in their Social Contents* |
| *Ait. Br* | : | *Aitareya Brāhmaṇa* |
| *AITM* | : | *Ancient Indian Tradition and Mythology* |
| Anu. | : | Anuṣaṅgapāda |
| Anu. P | : | Anuśāsana Parvan |
| *Āp. Śr. Sū* | : | *Āpastamba Śrauta Sūtra* |
| Aran | : | Araṇyakāṇḍa |
| Āśr. P | : | Āśramavāsika Parvan |
| *Āṣṭādh* | : | *Āṣṭādhyāyī* |
| *Āśv. Gṛ. Sū* | : | *Āśvalāyana Gṛhya Sūtra* |
| Āśv. P | : | Āśvamedhika Parvan |
| *Āśv. Śr. Sū* | : | *Āśvalāyana Śrauta Sūtra* |
| *AV* | : | *Atharvaveda* |
| *AV Pariśiṣṭa* | : | *Atharvaveda Pariśiṣṭa* |
| Ayo | : | Ayodhyākāṇḍa |
| Bāl | : | Bālakāṇḍa |
| *Baudh. Śr. Sū* | : | *Baudhāyana Śrauta Sūtra* |
| *Bhāg. Pu* | : | *Bhāgavata Purāṇa* |
| *Bhav. Pu* | : | *Bhaviṣya Purāṇa* |

| | | |
|---|---|---|
| BORI | : | Bhandarkar Oriental Research Institute |
| *Brahmavai. Pu* | : | *Brahmavaivarta Purāṇa* |
| *BSK* | : | *Bharatiya Sanskriti Kosha* |
| Dr. P | : | Droṇa Parvan |
| *Drā. Śr. Sū* | : | *Drāhyāyaṇa Śrauta Sūtra* |
| *DVR* | : | *Dictionary of Vedic Rituals* |
| ed. | : | Edition |
| fn | : | Footnote |
| *Gar. Pu* | : | *Garuḍa Purāṇa* |
| *Gautama DSū* | : | *Gautama Dharma Sūtra* |
| *Gop. Br* | : | *Gopatha Brāhmaṇa* |
| *HDS* | : | *History of Dharmaśāstra-s* |
| Intro | : | Introduction |
| *Jai. Br* | : | *Jaiminīya Brāhmaṇa* |
| *Jai. UB* | : | *Jaiminīya Upaniṣad- Brāhmaṇa* |
| *JAOS* | : | *Journal of the American Oriental Society* |
| *Kāt. Sam* | : | *Kāṭhaka Saṁhitā* |
| *Kāt. Śr. Sū* | : | *Kātyāyana Śrauta Sūtra* |
| Kṣkindhā | : | Kiṣkindhākāṇḍa |
| *Kū. Pu* | : | *Kūrma Purāṇa* |
| *Lāt. Śr. Sū* | : | *Lāṭyāyana Śrauta Sūtra* |
| M. Pu | : | Mahāpurāṇa |
| *Mānava Śr. Sū* | : | *Mānava Śrauta Sūtra* |
| *Manu. Sm* | : | *Manu Smṛti* |
| *Mārk. Pu* | : | *Mārkaṇḍeya Purāṇa* |
| *Mat. Pu* | : | *Matsya Purāṇa* |
| *Mbh* | : | *Mahābhārata* |
| MLBD | : | Motilal Banarasidass |
| Nār.Pu | : | *Nārada Purāṇa* |
| OUP | : | Oxford University Press |
| p. | : | Page number |
| P | : | Parvan |
| *Pad. Pu* | : | *Padma Purāṇa* |
| Prak | : | Prakṛtikhaṇḍa |
| Pu | : | Purāṇa |
| Pūrva | : | Pūrvārdha |

| | | |
|---|---|---|
| *Rām* | : | *Rāmāyaṇa* |
| Rep | : | Reprint |
| rev | : | Revised edition |
| *Rudra* | : | *Rudrasaṁhitā* |
| *RV* | : | *Ṛgveda* |
| Śal. P | : | Śalya Parvan |
| Śān. P | : | Śānti Parvan |
| *Śān. Śr. Su* | : | *Śaṅkhāyana Śrauta Sūtra* |
| Śat. Br | : | *Śatapatha Brāhmaṇa* |
| Satī | : | Satīkhaṇḍa |
| *Satyāṣāḍha Śr. Su* | : | *Satyāṣāḍha Śrauta Sūtra* |
| Sau. P | : | Sauptika Parvan |
| *Ska. Pu* | : | *Skanda Purāṇa* |
| Sundara | : | Sundarakāṇḍa |
| *SV* | : | *Sāmaveda* |
| *Tait. Br* | : | *Taittirīya Brāhmaṇa* |
| *Tait. Sam* | : | *Taittirīya Saṁhitā* |
| *Tān. MBr* | : | *Tāṇḍya Mahābrāhmaṇa* |
| tr | : | Translation |
| Ud.P | : | Udyoga Parvan |
| Umā | : | Umāsaṁhitā |
| Upa | : | Upasaṁhāra |
| Upo | : | Upodghāta |
| Utt | : | Uttarakāṇḍa/Uttarārdha |
| *Vaitāna Śr. Sū* | : | *Vaitāna Śrauta Sūtra* |
| *Vāj. Sam* | : | *Vājasaneyī Saṁhitā* |
| *Vām. Pu* | : | *Vāmana Purāṇa* |
| Van. P | : | Vana Parvan |
| Vid | : | Vidyeśvara Saṁhitā |
| *VSEN* | : | *Vedic Sacrifices: Early Nature* |
| *VVRI* | : | *Journal of the Viveshvaranand Vishvabandhu Research Institute* |
| *Yāj. Sm* | : | *Yājñavalkya Smṛti* |
| Yuddha | : | Yuddhakāṇḍa |
| Yud. | : | Yuddhakhaṇḍa |
| *YV* | : | *Yajurveda* |

# 1

# Introduction

Historically, civilizations have been understood better through rituals and practices followed by their people. Vedic civilization is one of the ancient civilizations of the world which had developed its own rituals and practices, in the form of sacrifices. Thus, sacrifice has been integral to the Vedic civilization. According to Bhattacharyya, "The beliefs and ideals in different civilizations are often formulated in their rituals more explicitly than in any other cultural trait, and this gives to the study of ritualism a deeper historical significance."[1] It is in this context that studies of Vedic sacrificial rituals form an important part of the study of the Vedic civilization.

The crux of Vedic civilization lies in its sacrificial rituals, which are predominantly based on the power of the utterances of the mantra-s incorporated in the texts. Rituals became complex and voluminous. Textual material developed in the form of Saṁhitā-s, Brāhmaṇa-s and Śrautasūtra-s have recorded and systematized rituals, so as to maintain them in their purest form. In spite of the tedious task undertaken by these texts, it is observed that the Vedic sacrifice has shown a significant change over a period of time. The present work aims at tracking these changes taken place in the Vedic sacrificial rituals.

It is important to understand some terms before proceeding to further details.

## EXPLANATION OF THE TERM 'VEDIC'

The term 'Vedic' stands for a language, i.e. Vedic Sanskrit, which is more archaic than that of the epics, viz. the *Rām* and the *Mbh* as well as the classical Sanskrit literature, the refined language bound by the rules of Pāṇini, the Sanskrit grammarian. The term 'Vedic' does not stand merely for language but also its culture. According to Jamison, "Given the nature of our evidence, what we primarily know about this culture is its religion. Political, social, economic and quotidian matters we know in general only as they were filtered through a religious lens, but 'religion' here is to be broadly defined. It profoundly affected most areas of what might today be considered secular life, and we are therefore luckily in possession of much incidental information in these areas"[2]. The crux of Vedic religion lies in its sacrificial rituals. The Vedic texts have to be the foundation of understanding the change and continuity of Vedic religion. Therefore, the term 'Vedic' needs to be understood in the context of a unique combination of language (of the Vedic texts) and religion and is therefore a *lingual-religious* term.

### DEFINITION OF THE TERM 'SACRIFICE'

Etymologically, the term 'sacrifice' (*sacer* – 'holy'; *facere* – 'to make') carries the connotation of the religious act in the highest or fullest sense. It can also be understood as the act of sanctifying or consecrating an object[3]. Sacrifice is seen as a structured performance of rituals in a specific order with a specific purpose. Smith has defined sacrifice as a coordinated and extended series of ritual actions, Vedic recitations and offerings of different kinds[4]. The dictionary meaning of 'sacrifice' is as follows: Primarily, the slaughter of an animal (often including the subsequent consumption of it by fire) as an offering to God or a deity. Hence, in a wider sense the surrender to God or a deity, for the purpose of propitiation or homage, of some object of possession.... In the primary use, 'a sacrifice' implies an 'altar' on which the victim is placed. Hence, the figurative uses are often associated with references to a metaphorical altar[5].

Sacrifice, i.e. *yajña* (√*yaj* + verbal derivative affix '*naṅ*[6]') or *yāga* (√*yaj* +verbal derivative affix '*ghañ*') comprises of three propositions: *dravya* (material), *devatā* (deity) and *tyāga* (offering)[7]. This is explained by the commentators as 'the offerings of oblations to the deities may be regarded as sacrifice'. This definition serves the purpose of giving a general idea of sacrifice. The sacrifice involves a deity, which is invoked during a sacrifice; a material, which comprises of milk or curds, clarified butter, cake made up of grains (rice/barley) known as the *puroḍāśa,* animal offerings, etc; the act of offering given to the deity with the help of mantra-s.

After discussing the connotations of the main terms, it is necessary to add that the term 'Vedic sacrifice' is understood in the sense of the sacrificial rituals incorporated in the Śrauta tradition [Kane has used the term 'Vedic sacrifice' as Śrauta (Vedic) Sacrifice] and not in the Gṛhya tradition[8]. Study of the Gṛhya tradition can be handled as a separate topic.

The Saṁhitā-s have recorded the sacrifices, and the Brāhmaṇa texts have served as manuals on the sacrifices. The nature of the Vedic sacrifice has never remained static. It has undergone many changes. By the period of the Śrautasūtra-s, it became complex and voluminous. In order to understand the nature of the sacrifice, it is essential to have an in-depth study of these three branches of literature on Vedic sacrifice.

This study would be incomplete without understanding the position of Vedic sacrifice in other branches of Sanskrit literature. Sanskrit language provides a vast panorama of literature. It is very difficult to cover every branch of literature. So the texts taken up for study are the *Rām*, the *Mbh*, the Mahāpurāṇa-s and classical Sanskrit dramas and Mahākāvya-s. The references to the Vedic sacrifice occurring in these texts are taken up for study.

## TIME SPAN OF THE TEXTS

The dates of the composition of these texts are discussed in the chapters of the work. The composition of the *Rām* seems to have been complete near about 300 AD. The *Mbh* with all its redactions seems to have been complete near about 1st century AD. The dates of these texts have been discussed in detail in their respective chapters. This indicates that *Rām* as a text is post-dated to the *Mbh*. However, the story of prince Rāma, i.e. Rāmakathā was well known even during the composition of the *Mbh* (Van. P. 273-91). Taking into account the existence of this story prior to the composition of the *Mbh* the rituals of sacrifice in the *Rām* have been discussed before those of sacrifice in the *Mbh*.

The eighteen M.Pu-s taken up for study are: 1) *Vāyu* 2) *Brahmāṇḍa* 3) *Mārkaṇḍeya* 4) *Viṣṇu* 5) *Matsya* 6) *Bhāgavata* 7) *Kūrma* 8) *Vāmana* 9) *Liṅga* 10) *Varāha* 11) *Padma* 12) *Nārada* 13) *Agni* 14) *Garuḍa* 15) *Brahma* 16) *Skanda* 17) *Brahmavaivarta* 18) *Bhaviṣya*. The date of the composition of the M. Pu.-s is broadly classified into two, viz. the upper limit and the lower limit. Apart from the *Mārk*, *Viṣṇu* and the *Bhāg* M.Pu-s, the lower limit of the M. Pu.-s is after

10th century AD. The upper limit of the *Brahma Pu* is 10th century AD. The time of the composition of the *Naiṣadhīyacarita* is 12th century AD. It is important to understand that the upper limit of the composition of the Mahāpurāṇa-s, barring the *Brahma Pu* is before 10th century AD. Besides this the Mahāpurāṇa-s are considered as one single branch of literature. Hence, the study of the Mahāpurāṇa-s has been taken up as one single unit.

The *Naiṣadhīyacarita* has its own place and importance in the five Mahākāvya-s of ornate Sanskrit poetry. It has been regarded as one among the five *prāṇa*-s, i.e. vital airs, of classical Sanskrit literature. In order to understand Vedic sacrificial rituals in ornate Sanskrit poetry, an Appendix has been added in this work, with a special focus on the Mahākāvya-s of Sanskrit literature, including *Naiṣadhīyacarita*. Therefore, to maintain homogeneity in the textual matter, the transgression of period is not taken into account.

## VEDIC SACRIFICE HAS A SPECIFIC TYPOLOGY ACCORDING TO WESTERN NOTION

To understand the nature of Vedic sacrifice it is necessary to know its typology. Typology is the study of types as in a systematic classification. Typology is also a theory of doctrine of types as in scriptural studies. Typology or morphology is also understood as a study of the structure and form of living organisms[9]. Western scholars have studied the nature of Vedic sacrifice. It is essential to understand the nature of Vedic sacrifice in order to elucidate a soteriological background of the texts referred to in this work. Therefore, it is necessary to present a typology of sacrifice[10].

- Sacrificer
- Sacrificial fire

- Offering
- External forms which belong to the act of offering, i.e. whether the sacrifice incorporates animal offering or offerings of milk products or the sacrificial cake.
- The place and time of the offering
- The recipient of the offering
- The purpose behind the sacrifice
- The fruit derived.

The following is an elaboration on each of these points.

## The Sacrificer

Most religions allow not only sacrifices offered by a group or community, but also individual sacrifices for entirely personal reasons; in an unstratified society, therefore everyone is in principle able to offer sacrifices. In fact, however, such purely personal sacrifices are rare and as soon as sacrifices become connected with a group, however, small, not every member of the group but only a representative may offer them. The sacrificer may be the head of a family or clan, an elder, or the leader of a band of hunters; in matrilineal societies, the sacrificer may be a woman. This is true especially of hunting and food-gathering cultures as well as nomadic pastoral cultures, even when these include individuals with specific functions. The more fully articulated the division in the society, the more often there is a class of cultic ministers to whom the offering of sacrifice is reserved. A priest may have other cultic or magical functions in addition to that of offering a sacrifice. He may for e.g. act as an oracle, exorcist, healer or a rainmaker.

The Vedic texts have prescribed certain rules regarding the right to perform sacrifices. Those belonging to the first three *varṇa*-s are entitled to perform the sacrifice[11]. It is to be understood that the right to perform a sacrifice is prescribed for those who are *gṛhastha*-s, i.e. householders.

Since there are no specifications about men from these classes, women belonging to these are also qualified to participate in the Vedic rites by the side of the sacrificer[12]. It is difficult to say that they actually participated in the ritual performance. However, their presence in the sacrifice was regarded mandatory. The Śrauta texts indicate that a person belonging to the caste of a *rathakāra*, i.e. chariot-makers has the rite to perform the *ādhāna*, i.e. setting up the three sacrificial fires[13].

Why do the Śrautasūtra-s make a special provision of the *rathakāra* caste? The reason is that the *rathakāra* is the son of *māhiṣya* and *karaṇī*. *Māhiṣya* is the son of *kṣatriya* husband and a *vaiśya* wife. *Karaṇī* is the daughter of a *vaiśya* husband and a *śūdra* wife (*Manu Sm*. X. 58). The leader of the *niṣāda* tribe is eligible to offer the *gāvedhuka caru*, i.e. a porridge of the *coix barbata* grains to Rudra. A *brahmacārin* i.e. a celibate, can perform the Gardhabhejyā, i.e. give an offering of an ass, if he is an Avakīrṇin, i.e. if he has violated the rules of celibacy. However, the offerings of the *niṣāda* leader and an *avakīrṇin brahmacārin* are to be performed in ordinary fires and not the sacred fires, prescribe the Śrautasūtra-s (*Kāt. Śr. Sū*. I. 1. 4).

The Vedic sacrifice has to be performed in the presence of priests. There are sixteen priests in a sacrifice[14]. Of these *hotṛ, adhvaryu, udgātṛ* and *brahman* are the principal ones belonging to the *RV, YV, SV* and *AV* respectively. Three that follow each of them in the enumeration are their assistants. The functions of the four principal priests are referred to in the *RV* X. 71. 11.

In the Agnihotra sacrifice only the *adhvaryu* is required; in the Agnyādheya, Darśapūrṇamāsa and other *iṣṭi*-s, i.e. one day sacrifices all the principal four priests are required. In the Cāturmāsya sacrifice, i.e. the four seasonal sacrifices, five are required, viz. the four principal and the *pratiprasthātṛ*, as the fifth one. In the animal sacrifices the sixth one, viz. the *maitrāvaruṇa* is added. The *soma*- sacrifices require all the sixteen priests[15].

## Sacrificial Fire

Vedic sacrifice has three fires for offering. They are the *gārhapatya*, i.e. the household fire, *āhavanīya*, placed in the eastern direction and the *dakṣiṇāgni* is the fireplace placed on the southeast of the *gārhapatya*. *Dakṣiṇāgni* is also known as the *anvāhāryapacana*. Plenty of rice is cooked on this fire and it is called *anvāhārya*[16]. There is a process for establishing the three fires, which is known as the Agnyādhāna or Agnyādheya. Before *ādhāna* the sacrificer should prepare *araṇi*-s, i.e. the sacrificial faggots, from the *aśvattha* tree, which has grown out of the natural grafting on the *śamī* tree. The abodes for the three fires have to be prepared on the day before the *ādhāna*. *Adhvaryu* brings together the seven items on the altar. They are the *sambhāra*-s. There are two types of *sambhāra*, i.e. objects comprising earth and those from the wood are mentioned in the *Tait.Br*. II. 1.3.9-12. (the text enumerates the list of *sambhāra*-s along with their Arthavāda). Before placing the *sambhāra*-s the surface of the ground chosen for sacrifice is dug out. Then the following materials are placed: sand, saline earth, earth dug up by rats, earth from the ant-hill, clay from a never-drying lake, pebbles and gold. These are the things related with the earth. Among the things related with wood; *aśvattha, udumbara, parṇa, śamī, vikaṅkata* tree and a tree struck by the lightning[17]. A householder who nurtures the three fires is termed as an '*āhitāgni*'.

## Offering

Anything which has a value for human beings can be the material of sacrifice, i.e. used as an offering, in the sacrifice.

This value can also be at times symbolic. An offering incorporates animate things as well as inanimate. According to van Baaren, 'if we look about in the history of religion, we find there are very few things that have not at some time or in some place served as an offering'[18]. An offering is the sacrificial gift given by a human being to the divine.

The nature of an offering can be made clear in this point. Vedic sacrifice comprises of various types of offerings. No sacrifice is complete without them. Offerings comprise of foodstuff, milk, milk-products and even a victim. Offerings of foodstuff comprises of '*puroḍāśa*' the sacrificial cake made up of flour of foodgrains like rice, barley, millet, etc[19]. This is baked on the potsherds. Sometimes an offering of a porridge (*caru*) is given to certain deities. Milk and milk products comprise of curds, fermented milk, i.e. *āmikṣā* and also clarified butter, i.e. *ājya*. The *ājya* is offered from a sacrificial ladle named *juhū*. The *ājya* is poured on the offering (*abhighāraṇa*) as a matter of purifying it. An animal victim is offered to certain deities. This offering is undertaken only after smothering the victim. Smothering is meant for keeping the breath of the animal in its body. Thus, a live offering is given. Therefore, this procedure is undertaken. Honey is also used as an offering. It is used in the formation of *madhuparka*, a combination made of honey, curds and ghee[20]. The victim is later on cut into parts, which are later offered in the sacrifice for e.g. the *vapā*, i.e. omentum, is offered in the sacrifice. The offering of *soma* is an important offering especially in the *somayāga*-s. In these sacrifices, the *soma* is pressed thrice, i.e. in the morning, at midday and in the evening. After discussing the various types of offering, it is essential to know the manner in which the offerings were undertaken. In an exceptional case like the Sautrāmaṇī sacrifice, wine is used as an offering. The ancient texts discuss the manner in which this offering is done. On the discussion of the 'Principle of Double Value', Dange has incorporated the manner in which wine is offered in the Sautrāmaṇī sacrifice. The rite of Sautrāmaṇī is prescribed by Sthapati Cākra for regaining of the lost kingdom (*Śat. Br.* XI. 9. 3. 4-13). In this rite two additional altars are made to the east of the usual *āhavanīya*. One of these is to the south of the other, which is to be made to its north. The Sautrāmaṇī requires an oblation of wine, i.e. *surā*. Wine cannot be offered into the *āhavanīya*. If wine is not offered, in this special rite meant for regaining of the lost kingdom, into the *āhavanīya*, it will serve no purpose[21]. In other words, the manner or gesture that expresses the offering is also important. This may consist of a simple deposition or a lifting up of the offering, without a change being affected on the object. The *Kāt. Śr. Sū* mentions two types of sacrifices, viz. *yajati* and *juhoti*. The *yajati*-s are offerings in which oblations are offered in a standing position with the accompaniment of a *vaṣaṭ* call, after the introductory verse, i.e. *puronuvākyā* and the offering verse, i.e. *yājyā*. The *juhoti*-s are offerings in which oblations are offered in a sitting position when the *svāhā* - call is uttered[22]. The offerings have to be given with the utterance of the *mantra*-s, as a mark of sanctification. *Mantra*-s serve the purpose of reminding the rite[23]. Secondly, a ritual coupled with the utterance of a *mantra* bestows higher merit than a ritual performed directly. The *Ait. Br* stresses the importance of the *mantra*-s (III. 12). When the *soma* was brought to the sacrificers, its powers and faculty of making the senses sharp moved from their place and scattered everywhere. The priests tried to collect and kept them together with one verse. But they failed. They failed and therefore tried to keep them together with two, and then with three, yet they failed. They succeeded with eight and recovered all the powers of *soma*. There are in those ceremonies which follow the bringing of the *soma* to the sacrificial compound, eight verses each time recited in order to collect and hold together the strength and those qualities of the *soma* shoots which give sharpness of senses. This is the concept of *rūpasamṛddha mantra*-s.

It is to be noted that the instruments used in the sacrifice in connection with the offerings are also of a specific type.

The waters play an important role in the entire sacrifice. They are of four types:

*Vasatīvarī*

These waters are taken from a flowing source, before sunset. The sacrificer distributes it all over the *savana*-, i.e. three *soma*-pressings[24].

*Praṇītā*

These waters are taken from the place of the *gārhapatya* to the *āhavanīya*.

*Ekadhanā*

*Ekadhanā* waters are carried in pitchers by the wife of the sacrificer. These waters are used for mixing with the *soma* juice.[25]

*Nigrābhyā*

These waters are in fact *vasatīvarī* poured into the Hotṛ cup. They are used for moistening the *soma* shoots at the time of pressing[26].

The offerings are given in the sacrificial fire and for this purpose the sacrificial altar is very important. The sacrificial altar, i.e. *vedi,* is used for keeping the material used for the sacrifice. The common shape of the sacrificial altar is said to be like a woman, in the act of embracing the *āhavanīya* fire. Her two shoulders are said to be *aṁsau* of the altar, which are the two corners of the eastern side. This side is smaller than the western one, the corners of which are said to be the buttocks, *śroṇi*. To make the likeness even clearer, the altar is prescribed to be contracted in the middle which would give the idea of a beautiful woman with a contracted belly (*Śat. Br.* I.2.5.16). Dange comments,

> Though the description does not clearly say, what exactly the pose of the woman would be, it is to be taken for granted that the pose has her legs contracted and folded under her buttocks; they are concealed under her buttocks with knees folded[27].

The general size of the altar is: three *aratni*-s[28] in the eastern side; one *vyāma* (the distance between the tips of the fingers of the two hands, extended to the two sides fully) in the western side; and the length be "that of a man" (*puruṣasammitā*) says the *Śat. Br* (I. 2. 5.14). Dange has explained this combination of man and woman. He opines,

> This would indicate that the expression *puruṣasammitā* has to be understood, not as meaning 'corresponding to the upper portion of a man' woman included. The altar was *puruṣasammitā* to indicate the general length, but it was the woman in respect of the *āhavanīya* fire, who is conceived as her mate to form a 'procreative couple', *mithuna* that would correspond to the procreative aspect of the sacrifice. This arrangement corresponds to the Prajāpati syndrome, and fits in the general structure of the Great He-She. Prajāpati is bi-sexual; hence, the sacrifice is bi-sexual; it is a procreative unit in itself. In mythology, the motif enters the concept of the bi-sexual Lord Brahmā, and other gods, that can produce and procreate from their own body.[29]

Such an altar is used in an *iṣṭi*, i.e. one-day sacrifice, like the Darśapūrṇamāsa. For *somayāga*-s, the altar which is built is much larger than that of the Darśapūrṇamāsa sacrifice. This altar is known as the Mahāvedi. According to the *Śat. Br*, the eastern side of this Mahāvedi should be twenty-four *prakrama*-s, the western side should be thirty *prakrama*-s and its east-west length should be thirty-six *prakrama*-s. According to Dange, the femininity of this altar is not prominent owing to its size[30]. At the Paśubandha sacrifice (the sacrifice of tying the sacrificial animal to the post), there is one altar to the east of the usual *āhavanīya*. There is one more type of altar raised for the purpose of Varuṇapraghāsa and Sākamedha *parvan*-s of the Cāturmāsya sacrifice. Two extra altars are raised to the east of the *āhavanīya* sacrifice. A similar procedure is followed during the Sautrāmaṇī.

## Place and Time of the Offering

The place for performing the sacrifice is called *devayajana*. The sacrificer prepares a raised place for the altar. Several rules are laid down about the choosing of the place of worship in the *Śat. Br* (III. 1. 1), *Ait. Br* (I. 3), *Drā. Śr. Sū* (I. 1. 14-19). It should be the highest place and in its vicinity there should be no spot which is on a higher level than it, it should be even and firm and should incline towards the east or north, being a little higher in the south. It should have many plants growing on it and in front of it there should be water (a well & c) or a large tree or a public road. The *Śat. Br* (III. 1. 1. 5). emphasizes that if one secures learned and skilful priests, it does not matter what kind of sacrificial ground one selects. The *Ait. Br* (I. 3). requires that the *dīkṣita* is to walk about and sit usually in the *devayajana*, and he must not leave it at all at sunrise, sunset and when priests are engaged in *āśravaṇa* (saying *Ā śrāvaya*)..... The *yajñaśālā* is called *dīkṣitavimita* in the *Ait. Br* (I. 3) and it is the same as *prācīnavaṁśa-śālā*. *Iṣṭi*-s are performed in the *prācīnavaṁśa-śālā*, but the Uttaravedi required an animal, *soma* and some other sacrifices are outside it.[31] The *devayajana* is prepared sloping towards the east. The sacrificer constructs a shed having the end of the principal bamboo or ridge turned northwards or eastwards. Beneath the middle of the ridge of the hut towards one end is the place (*āyatana*) meant for the *gārhapatya* fire; the place of the *āhavanīya* fire is to the east of the *gārhapatya* at a distance of eight *prakrama*-s for a *brāhmaṇa*, eleven and twelve for a *kṣatriya* and *vaiśya* respectively or all may have it 24 steps (*pada*) or at a distance found by the eye to approximate to the distances stated (without actual measurement). The place for the *dakṣiṇāgni* is near the *gārhapatya* to the south-east after a third of the distance between the *gārhapatya* and the *āhavanīya*. There are to be separate sheds for the *āhavanīya* fire and the *gārhapatya* in elaborate sacrifices but for the ordinary sacrifices like Darśapūrṇamāsa one shed only is usually constructed which houses all the three fires[32]. In the western portion of the *devayajana* from which all roots are uprooted, a pavilion (*vimita*, a four-cornered) is erected, the central ridge and the covering bamboos of which run from west to east, which has doors (two cubits wide) in all directions and which, slightly inclines towards the east, or a rectangular house (*śālā*) may be built, twenty *aratni*-s long and ten *aratni*-s wide.... A shed for cooking the *vrata* food is erected to the south of the pavilion and another to the west for the wife of the sacrificer[33].

Havirdhānamaṇḍapa is also an important sacrificial place. The carts in which the *soma* is carried during the *soma*-sacrifice are the Havirdhāna carts. A *maṇḍapa* is erected by having six posts in front of the two carts and six behind them and having two bamboos on the posts from south to north... The Havirdhānamaṇḍapa is higher in the east than in the west and has two doors one to the east and the other to the west.

Regarding the time of the offerings, the daily sacrifices like the Agnihotra are performed twice everyday, i.e. morning and evening. Morning offerings are given in the fire but for the Sun in (Agni form) and the evening offerings are given in the fire, i.e. Agni, after sunset. In *soma*-sacrifices, the pressings of *soma* are performed three times in a day, i.e. *prātaḥsavana, mādhyandinasavana* and *sāyamsavana*. No offerings are given after sunset, except the offerings given during a *soma*-sacrifice named Atirātra[34]. This sacrifice is performed by a sacrificer, who is desirous of attaining progeny or abundant cattle. Offerings of a draught of *soma* are given to Indra. These offerings are given at night.

## Recipient of the Offering

The offerings given during the performance of the Vedic sacrifice are assumed to reach gods. Gods have their share in the sacrifice. It is believed that by the power of the *mantra*-s chanted in a sacrifice, gods arrive on the sacrificial scene, so that they can have their share in the sacrifice. Gods are thought to dwell in the heaven. The smoke that rises from the sacrificial fire delivers the offering to the gods. Each deity has its specific share in the sacrificial offerings. For e.g. Pūṣan is offered *caru*, i.e. a mess of boiled rice, according to the *Śat. Br* (I. 7. 4. 7). Some gods were excluded from receiving a share in the sacrifice. In the *Śat. Br*, occurs an Arthavāda, i.e. an aetiological explanation, regarding the Āśvina *graha*, i.e. a cup of *soma*, offered to the Aśvins (IV. 1. 5. 13). The Aśvins were not invited in the sacrifice performed by gods. This sacrifice was headless. The Aśvins became *adhvaryu*-s in the sacrifice and restored its head. Hence a cup of *soma* is drawn out for them. Varuṇa receives a pap of barley. To have a better idea of the nature of the deities, who received the offerings of *puroḍāśa,* let us take the Rājasūya as an example[35]. The following is a list of deities, who are the recipients of the *puroḍāśa* offerings.

| *Deity/ies* | *Offerings* | *Explanation* |
|---|---|---|
| Agni and Viṣṇu | *puroḍāśa* of eleven potsherds | Agni is the giver for men. Men belong to Viṣṇu |
| Indra and Viṣṇu | *puroḍāśa* on three potsherds or pap for Viṣṇu | Indra is the sacrificer. Men belong to Viṣṇu. |
| Agni and Pūṣan | *puroḍāśa* of eleven potsherds | Agni is the giver and Pūṣan is the lord of cattle |
| Indra and Pūṣan | Pap for Indra and Pūṣan and a separate pap for Pūṣan. | By these offerings the sacrificer is bestowed with the cattle by Indra. By the grace of Pūṣan the sacrificer firmly establishes himself with the offerings |
| Pūṣan | Dark-grey bull | Pūṣan represents productiveness |
| Agni and Soma | *puroḍāśa* on eleven potsherds | |
| Indra and Soma | Pap and a separate pap for Soma. Brown bull is offered for Soma | Agni is the giver and Soma stands for glory. The bull represents Soma |

| Vaiśvānara | *puroḍāśa* of twelve potsherds. Bull is the fee. | Vaiśvānara stands for one year |
|---|---|---|
| Varuṇa | Pap of barley and a black cloth | Freedom of all creatures from the snare of Varuṇa |

## Purpose Behind the Performance of Sacrifice

Sacrifice is performed with a desire in mind. Generally the sacrificer performs it to maintain a continued favour of the gods and good fortune. But he may also perform sacrifices with certain desires in mind. For e.g. the sacrifice named Udbhid is performed for obtaining animals[36]. A king performs the Rājasūya or the Aśvamedha sacrifices to obtain sovereignty[37]. A sacrifice named Vājapeya is also performed with the purpose of attaining sovereignty[38]. There are certain *citi*-s, i.e. piles of bricks arranged in order to fulfill desires for e.g.; Chandaściti, Śyenaciti, Kaṅkaciti, Praugaciti etc (*Baudh. Śr. Sū.* 17. 24-30; 19. 1-10). Sacrifices are specifically identified with Kāmya *karman*-s, i.e. actions undertaken with desires.

## Fruit Derived

This point overlaps with the above point. However, it is to be understood that the fruit which is derived by the sacrificer is the fulfillment of the purpose with which a sacrifice is performed. Apart from this fulfillment each and every *karman* undertaken in the sacrifice accrues an unseen fruit, i.e. *adṛṣṭa* or *apūrva*. The *apūrva* plays an important role in assisting the sacrificer in attaining heaven, i.e. *svarga*. This concept of *apūrva* has been discussed in detail by the Mīmāṁsā School of philosophy.

## TWO PROMINENT SAṀSTHĀ-S

Vedic sacrifice is broadly classified in two *saṁsthā*-s, i.e. branches:

### HAVIḤSAṀSTHĀ

There are in all seven sacrifices in this *saṁsthā*.

#### *Agnyādheya*

This is the ritual of establishing the three fires. This has been dealt with, in the discussion on the typology of the Vedic sacrifice.

#### *Agnihotra*

From the evening of the day of the Agnyādheya, the householder has to perform the Agnihotra, i.e. burnt offering of cow-milk, etc. The *Śat. Br* has commented upon the mandatory nature of the Agnihotra. It says that those who offer Agnihotra indeed enter upon a long sacrificial session; Agnihotra indeed is a *sattra*, that ends with old age or death, since he becomes free from it only by old age or death (*Śat. Br.* XII. 4. 1. 1). The *Satyāṣāḍha Śr. Sū* permits the *rathakāra* and the *niṣāda* to perform the Agnihotra, which is opposed by the authors of the other Śrautasūtra-s. These texts prescribe the procedure of performing the Agnihotra, when the householder is not at home. He can perform the Agnihotra mentally. When he goes on a journey leaving his wife, he can entrust the fires to his wife and appoint a priest to perform the necessary rites. If accompanied by his wife, he should take the fires with him. If both husband and wife are away, without taking the three fires, a priest cannot perform Agnihotra in their absence. On return, the householder should perform Punarādhāna, i.e. resetting the three fires[39].

*Darśapūrṇamāsa*

This sacrifice is regarded as the archetype, i.e. *prakṛti* of the Haviḥsaṁsthā-s. It is a one day sacrifice, which is performed on the New Moon day, i.e. *darśa* and Full Moon day, i.e. *pūrṇamāsa*. Every *āhitāgni* has to perform this sacrifice with a desire of attaining heaven.

*Āgrayaṇa*

There are three Āgrayaṇa *iṣṭi*-s performed every year. In monsoon season, the Śyāmākāgrayaṇa using the *śyāmāka* grains, in autumn is the Vrīhyāgrayaṇa using *vrīhi*-s grains and in the spring season is the Yavāgrayaṇa using *yava* grains. This *iṣṭi* is performed either during New Moon day or Full Moon day. This sacrifice appears to be a harvest sacrifice, which incorporated newly arrived harvest of the grains mentioned in them.

*Cāturmāsya*

These are the seasonal sacrifices. The Cāturmāsya-s are three or four in number. They are a) Vaiśvadeva, b) Varuṇaprāghasa, c) Sākamedha and d) Śunāsīrīya. They are performed respectively on the Full Moon days of Phālguna, or Caitra, Āṣāḍha, Kārttika and on the 5th Full Moon from the day on which the Sākamedha is performed (i.e. on Phālgunī) or two or three days before it. They indicate the advent of three seasons, viz. *vasanta* (spring), *varṣā* (rains) and *hemanta* (autumn). The *Tait. Br.* (I. 6. 8.1, 2) states the reward secured by the performance of the Cāturmāsya-s[40].

*Nirūḍhapaśubandha or Paśubandha*

This sacrifice stands for the immolation of an animal in sacrifice. This is an independent sacrifice and it is also performed in *soma*-sacrifice as a constituent part, i.e. *aṅga*. The independent animal sacrifice is to be performed every six months or every year by the *āhitāgni* throughout his life (*Tait. Sam.* I. 3.5-11). If done once a year it was performed every six months in the rainy season on New Moon day or Full Moon day. A he-goat is sacrificed in this sacrifice. It is bathed in with scented water, is led between the *cātvāla* and *utkara* and brought in front of the *yūpa* to the east with the animal's face to the west. The animal is meant for Indra-Agni/Sūrya/Prajāpati and one has to dedicate the victim throughout one's life in every Paśubandha. After the animal is smothered, the wife of the sacrificer washes the animal with appropriate formulae. The omentum is offered in the fire. The different parts of the animal are cut and Paśu-puroḍāśa is prepared for offering. It is noteworthy that the blood of the animal is offered with the mantra addressed to the evil spirits (*Vāj. Sam* VI. 6). In various Kāmya *iṣṭi*-s, various animals are prescribed for securing desired objects[41].

*Sautrāmaṇī*

Sautrāmaṇī is that sacrifice in which *surā*, i.e. liquor is offered. It is divided into two a) Carakasautrāmaṇī: This sacrifice is performed in the context of the Rājasūya sacrifice and b) Kaukilasautrāmaṇī is incorporated in the Haviḥsaṁsthā. The first day witnesses the performance of an animal sacrifice to Indra. *Surā* is prepared and kept for three days. After giving offering of grain, milk and animal parts to the deities according to the various texts, *surā* is offered to all the deities. It is followed by offering of hairs of lion, tiger and wolf. Three animals are immolated and their omenta are offered to the fire. The Adhvaryu and Pratiprasthātṛ give offerings of liquor to Aśvins, Sarasvatī and Sutrāman Indra. The remaining liquor is given to a *brāhmaṇā* to be consumed or is poured on an anthill[42].

## Somasaṁsthā

The Somasaṁsthā is also a part of the Vedic sacrifice. They incorporate the seven *soma*-sacrifices of which the Jyotiṣṭoma/Agniṣṭoma is regarded as the archetype.

### *Agniṣṭoma*

The Agniṣṭoma is a one-day sacrifice and it is an integral part of the Jyotiṣṭoma so much so that the two are often identified[43]. The Jyotiṣṭoma occupies generally five days. Agniṣṭoma is so called because in it Agni is praised or because the last chant (*stotra*) is addressed to Agni[44]. It is to be performed in the spring every year and on the New Moon or Full Moon day. Kane mentions two views regarding the performance of the sacrifice. Firstly, one should perform a *soma*-sacrifice after having performed Darśapūrṇamāsa, Cāturmāsya-s, Paśubandha sacrifices. The second view is that it could be performed even before the Darśapūrṇamāsa, but after Agnyādhāna[45]. This sacrifice requires the presence of sixteen *ṛtvij*-s, Sadasya is the seventeenth according to some recensions. The Dīkṣaṇīyeṣṭi is performed so that the sacrificer can take the *dīkṣā* of the sacrifice. For this sacrifice, the sacrificer has to undergo the *dīkṣā* from three days to ten days. The sacrificer sends people to collect the *sambhāra*-s for the sacrifice. A Prāyaṇīyeṣṭi is performed on this day. Then follows the ritual of purchasing *soma*. When *soma* is brought at the sacrificial place, an Ātithyeṣṭi is performed. The ritual of Pravargya is optionally performed in the Agniṣṭoma sacrifice. Later on the sacrificial posts are erected. The fifth day is the Sutyā day when the pressing of the *soma* is undertaken. There are three pressings of *soma*, viz. the Prātaḥsavana, the Mādhyandinasavana and the Sāyamsavana. The concluding day is named the *avabhṛtha*, when the sacrificer, along with his wife, takes bath marking the end of the sacrifice[46].

*Ukthya/Uktha*

This is the second among the Somasaṁsthā. A person desirous of animals should perform this sacrifice. Some more rituals other than the Agniṣṭoma have to be performed. A goat is to be sacrificed for the dual deities Indrāgnī.

*Ṣoḍaśin*

In this sacrifice in addition to the fifteen *stotra*-s and fifteen *śastra*-s of the Ukthya, there is an additional *stotra* and a corresponding *śastra* called Ṣoḍaśin in the *tṛtīya savana* (both the *śastra* and the sacrifice have the same name, as the com. on *Āśv. Śr. Sū* VI. 2.1. says). There is an additional cup in the morning or at all pressings according to some (*Āp. Śr. Sū* XIV. 2. 4-5). It is made of Khadira wood and is quandrangular in shape. The *stotra* for the Ṣoḍaśin cup is begun to be chanted about sunset after the Adhvaryu hands over a piece of gold to the same *sāman* singer. Here the cow which is exchanged for *soma* is short in stature and has red, coloured ears or eyes. In this rite an additional victim, viz. a ram is sacrificed for Indra. The *dakṣiṇā* is a reddish brown horse or a female mule[47]. A sacrificer who is desirous of attaining vigour performs this sacrifice[48].

*Atyagniṣṭoma*

This is an addition to the Agniṣṭoma sacrifice. It is obtained by adding the Ṣoḍaśinstotra, the Ṣoḍaśin cup and an additional victim for Indra to what prevails in the Agniṣṭoma[49].

*Atirātra*

One who is desirous of progeny or cattle should perform this sacrifice. *RV* refers to this sacrifice (VII. 103. 7). As this sacrifice is not completed in one day but only after the day and night pass away, it is called Atirātra. The Atirātra has

29 *stotra*-s and 29 *śastra*-s. At twilight is chanted a *stotra* named Sandhistotra[50]. This sacrifice is well known in the *Jaiminisūtra-s* regarding the injunction or prohibition of the Ṣoḍaśin cup taken in the Atirātra (*Jaiminisūtra-s* X. 8. 6).

### *Aptoryāma*

According to Kane, this sacrifice is similar to Atirātra of which it appears to be amplification[51]. A sacrificer who is desirous of fulfilling all his desires should perform this sacrifice. According to the *Āśv. Śr. Sū* (IX. 11.1), one whose cattle do not survive or one who wishes to secure cattle should perform this sacrifice. The *Tāṇ. MBr.* gives the etymology of this sacrifice. This sacrifice has the root √*ap* to obtain, as its base. Therefore, it stands for obtaining all the desires. This sacrifice has four more *stotra*-s and *śastra*-s than Atirātra sacrifice[52].

### *Vājapeya*

This sacrifice literally means food and drink, or drink of strength or of food or of a race[53]. This sacrifice associates great importance to the number seventeen because this number is associated with Prajāpati. Along with *soma*, liquor is also used. The chariot race is an essential feature of the Vājapeya. Besides this the Yūpārohaṇa, i.e. ascending the sacrificial post by the sacrificer is another essential feature of this sacrifice. Vājapeya is performed by one who is desirous of attaining supremacy. The *Śat. Br* V. 1. 1. 13. eulogises this sacrifice as being superior to the Rājasūya. One who has performed the Vājapeya has the right of bearing a white umbrella. This sacrifice is of three types, viz. Āptavājapeya, Kuruvājapeya and Saṁsthāvājapeya[54].

## The Pākasaṁsthā-s

Smārta sacrifices are termed as the Pākasaṁsthā.: They are Aṣṭakā, Pārvaṇa, Sthālīpāka, Śrāddha, Śrāvaṇākarman,

Āgrahāyaṇī, Caitrī and Āśvāyujī according to some texts. They belong to the Gṛhya tradition.

*Aṣṭakā*

This ritual is performed on the eighth day of the dark fortnight of the four months of Hemanta, Śiśira, seasons. It is a rite for the dead ancestors. A *homa* is performed in the evening and a dinner is given to the *brāhmaṇa*-s. A *puroḍāśa* is given and a cow is sacrificed. If no cow is available, deer, buffalo, rhinoceros, boar, hare, pigeon are offered[55].

*Pārvaṇa*

This is also a ritual performed for dead ancestors for three generations on Amāvāsya of the month of Bhādrapada. *Brāhmaṇa*-s are invited and water is offered to them and *darbha* seats are given, sesame seeds are used to give offerings to the manes. A *sthālīpāka* is prepared, which is smeared with ghee and offered in the fire. Gifts are given to the *brāhmaṇa*-s and *svadhā* is uttered[56].

*Śrāddha*

These are rituals performed for dead ancestors. They are of different types. a) Ekoddiṣṭa: This is performed for only one person, who has recently died. b) Māsika: This is performed every month. c) Sapiṇḍīkaraṇa: This is performed on the twelfth day after a person has departed. d) Ābhyudayika: This is performed for prosperity. e) Kāmya: This is performed with a desire of a special reward[57].

*Śrāvaṇākarman*

According to the *Āśv. Gṛ. Sū*, this particular ritual is performed on the Full Moon day of Śrāvaṇa, whether the moon is in conjunction with the constellation of Śravaṇa or not. A new jar is filled with flour of unbroken grains of barley and he places it on a new *śikya*, which is an arrangement of strings for holding pots, etc. At sunset he prepares a mess of cooked food and *purodāśa* prepared on one potsherd and thus, offers an oblation. Out of the jar he fills the spoon with barley flour, goes out of the house with his face towards the east, pours down water on a pure spot and offers a sacrifice to the hosts of snakes (II. 1. 1-15)[58].

*Āśvāyujī*

According to the *Āśv. Gṛ. Sū*, this rite is performed on the Full Moon day of the month of the Āśvāyuja. On this day the house is cleaned, new clothes are adorned by the householder and a mess is offered to Paśupati (II. 2. 1-3)[59].

*Āgrahāyaṇī*

This ritual is performed on the Full Moon day of Mārgaśīrṣa. Pratyāvarohaṇa rite is performed to signalize the giving up of the use of cots and high couches recommended from the Full Moon of Śrāvaṇa for the fear of snakes. Oblations of *pāyasa* are offered to serpents[60].

*Caitrī*

This rite is performed on the Full Moon day of the month of Caitra. The householder and his wife clean the house and adorn themselves with new clothes and flowers, etc. Then two *āghāra*-s are made in fire and rice is cooked in a vessel for deities and offerings of clarified butter are given. The deities are Madhu, Mādhava, Śukra, Śuci, Nabhas, Nabhasya, Īśa, Ūrjā, Sahas, Tapas, Tapasyā, to the deities of Ṛtus, to herbs, Viṣṇu, etc. Sacrificial food is offered to Lord Śrīpati and Śrī, his consort. *Brāhmaṇa*-s and the *sapiṇḍa*-s of the householder are fed by the householder[61].

## VEDIC SACRIFICE DOWN THE AGES

### VEDIC SACRIFICE OF THE PERIOD OF THE SAṀHITĀ-S

The early Vedic ritual is reflected in the *mantra*-s of the *RV*. According to Dange, 'About what was the nature of the Vedic ritual of the period of the *RV*, there is very little help; and from the mention of some terms it is difficult to get a comprehensive idea of such ritual or sacrifices.' He further points out that *yajña* was known but, its types, as mentioned in the (later texts of the) *YV* tradition are not mentioned. Also the names of the three fires are not mentioned.[62] Though fire is mentioned to have been established in the three altars, their specific nature is missing (*RV* II. 34. 4). *RV* (II. 1. 2) and (I. 162. 5) mention the priest *agnīdhra*. This indicates that there was a specific office for the fire-kindler. Though the term *'vedi'* exists in the *RV* (X.61.2), no exact measurements appear. Dange points out certain rituals which were no more practiced in the later Śrauta tradition.

> 'There is a reference to the cooking of a bull (whole) and a ram. Cooking of the whole beast was never heard of. Similarly cooking of the entrails of a dog was never formed part of any regular ritual in the later sacrifices. But in the RV it refers to the rain-charm. The horse-sacrifice is not elaborate in the RV. Dange points out to the hymn of Vṛṣakāpi and comments that 'ape-sacrifice appears fossilized in the form of a myth and riddle'. The offerings of ghṛta appear to be the commonest of all offerings, inasmuch as it seems to have been offered with some other offerings[63].

Potdar analyses this as:

> the sacrifice has originated and grown on account of the peculiar role of Agni, who is said to be conveying the oblations and sacrificial performances to the gods. The offerings of ghee would keep the fire blazing and would facilitate the offerings of other oblations as well[64].

Apart from the offerings of clarified butter, i.e. *ghṛta*, *soma* was also offered. Potdar points out that 'it would be no exaggeration to say that the Ṛgvedic sacrifice is what is mainly on account of the *soma*-offering'[65]. These instances indicate that the nature of the sacrifice in the *RV* was of a beginning of the Vedic sacrifice or it was the early Vedic sacrificial ritual.

## Sacrifice Occurring in the *YV*

The *YV* is divided into two schools, viz. *Kṛṣṇa* (Black) and *Śukla* (White) *YV*. These two schools of the *YV*. display a developed institution of sacrifice. It is not an exaggeration to say that the entire Vedic sacrifice has at its edifice the *YV* for the term *yajus* has at √*yaj* as its root. The *yajus mantra*-s are systematically mentioned for their direct application in the sacrifice. The *Vāj. Sam.* of the *Śukla YV* discusses the *mantra*-s related to the sacrifices like the Darśapūrṇamāsa, Pitṛyajña, Agnyādhāna, *soma*-sacrifices, Agnicayana, Śautrāmaṇī sacrifices, Aśvamedha, Puruṣamedha, etc. It also discusses the various animal offerings in the sacrifices and also the different altars piled for the performance of sacrifices[66]. *Kṛṣṇa YV* school has four books, viz. *Kaṭha*, *Kapiṣṭhala*(not fully available), *Maitrāyaṇī* and the *Taittirīya Saṁhitā*-s. The texts discuss in detail the various sacrifices and the offerings incorporate in them, the different altars, etc[67].

## Sacrificial Ritual in the *SV*

The *SV* is the collection of *sāman*-s or chants, also to be recited in the course of the ritual. The *sāman*-s themselves are tunes, melodies to which a variety of different verses can be sung of a large number of the mantra-s from the *RV*. Though the *sāman*-s are based on the *RV*, each *sāman* has a different name. Some *sāman*-s are named on the basis of the metre, like *sāman* recited in the *gāyatrī* metre is named *gāyatra sāman*. A *sāman* arranged by a sage named Ruru is named *raurava sāman*. Many *sāman*-s are recited during the Gavāmayana. Many *sāman*-s are sung by the *prastotṛ* during the Pravargya ritual.

## Sacrificial Ritual in the *AV*

The *AV* comprises of hymns, which have black and white magic as their subject. Therefore, *AV* appears to be different in nature. It is divided into two schools, viz. Śaunaka and Paippalāda. The Paippalāda, though available, is corrupt in form. Approximately, one seventh of this Veda comprises of hymns from the *RV*[68]. Taking into consideration the subject matter of the *AV*, scholars differ in opinion about the ritualistic nature of the *AV*. Some scholars are of the opinion that the hymns are 'ritualistic in flavour'. Jamison comments:

> Though we can, I think, reasonably call it a ritual text under the characterization of ritual, (Ritual is patterned and repeated religious observance that involves physical activity and the manipulation of objects as well as words), it is not generally concerned with the great, solemn, Śrauta rituals on which the other three Vedas converge[69].

The task of incorporating the *AV* in the ritualistic tradition has been fulfilled by the *Gop. Br* and the *Vait. Śr. Sū*. The *mantra*-s of the *AV* are recited during the Darśapūrṇamāsa sacrifices. However some awareness regarding the Agniṣṭoma, Agnicayana rituals, preparations of the sacrificial altar, anointing the *barhis*, i.e. specific grass, etc. is seen in the *AV*. According to Devasthali, there are numerous references to the sacrifices in the *AV*. Thus, for e.g. there is a statement about the reward accruing to one who properly honours a guest; offering milk to a guest yields the same result or fruit as accrues from a full and large scale performance of the Agnihotra, similarly offering gruel yields fruit of a similar performance of the Atirātra; offering honey yields the fruit of a *sattra* and offering flesh yields to the fruit of Dvādaśāha sacrifice. From these references, it is clear that these sacrifices had become quite established so much so that the rewards accruing from them were too well-known to require any direct mention. It is also quite clear that these results were sumptuous enough to be quite covetable by all, but at the same time it is also evident that people ordinarily had begun to find it very difficult to perform these elaborate sacrifices and sought for some easier means of securing the same results. This, in other words, means that the concept of sacrifice has not only been impressed on and rooted into the society of those days, but had rather overgrown itself to such an extent that it had gone almost if not wholly out of the reach of a major part of the society. Such a conclusion finds full collaboration in the promulgation of the concept of *sava*-s in the *AV*, which ultimately appear to have supplanted the cumbrous sacrifices and sacrificial sessions altogether or at least to a very large extent[70].

## Sacrificial Ritual in the Brāhmaṇa-s

The Brāhmaṇa-s are manuals regarding the sacrifices. The sole purpose behind the composition of these texts was to give the institution of sacrifice a systematic structure to document the elaborate performances of the sacrifices and to justify the detailed ritualistic performance. They explain the application part of the mantra-s in the Saṁhita-s during the performance of the sacrifices. The Brāhmaṇa-s are broadly classified into two sections a) Vidhi, i.e. Injunctions which direct the performances of sacrifices. b) Arthavāda, i.e. aetiological explanations justifying the performance of rituals or condemnation for abstaining from performing rituals or performing them in an incorrect manner. The Brāhmaṇa-s have explained the functional application of the mantra-s of their respective Veda in the Vedic sacrifice[71].

## Sacrifice in the Āraṇyaka-s

The Āraṇyaka-s stand as a link between the Brāhmaṇa-s and the Upaniṣad-s taking their sap from the former, i.e. the Brāhmaṇa-s and culminating in the philosophical doctrines of the latter, i.e. the Upaniṣad-s. According to Dange (Mrs.), there are references to the ritualistic details of certain sacrifices in the Āraṇyaka-s[72]. They also deal with the concept of Brahman or *puruṣa*, which is further developed in the Upaniṣad-s. According to Jamison, the Āraṇyaka -text type seems like a lopsided Brāhmaṇa with a mystic bent[73].

## Sacrifice in the Upaniṣad-s

The Upaniṣad-s are the concluding sections of Vedic literature. They are regarded as a contrast to the thought expressed in the Brāhmaṇa-s, which give paramount importance to the sacrificial rituals. The Upaniṣad-s incorporate rigorous metaphysical thinking, which marks the culmination of all the knowledge of Vedic literature. It would be incorrect to regard the Upaniṣad-s as a revolution against the ritualistic order for the Upanisadic philosophy has a ritual setting. Some references to the ritual-setting of the Upaniṣad-s are cited here. Dange has marked three stages in this process[74].

a) Clear-cut mention of the terms, such as, *sāman, stobha,* etc; the importance of the gods like Indra is pointed out, following the point of view;
b) Upanisadic philosophy is laid down, but the imagery is clearly of the sacrifice; and

c) The highest Upanisadic philosophy is presented in the traditional ritualistic terminology.

The instruction given to Naciketas by Yama about the establishment of the three fires indicates the society accepting a new type of fire and a renovation of the sacrificial method[75]. Dange comments that this seems to be in addition to the then prevalent belief in the gain of the heaven by the performance of the sacrifice. The statement clearly indicates a sort of propaganda in the priestly community to lead one to heaven *quicker* than the traditional way. In the *Chāndogya Upaniṣad* we have the five householders going to Uddālaka Āruṇi for the gain of the knowledge of the Ātman. The latter, however, directs them to King Aśvapati Kekaya, himself accompanying them to Aśvapati. Aśvapati expounds the doctrine of the Vaiśvānara Ātman for them. The Vaiśvānara Ātman has the altar (Vedi) for the chest, the sacrificial grass for its hair, the Household fire, i.e. (*gārhapatya*) for its heart, the *anvāhārya* fire for its mind and the *āhavanīya* fire for its mouth. It is clear that sacrifice is not being symbolized here as the cosmic Fire. On the contrary, the Fire (Vaiśvānara, which is equally the microcosmic and the macrocosmic) is said to be not beyond the traditional sacrifice[76]. The *Praśna Upaniṣad* equates the vital breath, i.e. the Apāna with the *gārhapatya* fire, Vyāna with the *anvāhāryapacana* fire (which is also called the *dakṣiṇa* fire,) and the Prāṇa with the *āhavanīya* (V. 3. 4). The *Chāndogya Upaniṣad* (III. 6) identifies the very *puruṣa*, i.e. man, with the sacrifice. The first twenty-four years of his life amount to the morning *soma*-pressing (*prātaḥsavana*), which is associated with the *gāyatrī* metre having twenty-four syllables (three feet having eight syllables in each). The next forty-four years of a man's life amount to the mid-day pressing of *soma*. This part is associated with the metre *triṣṭubh,* having forty-four syllables (11x4). The last forty-eight years of a man's life stand for the evening pressing, which is associated with the *jagatī* metre, having forty-eight syllables (12x4). Basing the life of a man on the number of the syllables of the principal metres indicates the belief that the normal life of a sacrificer was believed to be 116 years (24+44+48)! Other details of this symbolic sacrifice are also given in the same text (III. 17. 1.5). Thus, whatever one desires to eat and drink but does not enjoy (i.e. he does not get it and thus abstains from it) stands for his initiation. Whatever one eats, drinks and enjoys stands for his *upasad*-s (which are rites that form part of the Jyotiṣṭoma sacrifice), which last for several days. As he laughs, eats and enjoys sexual union, all these amount to the mantra-s chanted in the sacrifice. One's patience, gifts, simplicity (*ārjava*), non-injury and truthfulness, are the gifts at this sacrifice. Whenever they say that a certain woman has delivered, that is one's re-birth; and death, verily, is his *avabhṛtha*[77].

## Sacrifice in the Śrautasūtra-s

Although, the Śrautasūtra-s do not fall in the section of Śruti-s, i.e. Vedic literature, it is important to take a view of this part of literature to know the position of Vedic sacrifice. The Brāhmaṇa texts are termed as manuals regarding Vedic sacrifice, yet there existed a considerable time gap between the Brāhmaṇa-s and Śrautasūtra-s. The style of the Śrautasūtra-s is aphoristic, therefore simple and unambiguous. They give minute and detailed descriptions of the procedure of sacrifice. Ram Gopal has discussed the probable dates of the Śrautasūtra-s and he prescribed the Śrautasūtra-s to a date as early as 800–500 BC[78].

## VARIOUS INTERPRETATIONS OF VEDIC SACRIFICE

The study of Vedic sacrifice has been undertaken by mythologists, historians of religion, anthropologists as well as sociologists.

### Interpretation Based on the Typology of Sacrifice

Anthropologists, Hubert and Mauss mention their view regarding Vedic sacrifice, 'Sacrifice consists in establishing a means of communication between the sacred and the profane worlds through the mediation of a victim, that is, of a thing that in the course of the ceremony is destroyed'[79]. They have stressed on the animal sacrifice and focused on the destruction of the animal victim, which is offered in the fire. The victim acquires its sacred character in the rite, and does not possess it normally *ab extra*, a fact which makes it well adapted for the accomplishment of the most varied ends[80]. The dichotomy between the sacred and the profane is "the foundation of all societies, the sacred being a set of symbolic figures, radically separated from the world of men, through which the group expresses its own transcendent existence, its moral values."[81]. The two scholars are of the opinion that sacrifice produces a definite effect in the performer and the means which he employs: he is filled with a sacred spirit as is the victim which he offers. This view can be extended to the fact that any oblation irrespective of it being animal or any other, the offering is destroyed in the fire. Moreover, the notion behind giving an offering is not of destruction but reaching it to the desired deity to obtain desired fruit from it. The study undertaken by the two scholars is considered as a landmark in the studies undertaken on sacrifices.

Keith was of the opinion that Vedic ritual was merely an elaborate way of giving gifts to the gods. However, he denied authenticity of the nature of Vedic sacrifice as expressed by the texts themselves[82]. This indicates that he considered a gulf existing between the texts documenting the sacrifice and the performance of sacrifice itself.

Bergaigne and Geldner opined that priests claim to control gods, to capture them in the net of the sacrifice, and make them do their bidding[83]. Sacrifice was a human effort to control the Supreme.

Sir J.G. Frazer is of the view that sacrifice is really not a gift at all, but an effort to secure the propagation of the life of the herds and of the world of vegetation by the periodic slaying of the spirit of vegetation, or in the case of animals of a representative of the species, in order to secure the freshness of the life of the vegetation and of the beasts of the earth. Sacrifice in the long run is reduced purely and simply to a piece of magic: it represents a period before man ceases to believe himself as the lord of nature and master of all that he desires, and recognizing his futility of high belief in humanity, turns to the conception of supernatural powers, whom he supplicates for the results, which he thought formerly to bring about by his own magic powers[84]. Initially, Sir Frazer focused on the pastoral aspects of the sacrifice and later on, on the magical elements derived from the sacrifice.

Levi has studied the sacrifice as represented in the Brāhmaṇa texts except the *Jai. Br* and has maintained the theories of sacrifice containing an idea of *ṛṇa,* i.e. debt of generation[85].

Basham writes,

> The chief purpose of the sacrifice was gratification of the gods in order to obtain boons from them.... the ceremony must have had its element of awe and wonder. The worshippers, inebriated with *soma*, saw wondrous

> visions of the gods: they experienced strange sensations of power; they were gods themselves[86].

Basham relates the sensation of awe or wonder with the sacrifice. Kramrisch brings out the symbolic meaning hidden in the Vedic sacrifice. She sees continuity from the primordial myths of the sacrifice recorded in the *RV* to their 'ritual reenactment' in the *YV* and the Brāhmaṇa-s[87]. Performing a sacrifice is the re-enactment of the cosmic occurrences.

## Historical Origin of the Vedic Sacrifice

Kane opines that the origin of the Vedic sacrifice lies in the fire because of the importance given to fire in its performance, which resembles the fire-worship prevalent among the Zoroastrians. He says:

> the fundamental conceptions of the Yajña (sacrifice) go back to Indo-European antiquities though the traces are rather faint. But it is quite clear that the cult of the sacrifice had been much developed in the Indo-Iranian period. There are numerous words indicative of the cult of the sacrifice both in the Vedic language and in the ancient Parsi religious books[88].

He has highlighted the historical origin of the Vedic sacrifice with that of the Avestan fire-rituals. Historical links of the Vedic sacrifice with other civilizations have also been attempted by many scholars. Basham has proposed a theory that there are connections between the Vedic fire altar and the platforms of fire altar found in the Indus valley[89]. Bhattacharyya has developed a theory that the Vedic sacrifices were originally the inseparable aspects of the 'primitive productive technique' related to agriculture and fertility. He points out to the references to the importance of food in the Vedic texts[90].

## Interpretation Based on the Rituals

According to Staal, the sacrifice is meaningless, at least in the two senses that its original meaning has been long forgotten by ritualists and that the actions performed in the rituals do not really reflect the possibilities those actions assume in the "real" world. He denies the assumption that ritual consists of symbolic activities referring to some external meaning. He considers that ritual is pure activity, without meaning or goal. Ritual is for its own sake.... that is meaningless, without function, aim or goal. It does not follow that it has no value: but whatever value it has its intrinsic value. Ritual exhibits its character of pure activity most readily when it is contrasted with the applied activities of our ordinary everyday life. In ritual activity, the rules count. But not the result....[91] Burde summarizes the main conclusion of Staal as follows:

1) Vedic ritual is pure activity without meaning or 'goal' performed for its own sake.
2) Language developed from the mantra-s.
3) There was in Ancient India a science of ritual[92].

The opinion of Staal in the context of present times may be true. But this does not mean that at the time of the origin of the Vedic sacrificial ritual, the ritual embedded in sacrifice was meaningless. The purpose behind ritual has been long forgotten. Moreover, one has to ponder over the reasons as to why the meaning of the rituals has been long forgotten by the ritualists. Certain socio-economic reasons might be behind this loss, which can be dealt with independently, since there is a requirement of a separate study for this. Heesterman has suggested that the central theme of the solemn Śrauta ritual is the periodical regeneration of the cosmos, the winning of life out of death. In the classical system of the ritual, as presented in the

Brāhmaṇa-s and the Sūtra-s, the pivot of the ritual is the *yajamāna*, the patron at whose expense and for whose sole benefit the ritual is performed. He is supposed symbolically, to incorporate the universe- identified with the cosmic man, Prajāpati. The ritual culminates in his ritual rebirth, which signifies the regeneration of the cosmos. He considers that there are two poles to the ritual, i.e. death and birth and these are resumed in the complementary pair patron-*brāhmaṇa*. He argues that this pair stands for the two opposed groups cooperating in the life-winning ritual. The chariot races and the verbal contests in the Māhavrata, the Vājapeya, the Rājasūya, the Āśvamedha stand for the same. The reason as to why the two, namely patron and the *brāhmaṇa* be complementary to each other is termed by Heesterman as a 'radical reformation' or 'an axial breakthrough'[93]. According to Selvanayagam, this theory provides some useful insights but is ambiguous[94]. Heesterman's theory is criticized as an imaginative construct which lacks objective literary evidence and perspective[95]. Haug has observed the development of the Vedic sacrifice. The term for the beginning of the sacrificial operations is 'to spread the sacrifice'; this means that the invisible thing, representing the ideal sacrifice which was lying dormant, as it were, is set into motion, in consequence of which several parts or limbs are unfolding themselves, and thus the whole becomes extended'[96]. Selvanayagam connects this with the socio-economic development of the Vedic Aryans as was observed by Dandekar[97]. According to Dange, the Vedic sacrificial ritual evolved with the passage of time. Vedic sacrificial ritual throws light on the fusion of the rites and rituals caused by the co-mingling of the Harrapan and the Aryan races. The fusion of all such rites and rituals, practices and beliefs gave rise to the religion of the society which came to be called Hindu[98]. This indicates that in the course of the mobility and migration of the Aryan tribes, there was continual assimilation of local and popular cultic elements into the sacrificial cult. Brāhmaṇa-texts unified different rites, which were practised by different communities. The Brāhmaṇa -texts adapted, enlarged, legitimized the ritual practices and provided sanctity to the customs and practices of different communities, which otherwise would have been lost.

According to Gonda, Vedic ritual has some important psychological and soteriological aspects[99]. These aspects have to be taken into consideration while studying the Vedic sacrifice.

## Sacrifice and Cosmic Order

Dange has established the relationship of sacrifice with the universal order, which stands for Ṛta. All the occurrences depend on Ṛta. The term Ṛta, has the root $\sqrt{}$*ṛ*, which means to go, i.e. that which continues, or that which is eternal. The sacrifice is the symbol of Ṛta, rather the physical form of Ṛta[100]. According to Dange (Mrs.),

> Sacrifice is a replica of cosmic activity. Any smallest ritual detail compliments the sacrifice. Any action like reciting the *mantra*-s, is undertaken to perfect the sacrificial performance. Sacrifice is a human effort to connect the terrestrial plane with the cosmic plane[101].

This relation between sacrifice and cosmos has been asserted by Dharmadhikari. He has highlighted the verse of the *RV* (X. 90. 16), which refers to the cosmic sacrifice. Imitating the cosmic sacrifice, the gods performed their sacrifices. Sāyaṇa on this verse names this cosmic sacrifice as *mānasa-yajña*... The concept that *yajamāna*, the sacrificer, who is often identified with Prajāpati and is expected to offer himself as an oblation in sacrifice owes its origin to the cosmic Puruṣa in the cosmic sacrifice[102]. Dharmadhikari quotes the observation of Yogi Aravinda (Aurobindo), "The whole process of the universe in its very nature is sacrifice". Thus he referred to the cosmic sacrifice ever-rotating in the creation of Prajāpati and probably suggested that the practice of the *dravya-yajña*, represents the cosmic one[103]. Thus scholars, both occidental and oriental have interpreted the Vedic sacrifice adopting different approaches ranging from the anthropological approach to the psychological approach. To specify the approach of the present study one has to take into consideration the different methodological considerations and constraints for studying the Vedic sacrifice.

The interpretations regarding the nature of Vedic sacrifice have been based on the study of specialized literature on Vedic sacrifice, namely the Saṁhitā-s, the Brāhmaṇa-s and the Śrautasūtra-s. Regarding the interiorization of Vedic sacrifice, scholars have taken into account the Āraṇyaka-s and the Upaniṣad-s. It is obvious that specialized literature pays attention to the minutest details of the Vedic sacrifice. Yet to know the position the sacrifice enjoyed apart from these texts, it is essential to take into account the references given in literature other than these sacrificial texts. Such literature provides us with valuable inputs to understand thought-processes of an evolving society and their practices. Hence, apart from specialized textual material on the Vedic sacrifice, it is critical to analyze how sacrifice gets reflected in literature, viz. Epics, i.e. the *Rāmāyaṇa* and the *Mahābhārata,* and the Mahāpurāṇa-s and classical Sanskrit literature.

The Epics and the Mahāpurāṇa-s form a large component of Indian narrative literature. Narrative literature begins with stories and myths that were told orally or through some texts. Narratives are formed in due course of time as a way to extract and circulate information, encourage interaction between different social groups, float new ideas and give impetus to change. Narrative literature like the Epics and the Mahāpurāṇa- s have been composed, arranged and re-arranged by the Suta tradition. The Suta-s, though highly respected in the Epic-Puranic tradition, did not play a significant role either as a priest or sacrificer in the ritual tradition. They were passive observers on one hand, but did uphold the Vedic sacrificial tradition. Their observations found place in the Epics and the Mahāpurāṇa-s, which are strewn with various references of Vedic sacrifices. These references are significant in understanding the position enjoyed by the Vedic sacrificial tradition amongst the non-sacrificing groups, i.e. the masses.

The Vedic sacrificial ritual as documented in the Brāhmaṇa-s and the Śrautasūtra-s is taken up as parameter in tracing the authenticity of the references to the sacrificial ritual mentioned in the abovementioned texts. This methodology takes into consideration the historicity of the composition of the texts taken up for study, as well as takes into account the hermeneutical process of accepting the Vedic literature as the ultimate authority. In the words of Selvanayagam, 'This is a historical process and a hermeneutical process too in which we may recognize tradition, continual change and even mutation'[104]. The word 'hermeneutics' has originated from the Greek word *hermeneuin*: 'to interpret'[105]. This science of interpretation appeared first in the Hellenic period in connection with the study of classical texts and it was later used for biblical interpretations. Burde analyzes system of hermeneutics, "The interpretations are believed to have two aspects. The objective side deals with the grammatical meanings and their historical variations, while the subjective approach tries to understand the author's intention"[106]. According to Schleiermacher (1768–1834), 'we should try to understand the specific part of the text not only in the light of the author's entire body of work, but in light of the author's personal life, intellectual life and career'[107]. He emphasizes that the spirit that permeates the whole (such as a text) sets its mark on the individual parts. The parts are to be understood on the basis of the whole, and the whole is to be understood as an internal harmony of the parts[108]. The basic problem of understanding is connected with our distance in time and space from the object being studied. This gap between the present researcher and the text to be studied is widened because of the impact of the values and principles of the present times. These values come in way in critically understanding the texts of the yonder years. Hermeneutics not only assists in bridging the historical gap but also the gap caused by laying the present century parameters to the ancient texts. As mentioned earlier hermeneutical process does take into account historicity of the textual matter.

Panikkar has also used this methodology. He defines hermeneutics as "the art and science of interpretation, of bringing forth significance, of conveying meaning, of restoring symbols to life and eventually of letting new symbols emerge"[109].

Historicity or historicism assumes that historical phenomena have their own intrinsic worth and must be evaluated on the basis of their own premises. This was the opinion of Herder (1744–1803), who would say that we must distinguish between understanding a phenomenon (such as the blood feud or widow immolation) and accepting it (on the basis of our moral criteria). His idea of humanity as the goal of history is, in sense, an anti-relativistic stance, but it seems to be incompatible with a radical version of the principle of individuation. Historicism propounded by Herder is characterized by understanding the historical phenomena as exceptional, unique, and particular. Methodically, historical understanding be based on the epoch's own premises, and all evaluations should proceed from internal rather than external criteria[110]. This understanding of Herder can be extended to evaluating the textual matter taken into consideration with its own intrinsic worth. One has to understand the time span behind the composition of the texts. The term time span assumes that the texts are not the creation of one single author but many additions/interpolations which have taken place in it. The treatment towards the textual matter should take into consideration the various stages in the composition of the texts. Thus one can proceed from internal criteria rather than external as mentioned by Herder. Thus, this analysis can be concluded with the note that historical approach must be *hermeneutically empathetic*.

One needs to hold this approach to achieve a twofold purpose

a) Firstly, to avoid ahistorical perspective; because many Indian texts are considered to have a universal appeal. They can be judged on the basis of individual experience and historical questions raised by are therefore ignored. Moreover, there are scholars like Bairdeau, who claim that it is essential to take a structuralist approach towards the study of Indian texts. Questioning the historicity of the epics, she says:

> It is no doubt more appropriate- and it is the position I have adopted in this book- to follow the hypothesis put forward some time ago by Georges Dumezil,...: whatever the advances of archaeological research in India, one will never find sufficient traces of the epic events or their cultural context, simply because these are mythical events without even the most elementary historical basis.... What is true of the epic is no doubt even more valid for even the

most explicit Vedic texts, those which abound in the proper names of persons and places; if these had many historical foundations, we can be sure that it has long since been lost when the epic narratives re-use them to say something else. So whatever the specific history of these texts, one can argue that it is forever impossible to reconstitute it, and that in any case this is not the most important task. In one way or another, by a more or less distant reference and through endless re-interpretation, these texts live in the Indian collective consciousness[111].

b) The second purpose is to avoid historical reductionism. This occurs when history of India is assumed to be the history of class struggles. The sacrifice is understood in light of class struggle between the *brāhmaṇa* priests and the laity. According to Kosambi, *bhakti*, i.e. devotion, perpetuates feudalism (however, his contribution to mythology and interpretative methods of social anthropology is revered) [112]. The Upaniṣad-s are also regarded as revolution against the sacrificial order. Texts of religious importance are reduced to mere matter of deriving aesthetic pleasure. It is true that socio-economic conditions have to be taken into consideration for studying the change in beliefs, customs and practices in general and ritual in specific. But this should not attribute to the socio-economic conditions. According to Selvanayagam:

'But to reduce it to a one-way traffic is unjustified because, first, transcendental awareness has been part of human history; second, new kinds of religious awareness have often contributed to the transformation of socio -economic conditions as we note in the development of religious traditions in India'[113].

Therefore an integrated approach of historical-hermeneutics is required for the study of ancient Indian texts. The methodology used in this study is to locate the references to the Vedic sacrificial rituals in the abovementioned texts. These references are compared and contrasted with the source material namely; Saṁhitā-s, Brāhmaṇa-s, and Śrautasūtra-s to find out whether they agree or deviate from the source. An analysis is made as to why do they either agree or deviate from the original source. In the process of analysis, the study assumes that the composition of these texts (apart from the classical Sanskrit literature) went on for centuries, since it is difficult to say whether each text was a composition of one person. It does not have a distinctive unitary form. Hence the study takes into account the various recensions and variations in the texts. Critical editions of the texts, especially the epics are taken into consideration. It is to be noted that critical editions of the Mahāpurāṇa-s were not available to the author. This type of study has been termed as 'historical textual criticism'.

## NEED FOR THE STUDY OF VEDIC SACRIFICIAL RITUALS IN THE SANSKRIT TEXTS

The present work is based on the assumption that changes in the systems of expression and societal understanding about them are also seen to have an impact on the processes and purpose of rituals. According to Bhattacharyya:

> the study of any cult or ritual in itself is of no value unless it is used as a means to understand the vast and enormously complicated problems of social history[114].

Vedic sacrificial ritual can be used as a tool in tracing and understanding the changes taken place in the religious history of ancient India. The epics and the Mahāpurāṇa-s are to be regarded as texts, which are religious, but not ritualistic in character. The present work assumes that epics and the Mahāpurāṇa-s are not compositions of a single pen. They had additions and omissions in their form for centuries together, as they do not form a single homogeneous composition.

The classical Sanskrit texts are composed by poets and dramatists to cater to the tastes of the elite class. In spite of the fact that the above-mentioned texts are not specialized manuals of sacrifice, sacrifice was an integral part of the religion of the society. Therefore, references to sacrifice are strewn in this literature. They can play an important role in determining the date of the composition of the texts. To be more specific, these reflections can determine the date of the composition of a particular portion of the text. The study takes into account the various recensions and variations in the texts taken place in the epics, as per the Mahāpurāṇa-s (availability of the critical editions) and the variations in the texts on classical Sanskrit literature.

In the contexts of the discussions above and in order to achieve the objectives of research, this study analyses:

## The Manner of the Performance of Sacrifices

The work provided special attention to the ritualistic details of any sacrifice referred to in the above mentioned texts. For e.g. the Aśvamedha is referred to in many works. References regarding this sacrifice along with its procedural details are compared to and contrasted with the Brāhmaṇa-s and the Śrautasūtra-s. At some instances there are passing references to the Vedic sacrificial rituals. These references are collected and an attempt is made to determine, which sacrifices the texts are hinting at.

## The Importance of Sacrifices

The texts glorify the Vedic sacrifice. The sacrifice is regarded as the parameter of comparison of one's greatness or merits.

Merit or *puṇya* is calculated in the unit of sacrifice. For e.g. a dip in a particular *tīrtha* would yield the merit of ten Vājapeya sacrifices or hundred Agniṣṭoma sacrifices, etc. The glorification of a king depends on how many sacrifices he performs. In order to throw light on the religious inclination of the subjects living in a kingdom, the texts employ descriptions of the kingdom being strewn with sacrificial posts erected at various places.

## Changing Trends in Sacrifices

From the study of the texts, it is observed that the Vedic sacrifice has undergone various changes. These changes are in the form of

### *Interiorization of the Sacrifice*

According to Bentor:

> Even though the interiorization of Vedic rituals has been extensively discussed by such scholars as Eliade, Varenne, Biardeau and Malamoud, and Heesterman, it is essential to bear in mind that at times these writers refer to different forms of interiorized rituals. The term 'interiorization' may pertain to a mental performance of the ritual, to the replacement of the ritual with a continuous process of life such as breathing or eating, to a particular way of life such as renunciation, to an actual performance with an inner interpretation, to the replacement of the external ritual with an internal one, and so forth[115].

There are terms like *ātmayajña, tapoyajña, dhyānayajña,* etc. employed to show the interiorized forms of the Vedic sacrificial ritual.

### *Simplification and Replacement of the Vedic Sacrifice*

Vedic sacrifice has involved animal offerings in it. Certain portions of the texts denounce animal sacrifice.

The concluding chapter of the study will make an attempt to analyze this trend. It is to be noted that the changing trends occurring in the Vedic sacrifice are termed by some scholars as 'Hinduization of the Vedic sacrifice'. The socio-religious trends which emerged in the process of time influenced the Vedic sacrificial ritual. Smith has analyzed this process with an example of *soma*-sacrifice. He says:

> The shift from the Śrauta to the Hindu ritual occurred in the domain of complexity: i.e. the rites became simpler, from the participation of a multitude of officiants and the text sources to only one. A *soma*-sacrifice required the sacrificer, seventeen officiants, four principal fire-places and nine minor ones; a variety of offering material including rice, ghee, animals, and *soma*: a vast quantity of ritual recitation; and an extraordinary degree of precision, patience, and expertise in order to complete the sacrifice. On the other hand a Rudra Mahāyajña, one of the fairly common major Hindu sacrifices, employs either one or eleven officiants in addition to the sponsor, the offering of a simple oblation of rice or sesame seeds mixed with ghee into a single, while the officiants recite in unison, eleven times, the Rudrādhyāya (*Tait Sam* IV. 5. 1-11)[116].

Discussions regarding Vedism and Hinduism and also Vedic Hinduism have been made by Brian Smith[117]. The conclusion of the present work will tackle these issues, especially those which consider that Vedism and Hinduism are two different religions using the changing trends in Vedic sacrifice as the parameter. Changing trend in the Vedic sacrifice is not reflected by mere change or simplification in the mode of ritual. The Vedic sacrifice has also been replaced by visits to *tīrtha*-s, i.e. holy place or performing *vrata*-s, i.e. vows. A list of *tīrtha*-s and *vrata*-s is given in the appendices of this work. A visit to a *tīrtha* or performance of a *vrata* is said to be equivalent to the fruit of the performance of many sacrifices. It is to be noted that the Vedic sacrifice was replaced by these *tīrtha*-s and *vrata*-s, but the fruit which was bestowed upon the sacrificer for the performance of the sacrifice remained static in the course of time.

## THE SACRIFICE EXPRESSED IN FIGURATIVE SENSE

Apart from references to the sacrifices and rituals, the Vedic sacrifice is reflected through various figures of speech like simile, metaphor, etc. There are few allegories occurring in the texts. Classical literature abounds in such figurative expressions. This is one of the reasons as to why classical literature was involved in the study, although it was not religious in character. The figurative expressions also take into account the sacrifice and its ritualistic details incorporated in the cosmic form assumed by chief gods like Śiva and Viṣṇu.

Although Vedic sacrifice was regarded as obsolete and outdated, yet there are certain historical references, which indicate that horse sacrifices were performed by kings[118]. The list of kings performing the horse sacrifice/s indicates that the Vedic sacrifice is not to be regarded as obsolete or out of vogue. A study of the procedure of these sacrifices is essential to understand the position and nature of these sacrifices.

| *Kings* | *Horse sacrifices* | *Date* |
|---|---|---|
| Parīkṣit | 03 | 3101 BC–3065 BC |
| Sarvatāta | 01 | About 500 BC |
| Puṣyamitra Śunga | 02 | 186 BC–150 BC |
| Sātakarṇi | 02 | 21 AD–77 AD |
| Caṇṭamūla | 01 | 250 AD |
| Haritiputra | 04 | 240 AD–300 AD |
| Bhavanāga | 10 | 260 AD–320 AD |
| Samudragupta | 01 | About 350 AD |
| Kumāragupta | 01 | 420 AD–430 AD |
| Praharasena | 01 | 460 AD–470 AD |
| Vallabhāśva | 01 | Later part of the fifth century AD |
| Pulakeśin I | 01 | Early 6th century AD |
| Mahendravarman of Assam | 02 | Early 6th century AD |
| Mahābhūtivarman | 01 | Before 554 AD |
| Sthitavarman of Assam | 01 | Early 6th centuryAD |
| Mādhavavarman | 01 | Between 535 AD–585 AD |
| Ādityasenagupta | 01 | About 650 AD |
| Jayasiṁha of Mewar | 01 | Early18th century AD |

The above chart gives us a list of kings, who have performed the Aśvamedha sacrifices. There are a number of inscriptions, which record the performance of these sacrifices. Since the present work is focused on purely textual matter, these inscriptions have not been taken up for study. Secondly, the non-availability of the critical editions of many Mahāpurāṇa-s have come in the way of determining which passages were composed earlier and which passages were composed at a latter date. This study is not intended to make a catalogue of all the references of Vedic sacrifices occurring in the epics, Mahāpurāṇa-s and classical Sanskrit dramas and Mahākāvya-s. Hence some references which passingly mention sacrifice are not recorded here. However this has not at all hindered the present endeavour in knowing the rituals of the Vedic sacrifices, as can be vouchsafed from the last, i.e. the concluding chapter, which speaks of the positive results arrived at.

# 2

# The Rāmāyaṇa

Epics, viz. the *Rām* and the *Mbh* are regarded as important sources of understanding the nature of post-Vedic religion, society and culture in ancient India. There is a deep impact of Vedic religion on the two epics. The institution of sacrifice is an essential feature of Vedic religion. It has pervaded over the societal and cultural aspects of the Vedic times. The epics have incorporated descriptions and references to sacrifice. A study of Vedic sacrifice occurring in the epics is essential for the proper understanding of:-

a) the Vedic ritual in practice among the people at the time of the composition of the epics;
b) the transformation of the Vedic ritual in the post-Vedic period;

and

c) the influence, which the institution of sacrifice exerted over the society as depicted in the epics.

The epics were transferred from generation to generation through oral tradition. This oral tradition of narration of heroic legends was a constituent of sacrificial ceremonies. The daily discourse of rotating sagas of gods and heroes, i.e. *pāriplava* during the performance of the Aśvamedha sacrifice is an appropriate reference to this oral tradition[119]. This cycle composed of mini cycles of narration of ten days, lasted for one year, while the sacrificial horse was away from the sacrificial chamber. At the end of the daily ritual, when the *hotṛ* priest had finished for the day, the chief of the lute players sang the deeds of the past kings, thus bringing the present sacrificer king in line with the royal sacrificers of the past[120]. It is noteworthy that the *Rām* was first narrated at the Aśvamedha sacrifice performed by King Rāma[121].

The *sūta*-s were the first composers, reciters and preservers of epic- poetry[122]. They narrated the epics from generation to generation and thereby preserved the great works through oral tradition. According to Winternitz, the credit of composing the two great epics goes to the tradition of the *sūta*-s. An inexhaustible store of prose and verse narratives-Ākhyāna-s, Itihāsa-s, Purāṇa-s and Gāthā-s forming as it were literary public property was drawn upon by the Buddhists and the Jains, as well as by the epic poets[123]. Their narration carried descriptions of and references to the sacrifices performed by kings of the yonder years. The details of the *sūta* tradition will be discussed in the chapter on the M. Pu-s which incorporate the myths relating to the origin of this community.

Among the Vedic sacrifices, the Aśvamedha has received the foremost position in the *Rām*[124]. However, the references to sacrifices like the Agniṣṭoma, Vājapeya, etc. occur by their names only. There is no description found of rituals performed in these sacrifices. This trend is seen in the *Mbh* also. The reason for the epics maintaining silence over the sacrifices other than the Aśvamedha might be that the *sūta*-s were the close associates of kings. Their narrations were based on the exploits of heroic and sovereign kings. Aśvamedha was regarded as the parameter of sovereignty; hence among the sacrifices performed by kings in the epics, the Aśvamedha dominates the scene.

## DATE OF THE *RĀM*

Before discussing the nature of the Vedic sacrifice occurring in the *Rām* text, it is important to discuss the date of its composition. The *Rām* appears to reveal the trend that Vedic sacrifices were getting more and more obsolete in practice, yet their importance as an institution was prevalent. Hence, the sacrifice described in this epic deviates from the original sacrifice recorded in the Śrauta tradition. One has to note that the *Rām* is different from the Rāmakathā recorded in the Van. P. of the *Mbh*. Rāmakathā, an older form of the *Rām* was in the form of floating mass of literature circulated from mouth to mouth. To have a clear idea of the difference between Rāmakathā and the *Rām* of Vālmīki, one must take into account the opinions regarding the date of the composition of the *Rām*.

According to Jacobi, Keith and Macdonell, the core *Rām* was composed before 500 BC. Bulcke and Gonda opine that the date of the *Rām* composition is the end of 400 BC. Guruge has proved the date of *Rām* to be 300 BC. Sankalia indicates the date to be as old as 1,500–1,000 BC. According to Lal, *Rām* is posterior to the original *Bhārata* of Vaiśaṁpāyana[125]. Dange (Mrs.) opines that the last edition of the *Rām* has been formed by the end of 300 BC[126].

## VARIOUS STAGES OF THE COMPOSITION OF THE *RĀM*

According to Yardi, Valmiki's original *Rām* was expanded in five successive stages by Sūta, his son Sauti,

Harivaṁśakāra and Parvasaṅgrahakāra and one more anonymous author christened as U-style author in the form of imaginary characters, events, myths and legends[127].

Bhatt admits that the original *Rām* consisted of only five *kāṇḍa*-s (II-VI) and that the Bāl and the Utt were added later on[128]. The subject matter of the present study being the Vedic sacrificial rituals in the *Rām*, irrespective of the statement made by Weber, 'as many Rāmāyaṇa-s as there are manuscripts' (q. 'soviel Handscriften soveil Rāmāyaṇa-s)[129] the edition taken into consideration is that of Panshikar with the commentary named *Tilaka* and the variations are noted from the critical edition of Baroda.

The period of the composition of the *Rām* indicates the rise of Buddhism. The institution of Vedic sacrifice was no longer dominant on the religious scene. Hence, elaborate Vedic sacrifices were not in vogue. Therefore, the descriptions of Vedic sacrifices are infrequent in the *Rām.*

## SACRIFICES OCCURRING IN THE RĀM

The *Rām* mentions the performance of two Aśvamedha sacrifices.

The Bāl of the *Rām* refers to the performance of the Aśvamedha by King Daśaratha. The king approached Sage Ṛśyaśrṅga to perform the Aśvamedha sacrifice. The Aśvamedha, as a ritual is an *ahīna* type of sacrifice, i.e. a sacrifice, which extends from two days to twelve days. The Aśvamedha has three pressing days, i.e. three days during which the Soma is pressed[130].

The origin of this sacrifice can be traced to the *RV* (I. 162, 163). The *Ait. Br.* (VIII. 2. 3) and the *Śat. Br.* (XIII. 5. 4), which refer to this ancient and famous rite, which kings alone performed to increase their realms. It is to be noted that the *Ait. Br.* does not mention about Aśvamedha sacrifice but another rite called the Aindramahābhiṣeka.

In these Brāhmaṇa-s a list of kings is enumerated, who were consecrated to perform this sacrifice. According to Kane, *Tait. Br.* identifies Aśvamedha with kingdom[131]. The Śrautasūtra-s also follow the line of the Saṁhitā-s and the Brāhmaṇa-s. The *Āśv. Śr. Sū, Kāt. Śr. Sū.* deem Aśvamedha as an *ahīna* with three pressings of Soma. *Āśv. Śr. Sū.* agreeing with the *Ait. Br.*, about the Aindramahābhiṣeka says that one who desires to secure all objects, to win all victories (including the one over his senses) and to attain all prosperity may perform Aśvamedha (*Āśv. Śr. Sū.* X. 6. 1).

King Daśaratha, who was childless, performed the Aśvamedha for progeny on the banks of river Sarayu (*Rām* Bāl 8. 1-2). One should perform the sacrifice following the rules, lest the sacrificer should perish says the *Rām* (Bāl 8. 18. and 12. 16).

Sacrificial material was collected (*sambhāra*) and 21 sacrificial posts i.e. *yūpa*-s were erected of the height of 21 *aratni*-s. Each six ones among the sacrificial posts were of *bilva, khadira* and *palāśa,* and one of *śleṣmātaka* and two of *devadāru* (Bāl 14.22-24ab). The erection of the sacrificial posts agrees with the information from the Śrautasūtra-s (*Āp Śr. Sū.* XX. 9. 6-8)[132].

According to the *Tait. Br.* the number of the *yūpa*-s was symbolic of twelve months, five seasons, three worlds and the sun (III. 8. 20. 2). There are two types of *sambhāra*-s i.e. objects comprising earth and those from the wood as mentioned in the *Tait.Br.* (II. 1.3.9-12). The Brāhmaṇa text enumerates the list of *sambhāra*-s along with their Arthavāda. Before placing the *sambhāra*-s the surface of the ground chosen for sacrifice is dug out. Then the following materials are placed: sand, saline earth, earth dug up by rats, earth from the anthill, clay from a never-drying lake, pebbles and gold. These are the things related with the earth. Among the things related with wood; *aśvattha, udumbara, parṇa, śamī, vikaṅkata* and tree struck by the lightning[133].

King Daśaratha commenced the Aśvamedha in the spring season and it lasted for one year, i.e. till the next spring season[134]. He underwent *dīkṣā,* i.e. consecration, for the performance of the sacrifice and then performed the Pravargya and the Upasad rites. In the Śrauta tradition, Pravargya is dealt with independently. It was supposed to provide the sacrificer with a celestial body. The Śrauta tradition does not mention the Pravargya rite to be performed at the commencement of the Aśvamedha. It is interesting to note that the critical edition accepts the version- *pravargyam śāstrataḥ kṛtvā tathaivopasadam dvijāḥ.* The Nepali, Maithili, Bengali, Devanagari (Mss. No. 10) and Ujjaini versions have incorporated the verse as— *pravargyādikramam cakruḥ kalpasūtravidhānataḥ*[135]. The priests (*ṛtvij*-s) well versed in the science of the ritual made sacrificial bricks blazed (*iṣṭakā*-s) and enkindled the fire. The fire blazed like a mighty eagle facing the east and with a tail. The ritual of the Aśvamedha, according to the *Tait. Sam.* (*kāṇḍa*-s IV-V) refers principally to the five layers of bricks. In the composition of the *Rām,* the Aśvamedha recorded in it strictly adhered to the rules of the Śrauta tradition[136].

It is to be noted that the Aśvamedha site located near Kalsi situated in the district of Dehra Dun displays some parts of Cayana, i.e. the piling up of bricks, for the sacrificial altar of recognizable measurements. They were utilized in the construction of *caitya* during the fourth Aśvamedha performed by king Śīlavarman in the 25th year of his reign[137].

The *Rām* mentions the three queens, viz. *mahiṣī, vāvātā* and *parivṛktī.* Kausalyā, the *mahiṣī,* immolated the horse with three swords[138]. It is to be understood that Kausalyā did not immolate the horse, this immolation took place on behalf of Kausalyā. According to the Śrauta tradition the queens tuck beads of gold into the mane and tail of the horse. They anoint the horse and then the horse is smothered with a large cloth, i.e. *tārpya* point the *Tait. Br.* (III. 9. 4. 4. ff.) and *Śat. Br.* (XIII. 2. 6. 8. ff.). However, the commentator Govindarāja justifies the procedure in the *Rām*[139]. The queens drew lines on the body of the horse. It is explained that the lines, which are drawn on the body of the horse serve the sacrificer as bridges to the heavenly world and secure people and royal power for him (*Śat. Br.* XIII. 2. 10.1). The swords are made up of gold, silver and copper, standing for the people, the Aśvamedha sacrifice itself and the royal power respectively.

King Daśaratha offered the marrow/omentum of the horse in the sacrificial fire and inhaled its smoke. The *Rām* further adds that on inhalation of this smoke, Daśaratha was freed from impurities (Bāl 14.34-36). The Śrauta tradition mentions differently. Along with the horse, the *tūpara* (hornless he-goat) and *gomṛga* (bovine deer) are immolated. Their omentum is offered. But as the horse does not have omentum, its fat is offered, says the *Tait. Br.* (III. 8.20.3) and *Śat. Br.* (XIII. 5. 2. 10). The *Rām* observes the ritual minutely and says that the offerings of other animals are to be placed on the mat of Plakṣa tree (*Ficus infectoria*) and that of the horse on a cane mat (Bal 14. 38).

The offerings of the Aśvamedha are spread out over three days, i.e. the Sutyā days. The first day is called the Agniṣṭoma and on this day the Catuṣṭoma laud is recited. According to the *Śat. Br.* (XIII. 3. 4) and the *Tān. Mbr.* (XXI. 4. 4) a honeybee tore the thigh of the horse. The Catuṣṭoma laud made the thigh whole. On the second day, i.e. the Ukthya day domesticated animals are sacrificed and non-domesticated animals are released. The third day is the Atirātra day. On this day is the horse immolated. However the *Rām* has changed the order. The immolation of the horse takes place after the Sutyā days. This is followed by Jyotiṣṭoma, Āyuṣṭoma, Atirātra, Abhijit, Viśvajit and Āptoryāma. According to the *Aśv. Śr. Sū.*, Abhijit should be performed for obtaining cows and Viśvajit should be performed by one desirous of animals[140].

King Daśaratha gave donations in the form of land and wealth to the priests. According to the Śrauta tradition, king should donate to the *hotṛ* wealth of the eastern part of the country, southern, western and northern parts respectively to the *brahman, adhvaryu* and *udgātṛ*. The *Rām* follows the rule perfectly[141].

Dange states the purpose behind the performance of the Aśvamedha in accordance with the *RV*, which is as follows:

I) general weal;
II) plenty in cattle, horses, sons and nourishing wealth and martial spirit
III) the fortune of women (both married and maidens)

There is no trace of royal glory in the ritual at this stage. From *RV*, it would appear that the sacrifice of the horse was initially for Tvaṣṭṛ who was believed to be the older god and the father of gods and that it was also a seasonal sacrifice and not very special. It was more for the people at large, unlike its later version, which was meant only for powerful king, and performed at long intervals. However, there is an indication that it was also performed for royal sway, when king Sudās of the Bharata clan, is said to have released his horse and had to clash with ten kings[142].

It is to be noted that the purpose of the Aśvamedha in the Bāl of *Rām* is for progeny. This episode does not associate any pomp, sovereignty, display of power, etc., with the sacrifice. The Aśvamedha performed over here is merely a fertility ritual, which is no. II as stated earlier.

Bhattacharyya opines: 'even the Rgvedic form of the horse sacrifice is not its original form because, one should not fail to recall in this connection that the *AV* regards Aśvamedha, the Rājasūya, the Vājapeya, the *sattra*-s and several other sacrifices as *utsanna*, i.e. gone out of vogue. The *Tait. Sam* and the *Śat. Br* also hint at the original purpose of the Aśvamedha and feature it to have sunk into oblivion'[143].

Keith highlights various opinions by scholars about the Aśvamedha. The meaning of the sacrifice is in the former view of Oldenberg the offering to Indra, the god of the warriors, of swift strong steed from which the sacrificer would thus derive magic power, whether directly or indirectly through the fact that Indra would thus be made strong to aid him. His later view makes the rite magical; the horse embodies royalty, and by its consecration is made especially sacred so that its slaughter gives strength to the sacrificer. The relation of the queen and the horse is clearly a fertility spell, while the obscene language, he thinks, might be explained in the same sense or as an amusement of the gods, or a mere relic of the plain speech of the crowd. In the view of Eggeling, the horse, the animal next to man in the scale is an appropriate offering on great occasions at the sacrifice; the steed can be identified with Prajāpati and so Prajāpati comes properly into the ritual. In view of von Negelein, the offering was made to the sun conceived as a steed, in order to strengthen him for his course in the heaven. Keith concludes, "the most attractive alternative to this view as the sun horse, offered originally to the sun as a spell to strengthen it, and the chief difficulty in that view is merely the fact that the sun is not the recipient of the offering, in any measure"[144].

According to Kak, the Aśvamedha rite has several functions. These are enumerated as follows:

a) It represents an equivalence of the Nakṣatra year to the heaven implying that it is a rite that celebrates the rebirth of the Sun.
b) It is symbolic of the conquest of Time by the king in whose name the rite is performed.
c) It is a celebration of social harmony achieved by the transcendence of the fundamental conflicts between various services of power[145].

After taking into account the opinions of scholars on the nature of the Aśvamedha sacrifice, it is necessary to examine the nature of the Aśvamedha performed by King Daśaratha in the Bāl of the *Rām*. The episode of the Aśvamedha in the Bāl of the *Rām* has procuring progeny as its purpose. This episode does not associate any pomp, sovereignty, display of power, etc. with the sacrifice. The Aśvamedha over here is merely a fertility ritual, which is (pt. no. II) according to Dange. A minute observation of the rituals described in the Bāl of the *Rām* indicates that this sacrifice hints at the primary function of the Aśvamedha, i.e. fertility.

The Bāl mentions of Kausalyā sleeping next to the silenced horse for one night. King Daśaratha inhaled the fumes of the *vapā* of the horse after it was offered to the fire. This cleansed him of the sins and he became pure. It is important to note that the horse does not have an omentum. Therefore the fat around its intestine is offered to the fire[146]. This action on the part of Daśaratha indicates the development of potency to procure offspring. In the *RV* the silenced sacrificial horse is propitiated for male progeny (I. 162. 22). The *Śat. Br* mentions the horse being in its prime youth as a criterion for the selection of the sacrificial horse. The reason behind this criterion is that prime youth indicates unlimited vigour on the part of the sacrificer (XIII. 4. 2. 2). After the immolation of the horse, the queens encircle it nine times. The *mahiṣī* says, "I will urge the seed layer, urge thou the seed layer! Seed, doubtless, means offspring and cattle": offspring and cattle she thus secures for herself according to *Vāj. Sam* (XXIII. 20). The *mahiṣī* further adds, "May the vigorous male, the layer of seed, lay seed" according to the *Śat. Br* (XIII. 2. 8. 5).

According to Dange, "It appears that the sacrifice of royal sway was originally a separate one and the ritual of fertility equally current among the the Vedic peoples' tradition got mixed up"[147]. The composer of this section must have been aware of the 'other purpose' of the Aśvamedha. Therefore, he has described the ritual aspect as against the political purpose of sovereignty and the battles fought for it, in detail with little deviations from the earlier Vedic ritual. It is essential to understand the reasons behind this description.

After the commencement of the Aśvamedha, Ṛśyaśṛṅga instructed Daśaratha to perform the Putrīyā-iṣṭi. The text says that he performed this *iṣṭi* with the Atharvaśiras mantra-s[148]. The text does not give any more details of the procedure of this *iṣṭi*. But it describes that all the gods and *gandharva*-s arrived to receive their share in the *iṣṭi*. What was the role of Ṛśyasṛṅga in the two sacrifices? Rśyaśṛṅga was not included among the list of the court priests of Daśaratha (Bāl 8. 6). Yet he received a special invitation in the sacrifice in the capacity of a priest (*ṛtvij*), to guide the sacrifice. But no details about the position of Rśyaśṛṅga are indicated in the passage on the sacrifice.

The Bāl of *Rām* (canto 9) gives a short account of Rśyaśṛṅga. This information was provided by Sūta Sumantra in secret. Rśyaśṛṅga, the son of Vibhāṇḍaka, was a celibate. He lived in a forest and worshipped his father and the fire (i.e. he performed sacrifices). At that time the kingdom of Aṅga suffered from a severe drought.

Romapāda, the king of Aṅga, was advised by the *brāhmaṇa*-s to invite Rśyaśṛṅga in his kingdom as a solution to the drought. The king brought him to the kingdom with the help of courtesans and gave his daughter Śāntā in marriage. The Sūta told Daśaratha that Rśyaśṛṅga will be helpful in the birth of his sons, according to the prophecy of Sanatkumāra (Bāl 9. 2). This narration does not discuss the relation between the birth of Rśyaśṛṅga and the relation between his arrival and rainfall.

According to Altekar, the story of Rśyaśṛṅga and the two sacrifices, namely the Aśvamedha and the Putrīyā-iṣṭi following it, performed under his auspices are interpolated in the Bāl[149]. This means that the cantos 8-17 are interpolated. Bulcke is of the opinion that cantos 8-14 are genuine. After the distribution of *dakṣiṇā*, Rśyaśṛṅga, the chief officiating priest, assured that four sons will be born to Daśaratha (Bāl 14. 59). After this assurance the Putrīyā-iṣṭi sacrifice told in the cantos 15-17 stands superfluous. Besides that, canto 18 begins with a reference to the departure of the gods after the completion of the sacrifice. This conclusively proves that originally canto 18 followed immediately after canto 14[150]. The opinion of Bulcke seems to be convincing. However, Altekar comments that 'the king is described to have ruled righteously. He was growing old but had no son. He might have thought of performing the Putrīyā-iṣṭi sacrifice and got it done by the family priest Maharṣi Vasiṣṭha and got sons by the grace of God. There could not have been any vestige of any deification of Rāma or his brothers. Vālmīki has composed his epic true to his idealism expressed at the very outset of his epic and supported by the short story of Rāma narrated by Nārada. But later on when the deification of Kṛṣṇa inspired the interpolator, he thought of deifying Rāma as well. For that in his plan he wanted to enhance first the reputation of

Daśaratha by the performance of the Aśvamedha sacrifice and then to begin the Putrīyā-iṣṭi for getting sons as *avatāra*-s of Viṣṇu[151].

The reference to the Putrīyā-iṣṭi without many details occurs in the *Tait Sam* of the *KṛṣṇaYV*, in which the offerings are to be given to the dual divinities named Indra and Agni. According to the *Tait. Sam*, Prajāpati, created offspring. On his creation, Indra and Agni hid them away. By giving an offering of *puroḍāśa* of eleven potsherds, to Indra and Agni, Prajāpati restored the offspring. One who is desirous of offspring and is fit for offering should give an offering on *puroḍāśa* of eleven potsherds[152]. The *Baudh. Śr. Sū* of the *KṛṣṇaYV* tradition also follows the same tune (XIII. 2). However, the sacrifice is not known as the Putrakāmeṣṭi. The *Śān. Śr. Sū* refers to the Vaiśvadevastut for obtaining progeny (XIV. 60). This Śrauta text mentions of the hymns recited in favour of Mitra and Varuṇa. Kane refers to the Putrakāmeṣṭi mentioned in the *Āśv. Śr. Sū* (II. 10. 8-9). This is the sacrifice performed for one desirous of son or one adopting a son. He quotes the *Vyavahāramayūkha* quoted in the *Kālikāpurāṇa* which prescribes that on adopting a son who is about five years old or more, the adopter should perform this rite[153].

The reference to the Putrakāmeṣṭi does occur as a rite in the *Dharmasindhu*, an 18th century AD text to be performed if one gets only female progeny. The ritual refers to the offering of *caru* cooked in milk and sixty handfuls of rice grains. The mantra-s recited are from the *Āpastamba Mantrabrāhmaṇa* and the *Hiraṇyakeśi Gṛhyasūtra*. Stray references occurring in the Saṁhitā-s and the Śrautasūtra-s of this *iṣṭi* and the mention of this rite in the texts on the Dharmaśāstra-s, indicates that the rite is of a later origin. The *Rām* mentions that the ritual was performed with the Atharvaśiras mantra-s. The mantra-s of the

Atharvaśiras are not mentioned in the *Dharmasindhu*. Rather the mantra-s are to be recited from the *KṛṣṇaYV* tradition. Putrīyā-iṣṭi thus serves as an example indicating the deviations from the details of the authentic sacrificial rituals. The composer/reciter of the *Rām* added these details without verifying them with the original sources. It can also be explained that the reference to the Atharvaśiras mantra-s is an attempt for incorporating the *AV* tradition in this entire exercise for bearing progeny. Lastly, this particular section of the rite indicates the influence of Gṛhya tradition over the *Rām*[154].

If the purpose of Aśvamedha is accepted as a fertility ritual then the cantos 8-14 of the Bāl do not seem to be an interpolation. Rather, the Aśvamedha sacrifice in the Bāl. seems to be the reflection of early Vedic ritual of the Aśvamedha. The political purport of the Aśvamedha appears to be a secondary growth. This secondary aspect got a pivotal place amongst the Śrauta texts. If the opinion among scholars is taken into account, then as per the Śrauta texts the Aśvamedha has deviated from its purpose of sovereignty and royal sway but has retained the seed of the early nature of the ritual of fertility.

The *Rām* (Utt) mentions the sacrifice of Aśvamedha performed by Rāma. It does not furnish many ritual details. It notes that the horse, which was released was *kṛṣṇasāra* in colour, i.e. one with black spots (92. 1). The *Śat. Br* refers to different opinions regarding the colour of the sacrificial horse. According to the opinion of Bhāllaveya, the horse should be of two colours, black- spotted *(kṛṣṇasāraṅgaḥ)* (XIII. 4. 2. 1-4). The reason given is that it was produced from the eye of Prajāpati and the eye is of two colours, white and black. The commentary *Tilaka* says that black colour is the essence of all sacrificial animals. However, the colour of the sacrificial horse is in accordance to that which is specified in the texts. The horse must be all white with dark circular spots or the front part of its body may be dark and the rest of the body white. It has a tuft of black/bluish hair[155].

In the sacrifice, many actors, dancers and musicians arrived. The place for the sacrifice was the Naimiṣa forest (Utt 91.15). Among the sacrificial materials are rice grains, sesame, pulses, gram, *kulittha, māṣa* and salt (Utt 91. 20-22). The presence of Sītā was in the form of a golden effigy[156].

The point of discussion is that before the commencement of this sacrifice, Rāma had expressed the desire to perform the Rājasūya[157]. There was a discussion between Rāma and his brothers, viz. Lakṣmaṇa and Bharata and they advised him to perform the Aśvamedha in place of the Rājasūya. The reason given is that Rājasūya leads to bloodshed (*Rām* Utt 83. 13-14). The moot question is that why is the Rājasūya replaced by the Aśvamedha under the pretext of bloodshed? Heesterman says that, in the ancient Indian *corpus rituale,* the Rājasūya does not represent a special type of sacrifice nor was it surrounded with the pomp and prestige of the horse sacrifice, i.e. Aśvamedha, the king of sacrifices[158].

According to Dange, "the term *rājasūya* indicates the creation of new essence (*sava*) in the king..... It is clear that, through this sacrifice, the king assured himself of socio-political eminence together with divine protection... At the original stage it was not as elaborate as it is seen in the Śrautasūtra-s". He further adds, "at the Rājasūya the king is already a king. What, then, is the specialty of this sacrifice? It lies in the assertion, by a public ceremony, of this status of him. Hence, it is constantly stated that he is being created (*sūyate, savaḥ*) on various levels–the divine, the terrestrial and the socio-political level"[159]. Then the question arises that if the texts have lauded this sacrifice and that which creates the new essence in the king, why does Lakṣmaṇa and Bharata dissuade Rāma from the performance of this sacrifice?

Thite cites examples from the Vedic texts which describe this sacrifice as dangerous and leading to loss of valour. He interpretes this sacrifice as something is lost in the performance and then regained by the king[160]. Apart from discussing the textual details of this sacrifice, the problem of the rejection of the performance of the Rājasūya can be solved if it is compared with the Aśvamedha.

Firstly, the rejection to the Rājasūya is on the grounds that this sacrifice would cause bloodshed and lead to the annihilation of many kings.

Secondly, Aśvamedha is regarded to be superior to the Rājasūya. As seen earlier the Aśvamedha incorporates battles fought only if a king obstructs the horse from wandering in his territory. If the sacrificial horse goes unobstructed, it symbolizes the supremacy of the sacrificer-king over the other king. This type of symbolic assertion of supremacy in the Aśvamedha ritual is not devised in the Rājasūya. Hence to assert the supremacy of the king who is desirous of performing the Rājasūya, fighting battles and annihilating a number of kings becomes inevitable.

Aśvamedha is regarded as a far superior sacrifice to the Rājasūya. This is the sacrifice which washes off sins like that of *brahmahatyā*. No other sacrifice can be compared with this sacrifice. The description of the Aśvamedha in the *Rām* (Utt) incorporates the pomp and fervour associated with it. Therefore, the Rājasūya is replaced by Aśvamedha. The ritual of pacifying the horse and the queen sleeping next to it is dropped since a golden image of Sītā was made as a symbolic participation of the queen Sītā.

## SATTRA-S

The *Rām* mentions the performance of two *sattra*-s. *Sattra*-s are those sacrifices, which have a minimum time span of twelve days and no maximum time span. They can be performed up to any number of years.

1. The *Rām* (Utt 55-57) narrates the story of King Nimi, the son of Ikṣvāku. He had chosen Vasiṣṭha as the chief officiating priest (Utt 55. 8). However, Vasiṣṭha was engaged by Indra. He asked Nimi to wait till the sacrifice of Indra was completed. But Nimi performed the sacrifice with Gautama as the chief officiating priest. Considering this as an offence, Vasiṣṭha cursed Nimi that his sentience would desert him and in a fit of rage Nimi cursed him back. However, Vasiṣṭha approached Lord Brahmā and according to his advice regained his sentience by the lustre of Mitra and Varuṇa, the dual deities. Sage Bhṛgu agreed to help Nimi. But he helped the king in a different manner. He placed the sentience of Nimi in the eyes of living beings. The body of Nimi was changed to *araṇi*-s, i.e. wooden slabs used for churning fire. From the churning was born Mithi. Since he was born, he became a Janaka (the derivation of this word is non- Paninian). Moreover, as he was born from the bodiless sentience, he became Vaideha (Utt 57. 18-19). Thus the etymologies of the words 'Mithi', 'Janaka' and 'Videha' have their source in the sacrifice. The various implications of this myth are further discussed in this chapter.
2. King Marutta is one among the famous kings who performed sacrifices. He is referred to in the Brāhmaṇa-s and the Śrautasūtra-s.

In the *Rām,* Marutta occurs as a king performing the Māheśvara *sattra* with Sage Saṁvarta as the chief officiating priest. Many gods participated in the sacrifice in the form of birds and animals. When Rāvaṇa entered the sacrificial place, they became frightened and started running helter-skelter. King Marutta challenged Rāvaṇa for a dual combat. However, Sage Saṁvarta intervened and said that if the *sattra* was left unaccomplished it would reduce the sacrificer and his family to ashes. Marutta agreed and gave up the combat. However, his sacrifice was destroyed by Rāvaṇa (Utt 18.1ff).

King Marutta's association with Vedic sacrifices can be traced up to the *Ait. Br.* VIII. 4. 21, *Śat. Br.* XIII. 5. 4. 6, *Śāṅ. Śr. Sū.* XVI. 9. 14-15. Among the three texts, the *Ait. Br.* associated Marutta with Aindramahabhiseka, whereas the *Śat. Br.* and *Śāṅ. Śr. Sū* have associated him with the Aśvamedha, which was performed with the Atirātra and Mahāvrata sacrifices. However, all the three texts associate him with the Marut-s. This association does not occur in the *Rām*.

The reason can be explained that this association would have been out of place in the entire sacrificial context[161]. Besides, when it comes to the performance of *sattra*, it does not incorporate the choosing of a priest and all the officiating priests are the *yajamāna*-s. Therefore Marutta might have performed some other sacrifice, the details of which seem to have been lost.

Since the *Mbh* abounds in references to the *sattra*-s, the position and details of *sattra*-s are discussed in the next chapter.

## OTHER REFERENCES TO THE VEDIC SACRIFICE

### Offerings by Kausalyā

In the *Rām*, there is a reference to Kausalyā giving oblation in fire. Rāma saw Kausalyā clad in white silk giving offering to the fire with the *mantra*-s[162]. The offerings were curds, *akṣatā*(unbroken ricegrains), clarified butter, sweet-meats, *lājā* (parched ricegrains), white garlands, *pāyasa* (porridge prepared with milk), *kṛsara* (rice with combination of sesame and pulses) and *samidh*-s (sacrificial faggots). She had used pots filled to their brim (with water). Important point is that how can a woman single-handedly give offerings?

The commentator says that she being the chief queen is a priest (*ṛtvij*). There are certain questions which pose from this passage.

i) Is it the daily attending on fire?
ii) Does this indicate Daśaratha being away?
iii) Does this indicate that in the absence of the husband (gone on journey) the wife can attend on fire? Here, the husband is the sacrificer, i.e. *yajamāna* and his wife becomes the *yajamānapatnī*. In his absence she carries out the rituals. But, since, it was the occasion of the coronation of Rama, there is no possibility of the absence of Daśaratha.

There is a possibility that the composer did not feel it necessary to incorporate all the details of this minor rite. The description of Kauśalyā giving offerings has been used to convey her happiness on account of the coronation of Rāma. Therefore, the presence of any priest/*ṛtvij* to carry out this ritual has been ignored by the composer.

The items used by Kausalyā in this ritual are not fully Vedic hence the sacrifice seems to be Smārta.

This passage can be compared to another passage occurring in the *Rām.* When Rāma, Lakṣmaṇa and Sītā started for the forest, while crossing the rivers Gaṅgā and Yamunā, Sītā made a vow to the river for the successful completion of exile years of her husband. She said that on return from exile, she would offer ten thousand cows, garments and food along with thousand pots of liquor and rice mixed with meat to the *brāhmaṇa*-s as token of doing something in the memory of the river Gaṅgā (Ayo 52. 87-89). She would be offering thousand cows and hundred pots of liquor in the memory of the river Yamunā (Ayo. 52. 88-89). This reference has been incorporated because of the usage of the verb—*yakṣye.* Though the root is √*yaj,* here it means offering and not sacrificing. These offerings are tinged with the Tantric shade. This vow serves as an indication to the old practice of promising an offering to a deity and fulfilling the promise only on the accomplishment of a particular goal or desire. This is unlike the concept of Vedic sacrifice, which is performed with a desire in mind. It is assumed that after the performance, the desire of the sacrificer would be fulfilled.

## Head as an Offering

Another important sacrificial detail is that of Rāvaṇa offering his head as oblation to the fire. Rāvaṇa was a ten-headed demon. He performed penance for ten thousand years. After every thousand years, he offered one head in the fire. He thus offered nine heads. When he was about to offer the tenth head, Lord Brahmā appeared before him (Utt 10. 10).

Another strange reference regarding the sacrifice is in the Ayo. of *Rām*. After building a hut, Rāma asked Lakṣmaṇa to make preparations for the ceremony of appeasing the site, i.e. *vāstuśamana* by bringing the flesh of an antelope[163]. The *Rām* clearly mentions that this particular ceremony was performed in accordance with the traditional lore, i.e. *śāstradṛṣṭa*. This practice of offering an entire animal especially an antelope is not a Vedic practice. For, the aetiological explanation behind it is that the antelope is directly connected to Prajāpati[164].

Lakṣmaṇa cooked the deer and gave it to Rāma saying that all the limbs of the deer are cooked and therefore it is to be offered to gods. Rāma sacrificed it to the gods and then performed the Vaiśvadevabali to Rudra and Viṣṇu and established the sacrificial altar, *caitya*-s and other places(Ayo. 56. 28-31,33). One should note that there is a variation regarding this rite which is recorded in the critical edition of the *Rām*[165].

There is an Arthavāda for not offering the entire animal in the sacrificial fire. All animals belonged to Tvaṣṭṛ. But Tvaṣṭṛ thought that if all animals would be offered no animal would remain as his own. So, he spat on the head of the animal, in order to make it inauspicious. Thus, the spittle of Tvaṣṭṛ is the brain and the marrow, i.e. *majjā* of the animal-victim. They should not be offered according to the *Śat. Br* (III. 8. 3. 11).

The sacrificial ritual performed by Rāma and Lakṣmaṇa does not indicate cutting of the parts of the antelope. Moreover, the commentary *Tilaka* indicates the offering of an entire animal (*samastāṅgaḥ śiraḥ pādādisarvāṅgopetaḥ*). Yet, the ritual is *śāstradṛṣṭa*, i.e. pertaining to the traditional lore. Then which ritual can this be?

According to Dange, 'Vālmīki must have been aware of this tribal ritual'[166]. At the time of the composition of the *Rām*, various 'a-vedic' rituals had crept in the institution of sacrifice and the offering of an antelope appeared to be the right manner of performing the *vāstuśamana* rite. According to Dange, the practice of severing the head of the sacrificial beast, preserving it or burying it somewhere was prevalent in the hoary past. It came to be regarded as obsolete even in the times of the Brāhmaṇa texts[167].While offering his heads in the fire, Rāvaṇa in fact played the role of the sacrificial beast and sacrificer himself. Since the Rākṣasa culture seems to be closely associated with 'a-vedic' practices, this practice of severe physical torture seems to be prevalent among the Rākṣasas.

## SOCIETAL ASSOCIATION WITH THE INSTITUTION OF SACRIFICE

The *Rām* reflects co-existence of four societies through the institution of sacrifice. In order to get a clear picture of the position of Vedic sacrifice in the *Rām*, it is essential to observe the position of sacrifices in the societies.

### URBAN SOCIETY

By the term 'urban society', the society of Ayodhyā is understood. The performance of sacrifices was a matter of glory for the people of Ayodhyā. Sacrifices seem to be a part of urban culture and glory of kings. When Bharata saw Ayodhyā from a distance, he praised the city as a place where sacrifices were performed. But since the city was in mourning the places of sacrificial altar had a deserted look (Ayo 71.20,40).

Rāma has described the glory of Daśaratha as one who performed many sacrifices (Ayo 105.32). Agnihotra was also an essential aspect of the royal life. Kauśalyā described her plight to Bharata that she would follow Rāma along with Agnihotra(Ayo 75. 14). King Janaka, the father of Sītā, had performed the Dvādaśāha sacrifice (a sacrifice performed for twelve days) (Bāl 50.15). Viśvāmitra mentioned about the bow, which cannot be stringed, as the fruit of this sacrifice performed by King Janaka.

According to the commentary *Tilaka*, a bow wielded by Rāma during the Svayamvara of Sītā was gifted to Janaka Devarāta on the occasion of the sacrifice of Dakṣa by Śiva and other gods (*Tilaka* Bāl 31.8. comm). The commentary gives an explanation that the bow was not the result of the sacrifice, but it was an occasional gift. This sacrifice was attended by many *brāhmaṇa*-s from various countries.

The Ayo. of the *Rām* does not incorporate many details of the Vedic sacrifice. However, there occurs a reference to the Rājasūya sacrifice. Sītā, after knowing that Rāma would be soon crowned as a king expressed the desire that he would perform the Rājasūya. Sītā was looking forward to see him holding the deer skin. Holding the horn of an antelope during the sacrifice indicates the consecration of Rāma for the sacrifice. She expressed the wish that the eastern quarter be protected by Indra, southern quarter by Yama, western quarter by Varuṇa and the northern quarter by Kubera (Ayo 16. 22-24). According to the *Tait. Br.*, these are for protecting the sacrificer king from evil forces in all quarters. The offerings in each quarter (in the altar itself) are for gods residing in the particular quarter and led by a particular god; and the offerings run in a *pradakṣiṇā* mode, i.e.

- East: gods led by Agni,
- South: gods led by Yama
- West: gods led by All-gods (Visvedeva-s)
- North: led by Mitra and Varuṇa
- Centre: led by Soma, his follower gods being said to reside above, i.e. in the heaven or sky[168].

The *Rām* throws light on the position of the Rājasūya sacrifice. Earlier it was observed that the Rājasūya was replaced by the Aśvamedha. The term Rājasūya indicates the creation of new essence (*sava*) in the king (*Tait. Sam* I. 8. 1-22). The king assured himself of socio-political eminence together with divine protection. Thus, Vedic sacrifice was held with reverence in the urban society during the time of the composition of the *Rām*.

### Society in the Forest

Sacrifice performed by the society in the forest indicates the religious activities performed by the sages settled there. Viśvāmitra had asked Daśaratha to hand over Rāma and Lakṣmaṇa to him. The reason given was that he intended to perform a sacrifice and he wanted protection by Rāma and Lakṣmaṇa. A fear lurked in his heart that the Rākṣasa-s would destroy the sacrifice (Bāl. 29). The text is silent about the name of the sacrifice. Yet, it mentions the span of the sacrifice, which is of six days or ten days, the text is not clear about this[169]. Based on the time span of the sacrifice, this is an *ahīna* type of sacrifice. The sacrifice indicates the use of sacrificial materials, viz. *darbha* grass, *camasa*, i.e. a cup for drinking Soma, *sruc*, i.e. a ladle, *samidh*-s, i.e. the faggots and also flowers[170]. The use of flowers raises a question mark on the exact nature of sacrifice because the flowers are never mentioned in the Vedic sacrifice. No other details are mentioned about the sacrifice.

Since the narration is used to describe the prowess of the two brothers against the Rākṣasa-s, the details of the rituals are avoided. Daṇḍaka forest is described in the *Rām* as a place sanctified with offerings and filled with the sound of the chanting of the *mantra*-s (Araṇya 1.6). The details of the sacrifices are not given. But it seems that they may be certain minor rituals performed by the sages residing in the forest[171]. This can be substantiated by the mention of Agnihotra performed by the Sage Śarabhaṅga in the *Rām* (Ibid. 5. 25).

The institution of sacrifice was strongly upheld by the sages residing in the forests. They did not perform elaborate sacrifices probably because of the scarcity of resources. Agnihotra, a regular ritual, i.e. *nityakarman*, was performed and also certain minor sacrifices. This also bears testimony to the fact that the Vedic culture, of which sacrifice is a hallmark had at that time penetrated to the southern parts of India.

### Vānara Society

By the term 'Vānara society', it need not to be understood in the literal sense as the society of monkeys, but a tribe using the totem of monkey[172]. It appears that the tribe had close links with the Aryan community (which followed the institution of sacrifice). It regarded the performance of sacrifice as a parameter of greatness and glory. Lakṣmaṇa introduced Rāma to Hanumat, as the descendant of the kings of Ikṣvāku dynasty, who had performed Agniṣṭoma and other sacrifices, by giving sumptuous donations (Kiṣkindhā 4. 8).

Hanumat introduced Rāma to Sugrīva as one who performed the Rājasūya and Aśvamedha sacrifices and gave cows in charity (Kiṣkindhā 5.4). There is no reference in the *Rām* prior to this one about Rama performing sacrifices, yet in the *Rām* a similar reference occurs elsewhere[173]. The Vānara army approached Sugrīva with gifts of flowers from the sacrificial altar, says the *Rām* (*Ibid.*, 37. 32). Jāmbuvat described his prowess to the Vānara-s by saying that on the occasion of the sacrifice performed by Kubera (Vairocana) he encircled the earth(Kiṣkindhā 65. 15). The *Rām* does not indicate a direct reference to the performance of sacrifice by the Vānara-s. They regarded the institution with reverence. Though they did not directly perform the sacrifices, they participated in it.

### Rākṣasa Society

The *Rām* throws light on the two entirely opposite approaches of the Rākṣasa-s to the institution of sacrifice.

According to the *Rām*, Viśvāmitra requested the protection of Rāma for his sacrifice since he feared some disturbance on the part of the Rākṣasa-s, viz. Mārīca and Subāhu (Bāl. Ch. 29). The *Rām* also describes the destruction of sacrifices by the Rākṣasa-s (Ayo. 116. 17). Rāvaṇa is described as one creating obstacles in the sacrifice (Araṇya 32. 13). He had destroyed the sacrifices of the *brāhmaṇa*-s in which Soma was offered to the fire (*Ibid.*, 19cd- 20). Another reference to the Rākṣasa-s being hostile to the institution of sacrifice is that of Mārīca referring to the destruction of sacrifices and wandering amongst the *tīrtha*-s and *caitya*-s (*Ibid.*, 39. 4).

Kane explains, 'the path going to the *vihāra* is called *tīrtha*. The sacrificial ground where the fires are mentioned is called *vihāra*. Śabarasvāmin says '*vihāra iti gārhapatyādiragnistretocyate viharaṇāt*'. The way for going to or coming from the *vihāra* is between Praṇītā and *utkara* and the *cātvāla* pit in other cases'[174].

*Caitya* is a mound built in a far away and a secluded place, out of reach for people, normally beyond a river. It can also be a tumulous spot raised over the ashes of dead or a tree marking the spot[175]. The term *caitya* occurs in the Buddhist and Jain texts as *cetiya*. The term is also used in the Vedic sacrificial context. The *caitya* is referred to in the *Āsv. Gṛ. Sū* (I. 12. 1-4) as the *caitya-yajña*, which is an offering to *caitya*. As per the description in the *Āsv. Gṛ. Sū*, a sacrificer has to make an offering to *caitya* prior to the *sviṣṭakṛt* offering. To understand the exact position of the *caitya* in the *Rām* it is essential to understand the contexts in which it is used. The word *caitya* occurs 16 times in the *Rām*.

In the Bāl and the Ayo sections of the *Rām*, this term is used in association with *devāyatana* and *catuṣpatha* (where four roads meet). At times the term *caitya* is compounded with a tree as *caityavṛkṣa*. *Caitya* had an important place in the religious life of Rama for even in exile, he erected a *caitya, devāyatana* and built an altar. The *Rām* describes Hanumat searched for Sītā in huge *caityagṛha* (Sundara 12. 18). Indrajit performed a sacrifice at a *caitya* named Nikumbhilā (Yuddha 84. 4). Rāvaṇa, who was sleeping in his chamber, appeared very terrible like a *smaśānacaitya* (Sundara22. 25). The commentator on the *Rām* interpretes the term *caitya* differently in different contexts for e.g.; *Rām* Bāl II. 3. 18.

*i) Tilaka*: *caityaḥ rathyāvṛkṣaḥ.*

*ii) Rāmāyaṇaśiromaṇi*: *caityeṣu catuṣpatheṣu*. The etymological interpretations of the term *caitya* is as follows:

a) *citiḥ patrapuṣpaphalādīnāmupacayaḥ, cityā sādhu cityam, cityameva caityam udyānam.*: *Citya* means abundance of flowers and fruits. Therefore, *caitya* means a garden.
b) *citerlepyādicayanasya bhāvaḥ karma vā caityam*: *Caitya* means the state or action of raising an idol.
c) According to *Abhidhānarājendrakośa*, the verb *citi* means to know. *Caitya*-s are the images of deities, seeing which one is reminded of the original deity[176].

The references to the term *caitya* in the first three *kāṇḍa*-s of the *Rām* vis-à-vis the *kāṇḍa*-s fifth and sixth when studied comparatively, indicates three types of *caitya*-s

a) The earlier *kāṇḍa*-s indicate a constructed mound or a tree planted at a four square.
b) The later *kāṇḍa*-s indicate a well-constructed building or a place/garden spot away from the urban area specifically allocated for the performance of some rituals. The reference to the performance of rituals occurs in the sixth and the seventh *kāṇḍa*-s of the *Rām*. Indrajit reached the battlefield and performed a *homa*. But how can a battlefield be a place for performance of rituals?

This query is satisfied through the commentary *'Tilaka'*. It says that, the battlefield stood for a place, i.e. Nikumbhilā, where sacrifices for victory in the battles were performed[177]. Indrajit gave oblations of puffed rice flakes (*lājā*). He used weapons as implements; faggots of the Vibhītaka tree were used as *samidh*-s, arrows were also essential implements, red garments and a *sruva*, i.e. sacrificial ladle, made up of iron were the other implements. A live black goat without horns was held by its neck and a one time offering of that goat was given in the fire. By performing such a rite he received divine weapons and missiles (Yuddha 73. 21, 24). According to the *Rām*, Indrajit performed another sacrifice in a similar manner (*Ibid*. 80.5-11). Moreover, before his last battle, he performed a sacrifice at the *caitya* named Nikumbhilā, which was obstructed by Lakṣmaṇa.

Some motifs of this sacrifice agree to that of the Śyena sacrifice as discussed in the *Kāt. Śr. Sū*. XXII. 3. 1-23. Śyena sacrifice is a one-day Sādyaskra sacrifice, which is a *soma*-sacrifice. The *idhma* bundle should be of the Bidhīdaka tree. The *barhis* (sacrificial grass) should consist of the *śara* grass. The *savanīya* animal victim is a red he -goat to be offered to the Rudravat Agni. The priests wear red clothes and red headwares while officiating. They hold up the strings of their bows stretched with arrows on their backs. The sacrificer gives away sets of nine cows as priestly fees. They are squint-eyed, limping; their horns are broken and are mixed with those cows who suffer from fever.

Not all the details of the Śyena sacrifice agree to that of the sacrifice, which was performed by Indrajit. But some motifs of the quiver of arrow and red garments agree with the *Kāt. Śr. Sū*. Besides, the intention behind performing this sacrifice as an *abhicārakarman*, i.e. the ritual performed as black magic is similar.

This ritual was performed at the *caitya* named Nikumbhilā. This garden was situated at the west of Laṅkā. It had *yūpa* and *caitya* in it. Nikumbhilā served as a place to perform Vedic sacrifices like Agniṣṭoma, Aśvamedha, Rājasūya for Indrajit, says the text (Utt 25.8). The female Rākṣasī-s, who encircled Sītā had expressed a desire to consume human flesh, drink liquor (*surā*) and dance at Nikumbhilā. The commentators understand Nikumbhilā as Bhadrakālī[178]. But this relation is not established in the *Rām*. Even then this relation is accepted by Hopkins[179]. Dikshitar has mentioned about *caitya*-s as temples protected by the tutelary goddess of Laṅka[180]. The critical edition of the *Rām* explains the dance of the Rākṣasī-s with a phrase which means 'dancing a goddess'[181]. One needs to mention an old custom prevalent in South India. The Kāli temples in this part of India have Neem trees planted in their vicinity. The trees enjoy absolute protection. Whosoever is desirous to please the goddess has to wear the Neem leaves on his body. It is believed that the goddess as well as the tree has the power of warding off evil spirits[182]. This indicates that the Nikumbhilā may be a place named after the goddess Nikumbhilā, where rituals were performed by the Rākṣasa-s.

There are some references regarding the hostility of the Rākṣasa-s towards the institution of sacrifice.

Mālyavat refers to Rāvaṇa destroying the sacrifices of the twice-born and also the Agnihotra of the sages(Yuddha 35. 19-20). The names of the Rākṣasa-s, viz. Yajñakopa (*Ibid.* 43. 11) and Yajñaśatru (*Ibid.* 44.20) also indicate their opposition to the Vedic sacrifice.

The funeral rites of Rāvaṇa are termed as Agnihotra. Here the term Agnihotra is used as a common noun but not as the sacrifice (*Ibid.* 111. 104-115). The corpse was placed on a cart and sandalwood was gathered; various aromatic items, gems, etc. were brought. The corpse, clad in silk, was placed on a golden mount, which was carried by Vibhīṣaṇa and others. A sacrificial animal was offered. An altar was raised for the Pitṛmedha, i.e. the ritual of the last rites of Rāvaṇa. A ladle full of speckled clarified butter was placed on the shoulders of the corpse. Roasted rice flakes were scattered all over the body and then it was consigned to flames by Vibhīṣaṇa.

The term Pitṛmedha has been used in this passage. According to the *Kāt. Śr. Sū,* Pitṛmedha is to be performed either after one year after the death of a person, on the third, fifth or seventh day during the constellation on which the person expired or as long time had passed since the death of a person because of being forgotten (Ch. XXI). This indicates that the terms Agnihotra and the Pitṛmedha are not used to point out specific rituals, which they stand for; on the contrary, they indicate unspecified rituals in general (ritual in the generic sense).

The description of Laṅkā in the *Rām* throws light on the religious practices of the Rākṣasa-s (Sundara Ch 4). The city of Laṅkā has been described as shining with *gṛhamedha*-s (sacrifices performed at home). However, there is no reference to the details of the sacrifices. The Rākṣasa-s recited the Vedic *mantra*-s and were engrossed in the study of the Veda-s. Some of the spies of Rāvaṇa were *dīkṣita, jaṭila* and *muṇḍa* (*Ibid.* 4. 15). The commentary *Tilaka* says that they are the householder, forester and mendicant respectively. *Tilaka* also poses an interesting question that since Laṅkā is situated outside India how can the Rākṣasa-s be consecrated for performing sacrifices? The explanation it gives is that regular rites (*nityakarman*-s) can be performed in foreign land also.

Rāvaṇa had performed severe penance and sacrifices and had the capacity to satisfy his desires. The commentary gives reference to the birth of Vṛtra through the sacrifice performed by Tvaṣṭṛ which is documented in the *Śat. Br,* in order to justify the capacity and power of the Rāvaṇa. The Rākṣasa-s performed sacrifices by offering handful of *darbha* grass in the sacrificial fire(*Ibid.* 4. 16). This is termed *abhicārakarman* for warding off evil. The commentary on this verse refers to the quotation from a *smṛti* as *yathā vajram hareḥ pāṇau tathā viprakare kuśāḥ.* In the *Rām,* Kumbhakarṇa gives Rāvaṇa a piece of his mind by using a simile regarding *abhicāra* rites. Any decision undertaken without proper counsel blemishes the glory of the doer just as offerings given in sacrifices regarding black magic make the sacrifices infamous (Yuddha 12. 31).

There are some contradictory references to the hostility of the Rākṣasa-s towards the culture of sacrifice. One important reference is that Rāvaṇa was an *Āhitāgni,* i.e. one who maintains the three fires[183]. They also performed sacrifices, for Vibhīṣaṇa has described the ill omens occurring during the sacrifices on the arrival of Sītā. He said that the sacrificial fire was emitting black smoke and it did not blaze with full effulgence. There were lizards and ants at the place of sacrifice and also on oblations (*Ibid.* 10. 21).

Thus, the Rākṣasa-s performed sacrifices, but the evidences indicate that some Vedic sacrificial rituals were incorporated in their society. Yet it is necessary to note that all the rituals were not Vedic. Certain *abhicārakarman*-s were specifically belonging to the Rākṣasa tribe. The Rākṣasa-s opposed the institution of sacrifice by destroying sacrifices performed or by creating obstacles in them. The belief behind the performance of the sacrifices was to strengthen the divine powers of gods, the rivals of the Rākṣasa-s. Thus to prevent the gods from becoming powerful, obstructing sacrifices was the only way. Hence, the Rākṣasa-s were hostile towards sacrifices. But, whenever they desired to achieve some powers from the gods, they resorted to the institution of Vedic sacrifice. Therefore the religious life of the Rākṣasa-s shows a composite texture of Vedic and Rākṣasa rituals.

## CORONATION OF RĀMA

The text describes two coronations of Rāma. Firstly, Rāma was coronate as the prince and secondly as the king. The ingredients referred to in the first coronation are—rice flakes, honey, clarified butter, chariot, weapons, white umbrella, chowries, pots made up of gold, bull with golden horns, tiger-skin etc (Ayo. Ch.3). According to the *Ait. Br.* VIII. 5, the king after the concluding *iṣṭi*, is besprinkled from the ladle made of Udumbara wood. The ingredients are, viz. curds, honey, clarified butter, rainwater fallen during sunshine, young sprouts of grass and of green barley, liquor and *dūrva* grass. He spreads tiger-skin on the throne made up of Udumbara wood. This indicates that some ingredients in the *Rām* agree to those in the *Ait. Br.* Moreover, Sītā described Rāma as one holding the deer-horn in his hand. This is somewhat similar to the ritual in a sacrifice in which the sacrificer has to tie the horn of a deer to his garment. According to the myth from the *Śat. Br*, the horn of the black antelope is the womb of the sacrifice (III. 2. 1. 18-28). After the coronation ceremony, Rāma would be declared the official heir to the throne of Daśaratha. Naturally, after succeeding Daśaratha, Rāma will have to perform duties of a king out of which performing sacrifices is an important duty on the part of a king.

The second coronation of Rāma occurs in the later portion of the *Rām*. For the ceremony, waters from the five rivers and four oceans were acquired in pots studded with gems. The besprinkling ceremony of the Rājasūya also incorporates the consecration of the king with different waters. The waters collected first are from some flowing source. The belief is that the waters that are flowing constitute a 'nation of water' (*Tait. Br.* I. 7. 5. 1). According to Dange, there is a sympathetic relationship between this *rāṣṭra* of waters and the *rāṣṭra* of kings. Other types of waters to be collected are—flowing against the current, flowing away from the main current, sea-water, from a whirlpool, from a steady sunny spot in a stream, from a stagnant pool, from a well, dew drops, honey, embryonic fluids, i.e. fluids from a cow that has given birth to a calf, milk, ghee, etc.[184] However, the passage from the *Rām* mentions only two types of waters, i.e. river water and oceanic water. According to the *Śat. Br*, waters have to be collected in a vessel made up of Udumbara (Ficus Glomerata)[185]. However, the passage describes a pot studded with precious stones. This can also be treated as a hyperbolic expression to indicate the prosperity of Rāma.

The passage refers to the presence of sages, viz. Vasiṣṭha, Vijaya, Jābāli, Kaśyapa, Kātyāyana, Gautama and Vāmadeva. Rāma was anointed with fragrant waters by the *ṛtvij*-s. This consecration took place in the presence of maidens, ministers, warriors, *vaiśya*-s. Thus the coronation ceremony of Rāma was performed with pomp and grandeur.

## MYTHS ASSOCIATED WITH THE VEDIC SACRIFICE

Narrations related to sacrifice are at times accompanied by myths. Myths related to sacrifice are of two types:

i) Sacrifice is incorporated in a myth.

ii) Myth is constructed in order to support the performance of a sacrifice.

## Sacrifice Incorporated in a Myth

### The Myth of Sagara Performing the Aśvamedha and Bhagīratha Bringing the Flow of the River Gaṅgā

In the *Rām*, Viśvāmitra mentioned the Aśvamedha sacrifice performed by king Sagara, the ancestor of Rāma (Bāl Ch. 39). No ritual details are mentioned about this sacrifice except the abduction of the horse. The chapter describes the search of the horse by the sons of Sagara. Further, the sons are reduced to ashes by sage Kaśyapa. In order to release the sons of Sagara, Bhagīratha undertakes severe penance and succeeds in bringing down the river Gaṅgā from the heaven. According to Dange, 'the memory of this great effort mixed with the later event of the usurpation of the sacrificial horse in the region; and the two events were joined up in a composite myth with, Sagara at the centre'. There is a possibility that the sacrifice became a latter addition to the entire mega-plan of changing the course of the river, which was undertaken by Sagara and his descendants. In fact, no sacrifice was performed by Sagara. The myth of the Aśvamedha was added to the saga of Sagara for changing the course of the river, only to enhance the greatness of the king and also to veil the geographical change[186]. Here sacrifice was associated in the myth only to sanctify the mega-plan devised by Sagara.

### *Myth of Triśaṅku*

Another interesting reference to the Vedic sacrifice which occurs in the *Rām* is that of the sacrifice performed by King Triśaṅku. Triśaṅku wanted to reach heaven with his mortal frame and hence wanted to perform a sacrifice (Bāl 58. 20-21). He approached Sage Vasiṣṭha, his family-priest, who refused to perform such a ritual. The king later on approached Sage Viśvāmitra. In order to score a point over

Vasiṣṭha, since there had been a feud for a long time between the two sages, Viśvāmitra readily agreed. However, the efforts of Triśaṅku were in vain, for the king had insulted the family priest. He did not succeed in reaching the heaven. It is noteworthy that the sacrifice mentioned here reflects the fact that sacrifice was used as a ready opportunity to prove a point of superiority between priests. This unnamed sacrifice is only for the purpose of stressing the importance of Vedic sacrifice as a means to reach heaven. It also preaches a moral that the sacrificing priest may be well versed with the technique of the sacrifice, yet offence against the family priest causes the fruit of the sacrifice decline.

*Myth of Śunaḥśepa*

Another important narration pertaining to the Vedic sacrifice, which is referred to in the *Rām* is that of the legend of Śunaḥśepa (Bāl 61. 1-20). According to the *Rām,* King Ambarīṣa started to perform a sacrifice. But his sacrificial animal was abducted by Indra. He was asked to replace the animal by another one. He started to search another animal and was ready to exchange a thousand cows for this animal. He met Ṛcīka, who had three sons and he agreed to sell his middle son Śunaḥśepa for ten thousand cows. Śunaḥśepa went to a *tīrtha* named Puṣkara and propitiated Visvāmitra. Śunaḥśepa sought resort to Visvāmitra, who accepted him as his son. He composed some Gāthā-s and with them pleased Indra. The myth of Śunaḥśepa occurs in the *RV* and it is fully developed in the *Ait. Br.* (VII. 13-18).

d) In the *RV*, there are seven hymns, which have Śunaḥśepa Ājīgarti as their seer (I. 24-30). At certain places in the hymns, the seer has requested Varuṇa to free him from fetters. Besides this, *RV* mentions Śunaḥśepa being released from the sacrificial post by Agni (V. 2. 7)[187]. The names of the king and father are changed in the *Rām*.

According to the *Ait. Br* Hariścandra is the king and Ajīgarta is the father of Śunaḥśepa. Rohita is the son of Hariścandra. Initially, Hariścandra was issueless. He prayed to Varuṇa to obtain a son. In case he got one, Hariścandra promised to offer him to Varuṇa. After Rohita was born, Varuṇa reminded him about the promise. But Hariścandra avoided fulfilling the promise under different pretexts. This angered Varuṇa and as a result Hariścandra was tortured with dropsy, an ailment caused because of committing an offence against Varuṇa. Meanwhile, on the advice of Indra, Rohita wandered in search of a suitable human being as his replacement. He came across Ajīgarta, a sage, who had three sons. Out of the three, Ajīgarta readily decided to part with the middle one named Śunaḥśepa for a hundred cows. When the boy was brought to the sacrificial place, the sages were horrified. They were not ready to tie him to the sacrificial post and treat him as a *paśu*, i.e. a sacrificial animal. However, Śunaḥśepa's father agreed to fetter him to the sacrificial post only for hundred cows. Śunaḥśepa prayed to different deities. Lastly, when he prayed to Goddess Uṣas, his fetters fell off.

Sage Viśvāmitra accepted him as the eldest son. Viśvāmitra had hundred sons. The first fifty sons did not accept Śunaḥśepa as their eldest brother. Viśvāmitra cursed them to be the Andhra-s, Puṇḍra-s, Śabara-s, Paṭiṇḍa-s and Mūtiba-s, the degraded castes. The myth of Śunaḥśepa in the *Ait. Br* achieves two purposes.

Firsty, it denies a human being as the sacrificial animal. Secondly, it indicates the creation of some tribes. There is a possibility that these tribes were not of a Vedic origin. The creation of these tribes by Viśvāmitra indicates the process of assimilation and integration of these non-Vedic tribes. The myth of Śunaḥśepa in the *Rām* occurs just as a narration. In the *Rām*, Śunaḥśepa was replaced for the sacrificial animal abducted by Indra. Rohita does not figure in. The reason behind Indra doing this act and creating an obstacle in the sacrifice of Ambarīṣa is unmentioned. The motif of Indra abducting the sacrificial animal is seen in the myth of Sagara.

At the time of the *Rām*, Indra, as a deity had lost his prominence. He was reduced to the status of merely a king of gods, protected by the trinity. He feared his position being taken away by any other king excelling him in the performance of sacrifice. Hence, he created an obstacle by taking away the sacrificial animal, which is a prime offering in the sacrifice. This myth appears to be in a fragmented form in the *Rām*. The narration of this myth is in the context of propagating the greatness of Sage Viśvāmitra. Therefore, the myth of Śunaḥśepa in the Bāl of the *Rām* has no other purpose except elevating the position of the Sage Viśvāmitra.

### *King Nimi and His Fued with the Sage Vasiṣṭha*

The myth of Nimi has been discussed earlier. Here a point has to be stressed that the fued between the Sage Vasiṣṭha and King Nimi resulted in the curse of Nimi. This myth is incorporated to highlight the sacrificial birth of King Mithi. The motif of churning the hand of Nimi is similar to the myth of the destruction of King Vena. When his right hand was churned, emerged King Pṛthu.

Some myths are incorporated in the *Rām* only for supporting the sacrifices. These myths can be compared to the Arthavāda statements in the Brāhmaṇa-s.

## MYTH OF INDRA AND VṚTRA

This myth has occurred in the Utt of the *Rām*, Vṛtra, the lord of the Daitya-s, ruled the earth. During his regime, there was peace and prosperity everywhere on the earth. He performed severe penance to obtain the position of Indra. Indra, with the help of Viṣṇu, entered into a combat with Vṛtra. The latter was killed.

This inflicted the sin of *brahmahatyā*, since Vṛtra was the son of the sage Tvaṣṭṛ, who was brother of Bṛhaspati. As a result the position of Indra was endangered. In order to eradicate the sin, Indra performed the Aśvamedha and wiped of the sin of *brahmahatyā*. This indicates the performance of Aśvamedha, as expiation (Utt 86. 9-10). The *Śat. Br.* also mentions the performance of Aśvamedha as a tool to wipe off the sins of *brahmahatyā* (XIII. 5.3.9). This myth was narrated by Lakṣmaṇa in order to stress the performance of the Aśvamedha in the place of the Rājasūya.

## MYTH OF ILA AND ILĀ

King Ila was the son of Karandhama. In the month of Caitra, he went on a hunting expedition. He entered a forest, which belonged to Pārvatī and every entity in the forest was feminine in nature. As soon as he entered, his masculine form disappeared and he became a woman. He propitiated Śiva and Pārvatī. As a boon he attained a male form for a month and the next month female form. When he attained the female form he was spotted by Budha. He became pregnant from Budha. He delivered a boy.

However, in order to solve the problem of King Ila, the sages suggested him to perform the Aśvamedha with the assistance of King Marutta (Utt 90. 12-13). As a fruit of this sacrifice, king Ila regained his masculine form (*Ibid.* 90. 19). Thus due to the Aśvamedha, Ila gained his masculinity. The myth has got two implications:

i) Aśvamedha sacrifice has the capacity to make impossible as possible.
ii) Due to the Aśvamedha sacrifice, Ila regained his masculinity, i.e. virile strength, to gain progeny.

## CONCLUSION

The sacrifice in the *Rām* indicates intermingling of various cultures in it. The Aśvamedha seems to be the most important and prestigious sacrifice. However, there is a great deal of difference between the Aśvamedha in the Bāl of the *Rām* and that in the Utt of the *Rām*. The purpose behind the two Aśvamedha-s is clearly stated in the text. The purpose of the first being progeny and the second being attaining merit. Therefore the descriptions in both the sections are different. The first section, i.e. the Bāl, gives great stress on the ritual part and the last section, i.e. the Utt, describes the roaming of the sacred horse.

The *Rām* discusses certain myths connected with the Vedic sacrifice. The myth of Śunaḥśepa, with some variations from the original text, the myth of bringing the river Gaṅgā from the heaven, Indra-Vṛtra myth and the myth of Ila and Ilā stress the importance of Vedic sacrifice prevalent in the times of the composition of the *Rām*. The Vedic sacrifice has served as a mere background in certain myths esp, Aśvamedha performed by Sagara and the Dīrghasattra by Nimi.

Performance of sacrifice was also a matter of prestige for sages. For e.g.; Viśvāmitra wanted Triśaṅku to attain heaven with a mortal frame. He had strife with the gods to attain this goal. Changing the sacrificial priest, i.e. (changing Vasiṣṭha and requesting Viśvāmitra to act as the officiating priest) was also an offence. Such an offence could ultimately culminate into a curse.

Certain gatherings were held by kings connected with sacrifices. These gatherings went by the name of *sattra*-s. A fear lurked in the minds of the kings, who arranged for them that if such a *sattra* was left incomplete, it might cause severe consequences to the family of the sacrificer.

Woman played a minor role in the sacrifices. In the Aśvamedha performed by Daśaratha, the three queens, viz. Kausalyā, Kaikeyī, and Sumitrā took the position of *mahiṣī*, *vāvātā* and *parivṛktī*. But in the Aśvamedha performed by Rāma, Sītā was absent. To compensate her absence a golden image of her was made. However, there is a reference to Kausalyā giving oblation in the fire. Such references can be stray references or exceptions. They can also stand for very minor rituals.

The sacrifice amongst the Rākṣasa-s seems to be mixed, i.e. Vedic and a-*vedic* elements are seen in their rituals. They performed the Agnihotra and other sacrifices and at the same time destroyed the sacrifices, the sages and the twice -born. The sages and the twice- born performed sacrifices for propitiating the gods. The gods and the Rākṣasa-s were arch -rivals. Therefore their approach towards the institution of sacrifice was hostile. They were experts in black magic and performed *abhicārakarman* and at times resorted to torturing their bodies.

The Vedic sacrifice has deviated to a certain extent in the *Rām*. At the time of the composition of the *Rām* the sacrifice was out of vogue. The glory of sacrifices was retained only in the form of mere memories. The transmission of the glorious sacrifices was done by the *sūta* tradition, who narrated the epics from generation to generation. So, of these narrations many references have been incorporated, lost or changed. The *sūta*-s retained names of sacrifices and took pleasure in narrating them to elevate the glory of the kings performing them.

Historically, around 400 BC the institution of sacrifice started suffering a decline. The composition of the *Rām* makes this decline evident yet its importance remained alive in the minds of the people. Therefore the time of the *Rām,* i.e. the last edition of the *Rām* seems to be by the end of 300 BC.

# 3

# The Mahābhārata

The *Mbh,* which means the story of the great battle of the Bhārata-s, has around its nucleus a huge mass of tales, legends and myths[188]. According to Oldenberg, 'the *Mbh* began its existence as a simple epic narrative. It became in course of centuries, the most monstrous chaos'[189]. Additions after additions seemed to be chaotic in nature in the eyes of this great scholar, yet such additions are a prominent feature of epic literature. Moreover, they have played a great role, in documenting ancient religious traditions.

The *Mbh* has grown from Jaya of 8,800 verses to Bhārata of 24,000 to the *Mbh* of one lakh verses. The epic itself agrees that it has come into being after two redactions in it. Linguistic studies mention five stratifications of the epic. These five strata or layers consist of the Bhārata of Vaiśampāyana and its four redactions by Sūta, Sauti, Harivaṁśakāra and Parvasaṅgrahakāra[190]. Understanding this stratification is essential for the present study, for it would help in estimating the date of the composition of this epic and would help in understanding the Vedic sacrificial ritual during the time of the composition of the epic.

## DATE OF THE *MBH*

Many scholars have attempted to estimate and establish the date of the *Mbh.* The epic has been dated in two ways: a) archeological evidence; and b) linguistic studies.

As the study is based on the text of the epic, the focus would be on the estimation of the date based on linguistic analysis. According to Weber, Holtzmann, Pischel, Rawlinson and Winternitz, the statement of Dio Chrysostomos that the Hindus possessed an *Iliad* of one lakh verses and were well acquainted with the sufferings of Priam, etc. constitutes an earliest external evidence of the *Mbh* of its existence in 1st AD[191]. Vaidya also agrees to the same[192]. The *Mbh* with all its redactions might have existed by 1st century AD. The third redaction, i.e. the role of Harivaṁśakāra might be placed around 2nd BC. This is based on the internal evidence in the Harivaṁśa, about a *brāhmaṇa* General, who was supposed to restore the Aśvamedha in the Kali age as *audbhijja,* i.e. plant born. This General is identified by Jayaswal as Puṣyamitra of the Śuṅga dynasty (187 BC–151 BC). The second redaction, i.e. the redaction of Sauti has been placed around 450 BC based on astronomical references[193]. Sauti has mentioned how Viśvāmitra, in creating a parallel world, arranged for the winter solstice, to begin in Śrāvaṇa month. This arrangement has come into vogue by about 450 BC (Ādi Parvan 65. 34).

According to Yardi, "Of these the Sūta and Sauti are separated only by a generation being father and son, and so their redactions may be considered together. It is seen that the description of the cities, palaces and *digvijaya*-s undertaken by the Pāṇḍava-s at the time of the Aśvamedha and the Rājasūya sacrifices occur in the addition made by

Sūta and Sauti"[194]. Hence the Rājasūya and the Aśvamedha sacrifices described in the *Mbh* would reflect the position of these great Vedic sacrifices around 450 BC. Moreover, it is noteworthy to say that the rituals of these sacrifices mentioned in the *Mbh* should be studied vis-à-vis the rise of Buddhism.

As regards the archeological excavation undertaken at the sites mentioned in the *Mbh*, these sites seemed to be interlinked with the findings of Painted Grey Ware (PGW). While interlinking the PGW findings and the *Mbh* text, Yardi comments that, in view of the urban development, this interval between Sauti's *Mbh* and the Harivaṁśa may therefore be considered synchronous with the PGW period[195]. This indicates that the period of the composition of the Bhārata by Vaiśaṁpāyana needs to be placed before the PGW. The Bhārata was narrated in the Sarpasattra of Janamejaya. The dynasty of Janamejaya is the Paurava dynasty. To trace the time period of Vaiśaṁpāyana's narration, one has to follow the genealogy of Paurava kings. King Udayana (Pāli: Udena) was contemporary of Gautama Buddha. He outlived Buddha by nearly ten to fifteen years. The date of Buddha's *nirvāṇa* is 487 BC, then the date of Udayana's death can be taken as 475 BC. According to the genealogy of Paurava kings, Udayana was 24th descent from Janamejaya. Hence assuming 20 years as the average reign period of each king, the date of Vaiśaṁpāyana's narration can be placed approximately 955 BC[196].

The *Mbh* is a Great Encyclopedia; therefore there is a saying that whatever is mentioned in the epic is seen everywhere and whatever is unmentioned does not exist anywhere (*yadihāsti tatsarvatra, yannehāsti, na tatkvacit*). So, pertaining to this saying, there is no wonder that customs, beliefs and religious practices are referred to in this epic.

There are references to the Vedic sacrifices strewn everywhere in the *Mbh*. Therefore, with the discussion of the date and various redactions of the *Mbh*, it is essential to see how has the Vedic sacrifice been reflected in the great epic.

## SACRIFICIAL RITUALS

Two prominent sacrifices seen in the *Mbh* are the Rājasūya and the Aśvamedha. Sacrifices like the Vājapeya, Agniṣṭoma, etc. are merely mentioned.

### Rājasūya Sacrifice

Sage Nārada asked Yudhiṣṭhira to perform the Rājasūya sacrifice as it was performed by Indra too. The sacrificial place was dotted with golden sacrificial posts and also golden *citya*-s. The critical edition of the *Mbh* takes note of a variation to the term *citya*-s and that is *caitya*-s. (The term *caitya* has been discussed in detail in the chapter II). King Hariścandra also performed this sacrifice and all the kings gave wealth to Hariścandra and participated in the sacrifice as waiters serving food to the *brāhmaṇa*-s (Sabhā Parvan 11. 56). This pattern can be linked to the reference to the Marut-s acting in the capacity of waiters (*pariveṣṭṛ*)in the sacrifice of King Marutta as mentioned in the *Ait. Br.*(VIII. 29) and the *Śat. Br.* (XIII. 5.4.6).

However the word *'pariveṣṭṛ'* can also be understood as those surrounding the sacrificial place (*pari+ √veṣṭ* – to surround or to envelope). One cannot deny the possibility that the kings might have surrounded the sacrificial place to protect it from evil. Unlike the reference to the prevention of the performance of Rājasūya in the *Rām*, the Sabhā P does not indicate any antipathy to the performance of this sacrifice. Here, Vaiśaṁpāyana has narrated the fruit of the Rājasūya sacrifice. A king who performs it gets the qualities of Varuṇa. He also attains the position of a *samrāṭ*, i.e. sovereign king (Sabhā P 12. 11). During the sacrifice the entire *kṣatriya* prowess is under his control. The Rājasūya ritual mentions a rite named Darvīhoma (*Ibid.* 12. 14). This rite is performed in the Sākamedha *parvan* of the Cāturmāsya sacrifice. It is an oblation of boiled rice on a wooden ladle, i.e. *darvī*, to Indra[197]. Rājasūya is a sacrifice which was spread over for two years. The earlier Saṁhitā-s do not discuss this sacrifice in great detail. The *Ait. Br.* does mention the Rājasūya but describes the Aindramahābhiṣeka ceremony. This ceremony seems to be the earlier form of the Rājasūya sacrifice. However, the Śrautasūtra-s deal with this sacrifice elaborately. According to Dange, "Originally it must not have been so elaborate. But the fact that it also included the Four-seasonal sacrifices (Cāturmāsya) which are of the non-Soma type indicates its enlarged nature[198]. The Darvīhoma getting incorporated as a part of the description of the Rājasūya indicates its enlarged nature.

Yudhiṣṭhira was also urged by his brothers and other *ṛtvij*-s to perform this sacrifice. The glorification of the Rājasūya by Yudhiṣṭhira indicates the importance enjoyed by this great sacrifice[199]. Since Rājasūya indicates absolute sovereignty, the sacrifice performed by Yudhiṣṭhira would not have been successful without destroying Jarāsandha, the king of Magadha. Jarasandha had imprisoned many kings and he wanted to sacrifice them to please Lord Śaṅkara[200]. Hence for absolute supremacy, destruction of Jarāsandha became inevitable. The word *'samālambha'* means to pacify the sacrificial animal, in other words 'to kill it'.

Kṛṣṇa did not regard this sacrifice as proper or just. He was opposed to term the kings as *paśu*-s, i.e. sacrificial animals (*Ibid.* 20. 11). He questioned as to how can a *savarṇa* term the other *savarṇa*-s as *paśu*-s. Jarāsandha wanted to make the other captive kings his sacrificial animals. That was improper according to the opinion of Kṛṣṇa.

The human sacrifice undertaken by Jarāsandha may not be a poetic fantasy. Moreover it did not strictly adhere to the rules of sacrifice. Hence the mission to prevent Jarāsandha from sacrificing the kings was undertaken by the Pāṇḍava-s and Kṛṣṇa. After the destruction of Jarāsandha, the kings who were released were asked to assist Yudhiṣṭhira in this endeavour by Kṛṣṇa according to *Mbh* (*Ibid.* 22. 35-36).

The Rājasūya also incorporated conquest of directions. The northern direction was conquered by Arjuna, eastern by Bhīma, southern by Sahadeva and western direction by Nakula mention the *Mbh* (*Ibid.* 23. 9-10). Here the directions need to be observed. At the time the king moves in a clockwise direction, i.e. from east-north-west-south and then east. But the directions of the Pāṇḍava-s appear to be otherwise.

Invitations were sent to different kings to participate in this sacrifice. Kṛṣṇa was requested to take a very respectful position by being a *dīkṣita* according to the *Mbh* (*Ibid.* 30. 19-23). This does not correspond to the Vedic ritual, because it is the king who performs the sacrifice, is consecrated for the sacrifice. Kṛṣṇa's position in the sacrifice is indicatory to the process of his deification. The sacrifice had the participation of common people like artisans, dancers and actors. Yudhiṣṭhira gave sumptuous donations to the *brāhmaṇa*-s. He appointed all the family members to look after various tasks in the sacrifice, e.g. Duḥśāsana was appointed for maintaining food supply (*Ibid.*32. 2-6). Sage Dvaipāyana took the position of the Brahman priest, Suśaman took the position of Udgātṛ, Yājñavalkya became the Adhvaryu and Paila became the Hotṛ, says the *Mbh*

(*Ibid.* 30. 34). Yudhiṣṭhira performed the sacrifice using six fires. After the Abhiṣecanīya ceremony, Yudhiṣṭhira entered the *antarvedi* for the performance of rituals. No *śūdra* entered this place, says the text (*Ibid.* 33. 1,9). The Rājasūya also incorporated narration of stories. This appears to be a passing reference to the narration of the Śunaḥśepa legend during the performance of the Rājasūya sacrifice (*Kāt. Śr. Sū* XV. 6. 1-4). The sacrifice was performed systematically by giving offerings sanctified by the *mantra*-s[201]. People from all the *varṇa*-s rejoiced during the performance of the great sacrifice. The sacrifice concluded with the *avabhṛtha* bath and all the *kṣatriya*-s returned to their respective kingdoms. The Rājasūya sacrifice in the Sabhā P of the *Mbh* has more description of the pomp and celebrations associated with it rather than the ritual details. It is described more as a socio-political affair than a religious performance. The Rājasūya portion seems to be incorporated in the second redaction of the *Mbh,* since it involves a political purpose of extending the boundaries of the kingdom, which the Rājasūya as a ritual does not incorporate. Though the Rājasūya as a ritual does not incorporate battles for royal sway, it is assumed that battles are fought for establishing sovereignty of the sacrificer-king. The ritual named Kṣtradhṛti, i.e. 'wielding of the royal power', is one of the last rituals of Rājasūya (*Kāt. Śr. Sū* XV. 9. 20-21). This indicates that the assumption of political sovereignty implicitly mentioned by the texts on sacrifices was explicitly described in the Sabhā P of the *Mbh.*

The second purpose was the destruction of Jarāsandha and Śiśupāla. This was supplemented by the process of deification of Kṛṣṇa. Kṛṣṇa and Jarāsandha were arch enemies. Kṛṣṇa had to suffer defeat at his hands a number of times. The *Mbh* does not directly hint at the enmity between Jarāsandha and the Pāṇḍava-s. The Rājasūya sacrifice was a 'tool' used by Kṛṣṇa for destroying Jarāsandha to prevent him from performing the human sacrifice.

Another achievement of the Rājasūya was the destruction of Śiśupāla, the king of Cedi. In this way, the *sūta*-tradition of narrators has described the Rājasūya; less as a sacrificial ritual and more as a glorification of Kṛṣṇa.

However, like the Utt of the *Rām*, there are references in the *Mbh* regarding wars fought during the Rājasūya sacrifice (*Mbh.* Ud. P 166. 26. cf. Sal. P 43. 33-41& 48. 11-15).

The *Mbh* mentions of this sacrifice performed by Soma. It was followed by the Tārakāmaya war, in which Kārttikeya killed the demon Tāraka (Śal. P 50. 1). Battles were fought after Varuṇa performed the Rājasūya and even after Janamejaya performed this sacrifice. Thus, though unmentioned in the texts like the Brāhmaṇa-s and the Śrautasūtra-s, the Rājasūya incorporates battles in it.

### Aśvamedha Sacrifice

The second sacrifice which is described in detail is the Aśvamedha in the *Mbh* (Āśvamedhika Parvan Ch. 71). Kṛṣṇa advised Yudhiṣṭhira to perform the Aśvamedha sacrifices and give donations to satisfy gods and the Pitṛ-s with Soma and *svadhā* respectively. The full-moon day of the month of Caitra was selected for commencing this sacrifice (*Ibid.* 71. 4). All the *sambhāra*-s were collected for this sacrifice. Specialists in horse-lore were invited and a horse suitable for sacrifice was selected and released for wandering at will. Sacrificial instruments like *sphya* and *kūrca* were made up of gold (*Ibid.* 71. 10). The disciples of Yājñavalkya were invited for the purpose of the sacrifice. *Kṣatriya* and *viś,* i.e. commoners, arrived at the sacrificial scene (*Ibid.* 72. 17). This was an *ahīna* type of sacrifice and since lot of gold was used it was also known as Bahusuvarṇaka sacrifice (*Ibid.* 90. 13). Yudhiṣṭhira was asked to perform three Aśvamedha-s and give *dakṣiṇā* three times. By these sacrifices the sin committed by Yudhiṣṭhira of the destruction of kinsmen, would be washed off (*Ibid.* 90. 15).

Pravargya was performed and the pressing of Soma was carried out. All the priests performed the rituals very carefully and systematically. Sacrificial posts were erected, which comprised of Bilva (*Aegle marmelos*), Khadira (*Acacia catechu*), Devadāru, and Śleṣmātaka (*Cordia myxa* or *Cordia latifolia*). These references agree with those of the *Śat. Br* (XIII. 4. 4. 5). The same section also gives the Arthavāda for the usage of these trees. Other *yūpa*-s were erected for beautification. The *vedi* was of the shape of an eagle. Many animals were immolated for the sacrifice. There were three hundred animals used for this purpose (Āśvamedhika Parvan 90-91). The animals were pacified, which was followed by the pacification of the sacrificial horse. Draupadī was made to lie next to the sacrificial horse (*Ibid*. 91. 2). The fat of the horse was offered and then it was inhaled by Yudhiṣṭhira and his brothers. By this the Pāṇḍava-s were cleansed off their sins (*Ibid.* Āśv. P 91. 4).

The Aśvamedha performed by Yudhiṣṭhira also describes the wandering of the horse and Arjuna following it. Yet much weightage is not given to the political angle of this sacrifice. The purpose of Aśvamedha has been clearly stated as an expiation of killing kinsmen. The performance of this sacrifice has this as one of the inherent purposes of this sacrifice.

The *Śat. Br* (XIII. 3. 1. 1) states that, the eye of Prajāpati swelled and fell out. From the fallen eye, the horse was born.... By means of the Aśvamedha the gods restored it to its place; and indeed he who performs the Aśvamedha makes Prajāpati complete; and this, indeed, is the atonement for everything. Thereby the gods redeem all sin, even the slaying of a *brāhmaṇa*! He who redeems all sin, he redeems the slaying of a *brāhmaṇa*. Muṇḍibha Audanya discovered this atonement for *brahmahatyā* (*Ibid*. XIII. 3. 5.4).

Apart from few exaggerations like the *yūpa*-s made of gold and the golden sacrificial implements, the rituals of the Aśvamedha described in the *Mbh* agree with the Śrauta texts. The details of the sacrifice are similar to those of the Aśvamedha described in the *Rām* (Bal. 8-14). The chapter II of the present work discusses the sacrificial details in comparison with the Śrauta texts. To avoid repetition, this comparison is avoided.

### Sattra

The *sattra* sacrifice is to be performed by *brāhmaṇa*-s only. The sacrificers of the same Kalpasūtra and lineage are authorised to perform *sattra*-s, so that the sacrificial performances would become flawless. The *kṣatriya*-s and the *vaiśya*-s do not have the right to become the sacrificers of the *sattra*-s[202]. On these lines the *sattra*-references in the *Mbh* need to be examined. The very beginning of the *Mbh*, refers to a Dvādaśavārṣikasattra (twelve years long) *sattra*, Śaunaka, the Kulapati in the Naimiṣa forest (Adi. P 2. 29). The *Tāṇ. MBr* explains this *sattra* as a rite of Prajāpati[203]. The *Mbr* says that, the inhabitants of the Naimiṣa forest throve in all possible ways. Those who undertake this *sattra* become prosperous. This indicates that the reference to the sages performing *sattra* at the Naimiṣa forest is very old.

Sage Bandin also performed the twelve-year long *sattra*. However, it is mentioned that this *sattra* was of Janaka. This sacrifice had a great Ukthya sacrifice (one among the Soma-saṁsthā-s), recitation of *sāman*-s and consumption the Soma juice (Van. P 134. 24, 36). All the *sattra*-s having the span of more than one year have Gavāmāyana *sattra* as their archetype. Some *sattra*-s which are the modifications of Gavāmāyana do have Ukthya as the soma-sacrifice and also the recitation of *sāman*-s, e.g. the Utsargiṇāmāyana has four Ukthya sacrifices, according to the *Kāt. Śr. Sū* (XXIV. 7. 23).

There are references in the *Mbh*, to the *sattra* sacrifices performed by kings, viz. Nṛga and Dhundhumāra who performed *satra*-s till they become very old (Anu. P 6. 38 c-d, 39).

Duryodhana performed the Vaiṣṇavasattra. The text does not disclose any rituals performed during this *sattra*. However, this *sattra* was a replacement for the Rājasūya, for the Rājasūya could not be performed by Duryodhana, till Dhṛtarāṣṭra and Yudhiṣṭhira were alive. The Vaiṣṇavasattra competed with the Rājasūya, in glory. In the Vaiṣṇavasattra, all the kings became the tributaries of Duryodhana. Duryodhana ploughed land for this performance (Van. P 241. 26-27, 32-33). Such types of rituals are also practised in the sacrifices like the Agnicayana. As it is mentioned earlier, the Rājasūya is associated with pomp, glory and supremacy. It is performed by a king desiring sovereign power. According to Thite, in the ritual itself, the sacrificer overpowers his relative only symbolically. The real overpowering, it may be assumed, must be taking place before the ritual[204]. The *Lāṭ. Śr. Sū*, mentions a rite, in which the weak agnate of the king assemble at the sacrificial place along with their wealth. The king plunders their wealth. He shoots arrows at them. They return them back by expressing the wish that may the king be victorious. Such agnates are called Rājanya-s. They become permanently disqualified for royal consecration (*Lāṭ. Śr. Sū.* IX. 1. 14-22). Thite concludes that the king sacrificer, before performing the Rājasūya, subdues all and in the performance of the Rājasūya subdues his relatives also in a ritualistic way. But this kingship is at the cost of other relatives who also might have claims for being king. But not only the kingship is robbed from them, it is also ritually denied to them even in future. They naturally would feel insulted[205].

The kingly position of Duryodhana was subordinate to Dhṛtarāṣṭra and Yudhiṣṭhira. Since a sovereign monarch, in order to proclaim sovereignty performed Rājasūya, Duryodhana was not entitled to perform it. Moreover, as it is performed by one king of the Kuru clan, Duryodhana could not perform it. This indicates that Rājasūya was to be performed only by one sovereign king of a family. Its political significance does not permit another king from the same family to undertake a conquest for its purpose. Yudhiṣṭhira, the crowned king, who had already performed the Rājasūya was in exile and Dhṛtarāṣṭra, though a titular king still existed in the family of Kuru-s. Duryodhana was merely a prince! The attempt to equate Vaiṣṇavasattra, with the Rājasūya, indicates the rise of Vaiṣṇavism vis-à-vis Vedic religion. Vaiṣṇavism was placed on an equal footing with the Rājasūya. This also throws light on the later addition of this passage.

The *Mbh* refers to a *sattra* by the Sage Agastya. He offered the omentum of a deer as a magical rite, i.e. *abhicāra karman*[206]. As mentioned in the earlier chapter, the omentum of a deer is never used in the sacrifice since the deer is compared with Prajapati. *Abhicāra* are those rites belonging to the *AV*. They incorporate black and white magic. Moreover, the name of this *sattra* is not mentioned in this passage. The nature of this sacrifice is not clear in this passage.

King Samvaraṇa and Tapatī have also performed a sacrifice for twelve years. This is necessarily the twelve-year-old sacrifice, i.e. the Dvādaśavārṣikasattra (Ādi. P. 163. 21). Gods performed *sattra*, where Yama played the role of Śamitṛ, i.e. one who pacifies the animal to be offered (Ādi. P. 189. 1-2). This *sattra* projects the problem that since Yama was busy he could not play the role of taking away the lives of beings.

King Bṛhaddyumna performed a *sattra* (no name mentioned) in which sage Raibhya was the sacrificer. He had two sons, viz. Arvāvasu and Parāvasu. The sage Raibhya was killed by his son Parāvasu, who mistook him as a deer. The sage was sleeping covered in a deer-skin. Parāvasu performed the funeral rites of his father and returned. Since Arvāvasu was incapable of undertaking *sattra* single-handedly, he accepted to perform expiation on behalf of Parāvasu. Parāvasu managed the *sattra* singly. After performing the expiatory rites, Arvāvasu returned. However, Parāvasu blamed Arvāvasu for *brahmahatyā*. Arvāvasu repeatedly pledged for his innocence. The quarrel ended when gods became pleased with Arvāvasu and gave him upliftment along with his father, says the *Mbh* (Van. P 139).

Another *sattra* mentioned in the *Mbh* is the Rākṣasasattra (Ādi. 172. 1-9). This *sattra* was performed by sage Parāśara, in which he sacrificed the Rākṣasa-s young and old. Three fires were enkindled for this *sattra*. None of the texts on sacrifice mention such type of *sattra*. This sacrifice was stopped by the intervention of the sages. The myth of the Rākṣasasattra, seems to be carved out from the Sarpasattra performed by Janamejaya. Certain facts are highlighted through this myth.

a) It indicates a feud between the *brāhmaṇa*-s and the Rākṣasa-s.
b) It indicates the triumph of the *brāhmaṇa*-s over the Rākṣasa-s.

c) *Sattra* has been devised to sacerdotize the victory of the *brāhmaṇa*-s over the Rākṣasa-s.

This Rākṣasasattra is a mythical sacrifice to veil the genocide of the Rākṣasa–s, or subduing them, if taken metaphorically.

Janamejaya, along with his brothers, Śrutasena, Ugrasena and Bhīmasena, performed a Dīrghasattra. A dog (*sārameya*) arrived on the sacrificial scene. It was hit and driven away by the brothers of Janamejaya. Wailing in pain, the dog returned to its mother Saramā. She arrived at the sacrificial place and asked the king and his brothers for justification for this rash behaviour. The king and his brothers could not give an answer. Since her son had not committed any formidable offence like 'seeing or licking the oblation', Saramā cursed the king that he would be haunted by an unknown figure (Ādi. P. 3.1-10). The motif of licking the oblation can be traced up to the Brāhmaṇa-s.

According to the *Ait. Br*, the Soma offered to Maitrāvaruṇa was licked by Dīrghajīhvī, an Asura woman. By this act the oblation became impure, which was purified by an oblation of curds (II. 22). The same myth occurs in the *Tāṇ. MBr* in the context of the Saumitrasāman (XIII. 6. 8-9). The motif of regarding a dog as inauspicious occurs in the *Śat. Br* (XII. 4. 1. 4 & XIII. 1. 2. 9) and the *Tait. Sam* (III. 2. 6. 2).

Sarpasattra is another important sacrifice narrated in the *Mbh.* It is important because the first narration of the *Mbh* took place in this *sattra* (Ādi. P 1. 58). This sacrifice was performed for the destruction of the *sarpa*-s (serpents/ serpent-tribe) (*Ibid.* 13. 40). Those specialized in the performance of the Sarpasatttra were appointed as the chief officiating priests. The serpents thought of various ways and means of destroying this sacrifice. However, their efforts were futile. Janamejaya got consecrated for this sacrifice.

All the sacrificers (*yājaka*-s) wore black garments and had their eyes reddened with smoke. The black garments worn by the sacrificers are very significant, because in the sacrifices, the priests wear white garments[207]. In sacrifices performed as *abhicārakarman*-s, the priests wear red garments. Only in the Kārīrīṣṭi performed for rain, the sacrificers wear black garments to induce black clouds for rain. Many serpents were destroyed in this sacrifice. The priests for the sacrifice stated in the *Mbh* were as follows (Ādi P.48. 5-9):

| *Position of the priests* | *Name of the sage* |
|---|---|
| Hotṛ | Caṇḍabhārgava, belonging to the family of Cyavana |
| Udgātṛ | Jaimini |
| Brahman | Śārṅgarava |
| Adhvaryu | Bodhapiṅgala |
| Sadasya-s | Vyāsa, along with his disciples viz; Uddālaka, Śamaṭhaka, Śvetaketu, Asita, Devala, Nārada, Parvata, Ātreya, Kuṇḍajaṭhara, Kūṭighaṭa, Vātsya, Śrutaśravas, Kahoḍa, Maudgalya |

The Brāhmaṇa-s and the Śrautasūtra-s mention the Sarpasattra. The *Tāṇ. MBr* says, 'An overnight rite (Atirātra)at the beginning and the end of the year consists through tens and tens, only the middle day (the *viśuvat*) is twelve-versed: at the middle day, the *sāman*-s of the serpents are applied. Through this (rite), the serpents gained a firm support in these worlds. They who undertake it get a firm support in these worlds. The priests mentioned in the same section are as follows (XXV. 15. 1-4)'.

| *Position of priests* | *Name of the sage* |
|---|---|
| Gṛhapati | Jarvara |
| Brahman | Dhṛtarāṣṭra |
| Udgātṛ | Pṛthuśravas |
| Brāhmaṇācchamsin | Pṛthuśravas |
| Grāvastut | Arbuda Kādraveya |

The text enumerates in details the names of different *sarpa*-s (may be kings and princes of the Sarpa-tribe). Dange (Mrs.) observes that Arbuda, the Grāvstut is the seer of the *RV* hymn (X. 94), which praises the pressing stones. It is said that through this rite, the serpents vanquished death. Hence, it is that having left aside their old skins i.e. 'slough the serpents' vanquished death. This entire rite has been understood as assimilating the Sarpa-tribe in the sphere of rituals[208]. *Baudh. Śr. Sū* gives more details about the Sarpasattra. It states that Arimejaya and Janamejaya are the kings and princes of the serpents who performed the Sarpasattra, in human form at a place named Khāṇḍava. One who performs the Sarpasattra is protected by the serpents as they do not kill him (*Baudh. Śr. Sū.* XVII. 18). Caland comments, "So much is certain, that in this Sarpasattra, the *sattra* performed by the serpents, we have to see the prototype of the Sarpasattra (the *sattra*, where the *sarpa*-s are sacrificed) of Janamejaya in the *Mbh*. According to *Baudh. Śr. Sū*, they were the kings and princes of the Sarpa-s, who at Khāṇḍavaprastha, in the human form performed this *sattra*, desirous of poison"[209].

Winternitz understands the Sarpasattra of the *Mbh* as not a real sacrifice, but a magical spell by way of which the serpents are brought to 'self-annihilation'. He opines that a clear-distinction between magic and sacrifice is little possible in India as elsewhere[210].

There occurs a clear-cut distinction between the Sarpasattra performed by Janamejaya and the procedure and purpose of the Sarpasattra mentioned in the Brāhmaṇa-s and the Śrautasūtra-s. As mentioned by Winternitz, there is a possibility of some other magical spell utilized for the destruction of the Sarpa-tribe. But to get religious legitimacy for this spell, the term 'Sarpasattra' was used by the narrators of the *Mbh*.

In fact, the *sattra*-s in the *Mbh* are not true to the rules prescribed by the works on the sacrifices. The points of difference are:

1. A *sattra* is not performed by *kṣatriya*-s. But in the *Mbh* kings performed *sattra*-s. There is one possibility of justification, i.e. the kings, might have funded these *sattra*-s. But this possibility is contradicted by the references to kings acting as sacrificers (*yajamāna*-s) for the *sattra*-s.

2. Certain *sattra*-s like the Rākṣasasattra-s are fictitious. They have been structured on the Sarpasattra.

3. The Vaiṣṇavasattra performed by Duryodhana is a sacrifice carved out as a compensation for being unable to perform the Rājasūya. The name Vaiṣṇava indicates the Visnuite influence on it.

4. The Sarpasattra in the *Mbh* has an inverted purpose vis-à-vis the sacrificial texts. The sacrificial texts mention two reasons for the performance of the Sarpasattra:

(a) Serpents perform it to become more powerful (as mentioned in the Brāhmaṇa-s).

(b) Sacrificers perform it, so that the serpents become harmless to them, probably to become more powerful than the serpents! (as mentioned in the Śrautasūtra-s)

There is a difference of opinion between the Brāhmaṇa-s and the Śrautasūtra-s. One can account for the time gap for such a difference. Pt. no. (b) seems to move closer to the Sarpasattra in the *Mbh.* One may not deny the possibility that Janamejaya might have performed the Sarpasattra to seek protection from the serpents. In other words, the 'protective magic' in the Sarpasattra would have served as a 'preventive device' against the serpents, to prevent the repetition of the history of his father. As far as the reference to Arimejaya and Janamejaya in the *Baudh. Śr. Sū* is concerned, it is difficult to say that Janamejaya referred to in the *Baudh. Śr. Sū* and Janamejaya in the *Mbh* are the same. The narrative style of Sūta Lomaharṣaṇa might have created the story of genocidal destruction of the serpent tribe through the Sarpasattra of Janamejaya. It is just to eulogise the king Janamejaya as one who avenged the death of his father Parikṣit at the hands of the serpent named Takṣaka and not as a king who sought protection to prevent the repetition of the history of his father. Lastly, the difference of opinion between the sacrificial texts and the epic indicates a wide time span between the compositions of the two.

## OTHER SACRIFICES

### Sādyaska Sacrifice

When the Kaurava-s undertook the *ghoṣayātra* (i.e. taking the cows for grazing), to observe the pitiful condition of the Pāṇḍava-s living in exile, Yudhiṣṭhira was performing the Sādyaska sacrifice. This sacrifice was also called the

Rājarṣiyajña. This was performed on the banks of a lake in the Dvaitavana with divine but forestal rituals (Van. P. 229. 13cd-15).

### Viśvajit

The reference to the Viśvajit sacrifice occurs in the episode of king Dhṛtarāṣṭra and Baka Dālbhya. In the Naimiṣa forest, sages performed the Dvādaśavārṣika *sattra,* at the end of which the Viśvajit sacrifice was performed (Śal. P 40. 3). This sacrifice is performed by one who is desirous of enjoying supremacy. Apart from this reference there is no explanation for the performance of Viśvajit. This episode mentions a very strange sacrifice. Baka Dālbhya, an old sage, asked for animals, for a sacrifice, to king Dhṛtarāṣṭra. The king who was annoyed with this demand gave dead cows to the sage. This angered the sage, who took the dead cows and offered their flesh in the sacrifice. He performed this sacrifice, a *sattra,* on the banks of river Sarasvatī, with the desire to destroy the kingdom of Dhṛtarāṣṭra (Śal. P 40. 4-'13). In this particular passage, the terminology used is essentially Vedic. But, the procedure of offering dead cows (not 'pacified' by sacrificial procedure) is essentially a-Vedic. Besides, the motive with which this sacrifice was performed is not constructive but destructive. What is the purpose behind incorporating such a passage? Dhṛtarāṣṭra had rejected the demand of Baka Dālbhya and had to face severe consequences for this. This passage throws light on the fact that if a demand from a sage who is desirous to perform a sacrifice is rejected by a king, it becomes a grave punishable offence. The sacrifice which has the death of Dhṛtarāṣṭra as its purpose is supported by offering flesh of dead cows. This can be compared to the ritual of placing the limbs of a dead cow, i.e. *anustaraṇī* cow, on the dead Āhitāgni person prior to his cremation. The following table gives a list of sources which mention about the sage Baka Dālbhya and the context in which the sage is mentioned[211].

BAKA DĀLBHYA

| | |
|---|---|
| *Kāṭ. Sam.* 10. 6.<br>Baka Dālbhya<br>Naimiṣa | *sattra* ritualist, lived in<br>Dhṛtarāṣṭra reluctant<br>patron (king) |
| Vaicitravīrya<br>*Jai. UBr* 1.9.3<br>Baka Dālbhya<br>Ajakeśin | Udgātṛ of the syllable Aum<br>rival ritualist |
| *Jai. UBr* 4.6-8<br>Baka Dālbhya | learned Udgātṛ among<br>Kurupāñcala-s |
| Bhagīratha<br>Aikṣvāka | asks about ritual/patron<br>(king) |
| *Chāndogya Upaniṣad* 1.2.13<br>Baka Dālbhya | Udgātṛ among those staying<br>at Naimiṣa forest |
| *Chāndogya Upaniṣad* 1.12<br>(Baka Dālbhya<br>Dogs reciting the<br>Bahiṣpavamānastotra | Udgātṛ<br><br>termed as poor singers |

## Cāturmāsya Sacrifices

The *Mbh* refers to the performance of Cāturmāsya sacrifices(*Mbh.* Anu. P 130. 15). However, no details are discussed regarding these sacrifices. The Cāturmāsya-s are seasonal sacrifices, which involve three *parvan*-s (parts or joints), viz. Vaiśvadeva, Varuṇapraghāsa, Sākamedha and Śunāsīrīya. They are called the Cāturmāsya-s because each of them takes place after four months. They are performed on the Full Moon days of Phālguna/Caitra, Āṣaḍha, Kārttika and on the 5th Full Moon from the day on which the Sākamedha is performed (i.e. on Phālgunī) or two or three days before it. The Cāturmāsya-s indicate the advent of three seasons viz; *vasanta* (spring), *varṣā* (rains) and *hemanta* (autumn)[212].

## Vaiśvadeva

Just as Cāturmāsya-s are merely mentioned similarly, the Vaiśvadeva is referred to by Draupadī. She has praised Yudhiṣṭhira for performing the Vaiśvadeva and other sacrifices (Van. P. 31. 13). The Vaiśvadeva *iṣṭi* is performed in the morning of the first day after Full Moon and is later followed by the Pūrṇamāsa iṣṭi[213]. However, the Vaiśvadevaparvan can be performed independently by one who is desirous of progeny[214]. The above reference in the *Mbh* may also point to an independent sacrifice and not a part of the Cāturmāsya-s.

The story of Jaigīṣavya in the *Mbh* refers to many sacrifices (Śal. P 49. 29-40). The Sage Asita Devala saw Sage Jaigīṣavya moving in different worlds which those performing the sacrifices attain, viz. a) Darśapūrṇamāsa, b) Agniṣṭuta, c) Cāturmāsya, d) Agniṣṭoma, e) Vājapeya, f) Pauṇḍarīka, g) Rājasūya, h) Sautrāmaṇī, i) Aśvamedha, j) Sarvamedha and k) Dvādaśāha

Performance of each sacrifice leads to the attainment of different worlds. However, this episode drives home the fact that in spite of attaining these worlds, *mokṣa* is the greatest fruit.

### Darśapūrṇamāsa Sacrifice

New-moon and Full-moon sacrifices is the archetype of other *iṣṭi*-s. Darśa is taken to mean 'the day on which the moon is seen only by the sun and by no one else'[215].

### Agniṣṭoma

This sacrifice is the archetype of the seven *soma*-sacrifices. It is a one-day sacrifice and is an integral part of the Jyotiṣṭoma so much so that the two are often identified with each other[216].

### Agniṣṭuta

Agniṣṭuta, i.e. Agniṣṭut is the modification of Jyotiṣṭoma sacrifice. There are four Agniṣṭut-s according to the *Tāṇ. MBr* (XVII. 4-9).

i) First Agniṣṭut is performed by him who deems himself impure. This Agniṣṭut is also performed by one desirous of priestly lustre.
ii) Second Agniṣṭut is performed by one desirous of cattle.
iii) Third Agniṣṭut is performed by him who goes amiss in a sacrifice.
iv) Fourth Agniṣṭut is performed by one who is desirous of food.

### Vājapeya

This sacrifice is said to be the form of Jyotiṣṭoma and follows the procedure of Ṣoḍaśin. It means food and drink or drink of strength or of food or of a race. The number 17 is very important in this sacrifice[217].

## Puṇḍarīka

There are references to a sacrifice in the *Mbh,* which is known in the Śrauta texts as Pauṇḍarīka. Pauṇḍarīka is meant for one who is desirous of all kinds of prosperity[218]. Pauṇḍarīka required a fee of 10,000 cows. According to the commentary (Devayājñikapaddhati) on the *Kāt. Śr. Sū,* this sacrifice has twelve *upasad*-s and also the performance of Daśarātra (an *ahīna*-type of sacrifice) sacrifice. The commentary mentions the name of Kṣemadhanvan (according to the *Mān. Śr. Sū*) and Kṣemavṛttama (according to the *Kāt. Sam*), the son of Puṇḍarīka, who performed this sacrifice and attained supremacy[219]. According to Kṣemadhṛtvan, the son of Puṇḍarīka having sacrificed with this (rite) at the northern border of Sudāman, throve in all respects. The *Mbh* text refers to the sacrifice Puṇḍarīka, and not Pauṇḍarīka[220]. There are three references to the Puṇḍarīka sacrifice in the *Mbh*[221]. In this reference given in the footnotes, Puṇḍarīka is accompanied with the Rājasūya sacrifice. Hence, it can be explained through the Daśapeya, rite performed during the Rājasūya. Daśapeya i.e. the drink of ten, has ten offerings. The *dakṣiṇā* at every offering is a white lotus, i.e. Puṇḍarīka. The purpose of this rite is to infuse the sacrificer with bodily strength, which he has lost during the lustration rites. Up to the seven offerings seven lotuses are given and five lotuses are given during the last three, which means twelve lotuses in all. The *Śat. Br* (V. 4. 5. 6-18) strikes an innovation with a golden lotus as *dakṣiṇā* at every offering. The sacrificer puts a wreath of twelve lotuses. This is a wreath of twelve lotuses because there are twelve months in a year, says the *Śat. Br* (V. 4. 5. 13-14)[222]. The association of Puṇḍarīka with the Rajasuya and the name of the sacrifice, i.e. Puṇḍarīka and not Puṇḍarīka may be because of the reference to the Daśapeya rite performed during the Rājasūya.

### Sautrāmaṇī

This rite is included among the seven forms of *haviryajña*-s. It is not a *soma*-sacrifice, but is a combination of an *iṣṭi* with animal sacrifice[223]. The chief characteristic of it is the offering of *surā*, i.e. wine, in it[224]. The Sautrāmaṇī sacrifice is to be performed by a *brāhmaṇa* desirous of prosperity[225].

### Sarvamedha

The Sarvamedha sacrifice is to be performed by one who is desirous of all kinds of achievements[226]. It consists of ten *soma*-pressing days. The *soma*-sacrifices taking place on the ten days of the Sarvamedha are Agniṣṭut, Ukthya, Suryastut, Vaiśvadevastut, Mahāvrata, Vājapeya and Aptoryāma according to the *Kāt. Śr. Sū* (XXI. 2. 2-5).

### Dvādaśāha

The Dvādaśāha is both an *ahīna* sacrifice and a *sattra*, since it is a sacrifice performed for twelve days[227]. *Kāt. Śr. Sū* (XII. 1. 6) indicates the difference between these two. The *sattra* sacrifice is indicated either by *āsate* or *upayanti* and *yajate* is used in connection with *ahīna* sacrifice.

The story of Jaigīṣavya has given a list of sacrifices. Asita Devala has seen the sage reach the abodes which are attained by those who have said to have performed these sacrifices even without performing them! Sacrifice vis-à-vis *mokṣa; mokṣa* is superior. The list of sacrifices and their fruits indicate that the *sūta*-tradition of the *Mbh* was well-aware of the sacrifices. However, did they have an in-depth knowledge of the sacrifices, still remains a doubt, for the list does not elaborate any rituals regarding these sacrifices. But the probability that the listeners were aware of the details and hence the narrators did not mention them cannot be ignored.

Draupadī has praised Yudhiṣṭhira for performing many sacrifices, viz. i) various *iṣṭi*-s, ii) Paśubandha, iii) Aśvamedha, iv) Rājasūya, v) Puṇḍarīka and vi) Gosava. She has also praised him for giving Vaiśvadeva offering, for performing occasional and desire-oriented *karman*-s and for giving large donations during these sacrifices. Yudhiṣṭhira gave offerings to the gods and manes (Van. P 31. 10, 13-15). There is an element of exaggeration in the praise by Draupadī. This exaggeration serves as an indicatory of a stronghold of the institution of sacrifice. The text is aware of certain rules regarding sacrifices, e.g. gods are offered oblations with the utterance of *svāhā* and the manes with *svadhā*. *Karman*-s are divided into three i) *nitya,* i.e. regular ii) *naimittika,* i.e. occasional and iii) desire-oriented, i.e. *kāmya*. The text speaks about occasional and desire-oriented *karman*-s. It also hints at the classification of sacrifices mentioned by the word Pākayajña-s. However, the text is silent about the remaining, viz. Haviryajña and Somayajña. The text is also hinting to its inclination towards the concept of sacrifice developed by the *Bhagavadgītā*. It speaks about consuming the remnant of the sacrifice and getting freed from sins (*Bhagvadgītā* 3.3). The same thought is upheld in the *RV* and the *Manu Sm*[228]. The text says that Yudhiṣṭhira offered food to the guests and servants and then consumed food (Van. 4. 7,9).

In this context; two sacrifices are to be discussed, viz. a) Paśubandha, b) Gosava

### Paśubandha or Nirūḍhapaśubandha

It means immolation of an animal in sacrifice. The animal sacrifice is an independent sacrifice and it is also performed in *soma*-sacrifices as a constituent part. The independent animal sacrifice is to be performed every six months or every year by an Āhitāgni, throughout his life[229]. An independent reference to the Paśubandha sacrifice in the *Mbh* is noteworthy because Draupadī mentioned it as an independent sacrifice and not an *aṅga,* i.e. the constituent part of the *soma*-sacrifice.

### GOSAVA

This sacrifice is performed for supremacy. A myraid (of cows should be given) as sacrificial fee; for that is equal to supremacy. The sacrificer is consecrated with milk. During this consecration the chanting of Bṛhatsāman takes place according to the *Tāṇ. Mbr* (XIX. 14. 1-10). The *Kāt. Śr. Sū* gives a different dimension to this sacrifice. Ten thousand cows are given as *dakṣiṇā* during this sacrifice. According to some, Gosava is to be performed by *vaiśya.* They regard the performer of the Gosava sacrifice as *'sthapati'*, i.e. head of the locality[230].

Pākayajña-s fall under the category of Gṛhya or Smārta *karman*-s. The given passage points out the influence (rather a confluence!) of Śrauta and Smārta traditions.

### PITṚMEDHA

There are references in the *Mbh* to the Pitṛmedha of Pāṇḍu (Ādi. 117. 31). The Pitṛmedha sacrifice is to be performed only when the death anniversary of the father is no longer remembered[231]. The *Śat. Br* also opines the same (XIII. 8. 1. 4). However, the connotation of the term Pitṛmedha is not death anniversary, but funeral rites performed after the death of Pāṇḍu. After the death of Pāṇḍu, his body was consigned to flames in the forest. His remains were brought to Hastināpura. A procession was carried with the white royal umbrella and chowries. Many people participated in this procession taking precious stones. Musicians participated in it. The sacrificers were clad in white garments. Beautiful garments were set aside for Pāṇḍu. Then Vidura, Dhṛtarāṣṭra, Bhīṣma and others performed the Śrāddha, with the utterance of *svadhā* (Ādi. P 118. 6-13). Participation of the *ṛtvij*s is also mentioned during the funeral rites of king Vicitravīrya(Ādi. P 96.59). However, the funeral rites of Pāṇḍu do not mention any ritual details.

Here ends the section on 'sacrifices'.

## REFERENCES TO THE SACRIFICIAL TERMS

### Somasaṁsthā

King Aṅga gave sumptuous *dakṣiṇā*-s to the priests and even gods and *gandharva*-s during the performance of the *soma*-sacrifices (Śān. P 29. 33). The details of the three sections of sacrifices, viz. Haviḥsaṁsthā, Somasaṁsthā and Pākasaṁsthā have been discussed in the introduction.

### Aśvasaṁjñāpana

This refers to the ritual of 'quietening' the sacrificial horse released during the Aśvamedha sacrifice (Ud. P 105. 13).

### Yajñasaṁstara

Performance of sacrifices leads to the *devayāna* at death. The word Yajñasaṁstara is used in the sense of sacrifice. Yajñasaṁstara is also used in the sense of ritual arrangements for a sacrifice[232].

### Paristaraṇa

The *brāhmaṇa*-s belonging to the Somaka dynasty gave offerings to the fire, after doing the Paristaraṇa ritual (Ādi. P 176. 31). It is the ritual in which the Adhvaryu strews the sacred grass around the Dakṣiṇāgni and places the utensils one by one[233].

### Avabhṛtha Bath

Yudhiṣṭhira took the *avabhṛtha* bath after performing the Rājasūya sacrifice (Sabhā P. 42. 35). *Avabhṛtha* bath is the bath undertaken at the end of the sacrifice.

### Agnipraṇayana

The lighted embers from the Gārhapatya fire are carried to the Āhavanīya which become two fires, similarly by the birth of Bharata one Duṣyanta became two(Ādi. P 68. 65). This is said by Śakuntalā on the birth of Bharata.

### Offering of Sesamum

Offering of sesamum is to be given to the manes (*Ibid*. Anu. P: 65. 8). However, *Śat. Br* prescribes wild sesamum offerings to Rudra during the Śatarudrīya offering. The text gives the reason that wild-sesame represents both kinds of food—cultivated and wild-growing (*Śat. Br*. IX. 1. 1. 3). The *tilaśrāddha* offerings possibly indicate the Puranic influence on this particular section.

### Abhiṣeka

After the great war Yudhiṣṭhira was consecrated as a king/ monarch (Śān. P 40. 10). Sage Dhaumya performed the ceremony. The consecration ceremony bears similarity with Vedic rituals of consecrating the sacrificer for the performance of the sacrifices like the Rājasūya, according to *Śat. Br* (V. 3. 5. 2). The Aindramahābhiṣeka of the *Ait. Br* bears ritual-similarity with the sacrifice (VIII. 25). During the consecration, offerings were given to the fire. Draupadī participated in the ritual. The sacrificial twigs were of Śamī, Palāśa, and Punnāga. The *sruva* was made up of Audumbara tree. The sacrificial altar was tapering to the north-eastern direction. It was anointed with ointments.

The Sarvatobhadra seat had a tiger-skin covered over it. Conches studded with gold were used. The Madhusarpiṣī offerings were also an ingredient in this ritual (Śān. P 40. 11-14). The procedure of the ritual if examined on the lines of the Aindramahābhiṣeka can surely throw light on the purpose behind the utilization of various ingredients[234]. However, the Sarvatobhadra seat is necessarily not Vedic, but Puranic[235]. Hence, one can conclude that the consecration-ceremony of Yudhiṣṭhira as a monarch was Vedic in nature with a tinge of Puranic elements in it.

### Reference to the Purchase of Soma

Bhiṣma had stated the importance of sacrifices and *dakṣiṇā*-s. No mantra without *dakṣiṇā* can be effective. Hence, Yudhiṣṭhira should perform sacrifices along with the first three *varṇa*-s. Bhīṣma further adds that it is the Vedic *śruti*, which says that Soma is the king of the *brāhmaṇa*-s. It should be purchased and by that the sacrificial ritual gets accomplished (Śān. P 81. 13). Similar thought occurs in the *Śat. Br* (III. 2. 4. 7)[236].

## SOME OTHER REFERENCES:

### Feud between Indra and Aśvins

In order to incorporate Aśvin-s in the share of the sacrificial offerings, Cyavana performed a sacrifice. This sacrifice was performed to teach Indra a lesson since, he refused to give a part of the sacrificial offerings to the Aśvins. The sacrifice gave rise to *kṛtyā*, the power of Sage Cyavana. Mada, a terrible demon, emerged from it (Van. P 124. 19). Śakra attacked Cyavana, but by the power of penance the latter held the hand of Śakra, i.e. Indra, to a standstill. Cyavana made offerings to the fire and from it arose *kṛtyā* (*Ibid.* Van. P 124. 18). The Śakti, i.e. prowess of the Pāṇḍava-s, was similar to the *kṛtyā* of the Atharvāṅgiras, which was radiant like the Samvartaka fire, says the *Mbh* (Śal. P 16. 43). The term *kṛtyā* occurs in the *AV*, as *kṛtyā aṅgirasaiḥ* (X. 1. 6, XII. 5. 52). The term Aṅgirasa refers to the hostile sorcery practices of the Veda. The *AV* Pariśiṣṭa XXXII. 2 refers to the term *kṛtyāpratiharaṇāni* as counter-witchcraft. *Kṛtyā* referred to in the *Mbh* indicates hostile, sorcery practices of the *AV*.

### Agnihotra

Performance of the daily ritual of Agnihotra is regarded as a *nitya-karman*. The *Mbh* says that Agnihotra if not performed causes fear (*Ibid*. Ādi. P 85. 24). The Vaikhānasa-s, who are desirous of performing sacrifice should perform them with faith. Here the discussion is of performing the sacrifice during sunrise or before sunrise (Śān. P 60. 47). This is an old argument regarding the performance of Agnihotra during sunrise or before sunrise. The *Kau. Br*, opines that, he who offers when the sun has already risen, offers to the god, who has already started on his journey. He who offers when the sun is not yet risen, but is about to rise, offers homage to god who is near him. Hence, one should offer to the sun, when he is about to rise and has not yet risen. The *Śat. Br* strikes a variant note. It says that the rays of the sun enter the fire as it sets. When the sun has arisen, its rays go out of the fire. In this context, the text refers to the view of Āsuri. According to him, if one offers to the sun after it has arisen, it is like bringing the offering to an empty abode. Hence one should offer prior to sun-rise, when its rays are still in their abode of the fire-altar (II. 3. 1. 9ff). This view says that the offerings of the *udita-karman* get broken[237]. The author(s) of the *Mbh* are aware of this old argument, but to them, this argument is immaterial until the sacrifice is performed with faith. Dhṛtarāṣṭra had carried the Agnihotra along with him, when he resorted to the forest (*Mbh.* Āśr. P 21. 3). The dialogue between Tārkṣya and Sarasvatī refers to the rules prescribed for performing Agnihotra (*Ibid.* Van. P 184. 3 ff). One should not perform Agnihotra when impure or when not learned or when not having the knowledge of the Brahman. Gods, who are desirous of eating and are pleased with pure behaviour, do not rejoice in oblations offered by one who is faithless. One whose education is incomplete should not perform Agnihotra. Sarasvatī says that she has emerged from the Agnihotra. She is nurtured by the offerings of excellent *brāhmaṇa*-s. Dhṛtarāṣṭra performed Agnihotra and other rituals. He ate the remnant of the food from offerings (Van. P. 184.1-18 58).

### AGNIHOTRA-COW

The *Mbh* accepts the importance of the Agnihotra-cow. The term Agnihotra- cow is used for that cow whose milk is used for offering during the Agnihotra. She is also termed as Homadhenu. The *svāhākāra* and *vaṣaṭkāra* are established in the sacrificial cow used for sacrifice. The *Mbh* eulogises the importance of cow as the mouth of the sacrifice (Anu. P 51. 28, 29). Karṇa's offence of killing a cow of a *brāhmaṇa*, was a grave offence because she was a special cow used for sacrifice (Śān. P 2. 20).

### SŪTASAVA

The *Mbh* has a passing reference to a sacrifice named Sūtasava. This was a specific sacrifice performed by the *sūta*-s (Ud. P 139. 14). The Sūtasava has been referred to in the *Śān. Śr. Sū* (XIV. 22.1). It is an Ekāha *soma*-sacrifice which takes the day of the Jyotiṣṭoma for the Sūtasava.

## CHANGING TREND IN THE INSTITUTION OF SACRIFICE

Vedic sacrifice involved large sums of wealth and also animal slaughter. One finds the face of this institution changing in the *Mbh.* The text is fairly eloquent about the changed approach to the institution of sacrifice.

a) Narrative of Somaka and Jantu: Somaka, the king, begot only one son, in spite of having many wives. Jantu, being the only son, the mothers gave excessive attention and had tremendous affection towards him. The king felt very insecure of having only one son. Hence, his *ṛtvij* advised him to perform the sacrifice with Jantu himself. The text describes in a pathetic tone, the lamentations of the wives of Somaka. At last Jantu was offered. Due to the inhalation of his *vapā,* the wives became pregnant (Van. P. 127. 20-21). After the death of the king, he went to the higher abode, but found the *ṛtvij* in the hell. When asked the reason, the *ṛtvij* admitted the sin of performing the sacrifice with Jantu, which led him to this misery. However, the place where Jantu was sacrificed became sacred and many kings performed sacrifices at that place. This story indicates the changing trend in the sacrificial institution. Sacrifice, which had the animal offering as a ritual in the later stage, started abstaining from violence.

b) Other references: Story of a *brāhmaṇa* who followed *uñcchavṛtti,* i.e. survived on the remnant of food-grains fallen in the fields. This story has arguments regarding sacrifices having violence and non-violence and non-violent sacrifices (Śan.P Ch. 264). At another place in the *Mbh,* the same tune is harped (Anu. P 128. 41). The *Mbh* narrates the story of Bhagīratha. This king had performed many sacrifices, to please gods. He performed Sādyaskra-s, Dvādaśāha-s,

Trayodaśāha-s, Aśvamedha-s and Ṣoḍaśin-s and many more sacrifices. But he did not reach the Brahmaloka through these sacrifices. He also performed Naramedha and Aśvamedha sacrifices and also the Viśvajit sacrifice. He performed a sacrifice with Śamyākṣepa. This is a ritual in which the sacrificial altar is located measuring the distance between a strong man who throws a *śamyā,* i.e. yoke pin, and the point on which the *śamyā* falls[238]. These sacrifices did not help Bhagīratha in attaining Brahmaloka. It is only attained through charity says the *Mbh* (Anu. P Ch. 106). The said passage has attacked the very philosophy behind the performance of Vedic sacrifices. Sacrifice is to be performed for attaining higher worlds. But in this passage Bhagīratha hardly gives any credit to the numerous sacrifices he had performed for this achievement of the higher world. But he has admitted that through charity, which is much simpler to the sacrifices, attaining the higher world is possible. This indicates the changing face of sacrificial religion.

c) The story of King Vicakṣu is also displaying the same changing trend in the nature of Vedic sacrifice. Seeing bulls and cows without any strength, the king thought in the interest of people consuming flesh that it was unrighteous to consume flesh under the pretext of sacrifices, trees and sacrificial posts (Śān. P 257. 8).

d) The story of Vasu Uparicara also reiterates the same trend. Vasu Uparicara performed the Aśvamedha sacrifice. Bṛhaspati played the role of Hotṛ, *sadasya*-s were the sons of Prajāpati, viz. Ekata, Dvita and Trita. Other sages were Dhanuṣākṣa, Raibhya, Arvāvasu, Parāvasu, Medhātithi, Tāṇḍya, Śakti, Vedaśiras, Kapila, Śālihotra, Kaṭha, Taittiri, Kaṇva and Devahotra. All the ingredients were collected for the sacrifice. It was a sacrifice, without animal-offerings, very pure in nature and without consumption of food. Lord Nārāyaṇa was pleased with such a sacrifice. Without manifesting his form he accepted the *puroḍāśa*. Having come to know this, Bṛhaspati lost his temper. Even the sons of Prajāpati, Ekata, Dvita and Trita said that they performed severe austerities to get a glimpse of Lord Narayana, however, they did not meet success. The passage ends with a note that to have a glimpse of Lord Nārāyaṇa, one needs to accumulate merit.

e) In another story of Vasu Uparicara in the *Mbh,* there was an argument among gods and sages regarding the offerings of the sacrifices. Gods said that *aja,* i.e. goat, should be the offering and sages said that grains should be used instead of goat. As the word *aja* signifies goat similarly it signifies grains[239].

f) The *Mbh* mentions some different types of *soma*-sacrifices. During morning-pressing, the essential ingredient is food, which is to be enjoyed by the *brāhmaṇa*-s, worshipping the three fires. Midday pressing should include cows and gold and evening pressing should incorporate Vaiśvadeva in it, which is to be given to the gods, manes and *brāhmaṇa*-s. Non-violence is very essential in the sacrifice and one requires, control of senses, patience and truthfulness while performing the *avabhṛtha* ceremony. Sacrifice should be conducted in this manner with faith and charity. Here, the injunctions and prohibitions of the sacrifice are seen in a totally new colour. A *soma*-sacrifice invariably has *soma*-pressing. But this passage denies such type of offerings (Anu. P 59.10-19).

## SOME OBSERVATIONS BASED ON THE ABOVEMENTIONED REFERENCES:

- The sages who participated in the Aśvamedha of Uparicara Vasu have Vedic origin.

- The sacrifice though, Aśvamedha, did not have animal sacrifice. The narration gave stress on the non-violent nature of the sacrifice.
- Non-violent sacrifice did not yield the fruit of the glimpse of Nārāyaṇa. Accumulation of merit is superior to the sacrifice.
- Point no. (b) indicates the changed trend of animal offering to offerings of grains.
- The power of the sages' vis-à-vis gods is superior. Since, by their curse Vasu loses his mobility.

A noteworthy point in this section is that the occurrence of passages is seen to be in specific *parvan*-s of the *Mbh* viz; the Śān. P and Anu. P. These passages seem to be composed in the later period since they indicate a shift in the nature of the performance of Vedic rituals. The passages propagate non-violence; they vehemently criticize violence and they argue over the true purpose of performing sacrifices. Seeking the grace of Lord Nārāyaṇa seems to be one of the chief purposes behind sacrifices. Not heaven, but the grace of Nārāyaṇa is the purpose behind sacrifice, which indicates the development of Viṣṇuite *bhakti,* i.e. devotion movement in the society. This can serve as a reference to the rise of Nārāyaṇa as an important 'godhead'.

## TIRTHA-S

A detailed discussion of *tīrtha*-s will be undertaken in Ch. VI of the present work. This point will discuss only the myths regarding *tīrtha*-s and their relation with the sacrifice. In the context of Udapānatīrtha, the *Mbh* narrates a myth of Ekata, Dvita and Trita (Śal. P. Ch. 35). The three brothers decided to perform a sacrifice. Ekata and Dvita made up their minds for the sacrifice and amassed a lot of wealth. Among the three brothers, Trita was an expert. Owing to jealously, the two brothers threw him in a dry well. Trita, determined to perform a sacrifice, mentally conceived three fires. He imagined the creepers in the well as Soma considered pebbles as limestones (used for anointing the altar), thought appropriate *mantra*-s to be chanted and conducted *soma*-pressings. These offerings reached gods and they were pleased with him. Udapānatīrtha became famous because of Trita. On visiting this place, one obtains the fruit of the Aśvamedha sacrifice.

Some observations: the story of the Trita brothers mentioned in the *Mbh* has its source in the *Śat. Br* (I. 2. 3. 1-4). Agni spat on the waters; from the waters sprang the Āptya deities, viz. Trita, Dvita and Ekata. They knew Indra going to slay Viśvarūpa. Trita slew him straightaway. The sin of *brahmahatyā* stuck to the three brothers. Trita has been a prominent deity of the early Indo-Iranian mythology. The name Traitana also occurs once in the *RV* (I. 158. 5). Eggeling comments

'Trita, the Āptya (i.e. probably 'sprung from or belonging to the *ap*, waters of the atmosphere), seems to have been a prominent figure of the early Indo-Iranian mythology, the prototype in many respects of Indra, the favourite god of Vedic hymns. The notion of wishing evil and misfortune away to Trita, or far, far-away is a familiar one to the Vedic bards. The name Traitona occurs in the *RV* (I. 158. 5), though a rather dark passage... Dvita and Ekata are no doubt later abstractions suggested by the etymology of the name Trita, although former Dvita occurs in the Veda-s'[240].

The story of the Āptya brothers occurring in the *Mbh* and *Śat. Br* can be compared and contrasted with each other:

- The brothers in the *Mbh* do not carry the common name 'Āptya'.

- No background about their origin (probably the narrator might have considered their origin out of context).
- No relation with water, except Trita falling into a 'well' full of dust and with little water.
- Eggeling has made a note that the notion of wishing evil and misfortune away to Trita is familiar amongst Vedic bards, yet the myth in *Mbh* is silent on it.
- The name Udapāna seems to have some affinity with water.
- The 'Āptya' brothers in the *Śat. Br* are valourous and are possessed with some mystic powers of knowing what is going on in others' mind. The three brothers in the *Mbh* do not possess such powers. However, they seem to be well-versed in the Veda-s. The utterances of Trita were so powerful that gods were compelled to arrive on the scene.
- Lastly, the *soma*-sacrifice was not a real sacrifice, but an allegorical one. Except for the *mantra*-s, all the ingredients were allegorical.

Apart from similarity of names, the story of the three brothers in the *Mbh* and the myth of the three Āptya-s in the *Śat. Br*, there is hardly any similarity. This seems to be a floating legend used for elevating the sanctity of the Udapānatīrtha, which was properly penned down or composed into a beautiful narrative by the narrator. It casts light on the sacrificial ritual, though allegorical suggestions and without any ingredients, bearing fruits. It elevates the power of the *mantra*-s vis-à-vis resources.

Importance of Puṣkara: The importance of Puṣkara has been highlighted in the *Mbh* (Śal. P. 37. 5-10). Lord Brahmā performed sacrifice at Puṣkara. Gods, *brāhmaṇa*-s, etc.

participated in the sacrifice. *Gandharva*-s and *apsaras*-es sang and danced with divine musical instruments as accompanists. He performed a *sattra,* which would fulfil all desires. The *sattra*-s had *puṇyāhaghoṣa* i.e. utterance that the particular day is auspicious for the performance of sacrifice. However, the sages complained that the greatest amongst rivers, i.e. Sarasvatī, did not arrive. Lord Brahmā thought of her and she arrived on the scene with the name Suprabhā. Here the arrival of the waters of the river Sarasvatī is connected with the sacrifice performed by Lord Brahmā. This narration follows the account of Kavaṣa Ailūsa occurring in the *Ait. Br.,* where Sarasvatī surrounds the (now-turned seer) Kavaṣa Ailūsa, when he saw the hymn to the deity Apām Napāt (II. 3).

## IMPORTANCE OF VEDIC SACRIFICE

The *Mbh* has taken note of the changing trend in the nature of sacrifice. Changing trend includes changes in the performance of sacrifice and also the change in the attitude towards sacrifice. The importance of *tīrtha*-s as an alternative to the sacrifice is also an important trend. But, it does not mean that the importance of sacrifice has been overlooked. In the *Mbh,* there is a discussion between Sage Kapila and a cow (Śān. P 26. 18 ff). A sage named Syūmaraśmi had entered the body of a cow. The passage says that, *śruti*-s repeatedly say that, one desirous of heaven should perform sacrifices. One should think of a fruit and then perform sacrifices[241]. Goats, horses, sheep, cows, birds, farm and wild animals, herbs and vital airs are the fruits, to be offered in a sacrifice. Animals and food-grains constitute the food of the sacrifice. This sacrifice constitutes Prajāpati, with it he gives offerings to the gods. Thus, by the sacrifice, the whole world sustains. All the above ingredients desire heaven through sacrifice. The seventeen constituents of the sacrifice are: herbs, animals, plants, creepers, clarified butter, milk, curds, oblation, earth, quarters, faith, time, *ṛc*-s, *yajuṣ*-s, *sāman*-s, sacrificers and Agni.

The eightfold path of righteousness has sacrifice in the first position (Van. P 2. 71). The *Mbh* says that it is through sacrifice and charity that the Pāṇḍava-s converted their sorrow into joy (Śān. P 14. 11). Giving donations is very important in the performance of sacrifice. No sacrifice can ever be successful without giving donations. Any king, who performs sacrifices, gives donations and undertakes penance can never fail; on the contrary, he will enjoy the fruits of these good deeds (Ud. P. 121. 21). Through sacrifices, penance and through the birth of son does a person repay the debts with which he is born (Ādi. P 220. 12).

Sacrifice is an indication of peace and prosperity in the kingdom. The commoners/subjects perform sacrifices when there is peace and prosperity in the kingdom (Ādi. P 102. 6-12). Śantanu's reign was peaceful because sacrifices were performed for gods and manes. No animal was slaughtered by unrighteousness (Ādi. P 94. 15).

Acceptance of the greatness of mantra-s during the performance of ritual was regarded as a parameter of righteousness. The dialogue between Nahuṣa and Agastya in the *Mbh* indicates that Nahuṣa expressed disbelief over the sanctity of the *mantra*-s chanted during the sacrificial ritual of sprinkling water in order to purify a sacrificial cow (Ud. P 17. 9). Sacrificial offerings are used for increasing the strength of the sages. Śacī increased the power of the sages by offering *havya* and *kavya*. *Havya* stands for the offerings given to gods and *kavya* stands for the offerings given to the manes (Ud. P.15. 2).

The *Bhagavadgītā* which is the part of the Bhīṣma P of the *Mbh* reiterates the importance of sacrifice. However, it gives stress on the following aspects of sacrifice[242].

1) *Karman*-s related to the sacrifice, which are performed with a desire to fulfil a desire/desires, lead to bondage. The *Bhagavadgītā* advocates the performance of *karman*-s without any desire behind them (Bhīṣma P. 25. 9).

2) According to Prajāpati, the living beings are created from sacrifice. Sacrifice is the desire fulfilling cow (Bhīṣma P. 25. 10).

3) Sacrifices impel gods and gods impel sacrifice, thus both of them are interlinked. One who enjoys the offerings bestowed on gods or will give it to others is a thief.

4) Eating the food, which is the remnant of food from the sacrifice, makes a person achieve fame. Such remnant cleanses off sins. One who cooks merely for oneself and does not give offerings is consuming sin (Bhīṣma P 26. 31).

5) *Bhagavadgītā* stresses the importance of sacrificial cycle. The cycle is as follows—Living beings-Food-Rain-Sacrifice-Karman-s- Brahman- Akṣara- and omniscient Brahman are all established in sacrifice. Here sacrifice becomes the centre-point of the universe (Bhīṣma P 25. 23-25).

6) Inclination to the performance of sacrifice is one of the qualities of a person endowed with divine qualities (Bhīṣma P. 38. 1).

7) Classification of sacrifice of those who are endowed with *sāttvika*, *rājasa* and *tāmasa* is as follows (Bhīṣma P 38.2 & 39. 11-12):

| *Nature of a person* | *Offerings of the sacrifice to gods* | *Desire* |
|---|---|---|
| *Sāttvika* | Gods | No desire, but sacrifice is for mental satisfaction |
| *Rājasa* | Yakṣa-s and Rākṣasa-s | With the desire to attain worldly pleasures and performance endowed with haughtiness |
| *Tāmasa* | Preta-s and Bhūta-s | No ritual, no faith to the offering of food, no mantra-s. |

8) Sacrifice having satisfaction of material desires leads to heaven. Yet, after enjoying the fruits, the sacrificers return to the earth (Bhīṣma P. 31. 21). Those who worship with faith ultimately and give offerings to Lord Kṛṣṇa, even though they do not know the rituals, the offerings reach the Lord (Bhīṣma P 31. 23).

The *Bhagavadgītā* does not accept the concept of sacrifice as having desire at its base, but takes the sacrifice to a different plane. Sacrifice without having desired fruit at its base is regarded as the best sacrifice. Sacrifice in the *Bhagavadgītā* indicates a shift from the ritual setting to a metaphysical plane. However, the importance of a sacrifice as an institution has remained. Sacrifice as an institution and sacrifice as a concept are two ways to understand Vedic sacrifice. Sacrifice as an institution includes the entire paraphernalia regarding the sacrifice, i.e. rituals, priests, ingredients, charity, the sacrificer, other resources required for the performance, etc. Sacrifice as a concept means the very idea of offering a concrete ingredient or abstract idea to the Supreme Lord, without any desire. However, the notion of giving up something is common in both these ways. In the *Mbh* we come across an increasing trend of giving importance of sacrifice as a concept, to make religion, as a practice more accessible to the common man. Since sacrifice is a hallmark of Vedic civilization, it is not possible for the priestly class to do away or go astray from it for alternatives are given with the framework.

*Anaśana* has replaced sacrifices at certain places in the *Mbh* (Anu. P 109. 33ff). One who eats twice a day, does not drink in between, gets engaged in non-violence and worships fire regularly for six years, gets the fruit of the Agniṣṭoma sacrifice. One who consumes food only once for one year gets the fruit of the Atirātra sacrifice, says the *Mbh*. One who eats only a quarter meal, engages in truthfulness, non-violence, controls senses for one year gets the fruit of the Vājapeya sacrifice and resides in the heaven for one thousand years.

### Sacrifice as Expiation

Sins are cleansed off by the performance of sacrifices(Van P 49. 18). Atonement of sin regarding the wife of one's preceptor requires the performance of Aśvamedha, Gomedha or Agniṣṭoma prescribes the *Mbh* (Śān. P 159. 48). Aśvamedha can be undertaken as expiation, for the performance of this sacrifice makes the sacrificer sinless. Indra performed this sacrifice a hundred times and by that he was called Śatakratu. He performed the sacrifice along with the Marut-s. The verse mentions the old relationship of Indra and the Marut-s. It also gives the etymology of the term Śatakratu (Śān. P 34. 26-27).

One who repents for the sin of alcoholism, he should perform the Agniṣṭut sacrifice for three years, give thousand cows and bulls, control food habits, be under celibacy and should develop forgiveness. Agniṣṭut is performed under the Sarvamedha sacrifice according to *Kāt. Śr. Sū* (XXI. 2. 4). However according to *Baudh. Śr. Sū*, Agniṣṭut is not included in the Sarvamedha sacrifice, but it says that one, who has committed oral sins, should perform sacrifice[243]. According to *Kāt. Śr. Sū*, this sacrifice is to be performed by one who is desirous of the *brahman*-splendour, virility, richness of food etc and status as well as by one who considers himself impure and wants to purify oneself (XX. 4). This chapter discusses the *dakṣiṇā* in the form of cows and bulls to be given on this occasion. Hence, Agniṣṭut sacrifice mentioned in the *Mbh* is indeed used for expiation according to the Śrauta tradition. In the passage of the *Mbh* attempts are made to convince Yudhiṣṭhira to perform Aśvamedha as expiation (Āśv. P 3-4 ff). One who commits sins gets purified by performing penance, sacrifices and by giving donations. In this section, there are references to sacrifices like the Naramedha, Rājasūya and Aśvamedha. The text cites the example of Rāma, the son of Daśaratha, who performed the Aśvamedha sacrifice (Āśv. P 3. 9). Yudhiṣṭhira was also confident of the fruits of the Aśvamedha. But he was doubtful about the large sums of wealth used during this sacrifice. Hence, it was quite clear that the Aśvamedha in the *Mbh* (Āśv. P) performed by Yudhiṣṭhira was an expiatory ritual, to cleanse off the sin of killing his kinsmen. The greatness of the sacrifice was that it wiped off the sin caused due to conquest of land(Van. P 34. 75). The *Mbh* regards the Aśvamedha as the means of regaining the position of Indra, because the Aśvamedha is regarded as giving an offering to Viṣṇu and pleasing him[244]. Thus the Aśvamedha purifies one who performs the concluding bath of this sacrifice. It cleanses off the sins which are committed by an individual[245]. The prose passage in the *Mbh* mentions the same story of Indra performing the Aśvamedha as a rite of purification (Śān. P 329. 39 ff).

The question is—Does the Aśvamedha, as expiation indicate the changing trend in the sacrificial institution or is it just another aspect of this great sacrifice, since yonder years ? When referred in the Śrautasūtra-s, the Aśvamedha is performed by a king yearning for prosperity and sovereignty. As far as the *Āp. Śr. Sū* is considered it hints at the different purpose of the Aśvamedha as discussed in the chapter of the *Rām*. But, if the *Śat. Br* is taken into consideration, it does point out to the other purpose of the Aśvamedha, i.e. atonement for *brahmahatyā*. The Aśvamedha advised by Viṣṇu for Indra, also harps on the same tune. But the Aśvamedha advised by Vyāsa to Yudhiṣṭhira as expiation for mass destruction of kinsmen is definitely the changed form of the ritual. One has to note the difference between *brahmahatyā* and mass destruction of kinsmen. The possibility for reaching to such a conclusion is that the passages of the myth of Indra and Vṛtra and Indra first losing the kingdom and then regaining it by the performance of the Aśvamedha are earlier passages of the *Mbh* because of the equation of atonement of *brahmahatyā* through Aśvamedha was already stated in the *Śat. Br*.

The narrator is to be applauded for having sound knowledge of the Vedic ritual. The passages which try to establish the position of Aśvamedha as an expiatory ritual indicate the position of Vedic religion. During the time of the composition of the *Mbh*, Vedic sacrifice was being well-documented and systematized on one hand yet, the general trend of the people was to go away from that institution because of violence and consumption of resources. Besides, the Aśvamedha is termed as a sacrifice, which was *utsanna*, i.e. no longer in vogue, since many years. Hence the passages pressing on the importance of this great sacrifice merely indicate the effort to re-establish the position of the great sacrifice, although in a changed form.

## Birth through Sacrifice

The *Mbh* gives reference to sacrifice as birthplace:-

### *Birth of Dhṛṣṭadyumna and Draupadī*

King Drupada did not have a son befitting himself. He had sons, but none of them were suitable to his personality and prowess. Since he and Droṇa were arch enemies, he wanted a son who could overpower and destroy Droṇa. Drupada appointed two priests named Yāja and Upayāja and gave them one hundred million cows. Yāja gave offerings to the fire for Drupada and the latter begot a son, who would kill Droṇa (*droṇahantāram*). At the last moment, he invited Pṛṣatī, the wife of Drupada. Pṛṣatī requested him to wait, for her face was fragrant with divine fragrances (Ādi. P 155. 35). Since the oblation was consecrated, offerings were made without the presence of Pṛṣatī. From that fire emerged a boy, terrible in appearance wearing a helmet and armour and having the colour of flames. In one hand he held a sword and in the other he wielded a bow and quiver of arrows. After him, emerged a very beautiful girl, of dark complexion and with black hair. Both the children were named Dhṛṣṭadyumna and Kṛṣṇā respectively. Dange has analyzed the account on the following lines: 1) "Kings had their own family priests. It is indeed strange that Drupada searches for another priest. This indicates that the task which the two priests were supposed to undertake is highly specialized. The names of the priests are also significant as they indicate helper at a sacrifice". Here, there is definitely the trait of artificialness and the narration leaves the track of history and holds the finger of myth.

2) The second significant fact is that the queen is ignorant about it and she remains 'conspicuously absent' during the final offering".

After these observations Dange explains that the pattern of the myth is that 'It is in the Vedic beliefs that altar is the 'womb' of good deeds according to *RV* (III. 29.8). The fire-god is born in the womb of Ṛta, i.e. the fire altar. According to the *RV* (I.65. 2), where the expression is *ṛtasya yonau garbhe sujātam*, about Agni. Agni lies, i.e. sleeps, in the altar which is the womb, says *RV* (III. 1.11 *ṛtasya yonau āsyad damūnāḥ)* and so on. The birth of the fire-god from the *araṇi*-s is also another aspect of this belief. He is kindled in the *araṇi* (one womb) and placed in another (the altar). This also follows the birth of fire and imitates the idea of the flames giving him a terrible appearance (*RV* I. 95. 8; V. 2. 3). Dange adds that Draupadī is dark, i.e. Kṛṣṇā, by name and her brother is flame-coloured according to *Mbh* (Ādi. P 166. 54). Both are aspects of the altar-fire, mythically. That is why, according to *Mbh,* Dhṛṣṭadyumna is said to have merged with the fire in the heaven after death (Svargā. 5.21)[246]. Another important aspect is the mention of the term *vaitāna karman*. This indicates that the sacrificial ritual was performed strictly adhering to the principles of Vedic sacrifice[247]. Vaiśampāyana wants to hint at two aspects:

a) The birth of Droṇa is supranatural. To destroy him, one requires someone equal in capacity. Dhṛṣṭadyumna's sacrificial supranormal birth satisfies this equation.
b) Draupadī's position as an unusual female character in the *Mbh* is projected right from the nature of her birth, i.e. through the sacrificial altar. It would not be

far-fetched to say that her fiery temperament is suitable to her fire-origin.

c) Vedic sacrifice has the capacity of producing strong and powerful characters. By this narrative, the greatness of Vedic sacrifice takes grip of the mind of the reader/listener.

Thus, two points are achieved through this passage: a) elevation of the character of Dhṛṣṭadyumna and Draupadī; b) Eulogising Vedic sacrifice.

*Birth of Viśvāmitra and Jamadagni*

Ṛcīka prepared *caru*, i.e. rice boiled in milk, for his wife and his mother-in-law, for obtaining male progeny. However, the *caru* was interchanged. Gādhi, the king begot a son i.e. Viśvāmitra. Though a prince, he renounced the world and resorted to the forest and Ṛcīka begot a son named Jamadagni, fiery in nature and having inherent prowess (Śal. P 49. 8-13). Dange interpretes this myth as an incentive to the natural semen[248].

*Birth of Droṇa*

According to the myth, Sage Bharadvāja was staying in the region known as Gaṅgādvāra. He saw the nymph Ghṛtācī by name, after he had a bath and he proceeded to the Havirdhānamaṇḍapa. Here Havirdhānamaṇḍapa means the place where the three fires are nurtured. Ghṛtācī was taking bath and moving. Her cloak rolled away from the body (Ādi. P. 121. 3-4). The ejected semen was collected in a *droṇa*, i.e. cup. Then a son was born named Droṇa. The Havirdhānamaṇḍapa is used for the two small carts in which the stalks of Soma are placed prior to their being pressed for taking out juice from. It is also used for the pandal in the Great altar (Mahāvedi) in which the carts are lodged, with the stalks of Soma and the wooden utensils required for placing the juice of Soma after the stalks are pressed. The *kalaśa* is a wooden vessel, so is the *droṇa*. Dange, has explained the word 'Ghṛtācī' in three different connotations:

a) of bounty (*rāti*)

b) offering ladle

c) she is also said to have many forms, as various types of offerings would be placed in it (her) to be offered into the fire. In this last image, she is conceived as secretly moving like a woman among assemblies, like Speech. Thus from the sacred surroundings of the sacrifice, she slips out and mixes with a bigger environment. This has to be taken as a stage where she gets mythical and obliges many a human hero to be adjusted in the pattern of mythical births and having birth with higher status[249]. One again comes across Ghṛtācī in the account of the birth of Śuka. Vyāsa is seen as producing fire through attrition with the help of the *araṇi*-s, when he saw the nymph Ghṛtācī arrived and was standing nearby. Dange compares this with a *ṛc* from the *RV* (VII. 84. 1). Vyāsa was smitten with passion on seeing her. On seeing the sage thus smitten, the nymph changed herself into a parrot. Vyāsa could not control himself and his semen got ejected on the *araṇi*. The lower *araṇi* is the female. Vyāsa proceeded with attrition, without knowing this; then a son Śuka was born. He instantly grew bigger. The river Gaṅgā came along and pacified him with her water. From the mid-region a staff and the black-antelope skin fell down for the use of Suka.

## Sacrifice and Kingship

The great sacrifices like Rājasūya and Aśvamedha described in detail were performed by great kings. The text has immortalized the names of great kings, who performed sacrifices, erected sacrificial posts and gave sumptuous donations to the *brāhmaṇa*-s. Food was also distributed during the sacrifice.

The very first chapter of the text begins with the descriptions of the sacrifice performed by Yudhiṣṭhira and the prosperity of the Pāṇḍava-s which created jealousy in the heart of Duryodhana (Ādi.P 1. 85-89). Apart from the sacrifices performed by Yudhiṣṭhira, there are descriptions of the sacrifices of other kings. King Yayāti had peformed great sacrifices and had erected *caitya*-s and *yūpa*-s (Ādi. 1. 169). Here the term *caitya* has been used in the sacrificial context. He performed sacrifices at the banks of the river Sarasvatī. All desires of the *brāhmaṇa*-s were fulfilled. Gods along with the *gandharva*-s, *apsaras*-es, etc. were pleased with this sacrifice (Śal. P 40. 34; Ud. P. 113. 1-2). Yayāti ascended the heaven because of the fruit of his sacrifice. But returned/fell down after the accumulation of merit was exhausted. Four kings, viz. Pratardana, Vasumanas, Śibi and Auśīnara performed Vājapeya and pleased Indra. By inhaling the smoke arising from these sacrifices, Yayāti faced a downfall from the heaven. A very different equation is mentioned here, i.e. the merit of other kings leads to the downfall of the other (Ud. P 119. 10-14).

Śaryāti had performed sacrifice in which the Aśvins obtained their share of Soma(Ādi. P 2. 118). This reference points out to the story which occurs in the *Śat. Br* (IV. 1. 5. 1-19). This is regarding the position of the Aśvins. The story comes under the topic of Āśvina *graha*. Cyavana, who belonged to the Bhṛgu–Āṅgirasa family was ghost-like in appearance. Śaryāta, the tribal leader just wandered along with his boys. The boys pelted him with clods. Due to the anger of Cyavana, the entire tribe faced lot of infighting. The king understood that such occurrences took place when a sage was insulted. As a token of atonement he offered his daughter Sukanyā to the sages. She being very beautiful, the Aśvins desired to win her love. But she refused. Cyavana realized this and told the Aśvins that they were neither complete nor perfect and they did not have any right to insult him. The Aśvins made Cyavana youthful. Cyavana pointed out to them, that they did not receive any share of Soma in the sacrifice. The Aśvins went to the sacrifice performed by gods and asked for their rightful share. Gods turned down their demand saying that they had mixed with men and thereby became impure. The gods were performing headless sacrifice. The Aśvins restored the head and then they received their rightful share.

King Mahābhiṣa of the Ikṣvāku dynasty performed thousand Aśvamedha-s and hundred Vājapeya-s (Ādi. P 91.2). King Gādhi performed the Puṇḍarīka sacrifice (Ud. P 117. 7). King Kṣemadarśin performed the Viśvajit sacrifice in which everything is to be given away (Śān. P 106. 21).

Indra rejoiced in the Soma offerings and the *brāhmaṇa*-s by donations in the sacrifice of Vyuṣitāśva. He performed many *soma*-sacrifices (Ādi. P 112. 9, 14).

King Bharata, the son of Duṣyanta, performed 1000 Aśvamedha-s and 100 Rājasūya-s. He had tied up 300 horses on the banks of river Yamunā and 20 on the banks of Sarasvatī and 14 on the banks of river Gaṅgā (Śān. P 29. 41-42). The *Mbh* also refers to a type of Aśvamedha named 'Govitata' performed by king Bharata[250]. There occurs a reference in the *Śat. Br.* of an Aśvamedha sacrifice named 'Govinata'[251]. King Śatānika Sātrājita performed this sacrifice after taking away the horse of the Kāśya king and since that time, the Kāśi-s do not keep up the sacrificial fires, saying 'The *soma*-drink has been taken away from us'. This section refers to the various *stoma*-s, *stotra*-s and *sāman*-s to be chanted during this sacrifice. It also mentions the Gāthā-s pertaining to the performance of this type of Aśvamedha. The 'Govinata' type of Aśvamedha was performed by the King Śatānika after seizing the sacrificial horse of the king of Kāśī and King Dhṛtarāṣṭra. The kingdom of Dhṛtarāṣṭra was in the periphery of the kingdom of Śatānika. This indicates that if any king obstructs and successfully seizes the sacrificial horse of the king performing the Aśvamedha, the victorious king performs an Aśvamedha of the 'Govinata' type.

King Aṅga performed *soma*-sacrifices. He gave thousands of girls, hundreds of bulls decked with ornaments made up of gold and thousands of cows in charity. He performed hundreds of sacrifices by spending sumptuous amount of wealth. Indra rejoiced in Soma and *brāhmaṇa*-s in charity. Kane gives details of the charity undertaken during Vājapeya, as one among the *soma*-sacrifices. *Āśv. Śr. Sū* says that 1,700 cows, 17 chariots to which horses are yoked-seventeen horses, seventeen animals which men ride, seventeen drought oxen, seventeen carts, seventeen slave-girls decked with golden *niṣka*-s round their necks, seventeen elephants with golden girths- these constitute the fee in Vājapeya. *Āp. Śr. Sū* (XVIII. 3. 4) is almost the same but adds seventeen goats and ewes. *Lāṭ. Śr. Sú* (VIII. 11. 16-18) is also practically the same as *Āśv. Śr. Sū*, but adds several alternatives about cows. In the Kuruvājapeya, cows donated are only 17, in other Vājapeya-s, 17or 17,000 cows may be given[252]. King Māndhātṛ performed hundreds of Aśvamedha and Rājasūya sacrifices. He gave Rohita fish to the *brāhmaṇa*-s in charity (Śān. P 29. 84).

King Dilīpa performed a great sacrifice and gave away the earth to the *brāhmaṇa*-s. The priest got thousand elephants decked with gold in charity. The *yūpa*-s and *caṣāla*-s (rings placed on the top of on the sacrificial post) were made up of gold. Thousands of gods and *gandharva*-s performed great sacrifices. Viśvāvasu, the *gandharva* personally played the lute. In fact, the *yūpa* and *caṣāla* are both made up of wood. But this passage is a piece of exaggeration. However, the passage throws light on dance and music played during the sacrifice (Śān. P 29. 65-69).

King Gaya performed many sacrifices like Darśapūrṇamāsa, Cāturmāsya and also Aśvamedha. He gave away earth during the Aśvamedha (Śān. P 29. 107, 110).

King Rantideva performed sacrifices in which he offered animals. The great river in his kingdom flowed carrying the skins of animals offered, hence became known as Carmaṇvatī (Cambal). Each and every item in the sacrifice was made up of gold (Śān. P 29. 118).

King Vainya performed Aśvamedha sacrifice. Sage Atri wanted some wealth. His wife suggested him to approach King Vainya. Atri praised Vainya as a first king. But he got angry, for the sage got the first place in the sacrifice (Van. P 183. 1-12).

King Yuvanāśva from the Ikṣvāku dynasty was sonless (Van. P 126. -24). He had performed thousands of Aśvamedha-s and other important sacrifices and had given lot of wealth in charity. He handed over the kingdom to the ministers. He performed each and every ritual according to the *śāstra*-s. One day, when the king had gone for hunting, he reached the hermitage of Sage Bhṛgu. The sage had performed the Saudyumnī *iṣṭi*. Mistakenly, the king happened to drink the waters consecrated during the *iṣṭi*. A child was born from the left thigh of the king. Indra offered to feed the child with his finger, so the child was known as Māndhātṛ. Dange comments, 'the left of a man is associated with a woman or his wife. The belief and practice is very old and in the Vedic ritual context the left (the north is the side of the woman) while that of the man (her husband or male partner) is her south (right), when both face the east or lie with their feet to the east[253].

The *Mbh* takes into account the story of Purūravas and Urvaśī and that Purūravas brings the three fires from the Gandharva-loka (Ādi. P 70. 21). There was a clash between Purūravas and the *brāhmaṇa*-s. The *brāhmaṇa*-s tried to win over him, but their efforts were fruitless. They cursed him. But he regained his status by bringing down the three celestial fires. Dange analyzes,

"Now, it is remembered that the *RV* does not mention three fires, viz. Gārhapatya, Āhavanīya and Dakṣiṇa. Out of these names indicating the fire, only Gārhapatya occurs in the *RV*, and that too only thrice; but at no place does it indicate the ritual-fire of that name (I. 15. 12; I. 35. 27, 36). *RV* mentions that it was the clan of the Bhṛgu-s that established the earthly fire for the benefit of men (II. 4. 2). But the fire is said to be one for the purposes of ritual".

Dange further explains the result of his unpopularity as follows, "The innovation was not fairly accepted in the Ṛgvedic period, though Purūravas was acclaimed to be a great seer sacrificer as noted above. It is also to be noted that Purūravas is mentioned in the later *RV* (I. 15. 12 & X. 95), a marked characteristic of which is the introduction of sex rituals, another pronounced ritual-hymn being that of Yama and Yamī (X. 10), which employs the motif-incest. This may be the reason why he was rather unpopular with the orthodox ritual-practisers"[254].

In the sacrifice of king Hariścandra, many *brahmaṇa*-s, were satisfied by different types of wealth. Different types of food items were offered along with wealth. By this sacrifice, which was necessarily the Rājasūya, Hariścandra shone with lustre. This refers to a ritual of giving the Samsṛp oblations during the Daśapeya ceremony.

When Varuṇa was consecrated for the sacrifice, he lost lustre. In search of it he stole after or tip-tread behind the deities. He found it behind Viṣṇu. As he stole behind the deities, the name became famous as *'samsṛpām havīṁṣi*. This passage refers to this in the term *prāsarpakāle samprāpte* (Sabhā. P 11. 58-61).

## CONCLUSION

The reflections of the Vedic sacrifice in the *Mbh* indicate the importance of this institution in the society. The Vedic sacrifice as reflected in the *Mbh* appears to have undergone series of changes. Moreover, understanding the process of sacrifices helps us to stratify the *Mbh* thereby providing a new lens of stratification of this Epic.

The passages which describe the greatness of the sacrifices like the Aśvamedha and the Rājasūya occurring in the *Mbh* (Āśv. P and the Sabhā P) respectively can be regarded as earlier passages because they pay attention to every minute details of the sacrifice. On the contrary, the references stressing non-violence, sacrifice to be performed with food-grains, etc. are to be understood as later passages. These changing trends in the nature of sacrifice indicate the influence of Buddhism and Jainism on Vedic religion. The passages which highlight the importance of *tīrtha*-s run parallel to those of the M. Pu-s. It is to be noted that the M. Pu-s also suggest the performance of *vrata*-s as alternative to the sacrifice, which the *Mbh* does not.

The *Mbh* shows a strong bond between sacrifice and kingship. Sacrifices were performed by the kings to enhance their glory and increase their political power. The *Mbh* maintains record of many kings which are referred to in the Brāhmaṇa texts. This maintenance of record is to be attributed to the *sūta*-tradition.

The references to the importance of sacrifice for the maintenance of the cosmos have been reiterated in the *Bhagavadgītā* while discussing the concept of Yajñacakra. These references appear to be an extension of the Vedic concept of integration between *yajña* and Ṛta. The interiorization of the Vedic sacrifice as propagated by the Upaniṣad-s is maintained in the *Bhagavadgītā*. Thus the references to the Vedic sacrifice in the *Mbh* indicate:

a) Respect to the institution of Vedic sacrifice; yet
b) Decline in the performance of Vedic sacrifice;
c) Rising alternatives to the Vedic sacrifice and;
d) Interiorization of Vedic sacrifice.

# 4

# The Mahāpurāṇa-s

The Mahāpurāṇa-s display a rich collection of various rituals practised in ancient India.

## THE TERM PURĀṆA

The term *purāṇa,* originally signified ancient or old narrative; but long before the beginning of the Christian era it designated a class of books dealing, among other matters, with old-world stories and legends of India. As the extensive *purāṇa* works handed to posterity included early and late as well as major and minor works, the name M.Pu was given in comparatively later days to that particular class of major Purāṇa-s, which commanded the highest respect of the people for their age and importance of their contents.

The name M.Pu is of a late origin. It is found only in the *Bhāg. Pu* (XII. 7. 10 & 22) and *Brahmavai. Pu* (IV. 131. 7 & 10). M. Pu-s were simply known as Purāṇa-s in their early formative stage. The references to the term *'purāṇa'* occur in the *AV* which contains the earliest mention of this term. It says that the *ṛc*-s, the *sāman*-s, the metres and the *'purāṇa'* originated from the residue of the sacrifice together with the *yajus*[255]. The *Bṛhadāraṇyaka Upaniṣad* on the other hand, ascribes the origin of the four Veda-s, Itihāsa, *purāṇa*, etc. to the breath of the Mahābhūta[256]. Some more references to the term *'purāṇa'* occur in the *Jaim. Br* (I. 53), *Śat. Br* (XIII. 4. 2. 12, 13), *Chāndogya Upaniṣad* (III. 4. 1. 2). It is difficult to say definitely how and when the M. Pu-s first came into being, though their claim to great antiquity, next only to that of the Vedas, cannot be denied. It is mentioned mostly in connection with Itihāsa, in the *AV*, *Śat. Br*, *Gop. Br*, *Bṛhadāraṇyaka Upaniṣad*, and a few other works of the Vedic literature. According to Hazra, these traditions, though fundamentally different, are unanimous in their recognition of the sacredness of the *purāṇa* [257]. It is the *AV*, which contains the earliest mention of the word *'purāṇa'*. These traditions, though somewhat different, are unanimous in recognizing the sacred origin of the M. Pu-s as also in giving a status almost equal to that of the Veda-s. In fact, in some of the works of the Vedic and early Buddhist literature, the *purāṇa* has been called the fifth Veda. The *purāṇa* has been connected with the sacrifice and with the *yajus* in the *AV*. The theory of the origin of the universe from sacrifice as expounded in the *Puruṣasūkta* of the *RV* and the topics constituting the Pāriplava *ākhyāna*-s or recurring narrations in the Aśvamedha sacrifice, tend to indicate that the *purāṇa*, as a branch of learning, had its beginning in the Vedic period and originated in the narrative portion (Ākhyāna Bhāga) of the Vedic sacrifice. In the extant Purāṇa-s, however, there is a verse which tells us that according to the traditional accounts, at the beginning of creation, Lord Brahmā had remembered the *purāṇa*, which was foremost of all the scriptures, even before the Veda-s came out of his mouth. This statement, however absurd it may appear to be, will have validity, if we take the word *'purāṇa'* to mean not the *Purāṇa* as a class of literature, but a storehouse of ancient stories and legends, which in every country, came into being much earlier than versified compositions[258]. The traditionally sacred character has been retained by the literature even to the present day; but it never attained the position of the Śruti, or Smṛti.

The famous lexicon *Amarakoṣa* contains an old definition, which is repeated in a number of Purāṇa-s[259]. A Purāṇa deals with the five topics:

1) Sarga—creation or evolution of the universe.

2) Pratisarga—again creating the world from the constituent elements, in which it had merged at the close of each aeon, i.e. *kalpa*.

3) Vaṁśa—genealogies of gods, demons, patriarchs, sages and kings, especially of the last two.

4) Manvantara—cosmic cycles, each of which is ruled over by a Manu, the first father of mankind.

5) Vaṁśānucarita—accounts of royal dynasties.

The roots of all these five characteristics can be traced up to the Ākhyāna-s, Upākhyāna-s, Gāthā-s, and Kalpokti-s.

According to the *Vāyu*, *Brahmāṇḍa* and *Viṣṇu Pu*-s, these topics were utilized by the ancient Sage Vyāsa in compiling the original Purāṇa Saṁhitā. Though the M. Pu-s are expected to deal with the five topics mentioned above, it is observed that most of the extant M.Pu.-s either omit some of these topics or deal with them very succintly. They incorporate on the other hand, extensive glorifications of one or more sectarian deities like Lord Brahmā, Viṣṇu, and Śiva. They add information on myths and legends and also multifarious topics concerning religion and society. Thus the Purāṇa-s have not come down to us with their early incorporations, because tradition demanded that they should be re-edited with the changes in society so that their importance as works of authority might not decrease. Now, the work of re-editing could be done in three ways, viz.

i) by adding fresh chapters to the already existing ones,

ii) by substituting the former by the later new chapters, and

iii) by writing new works bearing old titles. All these processes were equally practised with respect to the Purāṇa-s.

## LIST OF THE PURANIC TEXTS

Indian tradition accepts eighteen works as M.Pu.-s. The names of these works are: 1) *Vāyu*. 2) *Brahmāṇḍa* 3) *Mārkaṇḍeya* 4) *Viṣṇu* 5) *Matsya* 6) *Bhāgavata* 7) *Kūrma* 8) *Vāmana* 9) *Liṅga* 10) *Varāha* 11) *Padma* 12) *Nāradīya* 13) *Agni* 14) *Garuḍa* 15) *Brahma* 16) *Skanda* 17) *Brahmavaivarta* 18) *Bhaviṣya*. According to Shastri, many of these single Purāṇa-s claim to have come down in their original form. Besides these eighteen M.Pu.-s'-s, or principal Purāṇa-s, there are a number of works which style themselves *'purāṇa'* or *'upapurāṇa'*. The *Śiva Purāṇa* and *Devī Bhāgavata* also claim to be M.Pu.-s'[260].

The Puranic scholars are agreed upon the authenticity of seventeen M.Pu.-s but in regard to the eighteenth there is a difference of opinion. Most of the M.Pu.-s include *Śiva Pu* in the list, while a few others substitute *Vāyu* for *Śiva*. The substitution of either was inevitable for the traditional number has to be maintained. Therefore some voted in favour of *Śiva*, some in favour of *Vāyu*.

Now let us examine if any solution could at all be possible. We know that *Śiva Pu* is divided into seven Saṁhitā-s, one of which is the Vāyavīya. We have the testimony of the *Śiva Pu* itself that the original *Śiva Pu* consisting of one hundred thousand *śloka*-s was abridged into twenty-four thousand *śloka*-s. On the strength of this evidence it cannot be unreasonable to suppose that there was a proto-Śivapurāṇa and a proto- Vāyavīya. It is not unlikely that there was close affinity between the extant *Vāyu Pu* and the proto- Vāyavīya or that the extant *Vāyu Pu* is the recension of the proto- Vāyavīya and thus a part of *Śivapurāṇa* itself. Solution lies in assuming identicality of the two on the basis of this suggestion, not in accepting the one and rejecting the other[261].

## SOME REMARKS REGARDING THE TEXTS INCLUDED IN THE LIST OF THE M.PU.-S[262]:

1. *Brahma Pu:* This M.Pu is divided into chapters (*adhyāya*-s). It deals with the sacred places of India, especially Utkala and the worship of the Sun.

2. *Pad. Pu*: This extensive M.Pu is divided into five parts, viz. a) Sṛṣṭi *khaṇḍa* b) Bhūmi *khaṇḍa* c) Svarga *khaṇḍa* d) Pātāla *khaṇḍa* e) Uttara *khaṇḍa*. It is one of the leading Vaiṣṇavite M. Pu.

3. *Viṣṇu Pu*: It is divided into six parts named as *aṁśa*. It is an important Vaiśṇavite Purāṇa. The Viśiṣṭādvaita philosophy gives emphasis on this text.

4. *Vāyu Pu.*: This text preaches the worship of Śiva. The place of the *Vāyu Pu* is taken by the *Śiva Pu*. This text is divided into two parts and four *pāda*-s. The *pāda*-s are Prakriyā, Anuśaṅga, Upodghāta and Upasaṁhāra.

5. *Brahmāṇḍa Pu.*: In view of the facts that this work has sometimes been called Vāyavīya Brahmāṇḍa, is said to have been proclaimed by *Vāyu*, and that its chapters often agree almost literally with those of the *Vāyu Pu*, Pargiter has rightly said that originally these two Purāṇa-s were not separate.

6. *Bhāg. Pu*: This is regarded as the most famous M.Pu. It is divided into twelve *skandha*-s, which are further divided

into *adhyāya*-s. It is one of the leading Vaiṣṇavite M. Pu and is revered by the followers of Vallabhācārya.

7. *Nār. Pu*: This name has been given to the M. Pu. to separate it from the *Bṛhannāradīya Purāṇa,* which is an Upapurāṇa. It is divided into two parts.

8. *Mārk. Pu*: It is one of the oldest M.Pu-s, which is divided into 137 chapters. It appears to be one of the oldest texts because the text does not give much importance to the gods like Śiva and Viṣṇu; on the contrary, gods like Indra and Lord Brahmā are given importance.

9. *Agni Pu*: It is divided into 383 chapters. It is encyclopaedic in nature as it incorporates various branches of learning and details about arts and sciences. However, very few references to the Vedic sacrifices occur in the text.

10. *Bhav. Pu*: It is divided into five *parvan*-s. It tells the importance of solar worship.

11. *Brahmavai. Pu*: It is divided into four parts. One of the earliest references to Rādhā occur in this text.

12. *Vām. Pu*: It is related to the Vāmana incarnation of Viṣṇu. It is divided into 95 chapters.

13. *Kū.Pu*: This text earlier existed in the form of four *saṁhitā*-s out of which the Brāhmī *saṁhitā* is available at present. It is divided into two parts, which are further divided into chapters. The M.Pu highlights the importance of idol worship.

14. *Mat.Pu*: It is one of the oldest M.Pu-s dealing with a variety of subjects. It consists of 290 chapters comprising about 10,000 verses in a simple and lucid language. It has been named after the first incarnation of Viṣṇu.

15. *Gar. Pu*: It is divided into two parts, which are further divided into chapters. Like the *Agni Pu.* it is also encyclopaedic in nature.

16. *Liṅga Pu*: It is divided into two sections which are further divided into chapters. This text advocates the devotion of Śiva.

17. *Varāha Pu*: It is divided into chapters. It is a Vaiṣṇavite M. Pu.

18. *Ska. Pu*: It is the largest Purāṇa having lengthy geographical descriptions. It is divided into Kedāra *khaṇḍa*, Avantī *khaṇḍa*, Prabhāsa *khaṇḍa*, Maheśvara *khaṇḍa*, Viṣṇu *khaṇḍa*, Brahma *khaṇḍa*, Nāgara *khaṇḍa* and Kāśī *khaṇḍa*.

## DATE OF THE M. PU-S

There is no definite chronology in respect of the extant Purāṇa-s. There are different opinions of the scholars about the approximate date of the M.Pu.-s in general:

1. According to Gyani, the present form of the M. Pu-s was complete about the 7th century AD[263].

2. Pargiter thinks that the Purāṇa-s were compiled from 400 B.C. to 1000 AD[264].

3. Vaidya maintains that the present from of the Purāṇa-s is an output of the 4th century AD[265].

4. Bhandarkar and Smith agree in ascribing the Gupta period to the final phase of the Purāṇa literature[266], from 600 AD to AD 900 is the period when the Purāṇa-s were finally edited[267].

5. Hazra has fixed the date of the Purāṇa-s on the basis of the materials on the topics of Dāna and Dharma etc. He ascribes the date from 300 AD to AD 1200[268].

6. Kane also opines that the present form of the Purāṇa-s is a recast of the older ones made during the first centuries of the Christian era and all the M. Pu-s were in final form up to the end of the 7th century AD[269].

7. In the opinion of Majumdar, the period from 300 AD saw the full development of the Purāṇa-s. This view is accepted by Morgan[270].

8. Farquhar holds the view that present form of the M. Pu-s was under development during the Gupta period[271].

Scholars have attempted to establish the date of the M.Pu.-s. The date of the M.Pu.-s indicates the span of time of its composition.

Date of the M.Pu.-s based on the discussion of the scholars mentioned above:

| *Name of the M.Pu.-s.* | *Upper Limit* | *Lower Limit*[272] |
|---|---|---|
| *Mārk. Pu* | 3rd-4th century AD | 5th -6th century AD |
| *Vāyu Pu.* | 2nd century AD | 14th century AD (Gaya Mahatmya) |
| *Brahmāṇḍa Pu.* | 4th century AD (separated from the Vayu Pu) | |
| *Viṣṇu Pu* | 1st century AD –earlier half of the 3rd century AD | 4th century AD |
| *Mat. Pu.* | Last quarter of the 3rd century AD and the first quarter of the 4th century AD | Earlier than 1100 AD |
| *Bhāg. Pu* | 6th century AD | 8th century AD |

| | | |
|---|---|---|
| *Kū.Pu.* | 550AD-650 AD | Not later than 1250 AD |
| *Vām. Pu.* | 700 AD | 1050 AD |
| *Liṅga Pu.* | Not before 600 AD | Not after 1000 AD |
| *Varāha Pu.* | 800 AD | 1000 AD |
| *Pad. Pu.* | 600 AD | 1500 AD |
| *Nār. Pu.* | 850 AD – 950 AD | 1200 AD |
| *Agni Pu.* | 800 AD | 1500 AD |
| *Gar. Pu.* | 850 AD | 1000 AD |
| *Brahma Pu.* | 1000 AD | 1200 AD |
| *Sk. Pu.* | 700 AD | 1200 AD |
| *Brahmavai. Pu.* | 700 AD | 1000 AD |
| *Bhav. Pu.* | 500 AD | 1200 AD |

## CLASSIFICATION OF THE M.PU.-S

The eighteen M.Pu.-s can be classified in different ways. If they are classified according to their characteristics; the *Vāyu Pu., Mat. Pu, Brahmāṇḍa Pu* and *Viṣṇu Pu* are the earlier M.Pu.-s because their contents are pertaining to their characteristics mentioned above.

If the classification is according to the deities glorified, then according to the *Pad Pu;*

*(a)Mat. Pu, Kū.Pu, Liṅga Pu, Śiva Pu, Sk. Pu* and *Agni Pu.* are regarded as the Tāmasa Purāṇa-s.

*(b)Brahmāṇḍa Pu, Brahmavai. Pu, Mārk.Pu, Bhav. Pu., Vām. Pu.* and *Brahma Pu.* are the Rājasa Purāṇa-s.

*(c) Visṇū Pu, Nār. Pu, Bhāg. Pu, Gar. Pu, Pad. Pu* as well as *Varāha Pu* are the Sāttvika Purāṇa-s.

*Mat. Pu* categorizes the M. Pu-s as:

a) those describing *Viṣṇu* are Sāttvika

b) those describing Brahmā and Agni are Rājasa

c) those describing Śiva are Tāmasa

d) those describing Sarasvatī and Manes are miscellaneous.

These classifications discussed above have been done by the M. Pu-s themselves.

Shastri Haraprasad has classified the M. Pu-s as

1) M. Pu-s encyclopaediac in nature, viz. *Gar. Pu, Agni Pu* and *Nār. Pu,*

2) Those stressing upon *tīrtha*-s and *vrata*-s, viz. *Pad. Pu, Sk. Pu* and *Bhav. Pu.*

3) The M. Pu-s which have two recenssions, viz. *Brahma Pu, Bhāg. Pu* and *Brahmavai. Pu.*

4) Those M. Pu-s which describe the genealogy of kings, viz. *Vāyu Pu* and *Brahmāṇḍa Pu*[273].

The classification of M. Pu-s has been done in different ways by traditional and modern scholars.

This type of study of the M.Pu-s is essential to have a clear cut idea of the scope of the M.Pu-s and to understand their position as texts preaching religion to the masses. This study assists in estimating the position of Vedic sacrifice in the Puranic texts. The study of the sacrifice in the M.Pu-s is taken up on the following lines:

## SACRIFICES OCCURRING IN THE M.PU-S

This topic discusses the references to the sacrifices/sacrificial details occurring in the Puranic texts. These references include those which highlight the reference to the Vedic sacrificial ritual and also references to the various sacrificial terms.

## SACRIFICE AS A BACKGROUND (THE ROLE OF THE SŪTA)

The sacrifice has served as a background for the narration of many M.Pu-s. This narration has been done by the *sūta*.

### *Birth of the Sūta*

From the splendid sacrifice performed by Pṛthu, the *sūta* and Māgadha were born. *Sūta* was born from Sūti, on the Sutya day says the *Brahma Pu* (II. 33 ff). When his right hand was churned by sages like an *araṇi*, Pṛthu was born. He was the first amd the foremost of those whose coronations were performed with the Rājasūya sacrifice.

The *sūta* is regarded as the partial incarnation of Viṣṇu believes the *Kū. Pu* (I. 1. 16). According to the Smṛti-s, a *sūta* is the offspring of a *brāhmaṇa* woman from a *kṣatriya* male[274]. *Gautama DSu* (15-16) regards the *sūta* as a Pratiloma. Kauṭilya, in the *Arthaśāstra*, however notes that the *sūta* mentioned in the M. Pu-s is to be distinguished from the ordinary *brāhmaṇa*-s and the *kṣatriya*-s (III. 7. p. 165). He implies that though *sūta*-s of his times being a Pratiloma caste, were inferior to the *brāhmaṇa*-s and *kṣatriya*-s, the *sūta*, narrator of the M. Pu-s was different, i.e. was a great sage or a semi-divine person—a view endorsed by *Kū. Pu.* (I. 16). Such type of distinction made by Kauṭilya indicates the reducing importance of the *sūta* community. The M. Pu tells us that the word '*sūta*' has originated from the root $\sqrt{su}$, 'to extract Soma juice' and that in the sacrifice of god Brahmā, *sūta* was born on the day of Soma juice extraction, i.e. Sutyāha, for recounting the Purāṇa Saṁhitā[275].

The narration of *Kū. Pu* is after the sacrificial session, performed by the sages. Romaharṣaṇa, the *sūta* narrated this M.Pu. *Brahma Pu*[276] is introduced through the narration of the *sūta*, i.e. Romaharṣaṇa. *Nār. Pu* opens up with the narration of Śaunaka[277]. It has referred to the *sūta* named

Romaharṣaṇa who lived in the hermitage at Siddhāśrama. He performed different types of sacrifices to worship Janārdana. He was instructed by Veda Vyāsa to be competent in the knowledge of the M. Pu-s. The sages who intended to know how to worship Janārdana, the supreme God, approached Romaharṣaṇa. He was worshipping Narāyaṇa by means of the Agniṣṭoma sacrifice. The sages remained there till he performed the *avabhṛtha* rite (*Nār. Pu* I. 1. 15, 27, 28).

*Liṅga Pu.*[278] was also narrated by the *sūta* Romaharṣaṇa at Naimiṣa forest. However, the narration does not begin with a *sattra* performed by sages over there(I.1).

The narration of the *Śiva Pu* occurred at the sacrifice performed by all the sages at the confluence of the rivers Gaṅgā and Yamunā in the city of Prayāga. The M. Pu. was narrated by the *sūta* named Romaharṣaṇa (*Śiva Pu.* Vid. 1.2-3).

The *sūta* has played an important role with regards to the narration of the *Vāyu. Pu.* While Asīmakṛṣṇa, the valiant and excellent monarch was ruling over the earth righteously, the sages performed a sacrifice of long duration at Kurukṣetra on the banks of the river Dṛṣadvatī. They were within the precincts of Naimiṣa forest and had been initiated in accordance with the sacred scriptures[279]. The highly intelligent *sūta,* the foremost reciter of Purāṇa-s came there to see the sages. He became well-known to the world as Lomaharṣaṇa as he thrilled the members of his audience with delight by his excellent absorbing narration. He was the excellent disciple of the Sage Veda Vyāsa. The entire Puranic lore was established in him. His scholarship had become extensive through his study of the *Mbh.* On his arrival, the sacrificers requested him to expound the M.Pu. to the sages. He was strongly remembered by the sages, when they were consecrated for the sacrifice (*Vāyu Pu* Purva. Prak. 1. 13-41).

The first chapter of the Sṛṣṭi *khaṇḍa* of the *Pad. Pu.* opens up with the sages performing the *sattra* at Naimiṣa forest. Ugraśravas, the *sūta* narrated the Purāṇa to the sages as he was ordered by sage Vyāsa. The Purāṇa tells the origin of the *sūta* community. This is the duty of the *sūta* from ancient times, to record the genealogies of gods, sages and kings of unlimited prowess and the eulogies of the noble who are seen in the *itihāsa* and Purāṇa-s to be the declarers of sacred lore. The *sūta* has no authority whatsoever over the teaching or reciting of the Veda-s. When the sacrifice of the noble Pṛthu, son of Vena, was in progress, Māgadha and Sūta praised the king. He, being pleased with them, the large-hearted king granted them a boon. He gave the Sūta - country to the Sūta and Magadha country to the Māgadha.

Another etymology given in the text is that, one who is born from the rite named Sūti is known as *sūta*. When a sacrificial session in honour of Indra proceeded, and Bṛhaspati was conjoined with other planets, that offering to Indra was mixed up with that meant for Bṛhaspati and there the *sūta* was born. There arose the mixed castes due to the mixing up of lower and higher streams (I. 1. 27-35).

The origin of the *sūta* is attributed to the sacrifice. This has served for an elevation of the *sūta* -community. It is observed that some of the M.Pu-s are narrated by the *sūta*, who was revered by many sages. It is difficult for the M.Pu-s to convince themselves as to how a person can from the Pratiloma type of marriage be revered by sages and can be the disciple of the great Vyāsa. Therefore, the tool of 'divine origin' was devised by the M.Pu-s.

## THE SATTRA-S

The *Bhāg. Pu* says that the glory of Dhruva, an ardent devotee of Lord Hari was chanted in the form of three verses, by Nārada in the *sattra* performed by Pracetas (IV.

12. 40). The Brāhmaṇa-s mention various Gāthā-s sung during the sacrifices. Such types of references are devised only to sanctify the greatness of Dhruva as a devotee of Hari. It tries to emphasize that the sacrificial system could keep itself away from accepting the greatness of a person based on devotion. It also refers to the *sattra* performed by Parīkṣit, the son of Abhimanyu (I. 17. 33, 45). The *Bhāg. Pu.* also refers to the *sattra* performed by Parīkṣit, the son of Abhimanyu (I. 17. 33, 45).

A similar reference occurs in the *Mat. Pu.* Sage Nārada and a *gandharva* recited Gāthā-s in the sacrifice of Kārtavīrya Arjuna (XXXXIV. 19-24).

According to the *Viṣṇu. Pu,* sage Parāsara's father was eaten up by demons. As revenge he started performing the Rākṣasa *sattra,* in which a number of demons were reduced to ashes. (I. 1. 14).

According to the *Mat. Pu,* under the kingship of Adhīṣoma Kṛṣṇa, the sages were engaged in a *sattra* of which three years have passed in Puṣkara and two in Kurukṣetra (L. 58-67).

A *sattra* named Kuṇḍapāyinām Ayanam is mentioned in the sacrificial texts. The *Liṅga Pu.* refers to the name of a person related to the sacrifice. Sumedhas was born of the daughter of Cyavana. She became the wife of Naidhruva and the mother of Kuṇḍapāyin-s (I. 63. 52-54). Nidhruva was a seer according to the *Baudh. Śr. Sū*[280]. This text quotes the opinion of some scholars that Kuṇḍapāyinām Ayanam is one among the Haviḥ saṁstha-s. The *Kāt. Śr. Sū* refers to this sacrifice as a yearly *sattra,* the *dīkṣā* of which commences on the full moon day of the month of Phālguna or the fourth day of the black of Phālguna. The goblets employed for this sacrifice have no handle and they look like a round vessel, i.e. *kuṇḍa* (XXIV. 4. 33).

## SACRIFICIAL RULES PRESCRIBED FOR THE VĀNAPRASTHĀŚRAMA

Among the rules prescribed for the Vānaprastha, the *Bhāg. Pu* says that one should prepare the *caru* and *puroḍāśa* from wild corns and not from rice, barley and pulses (VII. 12. 20). One who has taken up the Vānaprastha should perform rites such as the Āgrayaṇa, enjoined at particular periods of time with oblations prepared out of wild products. The Āgrayaṇa *iṣṭi*-s are to be performed with *śyāmāka, vrīhi* and *yava* grains[281]. Since these are harvest grains, the person taking up Vānaprastha can perform these *iṣṭi*-s with products available in the forest. But he should on no account propitiate Viṣṇu, through the sacrifice of an animal as enjoined by the Vedas. Agnihotra offering to the sacred fire, Darśapūrṇamāsa, and the three sacrifices performed at the beginning of the three seasons of four months each (under the names Vaiśvadeva, Varuṇapraghāsa, and Sākamedha) should be performed by one who has taken up the Vānaprastha. This indicates that, apart from the Nirūḍhapaśubandha and Sautrāmaṇī sacrifices of the Haviḥsaṁsthā-s, the person taking up Vānaprastha, can perform the remaining Haviḥsaṁsthā-s. The texts are silent about the performance of the *soma*-sacrifices. Since the Nirūḍhapaśubandha and Sautrāmaṇī sacrifices enjoin immolation of animals, the M. Pu-s do not sanction these sacrifices for the person taking up Vānaprastha. If he becomes very old, he may withdraw the three fires and fix his mind on Śrīkṛṣṇa (XI. 18. 7-13). A person taking up Vānaprastha should perform Cāturmāsya sacrifices and also offer an oblation of the first fruits at the end of the rainy season (III. 58. 10-15). In the summer solstice and the winter solstice he should perform sacrifices with products of the spring and the autumn seasons brought by himself and should separately offer *puroḍāśa* and *caru*-s.

## DIRECT REFERENCE TO THE SACRIFICE

The *Agni Pu* refers to the seven Somasaṁsthā-s, viz. Agniṣṭoma, Atyagniṣṭoma, Atirātra, Ṣoḍaśin, Ukthya, Aptoryāma and Vājapeya sacrifices (166.14-15). The *Viṣṇu Pu* mentions the different *saṁsthā*-s of sacrifice, viz. Somasaṁsthā, Haviḥsaṁsthā and Pākasaṁsthā (III. 11. 24). The four Vedas and functions of the priests are also mentioned in the text (III. 4. 11-14). In the *Mārk. Pu*, there are references to the three fires namely the Gārhapatya, Āhavanīya and Dakṣiṇa. In this context, there is a story of the *brāhmaṇa* and an *apsaras*, Varūthinī by name. The parameter of the righteousness of the *brāhmaṇa* is nurturing the three fires (*Mārk. Pu*. LVIII. 65ab). When the *apsaras* asked him for physical pleasures, the *brāhmaṇa* refused because he was nurturing the sacred fires. The *apsaras* persuaded him and then he saluted the Gārhapatya fire: "You are the source of all rites, you are the source of Āhavanīya and the Dakṣiṇa fires. Gods subsist by the nourishment provided by the fire and then yield good rain and crops. Thus the world subsists because of the Gārhapatya fire". Due to this eulogy, the Gārhapatya fire appeared in human form and protected the *brāhmaṇa* (LXI. 75-79, LXII. 1-3).

The *Brahmavai. Pu* refers to sacrifices like the Aśvamedha, Rājasūya, Naramedha, Gomedha, Puṇḍarīka (Padmamedha), Putreṣṭi, etc. (II. 27. 119-124). The *Varāha Pu* refers to the performance of Gomedha sacrifice in the myth of Saramā (16. 11-40). No sacrificial details are given.

Chapter seven of the *Śiva Pu*, narrates the myth of Sandhyā. Sandhyā, the daughter of Lord Brahmā, went to the place where Medhātithi was performing the Jyotiṣṭoma sacrifice (*Śiva Pu* Rudra. Sati. 6. 60). The Gosava is said to have been performed for the growth of cattle at the bank of the Gautamī according to the *Brahma Pu.* (91. 6-11). The Gosava is said to be a Vedic ritual, wherein the sacrificer enacted the bull, approaching his near female relations[282]. This sacrifice is performed for increase in cattle. According to the *Jaim. Br* II. 13, it was performed by Janaka Videha (*Tait. Br.* II. 7. 6. 1).

The *Bhav. Pu.* also gives details of the sacrifice (*Bhav. Pu* I. 186. 5-7).

The classification of castes is mentioned in the *Kū. Pu.* The first three castes have the right to perform sacrifices. Only the *brāhmaṇa*-s have the right to act as officiating priests in the sacrifice. The *Kū. Pu* says that the *Śūdra*-s have right to perform Pākayajña-s (I. 2. 38-41). *Śūdra* is authorized to perform Pākayajña-s (122. 70) (*Brahma. Pu* 122. 70).

The *Kū. Pu* can be interpreted as giving *śūdra*-s the right to sacrifice, i.e. domestic sacrifices(I. 41ab). But as *Kū. Pu* in verse I. 2. 26, says that Lord Brahmā created the three castes for sacrifice, it will be inconsistent to interpret *Pākayajñādidharmataḥ* as allowing *śūdra*-s to perform domestic sacrifice according to *dharma.*

The *Sk. Pu* enlists the sixteen priests in the analogy of the Vedic sacrifice such as Hotṛ, Maitrāvaruṇa, Acchāvāka, Grāvastut, Adhvaryu, Pratiprasthātṛ, Neṣṭṛ, Unnetṛ, Brahman, Brāhmaṇācchaṁsin, Agnīdhra, Potṛ, Udgātṛ, Prastotṛ, Pratihatṛ and Madhucchandas, etc.(III. 1. 23. 24 ff).

## REFERENCES TO THE SACRIFICES

The *Bhāg. Pu* refers to King Bali performing the Viśvajit sacrifice. From the fire of this sacrifice arose a gold-plated chariot, a pair of quivers containing inexhaustible arrows

(VIII. 15. 4-5). Prahlāda performed the Aśvamedha sacrifices. Prahlāda had performed the Aśvamedha as an expiation for committing the sin of going against his kinsmen (ref. to the chapter on the *Mbh*).

The *Bhāg. Pu* refers to king Yudhiṣṭhira who had performed the three Aśvamedha sacrifices (I. 12. 34). According to the *Mbh,* Yudhiṣṭhira had performed two sacrifices a) the Rājasūya b) the Aśvamedha.

### The Aśvamedha Sacrifice of Bharata

According to the *Bhāg. Pu,* King Bharata took over the kingdom after the death of the father Duṣyanta. He bore the mark of a discus in his right palm and that of a lotus-bed on (the soles of both) his feet. Having been (duly installed on the throne after being) consecrated by means of a grand (religious) bath, the powerful emperor performed (as many as) fifty-five Aśvamedha sacrifices on the banks of the (holy) Gaṅgā in order of sequence (from the source to the mouth) and seventy-eight sacrifices (lit. he tied seventy-eight holy horses along the Yamunā) in the same order, choosing Dīrghatamas as his priest and freely gifting ample wealth. The sacrificial fire of Bharata was set up on an excellent (most sacred) sight where thousand *brāhmaṇa*-s divided among themselves, cows gifted to them. Through the performance of 133 Aśvamedha sacrifices, Bharata not only overcame Lord's Māyā (the deluding potency), but also attained to Lord Hari. In the sacrificial function called 'Masṇāra' Bharata gave away fourteen lakhs of dark elephants (IX. 20. 23-28). However, Bharata did not have any son suitable to his greatness. He propitiated the Maruts through a sacrifice named Marutstoma and they bestowed upon his a son named Bharadvāja (IX. 20. 34-35).

## The Aśvamedha Sacrifice of Bali

Bali went to Kurukṣetra to perform the Aśvamedha under the guidance of Sage Śukrācārya. In this sacrifice, the Bhārgava-s were the chief officiating priests. Śukra consecrated the king for the sacrifice. Wearing white clothes, putting on a garland, anointing the body, covered by the skin of deer at the back, the king sat for the performance of the sacrifice. His wife, Vidyāvatī was also consecrated for the sacrifice. A white-coloured horse endowed with good marks was released in the month of Caitra to roam over the earth. Tārakākṣa followed the horse according to the *Vām. Pu.* Ch. 62. 28-33).

According to the *Nār. Pu.* I. 10. 32. Bali the son of Virocana was a great devotee of Nārāyaṇa. In order to obtain his grace, he performed many Aśvamedha sacrifices.

## Aśvamedha Sacrifice Performed by Rāma According to the *Pad. Pu.* (V. 8. 5 ff):

On hearing the account of the birth and death of Rāvaṇa, Rāma felt that he had committed a sin of *brahmahatyā*. According to Agastya, it was the horse-sacrifice by which such type of sins would be washed off. A list of kings who had performed this sacrifice was enumerated by Agastya. It was king Dilīpa of this race who had performed the sacrifice. Indra performed hundred sacrifices and became the king of the heaven. Manu, Sagara, Marutta, Yayāti and many more kings performed this great sacrifice. [Sagara myth occurs in the *Brahmāṇḍa Pu.* (II. 52-55)].

*Pad. Pu* explains the procedure of the Aśvamedha sacrifice performed by Rāma (V. 9). The physical requirements of the sacrificial horse as denoted by the text are as follows: a) The complexion of the horse should resemble the waters of the river Gaṅgā, b) it should have auspicious marks on its physique, which include dark ears, red face and yellowish tail, and c) it should have the speed equivalent to that of the mind. The text states that these characteristics resemble those of Uccaiḥśravas, the celestial horse of Indra. Having worshipped the horse on the full moon day of the month of Vaiśākha, having written a note marked with one's name and power on his forehead, one should let him loose, carefully guarded by guards. The powerful guards should go wherever the horse to be sacrificed goes. The guards should forcibly bring back the horse from a person who binds him due to his own heroism and power. The sacrificer should remain practising the vow of celibacy. Till two years pass while the sacrificer was observing the vow, the poor, the blind, and the helpless should be satisfied by giving them wealth, etc.

Rāma did as he was told. He ploughed the land with golden plough. The land used for the sacrifice was four *yojana*-s. The king constructed temporary halls for the sacrifice. He prepared a basin with an altar and a girdle, decked with many gems and endowed with all charm. This was done by the Sage Vasiṣṭha. Nārada, Asita, Parvata, Kapila, Jātūkarṇya, Aṅgiras, Vyāsa, Ariṣṭasena, Atri, Āsūri, Hārīta, Yājñavalkya, Saṁvarta and Śuka participated in the sacrifice. As this was a gathering of all the sages, Rāma asked about the ways of life or the code of conduct for persons belonging to various castes. Rāma was consecrated along with the golden image of his wife. He slept on the ground, keeping the deer's horn on the waist, wearing a girdle, deer-hide and a staff. Here the M. Pu has explained the procedure of *dīkṣā* for the sacrifice.

The procedure of the *dīkṣā* is also explained in other M. Pu-s. Sacrificial consecration required the sacrificer and his wife to undergo certain rites. The sacrificer had to get his hair shorn and nails pared; his wife had to get her nails pared. It is said that when Lord Brahmā performed sacrifice, at his consecration Viśvakarman sheared his hair and pared his and Gāyatri's nails. Pulastya gave him the staff of Udumbara tree. An antelope skin and an antelope's horn were worn by Lord Brahmā. At his waist and that of Gāyatrī's there was a waist band of *muñja* grass according to the *Sk. Pu* (VI. 182. 5-7) and *Pad. Pu* (I. Ch. 16-17).

Agastya acted as the priest Brahman, Vālmīki acted as the Adhvaryu, Kaṇva was the door-keepr. There were eight gates to the hall which were auspicious with ornamental arches. At the eastern gate were Devala and Asita, southern gate Kaśyapa and Atri, western gate Jātākarṇya and Jābāli and at the northern gate were Dvita and Ekata guarding the directions. The courtesans offered him wishes of prosperity. The horse was seized by Vīramaṇi's son, after that king Suratha and lastly Lava, the son of Sītā. Lava has proudly proclaimed that he is brave because he is the son of Sītā and brother of Kuṣa, who is like a piece of wood called *araṇi* used for kindling the sacred fire and has fire in it too (V. 54. 23). Indra and other gods arrived on the sacrificial scene of Rāma to taste the oblations of the sacrifice. Along with Sītā, Rāma performed three Aśvamedha-s (V. 68. 25).

King Indradyumna had performed great sacrifices like the Aśvamedha. The *brāhmaṇa*-s in his kingdom were engaged in holy rites like the performance of the Agnihotra, etc. The king decided to perform the great horse sacrifice as worship to Lord Viṣṇu (*Brahma. Pu.* 45. 20). The king ordered the *brāhmaṇa*-s to find a suitable place for the performance of the sacrifice. The priest converted a fisherman's village into a sacrificial place. The king performed the sacrifice with great pomp and spent lot of wealth and food in charity. He concluded the sacrifice with all the injunctions and recited a eulogy to Viṣṇu. He was satisfied with the worship, but expounded the importance of idol worship to the king. As a part of the sacrifice and worship towards Viṣṇu, the sacred water reservoir named Indradyumnasaras was created, describes the *Brahma Pu* (48. 29).

The *Bhāg. Pu* mentions a prophecy that Janamejaya would perform a serpent sacrifice with Tura, the son of Kavaṣa as the chief officiating priest. His son named Śatānīka had deep knowledge of the sacrificial rituals, which was imparted to him by Yājñavalkya. The name of his son was Aśvamedhaja, which indicates the influence of Vedic sacrifice (IX. 22. 35-39).

King Janamejaya harassed Akrūra, the son of Garga. He attained the sin of *brahmahatyā*. He started to emit the odour of rusted iron. Under the guidance of Śaunaka the sage, he performed an Aśvamedha sacrifice, points out the *Nār. Pu.* (I.66.72-76).

According to the *Bhāg. Pu*, Yudhiṣṭhira worshipped Śrīkṛṣṇa through the performance of the Rājasūya (X.70. 41-42). This sacrifice can be performed only by a king who has conquered the four quarters (X. 71. 3). Sahadeva went along with Sṛñjaya warriors to conquer the southern regions, western regions were conquered by Nakula, northern regions were conquered by Arjuna and eastern regions were conquered by Bhīma (X. 72. 13-14).

The priests who participated in the Rājasūya, were Sage Dvaipāyana, Bharadvāja, Sumantu, Gautama, Asita, Vasiṣṭha, Cyavana, Kaṇva, Maitreya, Kavaṣa, Trita, Viśvāmitra, Vāmadeva, Sumati, Jaimini, Kratu, Paila, Parāśara, Garga, Vaiśampāyana, Atharvan, Kaśyapa, Dhaumya, Paraśurāma, Āsūri, Vītihotra, Madhucchandas, Vīrasena and Akṛtavarṇa. The priests ploughed the sacrificial ground with ploughs of gold and consecrated Yudhiṣṭhira, according to the scriptural injunctions, as the sacrificer. The utensils used in this sacrifice were all made of gold as they were in the sacrifice performed by Varuṇa in ancient times. Lord Brahmā, Śaṅkara, Indra and other guardians of the world, *siddha*-s and *gandharva*-s with their retinues came to the Rājasūya sacrifice of King Yudhiṣṭhira. All of them admitted without any hesitation that he was qualified to perform the Rājasūya, because to a devotee of Śrīkṛṣṇa nothing was impossible of achievement. Then the priests, who were as glorious as the gods, conducted for the king the Rajasuya sacrifice according to the scriptural ordinance, as in ancient times the gods did for Varuṇa. On the day which was fixed for extracting the Soma juice, the king honoured the blessed priests as well as the supervisors of the performance with due attention (X. 74. 6-15).

The *avabhṛtha* is described in text (X. 75. 8-15) While this ceremony was performed, various instruments of music like the conch, drum, kettledrum, tabor and trumpet were played upon. The courtesans danced in great joy, the songsters sang in batches. The sound of the lute, flute and cymbals reached the heavens. After the ritual known as Patnīsaṁyāja, (X. 75. 19) and the rites connected with the concluding ablutions had been over, the king performed Ācamana (sipping the water) and as directed by the priests bathed in the Gaṅgā, along with Draupadī. The *Bhāg. Pu* describes only the lavish celebrations of the Rājasūya, but hardly refers to the rituals of this great sacrifice. The M. Pu takes note of the conquest undertaken for the performance of this sacrifice. The *Brahmavai. Pu* refers to the Rājasūya performance of Yudhiṣṭhira (IV. Uttarārdha. 113. 25-61).

## The Aśvamedha of Rāma

After being coronate as the king, Rāma ruled the kingdom in a righteous manner. As a part of upholding *dharma*, he killed Śambūka, an ascetic who was performing rituals. On return to Āyodhya, he expressed a wish to perform the Rājasūya, as an act of merit. Formerly, Lord Brahmā performed 360 Rājasūya sacrifices. Soma, having performed the Rājasūya sacrifices, obtained an excellent position in the world. Mitra, having performed the Rājasūya, became Varuṇa. Bharata answered, "Rājasūya sacrifice should not be performed by a king like Rāma because, it leads to the destruction of all the beings on the earth. After the Rājasūya of Soma, a Tārakāmaya war took place, because Soma had abducted the wife of Bṛhaspati. When Varuṇa performed this sacrifice, all the aquatic animals perished. After the sacrifice performed by Hariścandra, the terrible war between Āḍi and Baka took place. All the beings on the earth turned to reptiles". Hearing this, Rāma gave up the idea of performing Rājasūya sacrifice and decided to install an image of Vāmana at Kānyakubja, says the *Pad. Pu* (I. 35. 154-71).

King Hariścandra had performed a Rājasūya sacrifice according to the *Pad. Pu* (6. 25). Śunaḥśepa was decided as a sacrificial animal (8. 65-68). This sacrifice was also performed by Soma. The priests for this sacrifice were Hiraṇyagarbha Brahman, Atri, Bhṛgu. After performing the sacrificial bath, his intellect became clouded due to ignorance. He abducted the wife of Bṛhaspati, i.e. Tāra. Tāra became pregnant from him and bore a son named Budha. Budha and Ilā bore a son named Purūravas (7. 13-33). Purūravas was also a great sacrificer (*Brahma. Pu.* 8. 1-2).

According to the *Mārk. Pu,* Hariścandra had performed the Rājasūya (Chap. VII). Sage Viśvāmitra appeared on the scene asking for *dakṣiṇā* on account of the performance of the Rājasūya (*Mārk. Pu.* VII. 25). Viśvāmitra demanded the entire earth surrounded with the oceans and all the wealth. Truth is superior to sacrifices, because a king named Kīrti, after offering seven Aśvamedha sacrifices and Rājasūya sacrifice, fell forth with from the heaven for falsehood (VIII. 21cd-22ab). The outcome of this Rājasūya sacrifice, which was the cause of the decay of the earth was the battle between Āḍi and Baka (*Ibid.* VIII. 286). The myth of Hariścandra and Śunaḥśepa also occurs in the *Bhāg. Pu* (IX. 7). The same myth of Śunaḥśepa, as being offered as the sacrificial animal in the sacrifice of King Hariścandra occurs in the *Vāyu. Pu* (Uttara. Anu. 29. 91-93). He became a sage named Devarāta since he was given by gods. The other Purāṇas which mention about King Hariścandra performing the Rājasūya sacrifice are *Brahma Pu.* (6. 25). and *Śiva Pu.* (Uma. 38. 20).

According to the *Brahmavai. Pu,* Utkala performed thousand Rājasūya sacrifices and was renamed as Suyajña (II. 50. 8-10).

Nābhi, the son of Priyavrata, had no issue. Therefore, he worshipped Lord Yajñapuruṣa. He worshipped Viṣṇu while performing Pravargya. The Lord appeared during the sacrifice and was waited upon by the officiating priests viz; the *ṛtvij*-s. They said that they do not perceive anything through the sacrifice, which is cumbrous with elaborate details. Nothing beyond Lord is fruitful (*Brahmavai. Pu.* V. 3. 7). Nābhi got a son named Ṛṣabhadeva. Ṛṣabhadeva bore a son named Bharata. After becoming the king, he worshipped the Lord Yajñapuruṣa with sacrifices. The *Bhāg. Pu.* enumerates a list of sacrifices, viz. Agnihotra, Darśapūrṇamāsa, Cāturmāsya, Paśusoma-s taking into account the Prakṛti-s and the Vikṛti-s along with the Cāturhotra rituals. When the Adhvaryu gave the offering to the fire, the king mentally offered the fruit of the sacrifice, the Dharma to Lord Viṣṇu (V. 7. 4-7). It is to be noted that it is not the ritual which bears fruit but by the grace of Lord Hari the desired fruit is achieved.

The *Mat. Pu* says that King Bharata performed various sacrifices for obtaining progeny. He obtained a son when he performed the Marutsoma sacrifice. He pleased the Marut-s by the performance of this sacrifice (XLIX. 27-30). The same text says that the wife of Ajamīḍha, Dhūminī performed severe austerities on the death of her son Somaka. She gave oblations in the fire and performed the Agnihotra. She gave birth to a son Ṛkṣa, who was smoky in colour (L. 17-19).

Action recommended in the Vedas is of two types: The *Bhāg. Pu.* mentions about two types of *karman*-s, viz. Pravṛtta and Nivṛtta. Through Pravṛtta *karman* one is likely to return to mundane existence in order to enjoy its fruit; while through Nivṛtta *karman* he is likely to enjoy Beatitude. A ritual having its object the destruction of an enemy or that conducted by means of material substances, such as Agnihotra, Darśapūrṇamāsa, Paśubandha, *soma*-sacrifices or even the Gṛhya rites like the Vaiśvadeva and also offering Bali and performing acts beneficial to the society are termed as Pravṛtta *karman*-s, if performed with an intention in mind. This path is characterized as the Pitṛyāṇa, which leads to rebirth. Those devoted to the performance of Nivṛtta *karman*-s also perform sacrifices, but in the fire of the senses lighted by Knowledge of the Self (VII. 15. 47-52).

The *Bhāg. Pu* mentions the fight which took place between the King Arjuna of the Haihaya dynasty and the sage Jamadagni, over the Agnihotra cow (IX. 15.25-26). After killing the *kṣatriya*-s, the sage performed a number of sacrifices to wash off the sin of genocide. At the end of these sacrifices he actually gave away the eastern quarter to the Hotṛ, the southern to the Brahman, western to the Adhvaryu and the northern to the Udgātṛ. He bestowed the intermediate corners on the other priests, the central region on the Sage Kaśyapa, the Āryāvarta to the Upadraṣṭṛ (the supervisor) and the region beyond the Vindhya-s to the *sadasya*-s. After that he washed away all his sins at the tank named Avabhṛtha on the banks of the river Sarasvatī (IX. 16. 20-23).

King Romapāda was issueless, he adopted Śāntā, the daughter of Daśaratha. There was no rain in the kingdom of Romapāda. The courtesans, when got Ṛśyaśṛnga in the kingdom of Romapāda, the kingdom received rains. Ṛśyaśṛnga performed a sacrifice in the name of Indra and secured progeny for the issueless Romapāda. The same sacrifice was performed by Ṛśyaśṛnga and he got four sons, points out the *Bhāg. Pu* (IX. 23. 6-10).

LIST OF YĀJÑIKA OṢADHI-S:

The *Viṣṇu. Pu* mentions Vrīhi, Yava, Godhūma, Caṇaka, Tila, Priyaṅgu, Udara, Koradhuṣa, Tinaka, Māṣa, Mudga, Masura, Niṣpāka, Kulathaka, Āḍhakya, Sana as the list of Grāmya Oṣadhi-s. The Yājñika Oṣadhi-s are Vrīhi, Yava, Māṣa, Godhūma, Caṇaka, Tila, Priyaṅgu, Kulatthaka, Śyāmāka, Nīvara, Jartila, Gavedhūka, Veṇuyava and Markaṭaka. (I. 6. 21-27)

Kṛcchra rite is performed as an expiation for performing sacrifice for Vrātya-s (*Kū*. Pu. II. 34. 44). King Navaratha worshipped Sarasvatī through sacrifice. The reference indicates the offerings given to the deity Apām Napāt on the confluence of the river Sarasvatī and Dṛṣadvatī (*Ibid.* I. 24. 26).

Sacrifice of Kārtavīrya Arjuna: He had performed ten thousand sacrifices. He had given immense wealth in charity during these sacrifices. The sacrificial posts and sacrificial altars were made of gold. Gods, *gandharva*-s and *apsaras*-es participated in his sacrifice. Through sacrifices, donations and penance the *kṣatriya*-s would achieve similar fame like that of Kārtavīrya Arjuna describes the *Mat. Pu* (XXXXIV. 19-24).

## Concept of Vedi According to the *Vām. Pu* (Chap. 23. 17. ff).

The gods asked Nārāyaṇa as to how many Vedi-s are there since he has referred to a Vedi named Sarvapañcakā as the Northern Vedi. The Vedi-s of Lord Brahmā are five in number which are equivalent to the bridges of religion, again equated with the sacrifices, which were performed by Śambhu, the Lord of the world. Prayāga is regarded as the middle Vedi and the Eastern Vedi is Gayā. The Southern Vedi is Virajā, the Western Vedi is Puṣkarā. This indicates that the concept of *tīrtha* is associated with the sacrifice.

## Sacrifice and Gods

Gods are the partakers of the offerings of sacrifice through the sacrificial fire. However, in the myth of the king Bali, the fire did not accept his offerings. Śukra, his preceptor said that Viṣṇu has incarnated as Vāmana to restore the glory of gods. Fire has not accepted the offerings because he has made the Dānava-s the partakers of the sacrifice. This indicates that if there is any change in the nature of the sacrifice, the sacrifice is not accomplished according to the *Vām. Pu* (Saromāhātmya 10 ff).

The Mitravindeṣṭi is to be performed by one who wants to procure good friends. A *brāhmaṇa* performed this sacrifice for seven times and by that King Uttama regained his wife (*Mārk. Pu* LXIX. 8-9). The reference to this sacrifice occurs in the *Śat. Br* (XI. 4. 3.1-20). It was Gotama Rāhūgaṇa, who discovered this sacrifice. This sacrifice is performed for obtaining a friend, kingdom and even for conquering death.

Jahnu, the son of King Ajamīḍha and Keśinī performed a great sacrifice called Sarvamedhamakha mentions the *Brahma. Pu.*(8.5).

## THE VARIOUS CATEGORIES OF PITṚ-S, BASED ON THE PERFORMANCE OF SACRIFICE

The Pitṛ-s who perform sacrifices are known as *soma*-sacrificers. Those who are mentioned as Yajvan-s are Barhiṣad-s, engaged in holy rites, who remain happy and contented till they take another body. Those who perform sacrifices and preside over them are known as Agniṣvātta-s. Those who adhere to their duties in virtue of their stages in life, those who closely follow their traditions, those who do not blunder in performance of their rites with faith, those who are engaged in holy rites with faith, those who are engaged in the holy rites till death, after being endowed with celibacy, penance, Yajña, progeny faith, learning and charitable gifts are also called Agniṣvātta-s (*Liṅga Pu.* 56. 63-65ab). According to *RV*, the Agniṣvātta-s are those who are tasted by the funeral fire (X. 15. 11), i.e. who are cremated and not buried.

Sacrifice performed by Sage Kaśyapa according to the *Brahma Pu* (6. 50 ff.). The word Kaśipu means a mat. The seat of the chief *ṛtvij* in a sacrifice is a golden mat. Kaśyapa performed an Aśvamedha. It was graced by the presence of deities and *gandharva*-s.

Five golden seats were kept ready. Three of them were sanctified by means of the Kuśa grass. The fourth had a bundle of Kuśa grass over it and the fifth a plank of wood. Diti, who was pregnant for thousand years, took the position of a wife. The boy came out of the womb and sat on the seat meant for the Hotṛ. He recited the Vedas as well as the Purāṇa-s. The sages gave him the name Hiraṇyakaśipu. How can Kaśyapa, the sage, perform the

Aśvamedha sacrifice? The probable answer is that he was a Prajāpati, the Lord of all offsprings, therefore he might be entitled to perform this sacrifice.

## MISCELLANEOUS REFERENCES

Śiva performed a sacrifice along with Pārvatī. On the completion of the sacrifice he gave *dakṣiṇā* to the *brāhmaṇa*-s according to the *Brahmavai. Pu.* (IV. Purvārdha. 45.1-2).

The *Nār. Pu* narrates the story of Triśaṅku, who performed the great sacrifice, under the guidance of Viśvāmitra. Viśvāmitra, raised him up to the heaven in his human form (I. 66. 7-8).

This text also mentions the destruction of Tārakāsura. In the three cities built for Tāraka, there were shrines of Rudra, and Agnihotra was performed everywhere. They followed the path of *dharma* and worshipped none else than Rudra. This worried Viṣṇu, for he was the form of sacrifice, the performer of sacrifice and partaker of the fruit of sacrifices. Sacrifice appeared before him in human form and advised him to perform the Upasad in worship of Rudra. Many goblins were created from the sacrifice and they were directed to kill the great demons. But they were destroyed by all the demons (I. 71. 28ff).

The *Śiva Pu* narrates the story of Guṇanidhi, the son of Yajñadatta which throws light on the life of a sacrificer. It refers to Yajñadatta who was born in the family of Somayājin-s. He had knowledge of Veda and Vedāṅga-s and he assiduously maintained the sacrificial fires and was devoted to the study of Veda-s. It points out that if the traditional code of conduct is not followed the title 'Dīkṣita'will be taken away. It also refers to the preparations made for the midday offerings to the fire (Rudra. Chap. XVII).

## SOME INJUNCTIONS AND PROHIBITIONS REGARDING THE SACRIFICE

1. At a sacrifice, the sacrificial fee is said to be a must, for, in the absence of the *dakṣiṇa*, the sacrifice would turn an enemy. Likewise if the required food is not available, it would burn the country, while if the proper *mantra*-s are not recited, it would kill the priests (*Sk. Pu.* VI. 182. 15). Not reciting the proper *mantra*-s gave the sacrificer as well as the priest the birth of a learned demon, i.e. Brahmarākṣasa says the *Varāha Pu.* (139. 28 ff).

2. For the performance of a sacrifice and for the construction of a tank a *brāhmaṇa* who has high moral values should be the priest, according to the *Mat. Pu.* (LVIII).

3. Gods are the partakers of the offerings of the sacrifice through the sacrificial fire. However, in the myth of king Bali, the fire did not accept his offerings. Śukra, Bali's preceptor, said that Viṣṇu is incarnated as Vāmana to restore the glory of gods. Fire has not accepted the offerings because he has made the Dānava-s the partakers of the sacrifice. This indicates that if there is any change in the nature of the sacrifice, the sacrifice is not accomplished *(Vām. Pu.* Saromāhātmya Ch. 10 ff*)*. This implies that as fire accepts offerings made to gods, a sacrificer should not offer to anyone else other than gods.

4. According to the *Pad.Pu*, a *brāhmaṇa* should hold a staff of bamboo or Palāśa and it should be high up to his hair, or a staff made of a tree fit for being used in a sacrifice and should be without a bruise (III. 51. 19).

5. According to the *Mārk. Pu*, one who sacrifices for an outcaste would go to hell and after he is released from hell, he may be born as a worm (XV.1). One should not kill a sacrificial cow of a *brāhmaṇa*. The text gives an example

of King Pṛṣadhra, the son of Manu who became a *śūdra* for doing so (CXLI).

6. While planning for the construction of a city, the sacrificial place was also taken into account. The main road in a village should be four steps wide; the space between two dwellings shall consist of three steps or paces. The side roads shall be half a pace wide. The way to the sacrificial room shall be a pace wide (*Vāyu. Pu.* 8. 116).

7. According *Nār. Pu.*, Sinīvālī, (the fourteenth day prior Amāvāsyā), should be accepted by the *brāhmaṇa*-s for the performance of sacrifice (I. 29. 27b). One who listens to the story of Sudharma attains the fruit of the Aśvamedha sacrifice (I. 40 58).

8. According to the *Nār. Pu*, Sage Nārada narrated the information of the Kalpa (II.51). Cowdung of certain types of cows should not be used in the sacrifice, i.e. the barren cow, the wicked or the defiled cow, the cow with afflicted limbs and the cow whose calf is dead (II. 51. 16).

9. One should scrape or scratch the ground with the *sruva* ladle or the Kuśa grass since this has been enjoined by Lord Brahmā for the achievement of Asthikaṇṭaka, i.e. bone and thorn, according to the *Nār. Pu* (II. 51. 18).

10. The *Nār. Pu* mentions that the sacrificial fire should be brought by women endowed with Saubhāgya in an auspicious earthen pot (II. 51.20).

11. According to the *Nār. Pu,* one should establish fire at the southern direction since there is fear from trouble created in this direction from the demons (II. 51. 22).

12. The vessels intended for consecration, and cooking should be placed in the north and the sacrificer should sit in the west instructs the *Nār. Pu* (II. 51. 23).

13. The *brāhmaṇa* and the Ācārya must be appointed from one's own *śākhā* in the course of the rite of Yajña.

There is no restriction in the case of the *ṛtvij*-s according to the *Nār. Pu* (II. 51. 24).

14. In order to make *sruva* and *sruc*, the trees used are Śrīparṇī, Śamī, Khadira, Vikaṅkata and Palāśa, says the *Nār. Pu* (II.51.41).

15. When there is rise of Gemini constellation, then invitation to the sacrifice is to be given, says the *Nār. Pu* (II. 56. 292).

16. The *Brahmavai. Pu.* enumerates a list of rules as to what type of beast is to be offered to the Goddess Durgā (Prakṛti. 64. 96-99).

17. A man, not having a surviving wife, is not authorized to perform the rites of gods, Pitṛ-s, guest and sacrifices (*Śiva Pu.* Rudra. Par. 54. 65-66).

## SOME OBSERVATIONS REGARDING THE INJUNCTIONS AND PROHIBITIONS

1. Not all the injunctions strictly adhere to the rules of the Vedic sacrifices.

2. The rules regarding correct utterance of the *mantra*-s indicate importance given to the minutest details of the sacrifice. If an utterance of a single syllable would go wrong, then the sacrificer will have to bear serious consequences after his death.

3. Appointment of the priest belonging to the same *śākhā* of the *brāhmaṇa* caste indicates the rigidity of the caste system at the time of the M. Pu-s.

4. Specifications of the type of cow used for the smearing of cow-dung, directions of placing utensils, etc. indicate attention to the minutest details of the sacrifice.

5. Importance given to married women by using the term Saubhāgya indicates that women with their husbands existing, had importance in the sacrificial rituals. Existence

of a wife is regarded as mandatory for the performance of sacrifices.

6. Lastly, for the construction of a city, the sacrificial place was taken into account. This indicates the importance enjoyed by the Vedic sacrifice in Ancient India.

## IMPORTANCE OF SACRIFICE

The Vedic sacrifice wielded great influence on the M. Pu-s. Following are the references which highlight the importance of Vedic sacrifice in the M. Pu-s.

The *Kū. Pu* mentions that performance of sacrifice was not only to obtain personal welfare, but also to obtain the welfare of the entire world (I. 20. 3-36). Those who perform sacrifices, observe holy rites and meditate on the great lord with devout feelings about the divine sports of the the Lord, attain immortality by passing through the Uttarāyaṇa, says the *Liṅga. Pu* (I. 34.18).

The *Kū. Pu* points out that the fruit of the performance of Agnihotra was the lustre of the sun (II. 8. 53).

King Vasumanas had performed the Aśvamedha sacrifice. He asked the sages as to what was beneficial to a person: Sacrifice, Penance or Renunciation. The answer given by sage Vasiṣṭha is that learning the Veda-s, procuring progeny and worshipping Viṣṇu through sacrifices and then resorting to the forest is beneficial. The answer given by Pulastya is that worshipping Viṣṇu through penance, performing sacrifices and then resorting to the forest is beneficial. These answers indicate that all the three modes of worship are beneficial for a human being (*Ibid*. I. 20. 31-36).

*Pad. Pu* says that a sacrificer or a donor plays in heaven with the gods in ponds having golden lotuses and at the root of the desire-yielding tree (V. 102. 14).

*Nār. Pu* says that those who maintain the sacrificial fires and serve their preceptors never undergo sufferings in this world (I. 13. 118b-119a).

*Pad. Pu* praises the sacrifice as follows: Gods are satisfied by sacrifices and human beings by the gift of rain. Therefore the text is of the opinion that the religious activity like that of sacrifice has to be performed (I. 3. 132)

## FOLLOWING ARE THE OBSERVATIONS BASED ON THE ABOVE REFERENCES

- Statistically, there are few references reiterating the importance of Vedic sacrifices.
- Most of the references combine sacrifice along with the other mode of worship or activity like penance, renunciation or serving one's preceptor, etc.
- The fruit gained by the performance of sacrifices is metaphysical and not material.
- Among the M. Pu-s quoted in this section, all the texts are Vaiṣṇavite in character.

Such references imply the changing trend in the nature of Vedic sacrifice. This trend indicates that the Vedic sacrifice is fast losing its grounds as the only mode of worship. It is considered on par with some other modes of worship like penance, renunciation or giving donations. However, these modes of worship do not fully substitute the Vedic sacrifice.

Mere comparison with Vedic sacrifice indicates an elevation in their position on the religious scene of the M. Pu-s. These references also indicate the change in the nature of fruit bestowed by the Vedic sacrifice. Performance of sacrifice yielded material gain like progeny, cattle, supremacy etc. and secured a place in the heaven after the death of the performer. The above references do not mention about material gains but discuss about achieving welfare of the world (philanthropic idea) and securing position in the heaven. To conclude, these references reflect on the decline in the position of Vedic sacrifice as well as change in the concept about the fruit accrued from the performance of sacrifice.

## CHANGING TRENDS IN THE INSTITUTION OF SACRIFICE

During the period of the composition of the M. Pu-s, the Indian society underwent many vicissitudes. As observed earlier, the Vedic sacrifice faced decline during the composition of the M. Pu-s. The changing face of the sacrifice does not mean that the sacrifice completely lost its significance. Instead of becoming obsolete, the institution of Vedic sacrifice thus was modified to exist in the course of time. The factors contributing to the change are:

- Sacrificial performances lead to heaven, but it is only through Jñānayajña that one obtains liberation (*Bhāg. Pu.* Discourse 2. 59,60).

The *Bhāg. Pu* discusses about the place of Jñānayajña. Therefore the very idea of Jñānayajña is modelled on the Vedic sacrifice, in which there is the concept of Yajñaśālā. Vājapeya and the Aśvamedha are the standards of merit (*Ibid.* 3. 1.ff.). The *Śiva Pu* is of the opinion that Tapoyajña is superior to thousands of Karmayajña-s, Japayajña is superior to thousands of Tapoyajña-s. Dhyānayajña is superior to thousands of Japayajña-s and there is nothing greater than Dhyānayajña-s (Rudra 1. 75. 13-14 c.f 10.45-46). The *Liṅga Pu.* also mentions similar thoughts (I. 75. 13-14).

All the ritualistic sacrifices, charitable gifts and austerities do not merit even a sixteenth fraction of the Japayajña. The other Yajña-s are attended with violence or killing but Japayajña-s have nothing to do with violence (I.

85.117-118 c. f. *Bhav. Pu* I. 4. 24-26). The importance of Japa is mentioned in the *Bhav. Pu.* to the extent that one who gives food to those who perform sacrifices gets the fruit of the sacrifices, performing *homa*-s and even visiting *tīrtha*-s (*Bhav. Pu.* I. 187. 84).

• Reading of the M. Pu-s lead to fruit which is superior to the performance of the sacrifice. Even one-sixteenth part of the merit accrued from these sacrifices cannot be compared with the reading of the *Bhāg. Pu.* (III.30,38,51). If we read half part of the verse or just one word from the verse of the *Bhāg. Pu*, we would obtain the merit of the performance of the Aśvamedha and the Rājasūya. Compared to a sacrifice, a Bhāgavata week is superior, compared to a week the vow of reading the Purāṇa is superior and compared to the reading of the Purāṇa, penance is superior and compared to the performance of penance, *tīrtha* is superior. Mere listening to the story of Śiva, a man secures that merit which results from the performance of Rājasūya and a hundred Agniṣṭoma-s (*Śiva Pu.* Śiva-Māhātmya. 1. 16). Thousands of Aśvamedha-s and hundreds of Vājapeya sacrifices do not merit even a sixteenth part of *Śiva Pu.*[283]. One who recites/listens to the *Pad. Pu* gets the fruit of the performance of the Aśvamedha sacrifice. The auspicious Aśvamedha does not exist in the Kāli age, therefore people do not get the fruit of this sacrifice. The recitation/listening to *Pad. Pu* is capable of yielding this fruit (II. 125. 13-14). By donating books like the *Rām*, one gets the fruit of the Vājapeya sacrifice. If *Bhav. Pu* is given in charity one gets the fruit of the Rājasūya and the Aśvamedha sacrifices (I. 93. 69-73).

• Omkāra is said to be the means of salvation. It consists of four Mātrā-s. One who worships with Aśvamedha every month for a hundred years, will not attain the benfit which accrues through a single Mātrā, says the *Vāyu. Pu* (Pūrva. Upo. 20.16). Obeisance as well as Omkara eulogise the lord. Yajña eulogises Omkāra, obeisance eulogises Yajña. Rudra eulogises prayer. Hence Rudra's region is auspicious, explains the *Vāyu Pu* (Upo. 20. 34).

- The M. Pu-s have raised voice against non-violence: The *Bhāg. Pu* preaches non-violence. Sacrifices cannot wash away the sins of killing the living beings (*Bhāg. Pu.* I. 8. 52). In the *Bhāg. Pu,* the dialogue between Sage Nārada and Pracīnabarhis indicates this changed trend of Vedic sacrifice. Pracīnabarhis was questioned by Nārada regarding the performance of sacrifices which involves the slaughter of animals. Nārada narrated the story of King Purañjana. This king had killed unlimited animals, when he went for hunting. The scriptures restrict the scope of hunting and lay down that a king (alone), if he is excessively fond of hunting, may kill on sacred occasions (Śrāddha, etc) animals recognized in the scriptures. The king killed bears, hares, boars, bisons, gayals, black antelopes and porcupines, fit for sacrifice and other animals. Nārada said that since the animals were slaughtered their anger has been aroused. They were waiting to tear the king apart with horns made up of steel. When the king was attacked by a Yavana king and dragged, all the animals mercilessly slaughtered by him chopped him with axes. Thus, the passage tells us about the changing trend in the sacrifice.

*Bhāg. Pu* mentions about a hell named Viśasana or Vaiśāsa, where the officers of Yama hack to pieces those hypocrites who actually slaughter animals in sacrifices performed for mere show to deceive others (V. 26. 25). Violence in the sacrifices leads to heaven no doubt but further bondage and then to the dreadful Varṇasaṁhāra, says the *Bhav. Pu* (III. 2. 39). Violence sanctioned by the

Śruti-s in regard to the *brāhmaṇa*-s, preceptors and sacrifice comes under the *ahiṁsā*, i.e. non-voilence. The *Liṅga Pu.* also harps on the same tune[284] (cf. I. 79.14).

The *Śiva Pu* narrates the greatness of Kumāra. One day a *brāhmaṇa* named Nārada approached Kumāra and requested him to search for his goat which had gone astray while he wanted to perform the goat sacrifice. Vīrabāhu, the attendant of Śiva, found the goat in the heaven with the sacrificial stake tied to his neck. On seeing Kārttikeya (Kumāra), the goat returned to the sacrificial place. Yet Kārttikeya said that this goat should be released and did not deserve to be killed. The sacrifice of the *brāhmaṇa* was declared to be complete, says the *Śiva. Pu* (Rudra. Kumāra. 6. 26, 32). The Vedic text encouraging the slaughter of animals cannot be held authoritative by the learned. To say that violence is allowed in Agniṣṭoma is an erroneous view of the wicked, states the *Śiva Pu* (Rudra. Yud. 5. 32).

According to the *Liṅga Pu,* the avocation of sacrifices was evolved in the Tretā Yuga. But persons of good holy rites did not resort to animal sacrifice. It was then that the seer Viṣṇu performed sacrifices forcefully. That is why, the *brāhmaṇa*-s praise a non-voilent sacrifice (I. 39. 51).

- Devotion is greater to Vedic sacrifice: *Bhāg. Pu* compares the fruits of *karman*-s offered to Hari with the offerings of sacrifices. It regards the fruits of *karman*-s offered to Hari superior to the offerings in the sacrifice (III. 15, 8). Devotion to Hari is superior as compared to the world attained by the performance of sacrifices, because these worlds are still impure observes, the *Bhāg. Pu* (VII. 7. 40).

- Changing nature of the performance of rituals: Sacrifice is performed for the occasion to consecrate a newly built tank, well and pool, grove and temple. The procedure is as follows: The altar, which is to be constructed, should be in the north-eastern direction with four openings made, near the tank. It should measure four hands in length. A pandal should be erected, which should have arches of the Aśvattha, Udumbara, Plakṣa and Vaṭa trees. According to the *Bhav. Pu*, the sacrificial post is to be made of Khadira, Śrīparṇika, Dhātrī trees and it should be sixteen *hasta*-s in measurements (II. 9. 82). A *brāhmaṇa* who has high moral values should be the priest, i.e. the Purohita, for the sacrifice. Water-pot and materials of the sacrifice should be placed at each of the pits, after which a fan and a white *cāmara* should be placed on a big plate of copper. The offerings of boiled rice and barley should be given to the gods. The sacrificial post should be made of the Kṣīravṛkṣa measuring three *aratni*-s in length of the hand of the sacrificer. It is also auspicious to get the sacrificial implements made of the size of the worshipper. The Hotṛ-s, Dvārapāla-s, Jāpaka-s, all eight in number and one Purohita are called *ṛtvij*-s in this sacrifice. They should be worshipped with the ornaments in gold. The Dvārapāla-s are those who are chanters of the *SV* and also experts in *AV*. They should perform the singing of the various *sāman*-s and the recitation of the Śāntika-s and the Pauṣṭika-s respectively. Performance of such rituals during the rainy season and autumn yields the fruit of the Agniṣṭoma sacrifice and of the Vājapeya and Atirātra sacrifice in the seasons of Hemanta and Śiśira. If this ritual is performed in the spring season, the performer gets the fruit of the Aśvamedha sacrifice and of the Rājasūya sacrifice in the summer season mentions the *Mat. Pu* (LVIII).

The performance of the rituals for the construction of a pond may not be fully Vedic in nature, but it does have a considerable influence of the Vedic sacrificial ritual on it. This indicates that though rituals have changed, there is a considerable continuity in this change. The change cannot be compartmentalized as 'Hinduized' rituals. Terming of such would indicate that they are different from the Vedic rituals. In fact they should be regarded as modified Vedic rituals.

According to the *Pad. Pu* on the occasion of planting trees one should perform a sacrifice with ghee, barley or even black sesamum. The sacrificial stacks of Palāśa are recommended (I. 28. 16). The Plakṣa tree is said to give the fruit of a sacrifice (I. 28. 25). Mere glimpse of Indra, the deity leads to the fruit of the Agniṣṭoma sacrifice and the Rājasūya sacrifice (I. 30. 111-12).

- Simplification of the performance of the sacrifice: He should perform the sacrifice with more than eight sesamum seeds, ladles of ghee and sacred woodsticks of the Palāśa tree. He should worship Gaṇeśa and Śāradā, stresses the *Pad. Pu* (II. 125. 39).

- Sacrifice as against *dāna* of food according to *Pad. Pu* (I. 34. 332-394): This passage narrates the greatness of giving food in charity as against the performance of sacrifices. King Śveta performed many Aśvamedha-s, gave the *brāhmaṇa*-s wealth and garments in charity. He thought that giving food as charity is insignificant. After death, he went to the heavens, but was tormented by hunger and thirst. He ultimately took the bones of his burnt body and licked them. King Vinītāśva also suffered in a similar way. He was liberated when he gave a cow of sesamum, ghee and liquid to a *brāhmaṇa*. This indicates that to attain a comfortable position in the heaven, performance of sacrifices is not sufficient. One requires giving of food also. According to the *Varāha Pu*, King Vinītāśva perfomed the Sarvamedha sacrifice and gave donations but no food (99. 81-81). After his death he became hungry. Therefore his priest made donations of *tiladhenu*, *ghṛtadhenu*, *jaladhenu* and *rasadhenu*. Giving *jaladhenu* in charity is equal to the performance of Aśvamedha (100.16). One who gives a hungry cow grass and water every day gets the fruit of the Gomedha sacrifice (111. 13).

- Agnihotra and the cow according to the *Varāha. Pu* (112. 5-11). The Kapilā cow is for the performance of the Agnihotra sacrifice. It was created from the effulgence of Brahman. *Brāhmaṇa*-s should perform the Agnihotra during morning and evening with the ghee, curds and milk of Kapilā. The cow is also used for entertaining guests. Greatness of the cow: *svāhā*, *svadhā*, *vaṣaṭ* and *hanta*, these four utterances are the teats of the cow (*Mārk. Pu* XXIX. 9).

- Greatness of a cow: The four nipples of the cow are *svāhākāra*, *svadhākāra*, *vaṣaṭkāra* and *hantakāra*. The *svāhākāra* nipple is sucked by gods, the *svadhākāra* by manes, the *vaṣaṭkāra* by other gods and presiding deity of the five principles and *hantakāra* by human beings. He who serves the cow with faith and reverence deserves to maintain the sacrificial fires, mentions the *Śiva. P* (Umā. 10. 44-46).

- Performance of sacrifice is considered as a Mayic act: While describing the evil portents and calamities in Yoga, the *Vāyu Pu* says that a Yogin, who is afflicted by evil may be enamoured of women and long for human enjoyments and fruits of learning. Such an afflicted person desires to perform Mayic, i.e. deceptive activities, such as maintenance of sacrificial fire, oblations in fire, performance of sacrifice, wealth and heaven (*Vāyu. Pu* Pūrva. Upo. 12. 3).

• Simplification of the Vedic sacrifice: The M. Pu-s reflect the increasing importance of Pākayajña-s which incorporate simple rules. As compared to the Śrauta sacrifices which are tedious, costly and cumbersome, the Pākayajña-s incorporate simpler rules and are cost-effective and do not require vast resources. According to the *Śiva Pu*, the offering made into the fire is called Agniyajña. In the case of persons in the Brahmacarya Āśrama, it is called Samidādhāna, i.e. collection of sacrificial twigs. All the persons in the first Āśrama perform their *vrata*-s with special sacrifices in the fire from sacrificial faggots. In the case of ascetics and forest-dwellers that have consigned the sacred fire to the Ātman, taking a restricted quantity of wholesome food is itself the sacrificial offering. Householders who have started their Aupāsana rite shall maintain the rite in the sacrificial fire kept in a vessel or pit. The sacrificial fire shall be maintained either in the Ātman or in the *araṇi*, or else the fire should be extinguished by royal or divine intercession. Offerings given in the fire in the evening for the firegod is for obtaining prosperity. The offerings in the morning for the sun-god are conducive to longevity. This is called Agniyajña in as much as it enters the sun during the day. The different sacrifices Sthālipāka, etc. for the propitiation of Indra and other gods by offerings in the fire are called Devayajña. The regular study of the Veda-s is called Brahmayajña (Vid. XIV. 2-10). The places suitable for Devayajña are cowshed, bank of a tank, Tulasī plant or Bilva or Aśvattha trees, temples, holy rivers, etc.

Ultimately, the place where one's mind is quite at home is the most excellent of all places (Vid. XV. 2-5). The above example highlights the fact that certain aspects of the Vedic sacrifice have been retained by the M. Pu-s in the course of simplifying religion. The reason for retaining some aspects of the Vedic sacrifice can be attributed to the fact that the religion in the M. Pu-s did not want to severe itself from Vedic religion, which was considered as their root.

- Opinion of heretics against Vedic sacrifice: The *Pad. Pu* narrates the story of king Vena. A heretic met King Vena and narrated the animal slaughter taking place in the sacrifice. When a guest goes to the house, a *brāhmaṇa* kills and cooks the flesh of a great bull or a goat. They kill a horse in a horse-sacrifice and a bull in a bull-sacrifice; a man in a human sacrifice and goats in a Vājapeya sacrifice. A great slaughter of many animals is done at a Rājasūya sacrifice. At a Puṇḍarīka sacrifice one would kill an elephant and at an elephant sacrifice one would kill an elephant. At the Sautrāmaṇī sacrifice a beast is seen to be fit for being sacrificed. Even a Cāṇḍāla or *śūdra* who is kind and would protect a life is said to be a *brāhmaṇa*. How can the *brāhmaṇa*-s be so cruel? (II. 37. 32-42). The *Pad. Pu* narrates the story of Lord Viṣṇu who created the Māyāmoha in order to infatuate the demons and take them away from the path of righteousness. He questioned the practices followed by the Veda-s. If oblations burnt in fire become fruitful or if it is laid down that a beast killed in a sacrifice obtains heaven, then why does the sacrificer not kill his own father in the sacrifice? If something eaten by one leads to the satisfaction of someone else, then *śrāddha* should be offered to those who are travelling (I. 13. 351-370).

- Apart from the importance given to devotion or recitation of the M.Pu-s, which appear to be the upcoming alteranatives to the Vedic sacrifice, the M. Pu-s have stressed the importance of *tīrtha*-s and *vrata*-s, which are discussed in the next chapter of this work.

## SOME PECULIAR SACRIFICES IN THE M. PU-S

The *Bhāg. Pu* refers to the performance of Śakramakha. Kṛṣṇa asked the purpose behind the performance of this sacrifice. He was told that this sacrifice was performed in honour of Indra because he is the rain-god. There is good harvest because of his grace and cows yield milk because of the lush green grass bestowed by Indra (V. 10. 18-24). The *Bhāg. Pu* refers to the Dhanuryajña performed by Kaṁsa. However, it does not reveal any details of the sacrifice (V. 15. 8). Kaṁsa performed a sacrifice named Dhanurmakha, supports the *Brahmavai. Pu* (IV. Purva.54.6). The M. Pu adds that this sacrifice was undertaken as per the advice of Sātyaka, the priest. This sacrifice destroyed bad dreams and enemies. This was the sacrifice unto Śiva. This was performed by Bāṇa, Paraśurāma, Nandin, etc. The bow was sanctified and was placed in the sacrifice. No one except Viṣṇu was capable of destroying the bow. When the bow was broken, it destroys the sacrificer (IV. Uttara. 1-13).

Gajamedha, Lohayajña, Svarṇayajña, Śiva, Rudra, Śakra sacrifices, Viṣṇuyāga, Varuṇayāga, etc. are some peculiar sacrifices mentioned in the *Brahmavai. Pu* (II. 43. 84-87). Gods performed a sacrifice but did not derive satisfaction from it. Then they worshipped Viṣṇu and Mahalakṣmī. Lord Brahmā gave *dakṣiṇā* and satisfied both of them and then derived pleasure of the sacrifice (II. 44. 37-40).

When Lord Brahmā created the seven sages, he asked them to sacrifice before him. Each sage sacrificed himself before Lord Brahmā. Seeing their rash action, Lord Brahmā cursed all the sages that they would be devoid of knowledge. The sages created their sons and went to heaven. The sons offered them oblations without delay, who had become manes. The manes of gods live in a world named Santānaka. Offerings are given by gods to the manes. Marīci and other sons of Lord Brahmā perform sacrifice for Marut-s. The Marut-s are pleased with sacrifices by those who are called Kalpavāsika-s, says the *Varāha Pu.* (13. 6-24).

## HEAD/BODY AS AN OBLATION (*VĀM. PU* 18. 41. FF.)

There were two dreadful demons named Rambha and Karambha. They performed austerities for birth of son for many years. Karmabha stood in the waters and Rambha in the midst of Five Fires concentrating on the Yakṣa Mālavaṭa. When he dived in water, Karambha was caught by the legs and dragged by none less than Indra who took the form of a crocodile. Rambha, who was enraged resolved to chop off his head as an oblation in the fire. The verb used over here is *hotum*. He was prevented by Agni and as a boon he was made invincible. This is some *Avedic* sacrifice, for a head is never an oblation in the sacrifice.

The demon Dhundhu, along with the other demons, approached Śukra, the priest to ask the means to reach the abode of Lord Brahmā. Śukra, the preceptor of the demons, directed him to perform the Aśvamedha sacrifice. He performed the great sacrifice with pomp and fervour. On smelling the odour of the oblations, gods became very dejected. On the request of the gods, Viṣṇu arrived at the sacrificial place in the form of a dwarf and asked for a space to take three strides. With one step he covered the earth, with the second he covered the heaven, but when no space was left for the third step, he fell on Dhundhu. This created a hole on the earth. Dhundhu fell in that hole which was thirty thousand Yojana deep. Vāmana covered it with sand (52. 32.ff).

The *Mat. Pu* narrates the story in which sacrifices were performed even by demons. Śukra had two disciples, viz. Śaṇḍa and Amarka. They assisted the demons in the sacrifices due to which they won victory over gods. Gods pursued Śaṇḍa and Amarka to join them in sacrifice, in which gods won victory in battle (XLVIII. 53-54).

The *Vāyu Pu* mentions the story of Gayā, a demon who had performed the sacrifice at the beginning of the Śveta Varāhakalpa. Every step taken towards Gayā will lead to the fruit of the Aśvamedha sacrifice. This demon was requested by the gods to give his body for the performance of sacrifice. This was agreed upon by the demon (Uttara. Upa. 44. 16-30).

## MYTHS ASSOCIATED WITH SACRIFICE

Myths regarding the creation of sacrifice/sacrificial fire: Yajña was born from Ruci and Ākūti (*Bhāg. Pu*. 1.3.12). Ākūti, the daughter of Svāyambhuva Manu, got married to Ruci, the Prajāpati and they got two offsprings, viz. Yajña, i.e. Viṣṇu and Dakṣiṇā, i.e. Lakṣmī. Yajña married Dakṣiṇā and the couple begot twelve offsprings out of which the names of two are associated with the sacrifice, viz. Idhma and Iḍaspati (IV. 1. 3-9). Pulastya's wife was known as Havirbhū (sacrificial name) whose sons were Agastya and Viśravas. The first wife of Viśravas was Iḍavidā, whose son was Kubera. Svāhā, the wife of Agni, bore three sons, viz. Pāvaka, Pavamāna and Śuci. The M. Pu says that these are the deities presiding over fire and they partake of the sacrificial offerings. From them sprang up other forty-five fire gods. Thus there are forty-nine fire gods, in whose names *iṣṭi*-s are undertaken during Vedic sacrificial performances by men well-versed in the Veda-s. Svadhā, the daughter of Dakṣa, is the wife of Pitṛ-s: Agniṣvātta-s, Barhiṣad-s, Saumya-s and the Ājyapa-s.

According to the *Mārk. Pu*, Svāyambhuva Manu had two daughters namely Prasūti and Ṛddhi. Ṛddhi was married to Ruci, the Prajāpati. They bore one son named Yajña and one daughter named Dakṣiṇā (L. 17-18).

According to the *Vāyu. Pu*, Manu gave his daughter Ākuti to Ruci, the patriarch. They begot twins Yajña and Dakṣiṇā by name. From them were born twelve sons (Purva. Upo. 10. 18-20 c.f. *Liṅga Pu.* I. 70. 273-78)

The variant of this myth occurs in the *Śiva Pu* in which, Svāhā, the wife of the fire-god, who was the mind-born son of Lord Brahmā in the form of Rudra, bore three sons of unmeasured splendour. They are Pāvaka, Pavamāna and Śuci. Pavamāna is the fire kindled by attrition. Pāvaka is the fire produced by lightning. The solar fire is called Śuci. Their sons in the order are Havyavāha, Kavyavāha and Saharakṣas. They are the deities, manes and gods. Their sons and grandsons are forty-nine. They are propitiated in the three rites, namely Kāmya, Naimittika and Nitya. These are in the form of Rudra and they are devoted to him. Householders are of two types, viz. sacrificers and non-sacrificers. Svadhā bore to the Pitṛ-s two daughters, namely Menā and Dhāriṇī. Menā is the daughter of the Agniṣvātta-s and Dhāriṇī is the daughter of Barhiṣad-s (Vāyavīya Sam. Section I. Ch. 17. 37-49).

According to the *Viṣṇu. Pu*, Svāyambhuva Manu and Śatarūpā gave birth to sons named Priyavrata and Uttānapāda and daughters named Prasūti and Ākūti. Ākūti married Ruci, the Prajāpati. They gave birth to Yajña and Dakṣiṇā, the twins (I. 7. 19-20).

Genealogy of the sacred fire according to the *Mat. Pu.* (LI): In the Svāyambhuva Manvantara, Agni was born from the mind of Lord Brahmā and Svāhā, his wife. This Agni stands for the presiding spirit of Fire. She gave birth to Pāvaka, i.e. the subterranean fire, Pavamāna, i.e. the terrestrial fire and Śuci, i.e. the celestial fire. Pavamāna or terrestrial Fire is produced by friction and Pāvaka Fire is lightning. Śuci is also called Saura, i.e. the Solar Fire. These fires are known as Sthāvara-s, i.e. Fixed Fires. Havyavāha is the son of Pavamāna. Pāvakin, Saharakṣa and Havyamukha are the sons of Pāvaka, Pavamāna and Śuci Fires. Pavamāna fire of the human beings is the first-begotten of Lord Brahmā. Brahmanandana known also as Bharata, was the son of Pavamāna. Havyavāha is also known as Vaiśvānara Agni. He died while carrying Havya offerings to the gods. He, being dead, the son of Atharvan (Aṅgirasa) produced the Fire Puṣkarodadhi (produced by the churning of the cloud), which is known as Atharva Alaukika Agni and also as Dakṣiṇa Agni. Atharvan was the son of Bhṛgu and Aṅgiras was the son of Atharvan. Pavamāna is produced from friction and the same is known as Gārhapatya Agni. He produced from Samśatī two sons, named Sabhya and Āvasathya. Havyavāhana was enamoured of sixteen rivers. This is known as the Āhavanīya fire. After dividing his body into sixteen different parts, he became desirous of Dhiṣṇya-s. Produced from them was the progeny known as Dhiṣṇu-s.

All the sons of the rivers made friends with these Dhiṣṇya-s. They are divided into two categories a)Viharaṇīya b) Upastheya. Vibhu, Pravahaṇa and Agnīdhra are fixed in their altars, while the remaining Dhiṣṇu-s are shifting and moving and taken from their places when some auspicious occasions arise. Vāsava and Kṛśānu are both the Agni-s of Dvitīyā and Uttaravedi-s.

Pāvakoṣṇa and Samuhya are the Agni-s found in the Uttaravedi. Havyasūda and Asamṛjya are both known as Śāmitra fires. Śatadhāman and Sudhājyoti are described as Raudraiśvarya Agni-s. Brahmajyoti and Vasudhāman are said to be Brahmasthānīya fires. The Upastheya Agni known as the Aja Ekapāt is known to be Śālāmukha. The Agni obtained by rubbing of *araṇi*-s went to dwell in the sacrificial fuel. This fire is called Āyu, in which the sacrificial victims are immolated. The son of Āyu is Mahimat and his son is Dahana, the presiding Fire in Pākayajña domestic sacrifices. Rakṣohayatikṛt is the presiding deity in all Kāmya sacrifices (Chap. LI. c.f. *Vāyu. Pu.* Purva. Upo. 29).

This type of genealogy, which occurs in the M. Pu-s indicates the attempt to personify fire and deify the various types of fires. Yajña, i.e. sacrifice personified, is regarded as Viṣṇu himself and Dakṣiṇā, i.e. sacrificial fee personified, is regarded as Lakṣmī, the consort of Viṣṇu, which established the strong relation between sacrifice and Viṣṇu.

The *Bhāg. Pu* describes the capital of Svāyambhuva Manu which was known as Barhiṣmatī. This capital was so called because it was created from the hair of Viṣṇu in the form of Yajñavarāha. As soon as the Yajñavarāha shook his head, his hair turned into the blades of Kuśa grass. The demons that interfered in the sacrifice were destroyed by the sages with this grass (III. 22. 29-30).

## VIṢṆU = SACRIFICE

In an attempt to establish absolute identification of the sacrifice with Viṣṇu, the *Bhāg. Pu* says Gāyatra, *ṛc*, Trivṛtstoma, Rathantara, Agniṣṭoma and other sacrifices were first created from the first face of Viṣṇu. The *yajus*, Triṣṭubh, Pañcadaśastoma, Bṛhatsāman, Ukthya were created from the southern face. *Sāman*-s, Jagatī,

Saptadaśastoma Vairūpa and Atirātra were created from the western mouth. Twenty-one *atharvan*-s, Aptoryāma, Anuṣṭubh, and Vairāja were created from the northern face. (I. 5. 53-56, c.f. *Liṅga Pu.* I. 70. 243-247, *Śiva Pu.* Vāyavīya Saṁhita Section I. Ch. 12. 58-62).

## ORIGIN OF SACRIFICE

According to the *Bhāg. Pu,* Lord Brahmā released the Ṣoḍaśin and Ukthya from the eastern mouth, Puriṣī and Agniṣṭuta from the southern, Aptoryāma and Atirātra from the western and Vājapeya and Gosava from the northern mouth (III. 12. 40).

## HOW DID PRAJĀPATI CREATE SACRIFICES?

The idea of the origin of sacrifice with its various constituents appears to have been influenced by the Puruṣasūkta of the *RV* (X. 90).

(*Kū. Pu.* I. 7. 57-60, c.f. *Mārk. Pu* XLVIII. 31-34, *Vāyu. Pu.* Pūrva. Upo. 9. 44-47, *Pad. Pu* I. 3. 105-114)

| *Mouth* | *Veda* | *Metre* | *Stoma* | *sāman* | *Sacrifice* |
|---|---|---|---|---|---|
| Eastern | *RV* | Gāyatrī | Trivṛtstoma | Rathantara | Agniṣṭoma |
| Southern | *YV* | Triṣṭubh | Pañcadaśa-stoma | Bṛhatsāman | Ukthya |
| Western | *SV* | Jagatī | Saptadaśa-stoma | Vairūpa | Atirātra |
| Northern | *AV* | Anuṣṭubh | Ekavīṁśa stoma | Vairāja | Aptoryāma |

The *Vayu Pu* narrates the myth of the origin of sacrifice differently.

When the whole world was a vast sheet of waters, Lord Brahmā came out of the navel of Viṣṇu just as fire comes out of *araṇi*. He laid down the process of preparing

Āhavanīya fire by means of Gārhapatya and Anvāhārya rites. He created the altar, the Kuśa grass, the sacrificial ladle with which the offering is taken or holy water is sprinkled and the materials for *avabhṛtha*. He made the gods partakers of the oblations and the Pitṛ-s, the partakers of *kavya*. In order to enjoy himself by the sacrificial procedure, he himself became Yajña, in the sacrificial fire. He created the requisite materials of the sacrifice like the *yūpa*-s, Samidh-s, *pavitra*, Paridhi, the sacrificial fires, *sadasya*-s, sacrificer etc (Uttara. Anu.35. 25-29). Viṣṇu created the world with the sacrifice. By the Gārhapatya and Anvāhārya rites, he created the materials essential for Yajña-s, while his hand was hanging downwards, Āhavanāya fire, Veda-s, consecration, sacrificial twigs, Prokṣaṇīya vessel, *sruva* ladle, *avabhṛtha* and the persons partaking of their share in *havya* were created. He made gods the partakers of *havya* and Pitṛ-s, the partakers of *kavya*. He assigned shares to them in the sacrificial rites and laid down rules regarding sacrifices. Lord created sacrificial implements, monetary gifts, consecration, *caru* offerings, *ulūkhala*-s, sacrifical posts, Soma juice, *pavitra*-s, Paridhi-s, articles required for sacrifice such as *camasa*, etc. He created the *sadasya*-s and Yajamāna-s (Uttara. Anu. 70. 29-33).

According to the *Varāha Pu*, Lord Brahmā created five great sacrifices: Divya, Bhauma, Paitra, Mānuṣa and Brāhma. These sacrifices are intended for the good of the *brāhmaṇa* and other castes. For other castes they are fruitful if got performed by *brāhmaṇa*-s (8. 31-32).

The *Varāha Pu* narrates the myth of the origin of sacrifice differently. Once, Nārāyaṇa was creating different living beings on his own. He became angry and the anger got converted into fire. He told fire to bear (*vaha*) the offerings, viz. *havya* and *kavya*. Thus the fire became Havyavāhana. But he was hungry; therefore Lord Brahmā said that he will be gratified in three ways. He will carry *dakṣiṇā*-s to the gods. Therefore, he will be known as Dakṣiṇāgni. His body is said to be *gṛha*, therefore he will be known as Gārhapatya. When propitiated by offerings, the fire will lead men to liberation. Therefore he will be known as Vaiśvānara. Fire will blaze when *idhma* is placed in it. And when air blows, it will be *idhma*. Lord Brahmā assured that those who propitiated through sacrifices will offer with the names in great sacrifices (18. 5-26).

The M. Pu-s attribute the creation of sacrifice either to Prajāpati/Lord Brahmā or Viṣṇu. There are hardly any references pointing out at Śiva being the origin of sacrifice. Such stray references mentioning Śiva being the origin of sacrifice occur only in the myth of the destruction of the sacrifice of Dakṣa. The M. Pu-s just recast the myths of the origin of sacrifice occurring in the Saṁhitā-s and Brāhmaṇa-s. The personification of Fire and the genealogy merely added up to superimpose anthropomorphic traits on the god.

## MYTHS REGARDING SUPRANORMAL BIRTHS RELATED TO THE SACRIFICE

There are two common myths in most of the M. Pu-s related to the birth of king Vena and Pṛthu and secondly the birth of Ilā.

### Birth of King Vena and his Son Pṛthu

According to the *Bhāg. Pu,* King Aṅga had performed the Aśvamedha sacrifice. Gods refused to partake any of the offerings in the sacrifice. Requesting the priests, the king broke the vow of silence and enquired to the Sadasyapati-s, the reason for this happening. The answer was that the king was issueless. An offering was given to the fire so that the king would beget a son. As a result, a being sprang up from the fire with boiled rice in his hand. This was given to the wife of the king. Soon a son was born. The *Bhāg. Pu* says that since he was a tyrant from his childhood, people named him Vena (IV. 13ff). Vena banned all the sacrifices as soon as he ascended the throne (*Ibid.* IV. 14. 6). The sages tried to convince the king that performing of sacrifice was nothing else but worship of Lord Viṣṇu and that would be beneficial to the king. The *Pad. Pu* says that Vena refused to get convinced and said that all the deities resided in the king. Therefore sacrifices were to be offered to him (II. 25. 24-25). King Vena was killed by the sages by a mere utterance of 'Hum'. Thereafter, the earth was without a king which caused anarchy. Hence, to create a new king, the sages churned the right thigh of the dead king. The *Bhāg. Pu* describes that at the beginning, a dark, short, meek man emerged and he asked, 'What shall I do'? The sages asked him to sit down. He became Niṣāda (IV. 14. 44-46). From further friction emerged a couple. Seeing them the sages were pleased. The man became the king of the earth and the woman became his wife (IV. 15. 3-6). Pṛthu performed hundred Aśvamedha-s. During these sacrifices the earth appeared in the form of a cow to provide milk as well as clarified butter. At the performance of the hundredth sacrifice, Indra became jealous and stole away the horse of Pṛthu. This act of Indra was detected by Atri, who advised the son of Pṛthu to have a combat with Indra. Pṛthu's son defeated Indra and got back the horse, therefore he was named Vijitāśva (IV. 19. 17-18). Creating a mass of darkness, Indra stole the horse again. Vijitāśva shot an arrow at Indra. Indra then released his garb and the horse and remained invisible. This particular passage tells the source of the emergence of the Jaina-s and the Buddhists. The garb released by Indra became those deceitful garbs worn by people who advocate hypocrisy. This garb was named

Pākhaṇḍa, i.e. sinful propensity (IV. 19. 22-24). Pleased with the sacrifices of Pṛthu, Viṣṇu, manifested himself in the sacrificial hall.

The myth of Vena also occurs in the *Brahma Pu* (I. 78 and II. 33). This text adds that the sages created Dhīvara, Tuṣāra-s and the Tuṇḍra-s from the body of King Vena. A similar account has been given by the *Vāyu Pu* with slight variations. The Niṣāda, who was born by churning the left hand of Vena, created the Dhīvara-s and the Khaśa tribes (Uttara. Upo.1. 95-146).

The myth of the destruction of King Vena highlights the following points:

- The anti-sacrifice approach of this king brought him an end.
- The sages did not find any other source apart from the body of Vena to create a new king. This indicates a belief that the body of a king, though lifeless, was capable of creating a new king. The idea obviously goes back to the Puruṣasūkta (*RV* X. 90), where creation comes into existence from the very Cosmic Puruṣa.
- Pṛthu, the son of Vena, performed sacrifices and revived the sacrificial religion.
- The left part of the body is impure. The Niṣada emerged from the left part of the body carrying all the impurities of Vena with him.
- The myth of King Vena assimilated not only the Niṣāda-s, in the Vedic fold but also the Tuṣāra, the Tuṇḍra, Dhīvara and the Khaśa tribes.

### Birth of Ilā:

The *Bhāg. Pu* gives an account of the birth of King Ila and how he did get transformed into Ilā, the female. Earlier, before Ikṣvāku and others were born, the glorious and powerful Vasiṣṭha conducted a sacrifice in propitiation of the gods Mitra and Varuṇa for the sake of a son to Manu, who was childless. During the performance, Śraddhā, the wife of Manu, requested the Hotṛ to perform rites so as to ensure birth of a girl. Hotṛ gave oblations to the fire with a similar intention in mind and from the fire sprang up Ilā. Later on by the grace of Lord Viṣṇu, Ilā got converted into a man known as Sudyumna (IX. 1. 13-22). According to the *Bhāg. Pu,* a female, i.e. Ilā, was born first and then she got converted into Ila, her masculine counterpart by the grace of Hari.

The *Kū. Pu* narrates this account differently. Mitrāvaruṇeṣṭi was performed by king Manu, with the desire to obtain progeny. He got a daughter named Ilā. She got a son for Manu by the grace of Mitrāvaruṇā (IV. 1. 8-10). The *Kū. Pu* somewhat follows the line of the *Bhāg. Pu* and notes that firstly a female, i.e. Ilā, was born from a sacrifice, who later on got converted into a male, i.e. Ila.

The *Mat. Pu* narrates the account differently. Agnīdhra, Agnibāhu and Savana are the sons of Svāyambhuva Manu apart from king Ila (IX.3). Ila becme Ilā as he entered the forest Śaravaṇa. His brothers searched for him. On knowing the situation from Vasiṣṭha, they propitiated Śiva. Śiva told them to perform the Aśvamedha, after which Ilā would become Kimpuruṣa.

Another variant occurs in the *Pad. Pu.* King Ila of the Ikṣvāku dynasty happened to wander in the forest Śaravaṇa by mistake. As per the stipulation, he who enters the forest becomes a woman, he got changed into a woman Ilā by name and the horse became a mare. Later on after the family members of Ila, performed the Aśvamedha, he became a Kimpuruṣa. For one month, he became a man Sudyumna by name and the other month, he became Ilā, the female. In his feminine form he was spotted by Budha, of the lunar dynasty who fell in love with her. She remained pregnant from Budha and from her Puru was born, the father of Purūravas. The story of Ilā throws light on the confluence of the solar and the lunar dynasties. (I. 8. 105-120). The Aśvamedha sacrifice was also performed as atonement of sin or for undoing a curse. The Aśvamedha sacrifice was performed with a wish to get male offspring.

The *Mārk. Pu* points out the mistake of the priest, which gave birth to Ilā the female, in the sacrifice of King Manu, who in spite of having sons like Ikṣvāku and others, in order to have a more distinguished son offered a sacrifice to Mitra and Varuṇa. Manu requested the deities that the daughter be changed to a son. The request was granted and Ilā became a son named Sudyumna. When Sudyumna had gone hunting, he again got converted into a woman due to the wrath of a god (the details are not given in the text). In this condition, she gave birth to a son Purūravas by name from Budha, the son of Soma (Moon). When a son was born Sudyumna performed the Aśvamedha and regained manhood (CXL. 4-15 and c. f. *Brahma. Pu* 7. 13-33).

The *Liṅga. Pu* does not mention the birth of Ilā due to the performance of a sacrifice. Manu, the Prajāpati, had nine sons and one among them was Ikṣvāku. The eldest daughter of Ikṣvāku attained the state of man, by the grace of Mitra and Varuṇa. She was known as Sudyumna. She entered Śaravaṇa and regained the state of woman at the behest of Bhava. Sudyumna, the glorious son of Manu, became a woman for carrying further, the lineage of the lunar race. It was at the time of the Aśvamedha sacrifice of Ikṣvāku that Ilā became a Kimpuruṣa. During the state of Kimpuruṣa, Ilā was called Sudyumna. She became a woman for one month and male for the next month. In the state of womanhood, Ilā resorted to the house of Budha, the son of Soma and begot a son named Purūravas. (*Liṅga. Pu*. I. 65. 17b-24 cf. *Śiva. Pu*. ch. 36).

The following observations are pointed out after analyzing the myth of Ila/Ilā.

- Manu/Ikṣvāku, the father of Ila/Ilā had to perform sacrifice for progeny. The sacrifice was either the Aśvamedha or sacrifice for Mitra and Varuṇa.
- In certain variants, a girl was born who attained manhood by the grace of the dual divinity Mitra and Varuṇa.
- The loss of manhood in certain variants is because of wandering in a forest prohibited for males. Another reason given is the expansion of the solar dynasty.
- After becoming a female, Ilā was the mother of Purūravas, another king who devised an innovative method of performing sacrifices with the help of three fires.
- Aśvamedha, the great sacrifice, also helps in regaining manhood.

With these observations, one can conclude that the myth of Ila/Ilā is developed in a ritual setting. All the distinctive stages in the life of Ila/Ilā are associated with the sacrifice. This myth has extended the function of Aśvamedha. The sacrifice, which was performed for male progeny, extends its function to being beneficial in regaining the lost manhood.

## OTHER SACRIFICIAL BIRTHS:

### Sacrificial Birth of the Marut-s

*Pad. Pu* throws light on the story of the birth of the Marut-s. Diti, the wife of Sage Kaśyapa, asked for a boon that she wanted a son who would destroy Indra. Kaśyapa agreed and performed the Āpastamba sacrifice for this and then deposited the semen in her. She remained pregnant. Knowing this, Indra came near her in order to know her weak points. One day she did not cleanse her feet, lay anywhere by day and with hair let loose and with her head raised. Taking this opportunity, Indra entered her body and cut her foetus into seven parts with his thunderbolt. The fetuses were crying and Indra cut each of them further into seven pieces. Thus cut into forty-nine, they cried more loudly. Indra realized that the fetuses were protected because of the Paurṇamāsī vow or because of the worship of Lord Brahmā. He begged for forgiveness to Diti and positioned the Marut-s among gods. Thus the birth of Marut-s has a sacrificial background (I. 7. 32-67). The Āpastamba sacrifice cannot be traced.

### The Myth of the Births of Jamadagni and Viśvāmitra According to the *Bhāg. Pu*: (IV. 8. 24-28).

King Gādhi gave birth to a daughter named Satyavatī. She married the sage Ṛcīka. In order to obtain offspring Ṛcīka prepared *caru* for her. She obtained one more *caru* for her mother so that she could also get a son. However, they interchanged the *caru*-s. The result was that Satyavatī would get a son terrible in nature as she had consumed a *caru*, which had the qualities of being prosperous, valorous, etc. Her mother would get a son who would be serene by nature and fix his mind on ascetism.

The *Vāyu Pu* narrates the account of the birth of Jamadagni. It tells that the *caru*-s pertaining to Rudra and Viṣṇu were interchanged. Jamadagni was born from the *caru* of Vaiṣṇava fire (Uttara. Anu. 92-94).

### According to the *Liṅga Pu*

Dvaipāyana begot of Araṇi, the son Śuka and the son Upamanyu from Pīvarī. Vasiṣṭha begot of Ghṛtācī, the son Kapiñjalya (I. 63. 84-91).

## Śiva Pu Narrates the Myth of Sandhyā

Sandhyā, the daughter of Lord Brahmā, went to the place where Medhātithi was performing the Jyotiṣṭoma sacrifice (*Śiva Pu.* Rudra. Satī. 6. 60). Vasiṣṭha had assumed the guise of a *brāhmaṇa* boy and was engaging the rites of the sacrifice. Sandhyā, who meditated on him as her future husband, cast off her body in the sacrificial fire without the knowledge of anyone. Her body became one with the *puroḍāśa*. She entered the zone of Sun, who divided her into two and she became the Prātaḥsandhyā and the Sāyaṁsandhyā. After the sacrifice was over, Medhātithi saw her in the pit, blazing like gold. He took her on the lap and then after she attained due marriageable age, married her to Vasiṣṭha. She became Arundhatī, i.e. one who does not hinder anyone in the sacrificial rites (*Ibid.* Rudra. Satī. 7. 17).

## Sacrificial Births of Sages

According to the *Vāyu. Pu* in the sacrifice of Lord Brahmā, he assumed the form of Varuṇa and with the desire for progeny consigned the semen to the sacred fire. In fact the semen fell on the ground. It was picked up by Lord Brahmā with the help of the *sruc* and *sruva*. From the first offering of semen, Venus, i.e. Kavi, sprang out. On seeing him, the Lord said that he was Bhṛgu (*Vāyu. Pu.* Uttara. Anu. 4. 37). Bhṛgu became the son of Mahādeva. A second ladleful of semen fell on the burning coals. Hence Aṅgiras was born. Aṅgiras became the son of Agni. During the third offering of semen six other sons were born. Marīci was born from the rays of the sacrificial fire. The second son was Kratu, i.e. born from sacrifice (*Ibid.* Uttara. Anu. 4. 44). The etymologies of Atri, Pulaha, Pulastya and Vasiṣṭha are not directly connected with the sacrifice. Bhṛgu, Aṅgiras, Marīci, Pulastya, Pulaha, Kratu, Atri and Vasiṣṭha were born. All the Aṅga-s, i.e. ancillaries and *vaṣaṭkāra* assumed corporeal forms. The *sāman mantra*-s, thousands of Yajus *mantra*-s and the *RV* with *pada* and *krama* were present. The other Veda-s including the *AV*, i.e. the Brahmaveda, was present along with its terrible rites. Due to the presence of Pratyaṅgiras, it appeared to have a single head with two bodies (Uttara. Anu. 4. 21-44). Bhṛgu married Divya, who gave birth to Śukra. Śukra had four sons. They approached Manu with the motive of spoiling sacrificial rites. Realising this, Indra said that he would have the sacrifice performed by Manu rather than these sages. The twelve sons of Bhṛgu were known as the twelve sacrificial Deva-s. Sadhyā, the wife of Dharma, gave birth to the Sādhya-s, who were the partakers of shares in sacrifices (Uttara. Anu 5. 4).

### Birth of Nimi

The *Bhāg. Pu* refers to the story of King Nimi. Nimi had decided to perform a *sattra* in which Vasiṣṭha had agreed to be the chief officiating priest. However, the sage was invited by Indra. Vasiṣṭha requested Nimi to wait for him. Nimi, however, remained silent and completed the sacrificial session, with the help of other priests. Vasiṣṭha felt insulted by this act and cursed Nimi that his body would fall. Nimi also pronounced a similar curse. Nimi gave up his body and Vasiṣṭha was reborn as the son of Mitra and Varuṇa, through Urvaśī. Fearing anarchy the sages churned the body of Nimi. From the body sprang up a son, who was named 'Janaka' because of his unique birth; 'Videha', because he was born in the line of Nimi, who lost his body; and 'Mithila' because he was born from 'churning' (the Sanskrit root of which is $\sqrt{}$*math*). The myth of Nimi is referred to in the *Vāyu. Pu.* (Uttara. Anu. 27. 1-5) in brief.

A variant of this myth occurs in the *Kū. Pu.* Nimi had performed a *sattra* of thousands of years. Vasiṣṭha was the Hotṛ. But he was selected as the priest for a *sattra* to be performed by Indra for about five hundred years. Instead of waiting for him, Nimi selected Gautama as the priest and performed the *sattra*. This angered Vasiṣṭha and he cursed Nimi that the latter would lose his body. Nimi cursed Vasiṣṭha the same. However, the subtle body of Vasiṣṭha entered the semen of Mitrāvaruṇa. Vasiṣṭha regained his body after the semen of Mitrāvaruṇa fell down on seeing Urvaśī. The body of Nimi did not decay. On the completion of his sacrifice, the sages/*ṛtvij*-s requested the gods to bless Nimi with a boon. Nimi expressed a desire of being placed in the eyes of all living beings. Hence all the living beings blink. (Etymology through the sacrifice). Nimi was sonless. His body was churned by the sages and from that Janaka was born. (These are all the etymologies from the sacrifice). Janaka tilled the land and from that Sītā was born (IV. 5. 7-28).

### The Birth of Māndhātṛ from Yuvanāśva is Mentioned in the *Kū. Pu*

Yuvanāśva was childless. He approached the sages. The sages sanctified water with the *mantra*-s and slept at night. The king unknowingly consumed that water and remained pregnant. Thus Māndhātṛ was born (IV. 2. 49-57).

## THE MYTH OF PURŪRAVAS

According to the *Viṣṇu. Pu*, the King Purūravas wanted to lead his life with Urvaśī. He wanted to be a *gandharva* and he was given a *sthālī*, i.e. a fire-pan, of Agni. He divided the Agni into three portions. Why was this *sthālī* brought by him and not Urvaśī, thus he repented. He left the *sthālī*. He thought at midnight that the *sthālī* was given to him for becoming a *gandharva.* But the fire left by him was converted into Aśvattha in the Śamī tree. He made *araṇi*-s from the wood of the trees. He decided their size and chanted in Gāyatrī metre. Thus he made three fires and then attained Sālokya with Urvaśī. The episode is concluded in the M. Pu-s as 'earlier there was only one Agni and now in this Manvantara there are three' (IV. 6. 76-94).

The myth of Purūravas and Urvaśī occurs in the ninth book of the *Bhāg. Pu.*. When Urvaśī disappeared for the first time, Purūravas found her. She was the mother of one son. He cohabited with her and could not tolerate separation. So Urvaśī told him to propitiate the *gandharva*-s. The *gandharva*-s bestowed upon him a vessel carrying fire. Purūravas thought that vessel to be Urvaśī, but when he realized this he left it on the ground and went away. When Tretā *yuga* commenced, the knowledge of the science of rituals dawned upon his mind. Going to the spot where he had left the vessel, and perceiving there a peepal tree sprouting from inside a Śamī tree, he hewed out of it a pair of *araṇi*-s for kindling fire by attrition. Then visualizing the lower *araṇi* to be Urvaśī and the upper one as his own self and the piece that intervened the two as their son, the king churned them with a longing to reach the realm of Urvaśī, uttering sacred texts (detailing the procedure of producing fire through such churning). As a result of his churning was produced a flame of fire, which is known by the name Jātaveda (that which has everything created in this universe by way of its property or food). Through the ceremony of consecration it was adopted by the king Purūravas in the three forms. He thus, propitiated Lord Hari, through sacrifice. The three Vedas, the cult of rituals expounded by them came into being from Purūravas alone at the dawn of the Tretā *yuga* and the king attained after death the realm of the *gandharva*-s by means of the sacred fire, adopted by him as his son (IX. 14. 40-49).

The myth of Purūravas and Urvaśī also occurs in the *Vāyu. Pu* (Uttara. Anu. 29). The condition laid down by Urvaśī has been mentioned. Urvaśī was cursed by Lord Brahmā that she would approach a human being. In order to redeem herself from the curse, she said that she should not see him naked except at the time of sexual intercourse or when swayed with passion. Two rams would also remain near their bed. She would take only ghee once a day. The king scrupulously adhered to her conditions. She stayed with Purūravas for nearly 64 years. Viśvāvasu, the *gandharva* hatched a plan to bring back Urvaśī. The *apsaras* saw the king naked and running behind the rams which were stolen by the *gandharva*-s. The condition was broken and Urvaśī left the king. Since he wanted to stay with Urvaśī, he chose the boon of Sālokya. The *gandharva*-s agreed and they gave him a *sthālī*, i.e. clay-pot, filled with Agni. Having performed a sacrifice with this fire, the king would attend the position of the *gandharva*-s. He took the fire and went back to the city along with the son. He placed the fire in the *araṇi* and went to his abode with his son. The fire was converted in an Aśvattha tree. The *gandharva*-s asked him to make use of the *araṇi* from that tree. The king churned and prepared three fires and performed sacrifices and attained heaven. Originally, there was only one fire, the three fires are fashioned out by Purūravas (Uttara. Anu. 29)[285]. The *Brahmāṇḍa Pu* also mentions this myth (I. 1.164-171).

### Purūravas was Slain by the Sages of Naimiṣa

The creator of the universe desirous of creating the universe, performed the holy *sattra* for thousand years. In the *sattra*,

Tapas was the householder, i.e. the sacrificer. Lord Brahmā assumed the office of the Brahman priest. Ilā assumed the position of the consort of the sacrificer. Mṛtyu performed the Śṛmitra rite. The sages performed the sacrifice for a thousand years in the place where the rim of the revolving Dharma *cakra* was shattered. Since, the sages performed the sacrifice at Naimiṣa, they were called Naimiṣeya-s. It was while the valiant King Purūravas was ruling over the earth that the sages performed the *sattra* for twelve years. He desired to perform sacrifice along with the celestial damsel Urvaśī. Viśvakarman made the sacrificial hall of gold for the sages. Seeing the hall, the king became greedy and he tried to seize it. This enraged the Naimiṣeya-s and they killed the king with Kuśa grass. Āyu became the king after the death of Purūravas. The Naimiṣeya-s resumed the performance of the *sattra*. The *sattra* was the place for discussions. Those who were well-versed in the philosophy of the *mantra*-s argued with one another. Some disputant overcame their adversaries by fallacious arguments. On this occasion the sages requested the God Vāyu to describe the various dynasties of kings. Thus the Purāṇa is narrated on a sacrificial background (*Vāyu. Pu.* Ch. 2).

According to the *Vāyu. Pu,* in the Tretā age, sacrifice was set in vogue. When there was plenty of rain the plants grew and agriculture became established. People set about building houses, hermitages and cities. Then Indra arranged the division of castes and stages of life and compiled *mantra*-s into Saṁhitā-s. He prescribed specific *mantra*-s for rites leading to fruits here, i.e. on this earth, and in the higher world. Indra along with the gods initiated sacrifice with all its procedures. When the Aśvamedha was instituted, the sages arrived there and began to perform sacrifices with the holy sacrificial beasts. On hearing about it, people assembled there to witness it. All the *ṛtvij*-s along with the Adhvaryu-s and Hotṛ-s performed their functions. When the animals were about to be sacrificed, the sages questioned Indra about this sacrifice. They said that animal-slaughter is not a desirable act. Violence can never be *dharma.* They recommended sacrifice without any violence. Seeds which were kept for the maximum period of three years and which did not germinate into sprouts should be offered in the sacrifice. There was a dispute regarding this for a long time. They decided to seek the advice of Vasu, the son of Uttānapāda. He said (with pondering over the strong and the weak points comments the Purāṇa) that sacrifice should be performed as laid down in the texts. It should be performed with sacrificial animals or seeds and fruits. Killing living beings (used as offerings) is the nature of sacrifice. This angered the sages and they cursed Vasu to attain the nether regions. Sacrifice consists of piety and *mantra*-s; *tapas* is of the nature of observance of fast; one attains gods through sacrifice and detachment through penance. Sacrifice can never excel penance. This was set in vogue in the Svāyambhuva Manvantara (Ch. 57).

## MYTH OF SLAYING VṚTRA

According to the *Brahmavai. Pu,* Tvaṣṭṛ,the father of Viśvarūpa, on his death, created a demon from the sacrifice named Vṛtra(IV. 47.50-51). The *Bhāg. Pu.* says that Viśvarūpa had three heads. With one he drank Soma, with the second he drank Surā and the third he consumed food. Since the gods were his fathers he gave the offerings to them and secretly gave offerings to demons. Indra, knowing this chopped off his heads. Knowing this, Tvaṣṭṛ became furious. He gave oblations to the fire and from the

Anvāhāryapacana fire emerged Vṛtra, the enemy of Indra (VI. 9. 1 ff.). Indra killed Vṛtra, but the sin of causing the death of Vṛtra could be washed away only by worshipping Viṣṇu, through the performance of Aśvamedha sacrifice (VI. 13. 6-7).

## SACRIFICE AND KINGSHIP

Great sacrifices like the Aśvamedha and the Rājasūya were performed by kings. The *Bhāg. Pu* says that the greatness of King Parīkṣit in performing sacrifices is beyond comparison with other kings. King Śibi had also performed great sacrifices (VIII. 8. 1-2). The same text mentions about King Śaryāti, the son of Manu Vaivasvata, who performed the *sattra* of Aṅgiras. He deviced the second day of this *sattra*. *Kāt. Śr. Sū* notes that the Śrauta texts do not speak about the Āṅgirasa *sattra* but they mention about Āṅgirasa *soma*-sacrifice which is of the *ahīna* type (XXIII. 2. 3). The *Kāt. Śr. Sū* says that a fortunate person, if loses his fortune, should perform the two-day Aṅgirasa sacrifice(XXIII. 2. 5). One cannot deny the possibility that the second day of this *ahīna* type of sacrifice was deviced by King Śaryāti under the guidance of Sage Cyavana. In this sacrifice a cup of Soma was offered to the Aśvins, says the M. Pu (IX. 3. 1.ff). This led to a conflict between Cyavana and Indra.

*Pad. Pu.* (V. 14-16) narrates the episode of Cyavana. Sukanyā, the daughter of Śaryāti, one of the Manu-s, got married to the old Sage Cyavana, who was unknowingly blinded by Śaryāti's men. Aśvins, the physicians of gods, helped Cyavana regain his youth, because they were pleased with the chastity of Sukanyā. In the *soma*-sacrifice of Śaryāti, Cyavana endowed with power made the Aśvins, who did not uptill then drink Soma, have a cup of Soma. Indra, seeing the two deities, allowed to sit in the line of those who were served Soma, though they were not fit to be in the line, took his thunderbolt to kill them. But Cyavana stupefied the arm of Indra with a mere utterance of *'hum'*.

The cup of Soma for the Aśvins was devised by Cyavana not for regaining youth, but during the sacrifice of Śaryāti.

According to the *Bhav. Pu.* (I. 19.1ff), the Aśvins demanded a share in sacrifice which is very rare to the gods. Cyavana made Śaryāti perform the sacrifice. Śaryāti was reluctant to give an offering to the fire for the Aśvins as he feared Indra. There was a small fight between Indra and Cyavana and finally, a share was given to the Aśvins.

Another king whose sacrifices are mentioned is King Sagara of the Ikṣvāku dynasty[286]. In the *Pad. Pu*, the King Sagara of the Ikṣvāku dynasty destroyed the Yavana-s, Kāmboja-s, Pallava-s, Pārada-s, etc. Then, he performed the Aśvamedha. His horse, moving near the south-east ocean, was taken away near the shore and then was taken into the interior of the earth. Afterwards, through his sons he got that region dug up everywhere. They could not find the horse in the great ocean. He obtained the horse from the ocean and later on performed hundred Aśvamedha sacrifices (VI. 20. 1-42). *Vāyu Pu.* also refers to Sagara who performed hundred Aśvamedha sacrifices (Uttara. Anu. 26. 151). This myth also occurs in the *Nār. Pu* (I. 8. 74-75) as well as the *Bhāg. Pu* (IX.8. 8).

In the *Pad. Pu* IV. 12, there was a king named Dīnānātha, who was childless. He approached Sage Gālava, who advised him to perform a Naramedha. For Naramedha one requires a man having a handsome body, charming face and who should be proficient in sacred texts. He, who is crippled, has a black complexion, is a fool would not be fit for sacrifice. In a place known as Daśapura, there was a *brāhmaṇa* named Kṛṣṇadvija with three sons. He was an ardent devotee of Viṣṇu. The messengers of the king asked Kṛṣṇadvija to hand over one of his sons to them. The *brāhmaṇa* refused to part with their eldest one and his wife refused to give the youngest one to them. The middle one went with the messengers. On the way they went to the hermitage of Sage Viśvāmitra. On hearing the account from the messengers, the sage asked himself to be replaced for the child. On hearing that Sage Viśvāmitra was ready to get himself replaced for the boy, the king said that he was willing to release the boy, if he would get a son without a sacrificial victim. The sacrifice without any victim was performed by the king. The boy was handed over to his father by the Sage Viśvāmitra.

It is to be noted that some of the account of the story corresponds with that of the Śunaḥśepa legend.

## FEUD BETWEEN THE PRIEST/S AND KING

The *Mat. Pu.* records a strife between Vaiśampāyana and Yājñavalkya. When Janamejaya favoured Sage Yājñavalkya and appointed him as the Brahman of the sacrifice, Vaiśampāyana cursed him that the innovations introduced by Yājñavalkya will not be respected. They would be honoured as long as he remained on the earth. Seeing the victory of the *kṣatriya*-s, the subjects flocked round the king Janamejaya. From that time the priests officiating at the sacrifices performed by the *kṣatriya*-s declined and refused to attend on the occasions of their sacrifices. When, after finishing the sacrifice of Prajāpati, on a full moon day, Janamejaya was entering the hall of the sacrifice, he was prevented from doing so by Vaiśampāyana, but the former did not pay any heed to him. On the contrary, Janamejaya performed two Aśvamedha sacrifices and then resorted to the forest. Janamejaya, the son of Parīksit, established the Vājaseneyika *brāhmaṇa*-s. This infuriated Vaiśampāyana and Janamejaya had to face many hardships. He worshipped Prajāpati through the offerings during the Paurṇamāsa sacrifice. He performed the Aśvamedha two times. Thereafter, he made the *brāhmaṇa*-s function for the performance of the sacrifice. Then Janamejaya was crippled thrice. He was known as Trikharvin. Śatānīka was crowned after Janamejaya. Aśvamedhadatta was the son of Śatānīka. The sages were performing the Dīrghasattra, when Adhīṣamarṣaṇa, the son of Aśvamedhadatta was the crowned king (L. 58-67 & cf. *Vāyu. Pu* Uttara. Anu. 37. 246-55).

*Brahmavai. Pu* (II. 45. 110) refers to the sacrifice performed by Janamejaya. Rambhā, an *apsaras*, was sporting with Nalakūbera, the son of Kubera. She was cursed by sage Devala that she would be the wife of Janamejaya named Subhagā. One day Subhagā was tending the horse used for the Aśvamedha of Janamejaya. She wandered along with the horse and was touched by Indra. Feeling ashamed of this act, she gave up her life and attained the original position of an *apsaras* (IV. 14. 46-54). King Janamejaya harassed Akrūra, the son of Garga. The above references associate Janamejaya with two sacrifices, namely the serpent sacrifice and secondly the Aśvamedha sacrifice. It is to be noted that the Aśvamedha sacrifice was performed by Janamejaya as an expiation either to cure a body ailment or to eradicate the sin of *brahmahatyā*. The king is also associated with a feud between Vaiśampāyana and Yājñavalkya. Here the king has supported Yājñavalkya. He was a king who was supportive to the Vedic sacrifice but also appreciated changes made in it.

Pertaining to the feud between the king and the priest on the background of sacrifice, there is another example of

King Sudās and his preceptor Sage Vasiṣṭha in the *Nār. Pu.* The son of King Sudās had killed the wife of a demon mistaking her to be a tigress. The demon threatened to avenge the death of his beloved wife. The king began to perform the horse sacrifice, under the guidance of Sage Vasiṣṭha. After the *avabhṛtha* bath was taken, the demon arrived there in the guise of Vasiṣṭha and declared that he wanted to have food in the palace of the king and desired to eat meat. The demon then took the form of a cook and cooked human flesh and gave it to the king. The king modestly offered it to the sage, who was enraged to see forbidden food served to him. He cursed the king to become a demon eating flesh (I. 9.15-30). He became the demon Kalmāṣapāda.

According to the *Vām Pu,* King Gaya had performed great sacrifices at Gayā on the banks of the river Mahānadī. He had performed Aśvamedha a hundred times, human sacrifice a hundred times and the Rājasūya a thousand times by giving lot of wealth in charity. He had performed the Aśvamedha, which was difficult to perform by gods as well as the demons. Viṣṇu has resided at this place. Those who take a bath at this place and give *tarpaṇa* to the Pitṛ-s, reap the fruits of the Great sacrifice, namely the Aśvamedha (50. 14-17). This highlights the importance of sacrifice for a king. It is because of the sacrifices performed by this king that the place became famous by his name. It also stresses that the Aśvamedha sacrifice was very difficult to be performed by celestial beings and even demons. But this king successfully completed these sacrifices many times.

According to the *Pad. Pu.,* King Kārtavīrya performed great sacrifices with his thousand arms. The sacrifices were well attended by gods. The earth was strewn with golden sacrificial posts and altars (I. 12. 110-112). This example has an element of exaggeration in it because the sacrificial posts are not made up of gold but they are made up of wood from different types of trees like Bilva, Khadira, Palāśa, etc. As mentioned earlier, this king is associated with the sacrifice in another context. Abducting the Agnihotra cow of Jamadagni by Kārtavīrya Arjuna was the root cause of the great genocide of the *kṣatriya*-s undertaken by Paraśurāma.

According to the *Vāyu Pu.*, Śaśabindu performed many Aśvamedha sacrifices (Pūrva. Upo. 32. 50). According to the *Mat. Pu.*, Suyajña, the descendant of Śaśabindu performed the Aśvamedha sacrifice. The descendant of King Marutta, Rukmakavaca, performed the Aśvamedha sacrifice (XLIV. 19-27). King Babhru, the descendant of Devavṛddha, performed a number of sacrifices. Nandanodaradundhubhi was his descendant. He performed the Aśvamedha sacrifice for progeny (XLIV. 57-65).

According to the *Liṅga Pu*, king Kuśaṅku performed great sacrifices for progeny. He got a son named Citraratha. Śaśabindu, the son of Citraratha, performed great sacrifices. He had twenty thousand sons out of whom Anantaka was very famous. His son was Yajña. Uśanas, his grandson, performed hundred Aśvamedha sacrifices. His son Sitāśu was the father of Marutta, a saintly king. His son was Kambalabarhis, whose son Rukmakavaca gave land to the *ṛtvij*-s in the Aśvamedha sacrifice (I. 68. 24-31). The *Liṅga Pu* mentions that, King Ambarīṣa performed great sacrifices like the Vājapeya and the Rājasūya in worship of Viṣṇu (II. 5. 48).

The *Pad. Pu.* gives a list of kings like Ṛtavīrya, Śantanu, Bharata, Yuvanāśva and also kings like Kārtavīrya, after having performed various sacrifices are rejoicing in the heaven (II. 64. 43).

According to the *Vāyu. Pu* the King Bharata had three sons. He felt that none among them is capable of ruling the earth. Then, the son of Bṛhaspati, Bharadvāja by name was handed over to the King Bharata by the Marut-s during a sacrifice (Uttara. Anu. 37. 135). Akrūra, the son of Gādhi performed great sacrifices with food and wealth as *dakṣiṇā*. This sacrifice became famous as the Akrūra Yajña(Uttara. Anu. 34. 82). Punarvasu, the son of Abhijit, had performed an Aśvamedha sacrifice for the sake of the son. In the course of that sacrifice, while the rites of Atirātra were being performed, a son was born admist the assembly (Uttara. Anu. 34. 118-19).

Reference to the fall of Marutta family: The *Bhāg. Pu* mentions the story of Diṣṭa's son Nābhāga, the ancestor of Marutta, who was degraded as *vaiśya* because of his profession (IX. 2. 23.ff). Greatness of the sacrifice of Marutta is mentioned in *Kū. Pu.* (IV. 1.17-34). In the sacrifice of Marutta, Indra rejoiced in consuming Soma. Everything became of gold in his sacrifice. The Marut-s played the role of waiters/encircled the sacrificial place of Marutta. A point to be noted is that the Purāṇa says that Nābhāga the ancestor of Marutta attained the position of a *vaiśya*. Nābhāga, the ancestor of King Marutta, fell in love with a *vaiśya* maiden. When his father realized this, he sought the advice of the sages, who suggested that Nābhāga could marry her provided he married a *kṣatriya* maiden earlier. Spurning the advice of the sages, Nābhāga married the *vaiśya* maiden. This angered King Karuṣa, who tried to overcome the prince by force. But he was thwarted by Lord Brahmā saying that Nābhāga had already degenerated to the position of *vaiśya*. Bhanandana, the son of Nābhāga, conquered the earth with the help of Sage Nīpa. However, Nābhāga himself, was denied to be the king as he had become a *vaiśya*. His wife Suprabhā told that she was *kṣatriya* by birth but had become a *vaiśya* since her father was cursed so. King Praṁśu and King Viviṁśa of the dynasty of Marutta also performed great sacrifices. Khaninetra, the ancestor of Marutta, was sonless. He went for hunting for a deer, in order to perform a sacrifice for the Pitṛ-s. He confronted with two deer in the forest one which had sons and the other which was sonless. The entire dialogue between the deer and the king is directed towards performing sacrifice without animal offerings (CXX). Marutta performed great sacrifices. Saṁvarta, the brother of Bṛhaspati, was his chief officiating priest. The sages said, "Equal to Marutta never lived a sacrificer on the face of the earth, at whose sacrifice his dwelling-house was cast and also golden palaces as large, Indra was made intoxicated with Soma and twice-born were given gifts. Indra and the Viśvedeva-s became waiters." Nariṣyanta, the son of King Marutta also performed great sacrifices. The entire account of the dynasty of Marutta is in the *Mārk. Pu* (CXIII-CXXXVII). The *Vāyu. Pu* refers to King Marutta, the son of Antara, who followed in the footsteps of the pious kings (Uttara. Anu. 32. 24). His son was Kambalabarhis.

According to *Varāha Pu*, Sage Tṛṇabindu had two sons: Jaya and Vijaya by name. They were invited by the King Marutta for his sacrifice. At the end of the sacrifice, they were given sumptuous. They had a fight over the *dakṣiṇā*-s and each cursed the other, one to become a crocodile (Jaya) and the other to become an elephant (Vijaya). After thousands of years they have a fight and by the grace of Viṣṇu they are freed from the curse (144. 133-56).

## SACRIFICE AND CHANGE IN RELIGION

The changing trends in Vedic religion have shown rise and fall of certain godheads. In the Puranic religion one sees the worship of Viṣṇu and Śiva as the two prominent trends. The M. Pu-s which preach the worship of Viṣṇu, associate the performance of sacrifice with obtaining the grace of Lord Viṣṇu. Sacrifice is regarded as an offering to Lord Viṣṇu. Śaivite Purāṇa-s do at times associate devotion of Śiva with sacrifice, but these references are very scanty.

Apart from these two prominent godheads, there is a minor reference of how the M. Pu-s show one deity being replaced by the other.

### Episode of Sāvitrī Getting Angry and Being Replaced by Gāyatrī Occurs in the *Pad. Pu*

Contents in brief: Lord Brahmā began to perform a sacrifice. At the time of consecration, Sāvitrī, the wife of Lord Brahmā, was asked to be present immediately. However, since her presence was delayed, Indra searched for another maiden to be the wife of Lord Brahmā. While wandering on the earth, he saw a cowherd maiden. Being impressed by her beauty, he seated her next to Lord Brahmā. This angered Sāvitrī, who pronounced curses on those who were present in the sacrifice. Rudra was present in the sacrifice in a very censurable form. He had kept the skull in the sacrificial place. The *brāhmaṇa*-s tried to object him. When Rudra showed his prowess, they accepted his greatness. This episode also narrates the importance of various *tīrtha*-s.

#### *Influence of Vedic Sacrifice on this Episode*

a) The position of wife was very important. Without her presence, the sacrifice was not accomplished.
b) Bhāgu was the Hotṛ, Pulastya was the Adhvaryu, Marīci was the Udgātṛ and Nārada was the Brahman.
c) Head of Lord Brahmā was shaved. Gāyatrī, who was consecrated along with Lord Brahmā, was holding the

deer's horn. This is an incorrect detail. It is the sacrificer, who holds the deer-horn. Lord Brahmā had the Audumbara staff in his hand and was covered with deer-hide. A girdle was tied around the waist of Gāyatrī.

d) Without the skull (*kapāla*), *puroḍāśa* cannot be prepared. As a mark of reverence to Rudra, *puroḍāśa* is prepared on potsherds. There appears to be a phonetic identity with the word *kapāla*. *Puroḍāśa* is prepared on *kapāla*-s. The episode of Rudra placing the skull (*kapāla*) in the sacrifice indicates his assimilation in the Vedic sacrificial institution.

e) There are references to rituals like the Pravargya.

f) Sacrifice was the occasion to discuss various branches of learning. The etymology of the words were discussed, pronunciations were discussed by those present in the sacrifice (I. 16-17).

## CONCLUSION

Sacrifices are merely mentioned in the M. Pu-s, devoid of any details. Therefore, it is difficult to compare them with the Vedic sacrifice documented in the Saṁhitā-s, Brāhmaṇa-s and the Śrautasūtra-s. The awe of the Aśvamedha and Rājasūya did not face any decline. Sovereignty of a king was measured in terms of the Aśvamedha-s and Rājasūya-s performed by him.

The Vedic sacrifice lost its rigidity and became simpler during the composition of the M. Pu-s. As seen earlier the M. Pu-s state the reason that the performance of the sacrifice is difficult for the poor. Therefore these texts have always made a deliberate attempt to give alternatives to the Vedic sacrifice in the form of giving importance to the recitation of the M. Pu-s, highlighting the importance of Bhakti, stressing on undertaking visits to holy places or practising vows. The M. Pu-s have never hesitated to reduce the importance of Vedic sacrifice as against the abovementioned alternatives. The reason given by many a scholar is that driven by the sway of Buddhism and Jainism, the M. Pu-s had a task of upholding the principles of Vedic religion. They identified the drawback of Vedic religion, which was rigid and cumbersome sacrifice which kept an eye on material gain. Ultimately, to uphold the Vedic religion the M. Pu-s had to forego the details or bypass the 'Vedic sacrifice' in due course of time. Yet the awe and reverence to the Vedic sacrifice did not perish. Sacrifice was always used as a parameter of comparison, for the effectiveness of any alternative was compared with the effectiveness or greatness of the Vedic sacrifice.

# 5

# Classical Sanskrit Dramas and Mahākāvya-s

The literature taken up for study earlier was predominantly religious in nature. Classical literature is secular in nature. The dictionary meaning of the term 'classical':

a) Of the first rank or authority constituting a standard or model; especially in literature.

b) Designating the language, art or culture of a period deemed to represent the most perfect flowering of the civilization that produced it.[287]

Yet, it is essential to take up this section of Sanskrit literature because it can give us a clear idea of the position of Vedic sacrifice prevailing in the society as well as in the mind of the learned ornate poet/dramatist. Though the Sanskrit language is a vast storehouse of classical literary works in prose, poetry and drama, the study here restricts itself to dramas and Mahākāvya-s.

## SECTION I: CLASSICAL SANSKRIT DRAMA

According to Winternitz, 'the most valuable testimony of court ornate poetry is the drama. And when the Indian poeticians say that drama is the best type of poetical composition, we should probably insert into their statement that it is the best for the reason that in it other types of poetical compositions too are included and epic, lyric and imitative representations of life are united into a single artistic whole.'[288] Moreover, the drama has to be the reflection of customs, practices and beliefs in the society[289]. Most of the plots of the dramas were based on the Vedic and Epic literature in which sacrifice was a prevailing practice. It is interesting to observe the extent to which the sacrifice is retained and at the same time the changes made in the same.

### PLAYS OF BHĀSA

The thirteen plays of Bhāsa known as *Bhāsanāṭakacakram* serve as storehouse of references pertaining to the Vedic sacrifice[290]. The date of Bhāsa can be placed through internal and external evidences, jointly in between 5th or 4th century BC.[291]

#### *Ūrubhaṅga*

The *Ūrubhaṅga* abounds in figurative descriptions of the Vedic sacrifice. It describes the battle as a sacrifice, i.e. *raṇayajña* (Urubhaṅga I. verse 4). The details of this allegory are discussed earlier. Duryodhana takes pride in describing himself as one who performed the coveted sacrifices as prescribed by the Veda-s (*Ibid.*, I. verse 52). The *Ūrubhaṅga* describes golden sacrificial posts, i.e. *yūpa*-s (Act I. verse 56). This should be understood as an element of exaggeration. The play also makes a passing reference to the Aśvamedha sacrifice and the conducting priest, namely Adhvaryu (*Ibid*. I. 55). The *Ūrubhaṅga* abounds in references to the Vedic sacrifice, however they are metaphorical.

### *Karṇabhāra*

The *Karṇabhāra* refers to the fruit of the Agniṣṭoma sacrifice. Śakra had appeared before Karṇa in the form of a *brāhmaṇa* and asked for great alms (*bhikṣā*). Karṇa said that he would give the fruit of Agniṣṭoma sacrifice (*Karṇabhāra* Act. I). This indicates that the fruit of a sacrifice can be transferred to someone else or given in charity. The *Karṇabhāra* also refers to Indra being satisfied by oblations offered by *brāhmaṇa*-s (*Ibid*. Act. I. 23).

### *Dūtaghaṭotkaca*

The *Dūtaghaṭotkaca* refers to the Pañcāgni-s, i.e. the five fires, viz. Āhavanīya, Gārhapatya Dakṣiṇa, Sabhya and Āvasathya (*Dūtaghaṭotkaca*: Act I. 6). This reference is also metaphorical. However, this metaphor indicates the awareness of not only the three fires but also five. The reference to the five fires occurs in the *Tait. Br.* [292]

### *Madhyamavyāyoga*

The *Madhyamavyāyoga* mentions a sacrifice named Śatakumbha (Act I). The *brāhmaṇa* family had gone to the hermitage of Sage Dhaumya to attend this sacrifice. The Vedic sacrificial texts do not mention any sacrifice of this name. There is a possibility that this is a reference to some Gṛhya rite performed at the time of Bhāsa.

### *Pañcarātra*

The *Pañcarātra* refers to the participation of kings in the sacrifice of Duryodhana along with their harem (*Pañcarātra*:

Act I.3). Duryodhana had performed this sacrifice with great pomp. The *brāhmaṇa*-s, those from the first three *varṇa*-s were given feasts; the flame of the sacrificial fire as if stole the fragrance of the flowers of the trees. The sacrifice of Duryodhana contented the entire world. The sacrifice had golden *yūpa*-s. The *caityāgni* was placed. The smoke arising out of the sacrificial fire entered the Prāgvamśa. The Prāgvamśa is the pendal in which Soma is kept during a *soma* sacrifice. Prāgvamśa or Prācīnavaṁśa is the chamber of fires at the Darśapūrṇamāsa sacrifice, in line with the set symbolism of facing the east (cf. *RV* X. 101. 2 *prāñcam yajñam pra nayatā sakhāyaḥ*)[293]. The bamboos sheltering the pandal are pointed eastwards; hence this structure is called Prāgvamśa(*Ibid.* Act I.6). It is significant to note that this sacrifice changed the mindset of Duryodhana (*Ibid.* Act I.23). He became very peaceful and rejoiced in getting the blessings from the elders. The drama has also referred to the *avabhṛtha* bath, which is taken at the end of the sacrifice. Karṇa has enumerated a list of kings, who were immortalized by the performance of sacrifices[294]. This list has been discussed in the chapter of the *Mbh.* However, the *Pañcarātra* does not mention the name of the sacrifice performed by Duryodhana. Since, the play is based on the *Mbh* one can conclude that this seems to be the Vaiṣṇava sacrifice performed by Duryodhana (*Mbh.* Vana. P 241. 22 ff.).

### *Avimāraka*

The *Avimāraka* refers to the performance of sacrifice, the name of which is not mentioned. The maidservant in the play expresses surprise over the absence of king Kāśirāja in the sacrifice (*Avimāraka*Act VI). It seems that since sacrifice was a social gathering, absence of any king/invitee was a matter of concern.

### *Pratimānāṭaka*

The *Pratimānāṭaka* refers to the items used for the coronation of a king, viz. umbrella, chowries, drum, Bhadrāsana, golden pots filled with *darbha* grass, flowers and waters from the holy places, chariot, ministers, subjects and the royal priest (here it is sage Vasiṣṭha) (*Pratimānāṭaka*: Act I. 3). The play records a strange practice that women can be viewed at the time of sacrifice, marriage, and calamity and in the forest[295]. Sumantra, the minister of Dasaratha, has described Aja as a performer of great sacrifices (Act IV.2). Lakṣmaṇa blessed Bharata to be like Raghu who gave rich donations during sacrifices.

Out of the thirteen plays of Bhāsa, Vedic sacrifice is reflected only in eight. The references to the Vedic sacrifice abound in the *Mbh* plays. The sacrifice performed by Duryodhana, in the *Pañcarātra* has served as a background for the play. The Udayana-plays hardly mention anything of the Vedic sacrifice. This non-mention indicates the historical decline in the performance of sacrifices by kings, leading to the loosening of the bond between sacrifice and kingship. The *Pratijñāyaugandharāyaṇa* has mentioned about a sacrifice, which falls in the category of the Pākasaṁsthā-s named Nīrājanāvidhi, i.e. circumambulating the horse. This ritual is performed during the Āśvayujī ceremony (Act. I.12).

The references to Vedic sacrifice reflect the pomp and fervour of the sacrifice; however no ritual details are mentioned. Moreover, the references abound in metaphors and exaggerations. This indicates that the Vedic sacrifice was declining at the time period of Bhāsa.

## Plays of Kālidāsa

Classical Sanskrit epics and Mahākāvya-s attained glory during the Gupta period. The great poet Kālidāsa flourished during this regime. He was patronized by King Chandragupta II, who bore the epithet Vikramāditya. The period of his regime is approximately extending 375–413 AD; hence the period of Kālidāsa is placed in between 350 AD and 472 AD[296]. The great poet-dramatist has authored three plays.

### *Mālavikāgnimitra*

This play is the story of Mālavikā, the princess of Malwa and King Agnimitra of the Śuṅga dynasty. The first act of this play compares the dramatic art to an agreeable sacrificial feast to the eyes of gods (Act I. v. 4). The play records a historical fact of the Aśvamedha sacrifice performed by King Puṣyamitra Śuṅga. However, the play mentions him as commander-in-chief Puṣpamitra[297]. It praises the bravery of Vasumitra, the son of Agnimitra, who protected the sacrificial horse and defeated the Yavana-s (*Ibid.* Act. V Praveśaka & Act. V. 15). The text has slightly modified the name Puṣyamitra to Puṣpamitra[298]. The play casts light on the historical fact of King Puṣyamitra of the Śuṅga dynasty performing this great sacrifice twice. He performed the Aśvamedha after defeating the Yavana-s and the Vaidarbha-s[299]. The modification of the name and the reference to Puṣyamitra as a commander-in-chief indicate that the time lapsed between Kālidāsa and the two kings, viz. Puṣyamitra and Agnimitra. However, Kālidāsa considers the Aśvamedha as a mark of glory. This indicates that he was patronized by the Gupta kings.

### *Vikramorvaśīya*[300]

This play is the story of King Purūravas and the celestial nymph Urvaśī. The plot can be traced up to the *Śat. Br* which narrates attempt made by the lovelorn Purūravas to become a *gandharva* in order to reunite with his lost beloved

Urvaśī, an *apsaras* (XI. 5. 1.1ff). The myth of Purūravas and Urvaśī as mentioned in the *Śat. Br* has its source in the dialogue hymn of the *RV* (X. 95). The attempt was in the form of a sacrifice. It was through this attempt that he introduced the performance of sacrifice using three fires[301]. Though the original story gives significance to the sacrifice, however, this significance seems to have been lost in the play. The play carries scanty references to the Vedic sacrifice in the form of *sattra* performed by sages of the Naimiṣa forest as well as the collection of sacrificial twigs (*Vikramorvaśīya* Act. V).

*Abhijñānaśākuntala*[302]

In the benediction of this play, Kālidāsa refers to the eight visible forms of creation, out of which one form is the sacrifice and its oblations and another one is the sacrificer himself (Act. I. Prelude). There are references to the preparations of the sacrifice in the form of collection of twigs (*Ibid.* Act. I. p. 18). The sages in the hermitage of Kaṇva performed certain *iṣṭi*-s. On a requisition made by the sages to protect the *iṣṭi*, the king replied that the Paurava dynasty to which he belonged to was ordained to officiate in the sacrifice by giving protection to the timid. Various sacrificial rituals like covering the altar (*vedisaṁstaraṇa*), pressing of Soma (*savana*) are mentioned (*Ibid.* Act III (interlude) & v. 25)[303]. The time span of the stay of King Duṣyanta in hermitage depended on the duration of the sacrifice (*Ibid.* Act IV p. 120). However, the context mentions an *iṣṭi*, i.e. one- day sacrifice. How could the king stay for a considerable time when an *iṣṭi* was performed? This indicates that series of *iṣṭi*-s were performed and the king stayed over to protect the *iṣṭi*-s. The text records a practice, which was prevalent at the time of Kālidāsa. This practice is of circumambulating the sacrificial fires (*Ibid.* Act IV p. 140). This action might be a token of reverence to the sacrifice performed. The plural term for fires used in this reference indicates the presence of three fires and not one. It means that the sacrifice was essentially 'Vedic' in nature. The benediction uttered by the Sage Kaṇva, the foster father of Śakuntalā, when she was about to leave her maternal home to meet her husband, has an interesting sacrificial reference (*Ibid.* Act IV v.8). The reference mentions the seats of the sacrificial fires, i.e. *dhiṣṇya*-s, having their places around the altar. It is noteworthy that the sage utters this benediction in the style of Vedic chanting. This indicates that Kālidāsa wanted to authenticate the sanctity of the benediction. However, the mention of these seats surrounding the sacrificial altar is incorrect. *Dhiṣṇya*-s are small fire-hearths. Eight in number raised for the Soma priests, viz. Hotrīyā, Āgnidhrīyā, Praśastrīyī and for the Brāhmaṇācchamśin, Potṛ, Neṣṭṛ, Açchāvāka (7 priests) and last for Mārjālīya. Of these, six are situated with the *sadas*, four to the north of the Pṛṣṭhya, the Hotrīyā on the Pṛṣṭhya in front of the eastern door of the *sadas* and the Praśāstrīya to the south of the Pṛṣṭhya. The Āgnīdhrīya and the Mārjālīya are situated to the north and the south of the Havirdhāna respectively. Fire is installed on them, and oblation can be offered on the Āgnīdhrīya[304]. This reference indicates that the original ritual seems to have been forgotten since the *dhiṣṇya*-s do not surround the sacrificial altar. This also indicates that the *soma*-sacrifices became more and more obsolete at the time of Kālidāsa. Another reference which leads to the similar conclusion occurs in the Prelude (Praveśaka) of the sixth act (*Ibid.* Act VI. v. 1). A verse in the Prelude states that a duty which is assigned to a person from birth, though condemned by others need not be given up. This premise is further strengthened with an illustration of a learned *brāhmaṇa*, who becomes cruel while discharging his duty of killing a sacrificial victim is in fact compassionate in nature. The thought reflected in this verse is that of the function of Śamitṛ, who 'pacified' animals during the performance of Vedic sacrifices. However, this function was not marked as an action of cruelty. The sacrificial animal was not slaughtered, but smothered and then pacified. The verse indicates the changed trend in the sacrifice for it highlights bloodshed (which is essentially non -Vedic) and secondly considers animal offered during sacrifice as a mark of cruelty. The blood was the share given to the evil spirits or *asura*-s and was not offered to gods. So the reference again harps the same tune of sacrifices becoming more and more obsolete at the time of Kālidāsa. The same act mentions the effort of gods for reuniting Śakuntalā with Duṣyanta because gods have a longing for a share of sacrificial offerings. The couple has to unite in order to perform sacrifices. The oblation and the *mantra*-s chanted during a sacrifice give strength to the gods[305]. Moreover, the reference is a reflection of the give -and –takes relation between the gods and human beings through the medium of sacrifice[306]. The sacrifice mentioned in the *Abhijñānaśākuntala* is the one performed by the sages in the forest and not the one performed in the capital by a king with pomp and fervour. The sacrifice is the form of *iṣṭi*-s, which are economical and can be performed with materials available in the forest. The *Abhijñānaśākuntala* has reflected a very peculiar nature of Vedic sacrifice.

## Plays of Bhavabhūti

Bhavabūti is revered as a dramatist, next to Kālidāsa. Compared to other dramatists and poets, who are silent about their life-history, Bhavabhūti has mentioned some details about his own self. He lived in the court of King Yaśovarman of Kanauj in the first of the 8th century AD[307].

All his plays were staged at the festival of the god, Kālapriyanātha.

### *Mālatīmādhava*[308]

The Prologue of the *Mālatīmādhava* refers to the family background of Bhavabhūti that he hails from the race of Kaśyapa. His forefathers have worshipped the five fires and have partaken of Soma, i.e. performed the *soma-* sacrifices (*Ibid.* Act. I. Prologue).

### *Mahāvīracarita*

The *Mahāvīracarita* refers to the birth of Sītā, who emerged from the sacrificial ground when it was ploughed (*Mahāvīracaritam* Act I.vv.15, 20). The text describes the closing of the sacrifice of Viśvāmitra and the attack of the Rākṣasa-s for creating an obstacle in it. This indicates the hostility of the Rākṣasa-s towards the sacrifice. The arrival of Paraśurāma is described by Rāma, as one who gave land to sage Kaśyapa in an Aśvamedha sacrifice (*Ibid.* Act II. v. 19). It is to be noted that the text refers a similar mention in the *Mbh* (Śan. P 49. 57). However, an Aśvamedha is not performed by a *brāhmaṇa*, but by a *kṣatriya* king. How could Paraśurāma perform such a sacrifice? The explanation can be given as follows: Since Paraśurāma had wiped out the race of *kṣatriya*-s twenty-one times, he has been regarded as sovereign by the dramatist. Therefore, Paraśurāma has been credited with the performance of Aśvamedha by Bhavabhūti. The text refers to the causes of the genocide carried out by Paraśurāma; one among them is the killing of the *brāhmaṇa*-s, who were performing *savana*-s, i.e. *soma*-pressings (*Mahāvīracaritam* Act III. v. 19). Paraśurāma made a striking remark about his *paraśu*, i.e. an axe, that it was used for the sake of the destruction of the *kṣatriya*-s and not used as an *idhmavraścana*, i.e. for the sake of cutting the *samidh*-s, used in the sacrifice (*Ibid.* Act III. v. 14)[309]. The lustre of Sage Āṅgiras is compared to the fire nurtured by the giving an offering of speckled clarified butter. The ritual mentioned over here is the *abhighāraṇa* ritual, which means the two pourings of clarified butter below and above the cuttings in the *juhū*, i.e. the sacrificial ladle used for offering clarified butter in the fire (*Ibid.* Act III. p. 106). The *juhū* is made up of wood from the Palāśa tree[310]. The same act refers to the distribution of thousand cows in the sacrifice of Janaka (*Ibid.* Act III.v. 30). The birth of Rāma is described as caused due to the *yājyā*-s chanted in a sacrifice (*Ibid.* Act III v. 47). The fourth act also throws light on the hostility of the Rākṣasa-s towards the institution of sacrifice. It refers to the Rākṣasa-s, viz. Virādha, Danuka and Kabandha, who caused trouble during the *sattra*-s performed in the Daṇḍākaraṇya. The draughts used for consuming Soma, the smell emerging out of clarified butter offered in the fire, the sacrificial faggots strewn around serve as an indication of proximity to the hermitage of Sage Mātaṅga (*Ibid.* Act. Act. V p. 174).

### UTTARARĀMACARITA[311]

The *Uttararāmacarita* refers to the Sage Ṛśyaśṛṅga as one who is a habitual drinker of Soma (*somapīthin*). Ṛśyaśṛṅga had performed a twelve year long *sattra*, i.e. Dvādaśavārṣikasattra and Kausalyā and others (Vasiṣṭha and Arundhatī) were present on this occasion (*Ibid.* Act I. v. 3). However, Janaka, the father of Sītā, had to leave Ayodhyā for Videha because extending the stay in Ayodhyā would mean discontinuing daily sacrifices (*Ibid.* Act. I v. 8). This was not permissible for Janaka since he was an Āhitāgni. This indicates that *sattra*-s were also regarded as festive occasions. The text also refers to the sacrificial procedure of releasing the horse during the Aśvamedha sacrifice (*Ibid.* Act. II p. 53). This sacrifice was performed by Rāma and Candraketu, the son of Lakṣmaṇa was appointed as a guardian to protect the sacrificial horse. The horse was released by Vāmadeva, a sage. Bhavabhūti also refers to the sacrifice of Sagara and the efforts undertaken by Bhagīratha to bring down the river Gaṅgā from the heaven (*Ibid.* Act. I v. 23). The memory of this myth was still alive during the time of Bhavabhūti.

The reflection of Vedic sacrifice in the dramas of Bhavabhūti can be analyzed on two levels.

a) Do these abovementioned references indicate the existence of sacrifice during the time of Bhavabhūti?

b) Do these references indicate that the dramatist had taken into account the Vedic sacrifice existing at the time of *Rām*?

Point no. (b) seems to be a possibility because taking into account the time of Bhavabhūti the Vedic sacrifice was in the declining state. Therefore, there are some incorrect quotations like Paraśurāma performing the Aśvamedha sacrifice. However, since, Bhavabhūti hailed from a family of *soma*-sacrificers, the usage of various sacrificial terms seems to be obvious.

### VEṆĪSAṀHĀRA OF BHAṬṬANĀRĀYAṆA

The plot of this drama is based on the *Mbh.* It starts from the envoyship of Kṛṣṇa up to the fall of Duryodhana. The period of the composition of this drama is in between 650 AD and 750 AD. The drama has only one allegorical reference to the Vedic sacrifice. This reference has been dealt with earlier.

- The other dramas, viz. the *Mṛcchakaṭika* of Śūdraka (2nd-1st BC) records only one reference of Aśvamedha sacrifice, which was performed by the dramatist, who was a king[312]. The *Mudrārākṣasa* of Viśākhadatta (500 AD) and the dramas of Śrīharṣa, viz. *Priyadarśikā, Ratnāvalī* and *Nāgānanda* (600 AD) do not have any references to the Vedic sacrifice[313].

## SECTION II: CLASSICAL SANSKRIT MAHĀKĀVYA-S I.E. EPICS

History of ornate court poetry could be dated up to the age of Pāṇini, to whom the two epics, namely *Pātālavijaya* and *Jāmbavatīvijaya* are ascribed to. The *Mahābhāṣya* of Patañjali refers to the secular lyrics composed in artistic metres and in the style of the ornate court poetry[314]. However, none of these works are available. *Saundarananda* and *Buddhacarita* of the poet-dramatist Aśvaghoṣa are regarded as the first classical Sanskrit epics. Yet these two works are not taken up for study since they are Buddhist in nature. The epics of Kālidāsa are taken up for study.

### Epics of Kālidāsa

Kālidāsa has composed two epics, viz. the *Kumārasambhava* and the *Raghuvaṁśa*[315].

#### *Kumārasambhava*

Himālaya was regarded as the source of sacrificial materials. Considering this factor, Prajāpati allocated him a share in the sacrifice (*Kumārasambhava* I. 17). Gods were regarded as the consumers of oblations (*Ibid.* XV.51). Lord Śiva was propitiated by the gods as one who is the utterance of the three syllables of Aum, personified. The utterances of these syllables results in the fruit, i.e. sacrifice. The fruit of the performance of sacrifice is heaven (*Ibid.* II.12). The Mīmāṁsaka approach towards sacrifices, i.e. performance of sacrifices, leads to heaven seems to be accepted at the time of Kālidāsa. It is the sacrifice due to which the cycle of life sustains (X.20). The utterances during sacrifices, viz. *svāhā, svadhā* and *hanta* are mentioned for gods, manes and human beings respectively (*Ibid.* X. 17).

*Raghuvaṁśa*

Kālidāsa has described the greatness of the kings of the Raghu dynasty as those who performed sacrifices (*Raghuvaṁśa* I. 6). The sages are mentioned as those who perform sacrifices and those, the fumes of smoke from whose sacrificial fires emerge from their hermitage (*Ibid.* I. 43). The practice of the preceptor maintaining the fires of the kings seems to be existent at the time of Kālidāsa (*Ibid.* II. 44). The text also refers to the *dīkṣā* (III.44) undergone by King Dilīpa. It also refers to the sacrificial horse of the Aśvamedha sacrifice being released [however, the sacrificial horse of King Dilīpa was caught by Indra (III.46)]. The *Raghuvaṁśa* refers to the Viśvajit sacrifice performed by King Raghu. It is this sacrifice during which the sacrificer distributes his entire property to the *brāhmaṇa*-s (*Ibid.* IV. 86). The greatness of the Ikṣvāku dynasty was because of performing sacrifices. The sages like Agastya acted as priests and asked the kings after their *avabhṛtha* (the concluding sacrificial bath) whether the rituals were duly performed (VI. 61). The text exaggerates the splendour of the sacrifice by describing a line of sacrificial posts made up of gold erected during sacrifices (*Ibid.* IX.20). The memory of the Aśvamedha sacrifice performed by Daśaratha for the sake of progeny in the *Rām* appears to have been lost at the time of the composition of *Raghuvaṁśa*. Rśyaśṛṅga performed the Putrakāmeṣṭi so that Daśaratha would beget an offspring. At the end of the rite, a divine form emerged from the fire to offer Daśaratha the desired fruit of the sacrifice (*Ibid.* X. 4, 19). Blood was taboo in a sacrifice.

During the sacrifice of Viśvāmitra, the Rākṣasa-s defiled the place with blood. The sages threw their ladles made up of the Vikaṅkata wood and fled away in fear (*Ibid.* XI. 25). The *Raghuvaṁśa* also mentions an aspect of the sacrificial ritual that the sacrificer should maintain silence (*Ibid.* XI. 30). The demon Lavaṇa committed atrocities on the sages by destroying their sacrifices, says the *Raghuvaṁśa* (XV. 2). The text refers to the hermitage of sage Śarabhaṅga who nurtured the three fires mentions the *Raghuvaṁśa* (XIII.45). It also refers to the Aśvamedha of Rāma. There are no details about the rituals performed, except that of an effigy of Sītā, which was created by Rāma to represent her in the sacrifice, since she was repudiated by Rāma. The absence of the wife of the sacrificer, i.e. Rāma, is compensated by her effigy. The Aśvamedha makes note of the gifts showered on Rāma by kings, Rākṣasa-s and Vānara-s and also other tributary kings (*Ibid.* XV. 58). The importance of sacrifice is accepted in the *Raghuvaṁśa* through the reference to the cosmic cycle being protected by sacrifice (*Ibid.* XVII. 80).

### *Kirātārjunīya of Bhāravi*[316]

The Aihole inscription of Pulakeśin describes Bhāravi as a renowned court poet. Bhāravi is placed before 634 AD[317]. Works on Sanskrit rhetorics regard Bhāravi as a very famous poet and his work, *Kirātārjunīya* has got a place among the five great Sanskrit classical epics. In the first canto of the *Kirātārjunīya*, Duryodhana is described as giving offerings to the fire along with his family priest. However, the verse lacks details regarding the sacrifice performed. A point to be noted is the presence of a priest during the offerings (*Kirātārjunīya* I. 22). The text also refers to the sacrifices as actions bearing fruit like the wish-fulfilling cow (*Ibid.* III.6). There are some more references to the sacrifices.

But since they are figurative they will be discussed in the next chapter.

### *Śiśupālavadha of Māgha*[318]

The great poet Māgha has modelled his epic on the *Kirātārjunīya* of Bhāravi. Though the usually accepted date of Māgha is 7th century AD, Winternitz is of the opinion that the lower inmost limit of Māgha is provided by the quotations from his poem by Vāmana (c. 800 AD) and Ānandavardhana (900 AD). In the stanza found in the *Śiśupālavadha,* he says that his grandfather Suprabhadeva was a minister of a king Varmāla, of whom an inscription of 625 AD exists. But this date and identification of the king have not been proved beyond doubt[319]. However, according to Upādhyāya, Māgha can be dated up to 7th century AD[320]. The *Śiśupālavadha* refers to the gods eating the sacrificial cake, i.e. *puroḍāśa*(Canto II.106). The term *saptatantu* refers to sacrifice (*Śiśupālavadha* XIV. 6). Mallinātha, a commentator of the *Śiśupālavadha,* is of the opinion that the term refers to the *saṁsthā*-s. However, the commentary refers to the *Amarakośa,* which accepts *saptatantu* as synonymous to sacrifice[321]. The same canto refers to the *sambhāra*-s, i.e. the items required for the sacrifice. It also refers to the offering of oblation by Śrīkṛṣṇa in the Rājasūya and then Yudhiṣṭhira would perform the concluding bath (*Ibid.* XIV. 10). This is unusual of the Rājasūya, though the text is following the *Mbh* Sabhā P. Therefore, it is to be taken as referring to the active participation of Śrīkṛṣṇa in the sacrifice. The same canto refers to the sacrifice of Yudhiṣṭhira, in which offerings were given on his behalf, by the *ṛtvij*-s. But the fruit was received by Yudhiṣṭhira (*Śiśupālavadha* XIV. 19). The text also refers to the *yājyā*-s and the *anuvākyā*-s chanted during the sacrifice (*Ibid.* XIV.

20). *Yājyā*-s are the invocation to the deity, during which the offering is given and *anuvākyā*-s are invocation to the deity in the form of invitation during the sacrifice[322]. The text indirectly refers to the function of the Udgātṛ priest who recited the chants with proper signs of hand (*Ibid.* XIV. 21). The same canto refers to the tying of the girdle (*mekhalā*) by Draupadī. The same verse refers to the *agnipraṇayana*, i.e. the lighted embers of the Gārhapatya were carried to the Āhavanīya (*Ibid.* XIV. 22).

### *Naiṣadhīyacarita of Śrīharṣa*[323]

The *Naiṣadhīyacarita* of Śrīharṣa is a story of love between King Nala and his beloved wife Damayantī. Śrīharṣa wrote this epic under the patronship of Vijayacandra and Jayacandra of Kanauj in the second half of the 12th century AD[324]. It is to be noted that considering the importance of the five great ornate epics, the sacrifice reflected in the *Naiṣadhīyacarita* has been taken up for study. The text refers to the famous myth of the deer-shaped sacrifice severed by Śiva (*Naiṣadhīyacarita* IV. 67). The Aśvins restored the head of the sacrifice. This reference points out to the myth recorded in the Brāhmaṇa texts of the head of the sacrifice being lost. This secret was told by Sage Cyavana to the Aśvins. The Aśvins told this to the gods and secured a share in the sacrifice[325]. Indra has been referred to in the *Naiṣadhīyacarita* as one performing hundred sacrifices, i.e. *śatamakhin* (V. 21). *Naiṣadhīyacarita* takes note of the doctrine of the Pūrvamīmāṁsā that gods do not exist independent of sacrificial formulas. Indra was pleased with Nala and he offered a boon that he would be present in the sacrifices performed by the couple and partake the share of oblations in a form visible to the human eye (*Ibid,* XIV. 73). In the *Naiṣadhīyacarita,* Agni is referred to as the one who is the mouth of gods, who is familiar to the taste of the sacrifices (XIV. 76). Advent of Kali in Nala's kingdom affected adversely on the sacrifices. This passage in the text refers to a number of sacrifices (XVII. 196-204). There are references to sacrifices like the Darśapūrṇamāsa, Agniṣṭoma, Aśvamedha, Mahāvrata, the sacrificer and his wife (*yajvabhāryā*). The poet has effectively used the sacrifices loosing lustre in order to heighten the intensity of the terrible effects of the advent of Kali. Considering the story of *Naiṣadhīyacarita*, which occurs in the *Mbh*, Śrīharṣa has incorporated some references to the sacrifice as an indicator of urban religious life. The myths related to the sacrifice, indicates the knowledge of the poet on this subject.

*Bhaṭṭikāvya or Rāvaṇavadha of Poet Bhaṭṭi*

The *Bhaṭṭikāvya* is a landmark composition in classical Sanskrit poetry. It is a unique composition of story based on the *Rām* and application of rules based on Paninian grammar. Bhaṭṭi flourished before AD 621[326]. The epic refers to the sacrifice of King Daśaratha for begetting sons. Sage Ṛśyaśṛṅga was the chief officiating priest. However, the work does not mention which sacrifice was performed by the king (I.10-14) Poet Bhaṭṭi has depicted the hostility of the Rākṣasa-s to the institution of sacrifice (I. 12, 17). In the forest life Rāma exercised his religious duties by performing daily sacrifices and offering to gods cooked meat. Gods are referred to as those eating lumps of meat offered to them during sacrifices. It also refers to the sacrificial beast killed by the priest (IV. 9). Śūrpaṇakhā mentions Indra visiting the hermitages of the *soma*- sacrificers. The epic makes a mention of various types of offerings, i.e. milk, curds, rice plant used for preparing the *puroḍāśa,* clarified butter and other items used for offering in the sacrifice (*Ibid*. V. 11,

12). There are references to other sacrifices like the Kuṇḍapāyana, Agniṣṭoma and the other Somasaṁsthā-s and those who maintain the sacred fires and those who preserve the *caityāgni*-s (*Ibid*. VI. 68). The Kuṇḍapāyana is referred to in the *Kāt. Śr. Sū.* XXIV. 4.23 as '*Kuṇḍapāyinām ayanam*'. This is a one-year long *sattra*. The *dīkṣā* for this sacrifice takes place in the month of Phālguna. An important belief is recorded through this work and that is of the sacrificial beast, if passed through the left is an ill-omen (*Ibid*. XIV. 99). This epic, the purpose of which is the practical application of the aphorisms of Pāṇini, throws light on the importance of sacrifice.

### *Jānakīharaṇa of Kumāradāsa*[327]

This epic composed by the Sinhalese poet Kumāradāsa is taken up for study because the theme of the epic is based on the *Rām.* Winternitz has attempted to estimate the date of this epic. 'Tradition ascribes the authorship of the poem to a Ceylonese king Kumāradāsa (517–526), who may have been a friend of Kālidāsa. But there are many indications that go to support the view that this poem of a mediocre merit is of a latter date... Finally, he was probably earlier than Māgha, who seems to echo a verse of his. Rājaśekhara, (900 AD) the poet asserts his fame....'[328]. Vyasa has established the date of Kumāradāsa around 700 AD[329]. The epic has only one reference to the sacrifice performed by Daśaratha. The poet says that king Daśaratha performed a number of sacrifices, which were futile. Lastly, he performed the Putrīyā sacrifice with the assistance of sage Ṛśyaśṛṅga (*Ibid*. IV. 1-2). A divine form emerged from the sacrificial fire carrying a *caru*. The *Jānakīharaṇa* says that the king then divided his lustre into four parts and entered the *caru*, which was later given to his wives and they bore the four princes (IV. 3-4). The poet has not mentioned any details of the Putrīyā sacrifice. He has described the lustre of king Daśaratha entering into the *caru*. This is indeed different from the original *Rām* and other works based on it. Lastly, the *caru* emerging out of the sacrificial fire seems to prove that the poet had little knowledge of the sacrificial system, as *caru* is an offering given to gods during a sacrifice and not the fruit of sacrifice.

Thite has commented on the references of Vedic sacrifice occurring in the works of Kālidāsa and Bhavabhūti[330]. Thite has attacked the concept of 100 Aśvamedha-s, "Even for the sake of argument, we accept that they lived extraordinary long life or that in fiction persons may live a very long life. Since Kālidāsa has not mentioned their age the problem remains unsolved. The only possible conclusion, in this connection is that Kālidāsa was not aware of the time required for the performance of the Aśvamedha sacrifice". Thite has taken up this concept of hundred Aśvamedha-s in the wordly sense. This concept can be understood as an exaggeration, by inflating the number of sacrifices. About the incidence occurring between Raghu and Indra, King Dilīpa has been mentioned to be present in the *sadas*. Thite has rightly observed this discrepancy, because from the day of preceding the release of the horse for wandering up to its return after one year, the sacrificer Dilīpa has to sleep in the hall called Prāgvaṁśa. Thite has pointed out to the monogamy advocated by Rāma, working as a hinderance in the performance of Aśvamedha, since Aśvamedha required the presence of four wives. But Bhavabhūti cannot be blamed for this inconsistency, for he was strictly adhering to the *Rām*, which described king Rāma performing the Aśvamedha, not even with the presence of Sītā in person. Since she was exiled, a golden effigy represented her. Neither did Daśaratha in the *Rām*, nor did Yudhiṣṭhira in the *Mbh* perform the Aśvamedha with the presence of four wives. Moreover, Bhavabhūti belonged to the family of Somayājin-s, so it is difficult to doubt his knowledge of the Vedic sacrifice. There is maximum number of references to the Vedic sacrifice in his works.

Thite concludes his arguments by mentioning the following points:

a) Kālidāsa and Bhavabhūti were not acquainted with the ritual.

b) These sacrifices were never performed liberally.

c) The performance of Aśvamedha might be one of such fictitious deeds.

The purpose of the writings of Kālidāsa and Bhavabhūti was to entertain the elite society with their monumental works and not to display the knowledge of the institution of sacrifice. Yet, following a critical approach, it is true that there are some discrepancies in their works in describing the Vedic sacrifice. Hermeneutics along with historicism does not permit blaming these authors for their incompetence in their knowledge of describing the sacrificial institution, on the contrary makes an attempt to analyze as to why this has occurred. The reason being that at the time of Kālidāsa and Bhavabhūti, the Vedic sacrifice had faced decline, in terms of performance. But the reverence for this institution has remained untainted over the years. It is wrong to conclude that the sacrifices like Aśvamedha were fictitious. A list of kings performing the Aśvamedha has been furnished in this work earlier, which bears testimony to the fact that the Aśvamedha was in vogue (though not frequently performed for obvious reasons) even till the medieval period.

Except from mentioning the sacrificial terms and sacrifices the classical Sanskrit works do not go into details about the sacrificial process. One of the reasons is that the institution of the Vedic sacrifice as a practice faced a decline during the period when compositions of classical Sanskrit works had reached their zenith, due to the influence of Puranic works, which emerged to counteract the thrust of Buddhism. However, the institution of Vedic sacrifice as a thought was still revered by the poets. They reflected the Vedic sacrifice through a) sacrificial names and b) figuratively, through metaphors and allegories, etc. These two points will be discussed in the next chapter.

# 6

# Miscellaneous

The Vedic sacrifice is seen in ancient texts in the form of references regarding direct mention of ritual procedure, sacrifices or elements used in sacrifice. As the Vedic sacrifice is directly mentioned in Sanskrit texts through references to various sacrifices, rituals, myths pertaining to sacrifices, etc., similarly there are indirect references to the Vedic sacrifice in the texts. Taking these references into consideration is important because it indicates the influence of the Vedic sacrificial institution on the thought process of the composer/narrator and his times. A study of figurative references is essential to understand the position of Vedic sacrifice in ancient India, because of two factors.

- Firstly, Vedic sacrifice as seen from the earlier study seems to be declined in due course of time especially regarding performance of sacrificial rituals.
- Secondly, set-back in practice does not mean that importance of sacrifice declined. That the importance of Vedic sacrifice still remained unchallenged in ancient India

can be proven through the figurative references occurring in various Sanskrit texts.

Study of figurative expressions regarding Vedic sacrifice is covered under two subtopics:

## SACRIFICE AS SEEN IN THE FORM OF SIMILES, METAPHORS, PERSONIFICATIONS AND ALLEGORIES

### Sacrificial Similes and Metaphors

Sacrifice has found an important place in the poetic and dramatic imagery of Sanskrit writers. These expressions appear in the form of similes, metaphors, personifications and allegories.

#### *Rāmāyaṇa*

The anger of Viśvāmitra blazed like the sacrificial fire sprinkled with clarified butter (Bāl 20. 28). This seems to be a favourite imagery in the *Rām* because the growth of Kubera, the son of Viśravas, is described as the fire which grows by offering oblations (*Rām* Utt 3. 9). The *Rām* describes the deserted look of Ayodhyā like the sacrificial altar deserted by the sacrificers along with its implements after the Sutya ritual (Ayo 114. 8). This is an incorrect reference to the ritual because the sacrificial place is deserted only after the performance of the *avabhṛtha* ceremony. In fact no trace of the sacrifice is left afterwards. Just as the fire blazes with oblations similarly, the bow in the hand of Rāma blazed by his mere glance (Sundara 47. 2). The greatness of Rāma is described as the fruit obtained by the Agnihotrin-s while performing the Agnihotra (Yuddha 105. 22-23). The fight between Lakṣmaṇa and Indrajit raised a heap of arrows just as there is a heap of Kuśa grass for the two blazing fires in a *sattra*. Though the reference is to a *sattra* with two blazing fires, this is incorrect because the *sattra* requires minimum three fires. The effulgence of Puṣpaka is compared with the radiance of the fire in the Agnihotra (*Ibid*. Utt 24. 10a). The three sons of Viśravas appeared terrible like the three fires (*Ibid*. Utt 5. 7-8, 6. 14).

### *Mahābhārata*

The birth of Abhimanyu from Subhadrā in the *Mbh* is compared to the birth of fire from the friction of wooden apparatus of the Śamī tree (*Mbh* Ādi.P 213. 61.c.f. Śān. P 47. 18). Penance yields knowledge; this thought is compared as follows: the preceptor is to be regarded as the upper *araṇi* and the lower one is his wife, the *brāhmaṇī*. When Tapas is churned the outcome is the fire of knowledge (*Ibid*. Asv P 34. 3).

Duryodhana surrounded by Aśvatthāman, Kṛpa and Kṛtavarman is described as *vedi* surrounded by three fires (*Ibid*. Sau P 9. 7). Aśvatthāman killed the sons of Pāṇḍava-s just as a Śamitṛ kills the animals in the sacrifice (*Ibid*. Sau P 8. 36). This is again incorrect because, Śamitṛ makes the sacrificial victim 'calm', i.e. *śānta*, by smothering it and not by actually killing it. (Etymlogically, the word Śamitṛ is derived from the root $\sqrt{}$*śam,* which means 'to be calm or to pacify'). After committing this terrible act, the son of Droṇa then gave offerings to Rudra. The bows became the *samidh*-s, sharp arrows became the *pavitra*-s, he offered his self as an oblation and requested Rudra to accept the same.

### *The Mahāpurāṇa-s*

The M. Pu-s also refer to sacrifice in a figurative sense. Varuṇa killed Virocana by tying him with the fetters and killing him with a mace, just as an animal is killed in the Aśvamedha sacrifice (*Vām. Pu* X. 37). It is to be noted that the simile is not clear, because the name of the animal is not mentioned. A horse is not killed in this way, but a dog is killed with a pestle of Sīdhraka wood.

The mind-born daughter of the Pitṛ-s, i.e. Menā, got united with Indra and was cursed by the Pitṛ-s. She resembled *araṇi*, the cause of sacrificial fire; she entered the womb of a fish, according to the *Pad. Pu* (I. 1. 37b-38).

A sage who moves about as a *'muni'* (quiet recluse), after granting freedom from fear to all living beings, need not be afraid of any living being at any place. The recluse performs the Agnihotra in his own body; it is through his mouth that he consigns the oblations obtained through begging alms to propitiate the bodily fire (*Nār. Pu* I. 43.126).

It is to be noted that the M. Pu-s give a number of allegorical references but do not abound in similes referring to sacrifice. The greatness of the parents and teacher is referred to in the *Bhav. Pu* (I. 4. 200). Mother is the Gārhapatya, father the Dakṣiṇāgni and the teacher the Āhavanīya. These three fires are the greatest in the world.

*Classical Sanskrit Dramas and Mahākāvya-s*

Classical Sanskrit dramas and Mahākāvya-s also give indirect references to Vedic sacrifice. Bhāsa in *Dūtaghaṭotkaca* refers to the Pāṇḍava-s as five fires which are the Gārhapatya, Āhavanīya, Dakṣiṇāgni, Sabhya and Āvasathya. The death of Abhimanyu has enkindled the five Pāṇḍava fires, says the text[331]. *Ūrubhaṅga* of Bhāsa, metaphorically refers to the war-sacrifice and compares the position of Dhṛtarāṣṭra as one re-entering the Aśvamedha without an Adhvaryu priest (*Ūrubhaṅga* Act. I. 55. c.f. I. 6). Here the background of this simile is the sad news of the fall of Duryodhana.

The *Kumārasambhava* of Kālidāsa compares Pārvatī deserving none else but Śiva as her husband just as except fire no other lustre deserves an oblation, consecrated by *mantra*-s (*Kumārasambhava.* I. 51). The *Raghuvaṁśa* mentions a hyperbolic expression regarding the sacrifice. The fame of the king reached the shore of the sea even before the surface of the sacrificial altar drenched with waters of ablution was dry (XVII. 37). Kālidāsa, in his prologue of the *Mālavikāgnimitra*, refers to the drama as an agreeable and beautiful sacrificial feast for the eyes[332]. The benedictory verse of the *Abhijñānaśākuntala* refers to that creation of the creator, which conveys to the gods the oblations offered according to the customary rites, i.e. fires, as well as the other creation, i.e. sacrifice.

In the *Kirātārjunīya* of Bhāravi, the dead boar in front of Śiva appeared like the dead animal lying in front of the *brāhmaṇa*-s in a sacrifice (XIV. 38). On hearing the greatness of Duryodhana, Yudhiṣṭhira maintained his calmness, seeing which Draupadī got furious. She asked him that how did his anger remain dormant and did not inflame him just as the fire in the Śamī tree though initially dormant does burst forth (*Ibid.* I. 32). This verse from the *Kirātārjunīya* is not directly connected with the sacrifice, but it refers to the fire remaining dormant in the Śamī tree. The wood of this tree is used as an *araṇi* to churn fire during the sacrifice because of bearing fire. The fourth act of the *Abhijñānaśākuntala* also refers to the fire-bearing quality of the Śamī tree.

The *Śiśupālavadha* has some indirect references to the Vedic sacrifice. Balarāma, Śrīkṛṣṇa and Uddhava seated in the counsel-hall appeared like three fires in the sacrificial altar (II. 3). Just as there were no errors in performing sacrifices by those performing the *sattra*-s, similarly during the rule of the king Yudhiṣṭhira, there were no errors in maintaining the welfare of the kingdom, according to *Śiśupālavadha* (XIV. 32). This reference indicates the period when the Śrauta rituals started to have a fixed order.

Thus the indirect references to the Vedic sacrifice, abounding in similes and with stray examples of metaphors and hyperboles, reflect on the fact that though the Vedic sacrifice was not in vogue, its influence as a great religious activity lingered in the minds of the poets and the *sūta*-narrators. The poets and the *sūta*-narrators took pride in associating their poetic imagery with the sacrificial institution.

• Sacrificial riddle: The *Mbh*, in a dialogue between Aṣṭāvakra and Bandin, has incorporated a sacrificial riddle (Van. P 133-134). The arguments between Aṣṭāvakra and Bandin took place in the form of a numerical riddle, in which there are references to the Vedic sacrifice. This passage incorporates references relevant to the Vedic sacrifice. According to Bandin, the number 3 stands for three Veda-s, through which the Vājapeya and other sacrifices are accomplished. It also stands for the three pressings of Soma. Aṣṭāvakra replied that the number 4 stands for the four priests of the sacrifice. Bandin said that the number 5 represents the five fires enkindled for the sacrifice. Aṣṭāvakra gave a reply that the number 6 stands for the six cows given as *dakṣiṇā* in Agnyādhāna and the six Sādyaskra sacrifices. Bandin answered that the number 7 stands for the seven metres used for a sacrifice. The number 8 stands for the sacrificial posts erected during sacrifices said Aṣṭāvakra. Sāmidhenī-s, 9 in number, are required in a Pitṛyajña, said Bandin. The number 10 does not mention anything about sacrifice. The number 11 stands for the sense objects which symbolize sacrificial posts for tying up the embodied soul which is symbolized as the sacrificial victim, said Bandin. Aṣṭāvakra said that the number 12 stands for the Dvādaśāha sacrifice. In this way the arguments lasted till the number 13 and at the end Bandin was defeated at the hands of Aṣṭāvakra. It is interesting to know through the numerical riddle the various components of Vedic sacrifice.

## Allegories Pertaining to the Vedic Sacrifices

Apart from the references which abound in similes and sometimes in metaphors, there are allegorical references occurring in the texts which highlight the influence of the Vedic sacrifice.

An allegory is a description of a subject under the guise of some other subject of aptly suggestive resemblance. It is a figurative sentence, discourse or narrative, in which properties and circumstances attributed to the apparent subject really refer to the subject they are meant to suggest an extended or continued metaphor[333].

One important aspect of this indirect mention is the allegory of battlefield as the sacrifice. The *Mbh* abounds in allegories of battlefield specially known as *raṇayajña* or *saṅgrāmayajña*. Janamejaya describes Bhīṣma as being permanently consecrated for the sacrifice in the form of war on the side of the Kaurava-s, and Dhṛṣṭadyumna was consecrated as the commander-in-chief on the side of the Pāṇḍava-s, mentions the *Mbh* (Ud. P 154.4, 12).

Duryodhana haughty as he was described the *raṇayajña* to Dhṛtarāṣṭra (*Ibid*. 57. 12-14), as follows:

| *Battle* | *Sacrifice* |
|---|---|
| Duryodhana and Karṇa | Consecrated for the sacrifice |
| Yudhiṣṭhira | Sacrificial victim |
| Chariot | Altar |
| Sword | *sruva* |
| Mace | *sṛuc* |
| Armour | *sadas* |
| Yoke | Cāturhotra |
| Arrows | Darbha |
| Glory | Oblation |

Duryodhana concludes the narration by saying that by such type of sacrifice Vaivasvata (Manu) made himself devoid of enemies. In the *Mbh,* Karṇa has given a detailed and graphic allegory of the sacrifice to the battle between the Kaurava-s and the Pāṇḍava-s (Ud.P 139.23-47).

| *Battle* | *Sacrifice* |
|---|---|
| Śakti | *samidh*-s |
| Mace | Paridhi |
| Tomar | Vat of Soma |
| Bow | *pavitra* or Darbha grass |
| Disciples of Droṇa and Kṛpa | *sadasya*-s |
| Arrows released from Gāṇḍiva | Stoma-s |

| Sātyaki | Pratiprasthātṛ |
|---|---|
| Sons of Dhṛtarāṣṭra and the wives | Consecrated for the sacrifice |
| Ghaṭotkaca | Śamitṛ |
| Dhṛṣṭadyumna | *dakṣiṇā* of the sacrifice named Atirātra |
| Karṇa killed in the battle | Piling or enkindling of this sacrifice |
| Kṛṣṇa | Adhvaryu |
| Arjuna | Hotṛ |
| Gāṇḍiva and prowess | *sṛuc* and *ājya* |
| Aindra, Pūśupata, Brahma and Sthūṇākarṇa are the names of missiles | *mantra*-s used by Savyasācī |
| Abhimanyu | Grāvastut |
| Bhīma | Udgātṛ |
| Yudhiṣṭhira | Brahman |
| Blood of Duḥśāsana | Sutya |
| Conch, tabor, etc. | Subrahmaṇya |
| Different types of arrows | Upabṛṁhaṇa |
| Chariots | *yūpa*-s |
| Nakula and Sahadeva | Śamitṛ-s |
| Great army | Wife of the sacrificer |
| Death of Duryodhana and the lamentations of the wives of the Kaurava-s | This is the *avabhṛtha* of the battle |

The Ud. P. of the *Mbh* abounds in such allegories. There is a possibility that the *sūta*-narrator of the *Mbh* was fond of such graphic narrations and also displayed the knowledge of the system of sacrifice. The mention of the Atirātra sacrifice and the term *vaitāna karman* are the striking references to the Vedic sacrifice. The Atirātra sacrifice is the one among the Somasamsthā-s which continues overnight. The battle of the *Mbh* on the day when Ghaṭotkaca was killed was also fought overnight. This similarity has been marked by the *sūta*-narrator.

There is another graphic description of this *saṅgrāmayajña* allegory in the *Mbh* (Śān. P 99. 12-38). King Ambarīṣa, the son of Nābhāga, had reached the heaven. There he saw his minister named Sudeva. Ambarīṣa questioned about this to Indra as to how could a minister who had performed not many sacrifices to please gods enjoy a position in the heaven. To this question Indra answered that though he had not performed sacrifices to please gods, being a *kṣatriya* he had performed sacrifices in the form of war and hence attained heaven (Śān. P 99.12-38).

| *Battle* | *Sacrifice* |
|---|---|
| Elephants | *ṛtvij*-s |
| Horses | Adhvaryu-s |
| Flesh of the enemies | Oblations |
| Blood | Clarified butter |
| Scavenging birds and animals | *sadasya*-s of the *sattra* |
| Weapons | *sruc*-s |
| Arrows | *sruva* |
| Sword | *sphya* |

| Bloodshed | Pūrṇāhuti |
|---|---|
| The enemy army | Havirdhāna |
| Own army | Altar of the shape of a hawk |
| Utterances like *chindhi* and *bhindhi* of the warriors | *sāman*-s of *sāman*-singers |
| Flesh of the elephants and horses | Havirdhāna |
| Headless bodies | *yūpa*-s |
| Trumpeting of the elephants | Vaṣatkāra |
| Dundubhi | Udgātṛ |
| Swords and other weapons | Grass strewn around the *vedi* of the sacrifice |
| River of blood | *avabhṛtha* |
| Shoulder bones of horses and elephants | Patnīśālā |
| Vyūha of both the armies | *vedi* |
| Own army | Havirdhāna |

The description further compares the army of the enemy as Patnīśālā and the warriors on the right as *sadasya*-s, from the north as Agnīdhra. It gives the position of Bṛhaspati in sacrifice and Viṣṇu in prowess to those who have killed the commander-in-chief of the enemy. The description displays beautiful poetic imagination and gives minutest details of the warfare during the time of the composition of the epic.

The *Ūrubhaṅga* has described the battlefield as a sacrificial altar for offering the oblations of life into fire (I. 4). The *Mbh,* through an allegory of the Vaiśvānara has depicted spirituality in a ritual-setting. The Vaiśvānara is divided into seven parts. These are the seven tongues of Vaiśvānara: nose, tongue, eyes, skin, ears, mind and intellect. These organs lead to sensory perceptions. The subjects of these sensory perceptions are the *ṛtvij*-s, e.g. one who smells or one who tastes; and the objects of sensory perceptions are the *samidh*-s, e.g. a flower whose fragrance is inhaled by the nose. The actions of smelling, seeing, tasting, etc. are the oblations. The world is created from these oblations (Āśv. P. 20. 18-22). There is one more interesting reference to the embodied soul, which is regarded as the Gārhapatya fire and the mind as the Āhavanīya fire (*Mbh* Āśv. P 21. 3).

The *Veṇīsaṁhāra* of Bhaṭṭanārāyaṇa refers to the *saṅgrāmādhvara* in brief as follows:

| Four Pāṇḍava-s | Officiating priests |
|---|---|
| Hari | Director of the ritual |
| Dharmarāja | Sacrificer |
| Draupadī | Sacrificer's wife |
| Kaurava-s | Sacrificial victims |
| Removing the affliction due to insult | Fruit of the sacrifice. |

This indicates that Bhaṭṭanārāyaṇa was influenced by the *raṇayajña* of the Ud. P, Śān. P and Sau. P of the *Mbh.*

A question arises as to why be the various facets of war combined with the institution of sacrifice. To answer this question, a practice is to be noted, i.e. whenever any king went for war he was consecrated. Performing the consecration ceremony indicates that war was regarded as an extension of sacrifice. The *RV* refers to the Dāśarājña war where the sacrifice is dedicated to Yama (VII. 18.6-8). Warfare is one of the essential aspects of kingship. Sacrifices like the Rājasūya and the Aśvamedha were performed by kings only. These sacrifices are closely associated with wars. Therefore poetic imagination in the yester years was tempted to associate warfare and Vedic sacrifice. This combination of the war with sacrifice is used even in the vernaculars of the present times. Giving up life for one's country is regarded as 'sacrificing life' or giving '*āhuti*' of one's '*prāṇa*-s'.

- The metaphor of *Yajñavarāha* is very famous in the M.Pu-s. The entire imagery of the *varāha*, i.e. the giant boar is set in the sacrificial system. While tracing the literary evidence to the emergence of *varāha* in Indian traditions, one has to refer to the *RV*. In the *RV*, a mention is made of a myth in which Viṣṇu carried away a hundred buffaloes and cooked rice-milk which were guarded by or at least had something to do with a boar called Emūṣa (I. 61. 7, and VIII. 77. 10)[334]. In the *AV* (XII. 1. 48), there is a short reference to the association of Earth with a *varāha* (XII. 1. 48). According to Nagar, this could be termed as the fore-runner of the subsequent developed story of the rescue of the Earth by a *varāha*[335]. According to the *Tait. Sam* (VII. 1. 5. 1), this universe in the beginning was water. On this, Prajāpati became the wind. He saw the Earth and took it up; becoming Viśvakarman, he wiped water from it. In the *Tait. Br* too it is Prajāpati, who, having assumed the form of a *varāha*, plunged into the waters (I. 1. 3. 5). Finding the Earth lying deep in the sea waters, he raised it to the surface. The *Śat. Br* (XIV. 1. 1. 2-11), testifies the salvage of the earth by the boar, who was none else than Prajāpati (XIV. 1. 1. 2-11). This Prajāpati has been described to be the husband of the Earth, who was initially as small as a thumb and grew abnormally subsequently.

The *Rām* describes Lord Brahmā, who became the boar initially and raised up the earth. The *Rām* also considers Lord Brahmā as the great boar who rescued the Earth from the ocean. The identification of Viṣṇu, i.e. as the *varāha,* began in the *Mbh.* His epithet Govinda is described in the *Mbh* as one who got hold of the Earth (*go*). The reference from the *Mbh* indicates that *varāha* has definitely been incorporated in the incarnation cycle of Viṣṇu. It is stated that Madhusūdana or Janārdana assumed the form of the great Varāha, Nṛsiṁha, and Trivikrama[336]. The first detailed account of the *varāha* -myth is found in the Harivaṁśa (III.34. 30-43). The text describes how Viṣṇu -Kṛṣṇa assumed the form of a roaring boar, penetrated into the nether regions and destroyed the demons.

The *Agni. Pu* refers to the Yajñavarāha, killing the demon Hiraṇyākṣa and thus protecting *dharma* and the gods simultaneously (IV. 2-3). The *Bhāg. Pu.* describes the Yajñavarāha bearing the entire sacrificial structure within its giant self (III. 13. 34-45). In this way the Yajñavarāha combines in person the sacrifice. Thus this boar is known as the Yajñamūrti (III. 14. 2) c. f. *Pad. Pu.* (I. 39. 77-83).

Mythology of *varāha* rescuing the Earth from the waters is observed in its initial stages in these passages from the Brahmanic literature mentioned above. It deserves to be noted that *varāha* is one of the forms of Prajāpati in its initial stages. His connection with Viṣṇu, whose important incarnation he became in the later period, is completely unknown at this stage.

The relation of the boar and the clouds is stated in the *Nirukta*[337]. *Varāha* is the designation of both, the cloud and the boar, for *varāha* is the one who eats the best type of food. The cloud and the boar are etymologically identified by the *Nirukta*.

Several scholars have dealt with the mythology of *varāha*[338]. Desai observes that *varāha* is the therimorphic form of Vṛtra which is the cloud. In spite of the tortuous way of reasoning and a fanciful etymology, the equation of *varāha* with the clouds or primordial waters seems a sound proposition according to Desai[339].

Shah opines that, in the Vṛṣākapi hymn of the *RV*, Vṛṣākapi stands for *varāha*[340]. With evidences from the *Mbh*, *Harivaṁśa*, and *Mat. Pu*, Shah has attempted to establish a relation between Vṛṣākapi and *varāha*. The relation is also established between the boar and the sun perhaps due to its connection with the clouds. *Varāha*, right from the time of the *RV* was referred to as Vṛṣākapi[341]. Rangarajan also supports this hypothesis which is discussed further in this chapter.

According to Agarwala, the concept of Yajñavarāha seems to have been formulated for the first time by the author of the *Vāyu. Pu*, which includes it in the proper context of Sṛṣṭivarṇana and from there it has been taken by the *Mat. Pu* which adds it at the fag end of the text (Ch. 238). He also adds that the version of Yajñavarāha given in the *Viṣṇu Pu.*, (I. 4. 32-35), is the combination of some epithets from the *Mat. Pu* with some new ones of its own and the whole thing is restated in a new metrical form[342]. The upper limit of the *Vāyu Pu*, is 2nd century AD and the *Mat. Pu* is 3rd century AD. The *Brahmāṇḍa Pu* also describes the Yajñavarāha (213. 33-37).

There are two aspects of the question, viz.

i) the real meaning of the *varāha* conception as applied to sacrifice, i.e. its significance as a symbol of Vedic cosmology;

ii) Secondly, the correspondence between the various elements of sacrifice and the different limbs of the body of *varāha* as an animal. In these texts they compare each and every limb of the body of the *varāha* to each and every component of the sacrifice.

Rangaranjan says that the concept of Yajñavarāha is based on two factors:

i) the real meaning of Yajñavarāha in the light of the Vedic cosmogony and

ii) the corresponding relationship of the various limbs of *varāha* with the various elements of Yajña[343].

Rangarajan further observes that:

> .....abovementioned Purāṇa-s use the expression Chāyāpatnīsahāya, which means Chāyā is his consort. Here Chāyā is compared to the female Śakti of Yajñavarāha. But Chāyā is the wife of Sūrya. She is also called Suvarṇā. She is the shadow of Saṁjñā, the real wife of Sūrya. Unless Yajñavarāha is treated as Sūrya himself, this description cannot be sustained.[344]

The orthodox explanation of the symbolism underlying the *varāha* - incarnation of Viṣṇu is given in the *Pad. Pu.* The *Vāyu Pu* reproduces the same passage word by word. This inference by Nagar appears to be incorrect because the date of the *Pad. Pu* is 6th century AD. He does not take into consideration the detailed description of the Yajñavarāha with all its components of sacrifice occurring in the *Bhāg. Pu.* The date of the *Bhāg. Pu* runs parallel to the date of the *Pad. Pu.* In the *Bhāg. Pu* it is stated that the sacrifice is as a whole symbolized by the boar and that its various limbs represent the limbs of the sacrifice (III.13. 34-45)

Agrawala has attempted to analyse the nature of Yajñavarāha. He believes that the Vedic conception of creative modality comprises the fivefold pattern of Svayambhū, Parameṣṭhi, Sūrya, Candra and Pṛthivī;

i) Svayambhū as Ādivarāha
ii) Parameṣṭhi as Yajñavarāha
iii) Sūrya as Śvetavarāha
iv) Candra as Brahmavarāha
v) Pṛthivī as Emūṣavarāha[345]

From the information occurring in the *Bhāg. Pu*, the following table can be made to explain the relation between the *varāha* and the Yajña, with the components of both:

| *Body of Yajñavarāha* | *Components of Sacrifice* |
|---|---|
| Skin | Vedic metres |
| Bristles | Kuśa grass |
| Eyes | Clarified Butter |
| Four legs | Four priests |
| Snout | *sṛuc* |
| Nostrils | *sruva* |
| Belly | Iḍā |
| Cavity of the ears | *camasa*-s of Soma |
| Mouth | Prāśitra |
| Throat | *graha*-s of Soma |
| Chewing | Agnihotra |
| Descent on the earth | Dīkṣaṇīyeṣṭi |
| Neck | Upasad-s |
| Tusks | Prāyaṇīyeṣṭi and Udayanīyeṣṭi |
| Tongue | Pravargya |
| Head | Sabhya and Āvasathya fires |

| Vital airs | Piling of the bricks |
|---|---|
| Procreating fluid | Soma |
| Sitting posture | Three pressings of Soma |
| Seven constituents of the body | The different Samsthā-s of sacrifice |
| Joints of the body | Sattra-s |

According to the *Vāyu Pu,* Viṣṇu assumed the form of the wild boar:

He entered the nether regions in order to lift up the earth[346]. He was the guide for the propounders of the Veda-s. The Yajñavarāha was lustrous and had undergone different initiations for performing sacrifices.

He was charming with the sacrificial rites of Upākarman.

| *Body of Yajñavarāha* | *Components of Sacrifice* |
|---|---|
| Sacrifice | Chest |
| Face | *citi*-s |
| Tongue | Sacrificial fire |
| Hair | Darbha-grass |
| Head | Brahman priest |
| Nose | *ājya* |
| Snout | Sacrificial ladle |
| Roaring grunt | Sāman-s |
| Masculine organ | Offerings of *ghṛta* |
| Seed of creation | Sacrificial spot |
| Inner soul | Sacrificial altar |
| Hips | *mantra*-s |

| | |
|---|---|
| Blood | Soma mixed with *ghṛta* |
| Velocity | Havya and Kavya |
| Body | Prāgvaṁśa |
| Heart | *dakṣiṇā*-s |
| Hair on the chest | Pravargya |

The analysis of the Yajñavarāha can be better understood by taking into consideration the iconographic depiction of the same. The iconographic description of *varāha* is found in the Pāñcarātra texts, the *Vaikhānasāgama*, the Purāṇa-s and the Śilpaśāstra-s. Gopinath Rao classifies them under three heads, namely, i) Bhūvarāha ii) Yajñavarāha iii) Pralayavarāha[347]. Among the Pāñcarātra texts, the Śeṣa Saṁhitā and the Sāttvata Saṁhitā describe the image of *varāha* in zoomorphic (Yajña) form. They refer to the image of *varāha* as Yajñapuruṇa. According to the Sātvata Saṁhitā, the body of the Yajñavarāha holds the *bhūḥ, bhuvaḥ* and *svaḥ,* i.e. creation of the universe; and *varāha* is the supreme[348].

According to the Vaikhānasāgama, the description of Yajñavarāha is that of an image with the face of a Boar and the body of a man. It should have four hands, two of which should hold *cakra* and *śaṅkha*. The Yajñavarāha should be seated in Lalitāsana on a *siṁhāsana* with left leg resting upon the seat. To his right the figure of Lakṣmī should be shown seated in Lalitāsana with right leg hanging. She should hold a lotus in left hand and the right hand should be resting on the seat. On the left of *varāha* the figure of Bhumidevī should be seated in Lalitāsana with left leg hanging.

She should hold a blue lotus in her right hand and left hand should rest upon the seat. She should be shown casting a wondrous look[349].

The icons of the *varāha* are classified under two heads following the findings of Rangarajan:

1) Zoomorphic form and
2) Zooanthropomorphic form.

In the zoomorphic form the images of *varāha*, which are called Yajñavarāha, have been sculptured to emphasize two important factors. They are:

a) *Varāha* as the creator of the Universe and
b) *Varāha* as the representation of Yajña or sacrifice.

The concept of *varāha* as the creator of the Universe is brought out on the body of *varāha* by the representation of various gods and goddesses, celestial beings, sages, river goddesses, earthly beings and the beings of the nether region. In some of the representations the three loka-s—*bhūḥ*, *bhuvaḥ* and *svaḥ* are also depicted on the vertebral column of the images of *varāha*.

The second aspect of *varāha*, the various elements of the sacrifice or Yajña are compared to the various limbs of the animal. For example, three *iṣṭi*-s of Jyotiṣṭoma Yajña are compared to the neck of *varāha*, which is represented in the Khajuraho Varāha. Similarly, two other *iṣṭi*-s called Prāyaṇīya and Udayanīya are compared to the tusks of *varāha* which are personified in human forms and are again presented in the images of *varāha* in the Madhya Pradesh. Again, the two *dharma*-s called Iṣṭapūrta are compared to the ears of *varāha*, which are being shown in the human form in the images of *varāha*[350]. Here there is a variation that the two *dharma*-s can be regarded as the Śrauta and the Smārta *dharma*-s.

On the body of the Varāha image at Khor, in the second row, starting from the neck on the right, seven figures of sages are seated in Yogāsana posture. They are two-armed. Their right hands are shown in Abhaya-mudrā and left hands are kept on the lap. They may be representations of seven sages. They are followed by a female figure. On the left, starting from the neck, there are figures of seven sages with two arms. The right hand is in Varada-mudrā and the left hand is holding water pot. They are the personifications of seven sacrifices, viz. Agnihotra, Atyagniṣṭoma, Ukthya, Ṣoḍaśin, Vājapeya, Atirātra and Āptoryāma[351].

The *varāha*-images have been analysed due to the painstaking efforts of Rangarajan. Yet there are some details to be clarified, regarding the *soma*-sacrifices, which Rangarajan has missed. Firstly, the three *iṣṭi*-s of the Jyotiṣṭoma sacrifice can be understood as the three pressings of the Soma. Secondly, the seven sacrifices as mentioned by Rangarajan, by giving the reference of the *Bhāg. Pu.* (III. 13. 38) are the seven *soma*- sacrifices, which do not incorporate the Agnihotra but the Agniṣṭoma, as the archetype of the Somasaṁsthā.

The allegorical depiction of the Yajñavarāha in the M. Pu-s is in the context of Vedic cosmogony. This imagery of the M. Pu-s is a confluence of:

a) Mythology of the Great Boar saving the earth from the clutches of the wicked demon Hiraṇyākṣa. This myth incorporates the theory of incarnation in which the Divine Lord descends on the earth to redeem her from the anarchy and to uphold the rule of righteousness.

b) It incorporates the principle of creation in the context of Vedic cosmogony. Here an attempt is made to establish the ancient principle of associating the sacrifice with the entire cosmos; the Vedic conception of the sacrifice equated with the cosmic order, i.e. Ṛta.

Moreover, the entire imagery of the Yajñavarāha appears to have been influenced by the Puruṣasūkta of the *RV* in which the entire cosmic Puruṣa encompasses the universe within Himself[352]. The Yajñavarāha indicates the shift from the importance of the godheads like Prajāpati to the rising godhead Viṣṇu. It also traces the relation of Viṣṇu to the Sun in the quote Chāyāpatnīsahaga.

The Āgama-s and the Tantra-s visualize Yajñavarāha in the anthropomorphic form with the face of a Boar and the body of a man. Even though they use the name Yajñavarāha, they do not make any reference to its relationship with Yajña or Cosmogony. Iconographic depiction of the Yajñavarāha depicts the Vedic sacrifice but in a personified form.

## SACRIFICIAL NAMES MENTIONED IN VARIOUS TEXTS

The influence of the Vedic sacrifice is seen in the names of various characters in different texts. The *Rām* refers to the names of demons like Yajñaśatru, Yajñakopa, which indicate the hostility of the demons towards Vedic sacrifice (*Rām* Yuddha. 44. 20). These references should not be inferred as absolute hostility towards the institution of sacrifice. For, there are names like Yūpākṣa given to the demons, which indicates their affinity to the institution of sacrifice (*Ibid*. Yuddha. 75. 47).

The *Mbh* refers to names like Suyajñā, the daughter of Janamejaya (Ādi. P 90. 19). It also refers to Aśvamedhadatta, the son of Śatānīka (Ādi. P 90. 96). *Bhāg. Pu* mentions that Janamejaya's son was Śatānīka and he obtained the knowledge of rituals through Yājñavalkya. His son was Aśvamedhaja (IX. 22. 35-39). *Vāyu Pu* mentions the name Aśvamedhadatta as the son of Śatānīka (Uttara. Anu. 37. 246-55).

The *Mbh* refers to Suhotra, Suhotṛ, Suhavi and Suyajus as the sons of Bhūmanu, the son of Bharata (Ādi. P 89. 18, 21). According to the *Bhav. Pu*, Suhotra, Vītihotra, Yajñahotra and Śakrahotra are the sons of Bharata (III. 3. 39-41).

According to the *Bhāg Pu*, Manu bore a son named Priyavrata, who married the daughter of Viśvakarman named Barhiṣmatī. She begot ten sons and a daughter named Ūrjasvatī. The names of the ten sons are Agnīdhra, Idhmajihva, Yajñabāhu, Mahāvīra, Hiraṇyaretas, Ghṛtapṛṣṭha, Savana, Medhātithi, Vītihotra and Kavi (V. 1. 25). For similar references cf. *Mārk. Pu* (LIII. 14-16), *Vāyu. Pu* (Pūrva. Upo. 33. 9), *Varāha. Pu* (7-9), *Liṅga Pu.* (I. 46.15-18).

Here these names indicate the affinity of Manu and his progeny towards the institution of sacrifice.

According to the *Mat. Pu,* sons of Cākṣuṣa Manu from Naḍvalā are Havi, Agniṣṭut and Atirātra (IV. 41b-42). One son of Pṛthu is Havirdhāna and his wife is Dhiṣaṇā (IV. 44-45). Agnīdhra, Agnibāhu and Savana are the sons of Svāyambhuva Manu mentions the *Mat. Pu* (IX.3).

According to the *Liṅga Pu,* Anantaka, one of the ancestors of Marutta, had a son named Yajña(I. 68. 27). Thus, the indirect influence of the Vedic sacrifice is reflected through the names of various personalities documented in the M. Pu-s.

Apart from the *Rām,* there are hardly any names in the other texts indicating hostility to the influence of sacrifice. The reason can be attributed to the fact that the portrayal of the Rākṣasa culture was anti-Vedic sacrifice. In the *Rām* one comes across descriptions of the Rākṣasa-s destroying sacrifices performed by sages. Therefore as a mark of achievement they bore names depicting their anti-sacrifice tendencies.

However, the *Mbh* and the M. Pu-s do not mention any names similar to those of the *Rām*. Yet there are references to the anti-sacrifice tendencies of certain demons and even kings, like Vena. This observation indicates that the nature of the composition of the *Rām* was more poetic (it is regarded as an Ādikāvya), rather than mere documentation of facts. Therefore through names like Yajñaśatru and Yajñakopa, the author has figuratively suggested the religion practised by the Rākṣasa-s.

## TĪRTHA–S

*Tīrtha*-s have come up over a period of time to serve as an alternative to the Vedic sacrifice. Vedic religion faced decline due to the rise of Buddhism and Jainism which attacked vehemently the long, expensive and tedious ritual procedures that kept an eye on the fruit to be achieved not in the world here, but in the yonder world.

It is essential to trace the development of the concept of *tīrtha*-s. The word *tīrtha* is derived from the root √*tṛ*, which means 'to swim, to cross waters'. The meaning assigned to this word is a watering place or a path to a watering place, ford of a river, and peeve of water, bathing place or place of pilgrimage on the banks of sacred stream[353]. According to the *RV*, the word *tīrtha* appears to have been used in the sense of a road or a way (I. 169. 6. & I. 173. 11). But at one place in the *RV*, its occurrence can be explained in the sense of a 'holy place' or 'place of pilgrimage, in which it is now popularly used[354]. The word *tīrtha* occurs 8 times in the *RV*[355]. Kane points out that the importance of holy places, visiting them and performing religious rites were known in the Brahmaṇa period, and the word *tīrtha* came to denote a locality or spot or expanse of water which gives rise to the accumulation of righteousness (merit) owing to its own peculiar nature without any adventitious circumstance. In the Vedic age, waters were considered to have purificatory and divine qualities. *RV* refers to the divine waters, which are requested by the seer to protect him in this world (VII. 49. 2). *Tait. Sam* also refers to the similar qualities of the waters (II. 6. 8. 3). According to Rudhart Jean:

> whenever they are found, waters are often bound up with divine powers... water fulfils a positive function. It bathes, dissolves and purifies. It symbolizes a generative and life-giving quality very similar to creative power and is thus divine and sacralizing. It has a positive trait of conferring purity and immortality[356].

Vedic *tīrtha*-s are first mentioned in connection with the performance of sacrifice, a ritualistic practice going back to hoary antiquity. In the ritual context, the term *tīrtha* is understood as a ford; the passage for moving along within the sacrificial area; the path lies, in all *iṣṭi*-s between the *utkara* and the spot where Praṇītā waters are kept (=sañcara) and between the *cātvāla* and *utkara* for a rite which requires an Uttaravedi according to the *Āp. Śr. Sū.* (XII. 5. 4). The *tīrtha* for driving the cows which are sacrificial fees lies between the *śālā* and the *sadas* and from there to the south of the Agnīdhra[357]. Kane explains the term *tīrtha* as:

> the way for going to or coming from the vihāra is between the Praṇītā and *utkara* in the case of *iṣṭi*-s (i.e. to the east of *utkara* and to the west of Praṇītā) and between the *utkara* and the *cātvāla* pit in other cases. This path for going to the *vihāra* is *tīrtha*. The sacrificial ground where the fires are maintained is called *vihāra*[358].

He has pointed out that 'all religions have laid great emphasis on the sacredness of certain localities and have either recommended or enjoined with great insistence pilgrimages to them'[359]. In the sacrificial context, thus the term *tīrtha* is associated with water.

*Śabdakalpadruma* explains *tīrtha* as *tarati pāpādikam yasmat*. *Tīrtha* is associated with the worship of sage, existence of water and preceptor[360]. The word *tīrtha* has been understood in the sense of pilgrimage, i.e. *tīrthayātrā* in the context of the *Mbh* and M. Pu-s. Agehananda Bharati is of the opinion:

> Vedic references are sparse, as indicated earlier; and to my knowledge there are no pilgrimages enjoined, nor even recommended, in any literature earlier than the *Mbh* and the Purāṇa-s. The Purāṇa-s and then of course the Tantra-s (both Hindu and Buddhist) are full of references and instructions pertinent to pilgrimage; apart from them, all these texts have abundant topography, and although the enumeration of holy places is not itself one of the *purāṇa-pañcalakṣaṇa*-s, it is subsumed under any of the five topics constituting a *purāṇa*[361].

The observation of Agehananda Bharati is correct. It is to be understood that no religious system is static. It evolves in due course of time. Although there is no direct mention of recommendations to *tīrtha*, the thought of associating sanctity to water already existed during Vedic age. In this section an attempt is made to establish how the concept of *tīrtha* in the sense of 'pilgrimage' evolved from the institution of Vedic sacrifice. The process can be understood as one religious institution giving birth to another religious institution. The *tīrtha*-s arose as a positive alternative as they are equated with the sacrifice or at times elevated above the Vedic sacrifice. A list of *tīrtha*-s is provided to have an overview of the relationship with Vedic sacrifice. (Appendix No. 2).

The *Mbh* explains the importance of *tīrtha*-s. Pulastya, the sage, has explained to Yudhiṣṭhira, the fruit for visiting *tīrtha*. One who has knowledge, who has undertaken penance, which has fame, who gives in charity, which is devoid of arrogance and has retired from worldly affairs, attains the fruit of *tīrtha*. The sage further adds that 'in this world the seers in the Veda-s have taught the sacrifices in due order and what exactly will be the result of each of them, in this world and in the yonder world. But those sacrifices are out of reach of the poor man. Sacrifices require tremendous wealth and other material resources. It is not possible for everyone to perform sacrifices because of these reasons. Visiting *tīrtha*-s is a rite, which is within the reach even of the poor and in merit equals the result of sacrifices. This mode of worship has been propounded by the seers. *Tīrtha*-s, at times even excel sacrifices in merit. Not paying any visit to the *tīrtha*-s, maintaining fasts over there for three days and nights and not giving gold nor coins, leads to sins and such a sinful person is reborn as a poor man. He who has performed the Agniṣṭoma and similar such sacrifices with liberal gifts does not reap such fruit as from the visit to holy places' (Van. P 80. 29-40).

From the above passage one can infer that performance of sacrifice became complicated and tedious in due course of time. It involved expenditure of wealth and at the same it was time-consuming.

An observation of the names of sacrificers in the texts indicates that only kings could perform sacrifices. *Tīrtha*-s not only replace sacrifice, but excel it in terms of fruit. Although the sacrificial institution is termed as Brahmanic religion, the texts describe sages performing sacrifices like Agnihotra and *sattra*-s. Thus performing great sacrifices was the privilege of kings. How can performing a religious act be accessible to the commoners? The chapter attempts to analyze how has this alternative arisen from the situation in the society.

The greatness of *tīrtha* is also indicated through various myths. For e.g. importance of Puṣkara has been highlighted in the *Mbh.* Lord Brahmā performed sacrifice at Puṣkara. Gods, *brāhmaṇa*-s, etc. participated in the sacrifice. *Gandharva*-s and *apsaras*-es sang and danced with divine musical instruments as accompanists. He performed a *sattra,* which would fulfil all desires. Sages complained that Sarasvatī, the greatest among rivers had not arrived. Lord Brahmā thought of her and she arrived on the scene with the name Sūryaprabhā. The same river arrived at Gayā when the King Gayā performed the great sacrifice. Thus, when the Grandsire performed a sacrifice, the great river arrived. Similarly, when king Gayā performed the sacrifice the river arrived on the scene. This can be interpreted as the origin of the river at a particular place (Śal. P 37. 5-10).

The *Sk. Pu* has associated *tīrtha*-s with the legends of Lord Brahmā. Once Lord Brahmā asked for some land from the Nāgara *brāhmaṇa*-s in the Hāṭaka Kṣetra. There he performed a sacrifice called Pañcarātra and also built a *tīrtha* named Dvitīya Puṣkara (the first one being in the sky). As their *dakṣiṇā,* the *brāhmaṇa*-s asked Lord Brahmā to purify that place by staying there. Lord Brahmā said that during the Pañcarātra, i.e. from Ekādaśī to Pañcadaśī of the month of Kārttika, whosoever bathed there would get the everlasting fruit of his bath or Śrāddha performed there. He further said that he himself would come and stay there during five days. The *brāhmaṇa*-s declared the sacrifice as completed. They propitiated Varuṇa through the *avabhṛtha iṣṭi.* Then Lord Brahmā said to Indra,' When I am performing this act in the water, people will not be able to see me from a distance. So you ride on your elephant, place an antelope's skin on top of a bamboo and when it is time for the bath, you throw it in the water, so that people will come to know that it is time for bath.' The boon bestowed by Lord Brahmā on Indra was that if a king riding on an elephant throws a deer-skin here, he should become unconquerable by his enemies and all those who bathe here should have their sins of the whole year destroyed; and they should get rid of all the diseases. The place became known as Yajñāvabhṛthayakṣmatīrtha. Savitri Kumar points out that the reminiscences of Vedic religion can be easily seen in the legend of Brahman's performance of the Pañcarātra sacrifice[362].

Certain places in the *Mbh* have attained the designation of *tīrtha,* because kings have performed sacrifice in those places.

- Nṛga performed sacrifices in the forest of sage Māṭhara. Indra rejoiced by the offerings of Soma and the *brāhmaṇa*-s rejoiced because of sumptuous donations (*Mbh.* Ādi. P. 86. 6).
- At Plakṣāvataraṇa, *brāhmaṇa*-s performed the Sārasvata sacrifices for king Sahadeva, with Śamyākṣepa (*Ibid.* Ādi. P. 87. 3-4).
- At the same place King Bharata performed the Aśvamedha-s.
- At the banks of the river Dṛṣadvatī, King Vaivarṇya and Varṇa performed many sacrifices.

This passage throws light on some rituals, which are connected with the *sattra* performed on the Sarasvatī and Dṛṣadvatī. Plakṣāvataraṇa is a place where Sārasvata sacrifices are to be performed. The *Tāṇ. Mbr* says that there are three sacrificial sessions to be performed on the banks of the river Sarasvatī. Consecration should be undertaken at the place where the river got lost. After the libation of the *sānnāya,* i.e. a mixture of milk and curds, the Adhvaryu throws a yoke-pin i.e. *śamyā,* in the eastern direction, from the place where the sacrifice has been performed. The spot where it falls down is the place for the Gārhapatya fire. From this spot, he makes 36 strides in the eastern direction; this is the place for the Āhavanīya fire. This procedure is known as the Śamyākṣepa (XXV. 10-12). *Kāt. Śr. Sū.* agrees with this procedure[363]. The same passage of the *Tāṇ. Mbr* refers to the sacrifice on the banks of the river Dṛṣadvatī. Caland remarks that this sacrifice on the banks of the river does not belong to the *sattra*-type of sacrifice, but consists of series of *iṣṭi*-s performed each day on a different spot[364]. One can comment that the passage of the *Mbh* carried the memories of the lost river Sarasvatī.

Indratīrtha is a place which was so named because Indra performed hundred sacrifices at that place. According to the *Mbh,* Balarāma worshipped the *brāhmaṇa*-s at that place, when he went for a pilgrimage during the great war. Rāmatīrtha is also that place named after Paraśurāma, who performed the Vājapeya and the Aśvamedha sacrifices. He distributed the entire earth amongst the *brāhmaṇa*-s. From this place Balarāma proceeded to the Yamunātīrtha, where Varuṇa brought the Rājasūya sacrifice (Śal. P 43. 33). At the Ādityatīrtha, Varuṇa performed the Rājasūya sacrifice, which had the potential to destroy gods and demons. On performing this sacrifice, the Sun god, got the power of lustre (*Ibid.* 48. 10). The Saptasārasvatatīrtha is that place where Auddālaka performed sacrifice. At the Aruṇatīrtha, Indra performed the Balabhid sacrifice and was cleansed of the sin of killing Vṛtra (*brahmahatyā*). The Udbhid and Balabhid sacrifices are one-day *soma*-sacrifices, which are connected with each other as the Darśapūrṇamāsa and they bring out the result of plentitude of cattle. These sacrifices are performed jointly. Once the former is performed the performance of the latter becomes compulsory[365].

Dharma performed the sacrifice at Kaliṅga on the banks of river Vaitaraṇī. The same place is associated with Rudra performing a sacrifice at, with an animal. The gods abducted that animal. This angered Rudra. In order to pacify him, gods asked him to perform an *iṣṭi*, with the animal. Then Rudra released that animal. The narration concludes with a note that any king who recites this Gāthā, attains heaven (Śal. P. 114. 4 ff). At this place Viśvakarman performed sacrifices and earth was given to Kaśyapa. When the earth showed discontent over been given to a mortal, Kaśyapa propitiated her. She entered the ocean, but then returned in the form of an altar. Sage Viśvāmitra, along with Indra performed sacrifice at the river Gomatī. The banks of Gomatī, became the sacrificial ground for gods. Lord Brahmā also performed a sacrifice at this place. Gayā is regarded as an important place for pilgrimage. The Pāṇḍava-s performed Cāturmāsya sacrifice at this place. King Gayā performed great sacrifices. He gave large donations in the form of food and wealth. All the gods arrived at the sacrifice to participate in it (Van. P 93.13-26). Thus the sacrifice has contributed to the sanctity of certain places. They became centres of pilgrimage because sacrifices were performed there by gods and kings.

The *Pad. Pu.* throws light on the concept of *tīrtha*. It gives an analogy of the human body. Just as some parts of the body are regarded as sacred, some regions of the earth are regarded as sacred due to some astonishing qualities of the land itself, some speciality of water or solely because the place has been resorted to by the sages (VI.237. 25-27). The places emerging as *tīrtha* is a process which has continued even in the present times. Places like Shirdi in Maharashtra have emerged as a *tīrtha* within a couple of centuries.

Bakre has classified *tīrtha*-s in two ways[366]:

a) Purpose behind the formation of a *tīrtha*:-

- Those that eulogise just the remembrances or visits to holy places.

- Those that applaud plunges or bathing into them.
- Those that glorify the act of making gifts and/or the performance of *srāddhakarman*-s at them.

*b) Tīrtha*-s can be divided as per the fruits they bestow:

- Those that lead to the acquisition of material pleasures and destruction or removal of all sins.
- Those that enable the visitors to reach the heaven or various other worlds such as Viṣṇuloka, Śivaloka, etc. or even the final beatitude.
- Those that confer Yajñaphala or are described as superior to various sacrifices.

The M. Pu-s have also considered the places of stagnant water as *tīrtha*-s. Most of the *kuṇḍa*-s are connected with the sacrificial altars. Sacrifices were performed there; and after the successful completion of the sacrifices, the deities blessed the performers as well as these *kuṇḍa*-s. It is clear that a water-place was dug nearby or the sacrifice itself was performed near a well or water-tank (*kuṇḍa*) which was already there. Or the *kuṇḍa* itself might have been constructed in view of the ensuing sacrifice and got filled with water. For instance, according to one tale, Daśaratha performed Putreṣṭiyajña. Agni appeared and offered him a golden pot full of sacrificial *pāyasa* to be given to the wives. Since the *kṣīra* was obtained from a particular *kuṇḍa*, it became known as Kṣīrodakuṇḍa. Savitri Kumar is of the opinion that the water of the *kuṇḍa* was known to be of a whitish milky hue; and a legend was attached to it later. As the water was milky, *Rām* account of the sacrifice of Daśaratha came handy to be used[367].

A statistical data of all these *tīrtha*-s and the fruits in the form of the performance of Vedic sacrifice reveals that among the sacrifices Aśvamedha tops the list. It seems to enjoy the favourite position which is followed by the Agniṣṭoma sacrifice. Vājapeya, Atirātra, Rājasūya, Gosava, Puruṣamedha, Puṇḍarika are also those sacrifices getting place in this list. Fruit of the performance of Puruṣamedha indicates that the memory of this sacrifice existed at the time of the *Mbh* and even the M-Pu-s.

Visit to the *tīrtha*-s does not seem to yield the fruits of performance of smaller or less important *iṣṭi*-s and *sattra*-s. Large, pompous and glamourous sacrifices are mentioned. One can say that these sacrifices were out of reach of the common people. This type of substitution of the sacrifice by visiting *tīrtha*-s and yet claiming the fruit of the sacrifice was to give satisfaction to the commoners of indirectly getting the fruit of the performance of a great sacrifice.

*Tīrtha*-s have provided a viable alternative and made religion palatable for the common people. This mode of substitution should not be understood as a revolt against the Brahmanic sacrificial institution. Had this been a revolt, no attempt would have been made to substitute it with sacrifice or regard the fruit of the performance of sacrifices as the parameter of merit of visiting these places. This mode of substitution can be understood as a successful attempt on the part of the composers of the *Mbh* and the M.Pu-s to harmonize pilgrimage with the Vedic religion. Dubey feels that the practice of pilgrimage was mainly introduced to simplify the otherwise complicated sacrificial routine[368].

The *tīrtha*-s deviced by the *Mbh* and the M. Pu-s portray a picture of India's religious, 'quasi-spiritual' geography[369], which ultimately became the basis of the development of the norms of Indian culture down to the age. The *tīrtha*-s have been strewn all over India and have served as a religious binding force to unify the country under a single umbrella of the Puranic religion, which later on shaped into Hinduism. This tradition was innovated by the *Mbh*, which laid down the foundation of India's religious and cultural geography which was later adopted by the various sects like Śaiva, Vaiṣṇava, Śākta and even Jaina and Bauddha.

One cannot ignore that by this mode of substituting the Vedic sacrifice with *tīrtha*-s, the performance of sacrificial rituals did get a set-back and then it declined in due course of time.

## VRATA-S

*Vrata*, i.e. an observance or vow, has been defined as a practice undertaken for a specific time or till death of the person observing a *vrata*. The antiquity of the word *vrata* can be traced up to the *RV* (I. 22. 19 & VIII. 11. 1). The word used in the hymns is Vratapāḥ, i.e. those protecting the sacrifice. *Tait. Sam* also refers to the term *vrata* (II. 5. 5.6)[370]. Kane has explained the meaning and the significance of the term *vrata* and stated that the derivation and semantic development of the word *vrata* have been the subject of great controversies. The word is to be derived from the root √*vṛ* 'to choose' and could mean the following:

i) will, command, law, prescribed order,
ii) subservience, obedience, service,
iii) domain,
iv) order, regulated succession, realm,
v) calling, office, customary activity, carrying on, custom
vi) religious duty, worship, obligation
vii) any undertaking, religious or ascetic performance or observance, vow, sacred work,
viii) vow in general, fixed purpose and
ix) other specialized senses[371].

This indicates that *vrata* as a term is having multiple connotations. Kane has traced the antiquity of this term. In the *RV*, *vrata*-s were the laws or ordinances supposed to be laid down by all gods or by individual gods. In the Saṁhitā-s other than the *RV*, in the Brāhmaṇa-s and the Upaniṣad-s, the word *vrata* is used in the sense of:

i) Religious observance or vow or restrictions as to food and behaviour undertaken as a religious vow.

ii) The special food prescribed for the sustenance, when a person is engaged in a religious rite or undertaking.

Yāska has given these meanings in the *Nirukta* (II. 14). The *Tait. Sam* (II. 5. 5. 6) uses it in the first sense and in one place (V. 7 6. 1) in the second sense. In the times of the Brāhmaṇa-s, the word *vrata* was also used in the secondary senses derived from the sense of religious observance and obligation', viz.

i) a proper course or pattern of conduct for a person as referred to in the *Ait. Br* (VIII. 28) and

ii) an *upavāsa* i.e. act of staying at night near Gārhaptya fire or fasting on the part of a sacrificer, according to the *Ait. Br* (VII. 2).

Kane has pointed out that *vrata* comprehends several items such as bath (*snāna*), the morning prayer (*prātaḥsandhyā*), mental resolve (*saṅkalpa*), enkindlement of the fire (*homa*), worship (*pūjā*) of the deity or deities in whose honour the *vrata* is undertaken, fasting (*upavāsa*), feeding of *brāhmaṇa*-s, maidens or married women or the poor or helpless, gifts (*dāna*), and the observance of certain rules of conduct during the period of *vrata*.

Kane has observed that there is universality in the nature of *vrata*-s. The Jainism lays down the five great vows (*mahāvrata*-s) and five small vows (*aṇuvrata*-s). The Buddhists have the *pañcaśila*-s. The contents of the Testaments, Old and New, reveal the sacredness of vows. Buddhism and Jainism were influential rivals of the Vedic-Brahmanical sacrificial system. It was in order to wean away common people from those two schisms that probably learned followers of the Vedic system glorified *vrata*-s and promised heaven and other worldly and spiritual rewards[372].

Among the multiple connotations given by Kane and noted above, connotation no. v) and vi) appear to be acceptable in accordance with the sacrificial system.

To understand the need for the concept of *vrata* during the Puranic period, the term is understood in the abovementioned connotation only. Surprisingly, the *Mbh* does not substitute the *vrata*-s for the sacrifice as it has substitute sacrifices with *tīrtha*-s. We come across *vrata*-s substituting sacrifice only in the M. Pu-s. Not all M. Pu-s make such an attempt. It is noteworthy that the *Bhāg. Pu* and the *Viṣṇu Pu* which are the popular Vaisnavite M. Pu-s and the *Liṅga, Śiva* and *Sk.* M.Pu-s do not substitute the Vedic sacrifice with the *tīrtha*-s and *vrata*-s. The religion of the *Sk. Pu* is predominanatly tantric in nature[373]. The M. Pu-s which have attempted to substitute sacrifice by *vrata*-s and *tīrtha*-s are:

| Name of the M. Pu. | *Tīrtha* | *Vrata* |
|---|---|---|
| *Mat. Pu* | ✓ | |
| *Kū. Pu* | ✓ | |
| *Vāyu Pu* | ✓ | |
| *Brahmāṇḍa Pu* | ✓ | |
| *Vām. Pu* | ✓ | |
| *Varāha Pu* | ✓ | |
| *Pad. Pu* | ✓ | ✓ |
| *Nār. Pu.* | ✓ | ✓ |
| *Brahma Pu* | ✓ | ✓ |

| | | |
|---|---|---|
| *Brahmavai. Pu* | | ✓ |
| *Bhav. Pu* | | ✓ |

The Vedic sacrifice is substituted by *vrata* on the following lines:

(a) Giving an offering to a particular deity: According to *Mat. Pu* (CLXXX. 75), if one worships Śiva by giving offerings of golden flowers, then a person gets the fruit of the Agnihotra sacrifice (CLXXX. 75).

(b) Paying obeisance to a deity: By paying obeisance to Kṛṣṇa one gets the fruit of thousands of Aśvamedha-s according to the *Brahma Pu* (54. 38).

(c) Recitation of a hymn or chant: Aghamarṣaṇa hymn of the *RV* (X. 190), washes of sins just as the Aśvamedha cleanses the performer of his sins according to the *Brahma Pu* (57. 38).

(d) Wearing some auspicious item: One who wears a necklace of beads made up of Tulasī gets the fruit of one lakh Aśvamedha sacrifices according to the *Brahmavai. Pu* (II. 21. 47).

(e) Performance of a *vrata*: Rasakalyāṇīvrata leads to the fruit of 1000 Agniṣṭoma sacrifices, according to the *Pad. Pu* (I. 22. 134).

By casting a glance at the M. Pu-s which substitute the sacrifice with the *tīrtha*-s and *vrata*-s, it appears that they have the upper limit of their date of compositions as 2nd AD. To be more specific, *Vāyu Pu* and the *Brahmāṇḍa Pu* (same as *Vāyu Pu*) have mentioned about *tīrtha*-s but not *vrata*-s. This indicates the influence of the *Mbh* on the two texts. The M. Pu-s which mention the *vrata*-s appear to have been composed at the beginning of the 4th century AD. This indicates that the substitution of the *vrata*-s for sacrifices was a later development. *Vrata*-s appear to be a simpler alternative to the *tīrtha*-s. Visiting holy places and performing rituals over there was a tedious, costly and at the same time difficult to carry out matter. M. Pu-s attempted to give a simpler alternative to the *tīrtha*-s. A list of *tīrtha*–s and *vrata*-s as well as the sacrifices they replace is given in two appendices.

## THE MYTH OF ŚIVA DESTROYING THE SACRIFICE OF DAKṢA

There are many recurrent myth motifs occurring in the Epics and the M. Pu-s. A prominent myth that recurs frequently is that of Śiva destroying the sacrifice of Dakṣa. The myth of Śiva's wife Satī immolating herself on her father Dakṣa's sacrificial altar finds mention in the *Rām, Mbh,* and the M. Pu-s. The need for analyzing the myth separately is that there are many dimensions to this myth. There is a possibility that this myth might highlight a cultural or mythological phenomenon.

- The *Rām* points out the destruction of the sacrifice of Dakṣa in just a couple of verses. Here Śiva points out that the gods did not design any share for him in the sacrifice (Bal. 66. 9-10).
- The *Mbh* has narrated this myth in the context of how Vṛtra was tortured/confused (*mohita*) because of *jvara* and was slain by Indra. In the context of the origin of *jvara,* this myth is narrated. Dakṣa performed the Aśvamedha sacrifice but did not invite Maheśvara. When Maheśvara was questioned by Umā, he said that in all the sacrifices gods did not assign any share for him (Śān. P. 274. 25). Umā was aggrieved to know this fact and she maintained silence. Maheśvara got angry and destroyed the sacrifice. Then, the sacrifice took the form of a deer and leapt in the sky. Maheśvara shot a dart at the sacrifice. From the sweat

of Śiva sprang up a terrible form which became known as *jvara* (Śān. P. 274. 1-42).

The *Mbh* refers to same myth where Rudra=Śiva=Mahādeva destroyed the sacrifice of Dakṣa. Here there is a reference to the eyes of Bhaga being pulled out, Pūṣan's teeth being knocked off by Śiva. In both these myths there is no reference to the immolation of Satī (Sau. P.18 1ff).

- Myth of the destruction of the sacrifice of Dakṣa according to the M. Pu-s:

### Destruction of the Sacrifice of Dakṣa According to the Bhāg. Pu (IV. 2. 1. ff.)

Once all the seers, sages as well as gods presiding over the sacred fires assembled with their attendants in a sacrificial session held by the Prajāpati-s. Dakṣa Prajāpati appeared on the sacrificial scene. Everybody except Lord Brahmā and Śiva, stood up to receive him. This gesture of Śiva angered Dakṣa and he cursed Śiva that the latter will not get any share in the sacrifice. As Śiva was cursed, Nandin, the vehicle of Śiva, became furious. He cursed Dakṣa that his face would turn into a goat. This enraged Sage Bhṛgu, who cursed that those who worship Śiva will become heretics and will be termed as acting contradictory to the Veda-s. Later on the sacrifice of the Prajāpati-s was accomplished. This was the sacrifice in which Hari was duly worshipped. King Dakṣa had performed the Vājapeya and then the Bṛhaspatisava sacrifices (IV. 3. 3). Satī, the wife of Śiva joined the sacrifice of Dakṣa, but was furious to see that there was no share of Rudra in the sacrifice. Later on Satī cast her mortal frame in fire. Seeing this, the attendants of Śiva, who were the escorts of Satī, proceeded to attack Dakṣa. Bhṛgu gave offerings in the Dakṣiṇāgni and from it arose the Ṛbhu-s. Ṛbhu-s beat back the attendants of Śiva. This enraged Śiva and from his matted locks arose

Vīrabhadra and Śiva ordered him to destroy the sacrifice of Dakṣa. The attendants of Śiva led by Vīrabhadra destroyed the sacrificial grounds. They broke the Prāgvaṁśa, Patnīśālā, *sadas*, Agnīdhraśālā, sacrificial instruments, etc. Some destroyed the sacrificial fires and urinated in the sacrificial pits. Vīrabhadra pulled out the moustaches and beard of Bhṛgu, knocked off the teeth of Pūṣan, and setting his foot on the chest of Dakṣa attempted to cut off his head. But his head could not be cut by any weapon. Then observing the way the sacrificial beast is offered in the fire, Vīrabhadra immolated Dakṣa assuming him to be the sacrificial animal. He threw the head of Dakṣa in the Dakṣiṇāgni as an offering (in fact a head is never offered in the Vedic sacrifice). Lord Brahmā and other gods propitiated Śiva and requested him to favour the gods and Bhṛgu, who had lost their limbs during the destruction of the sacrifice. Śiva replaced the limbs of gods in the following way: Bhaga can see through the eyes of Mitra; Pūṣan can eat flour and chew through the teeth of the sacrificer; Dakṣa's head be replaced by the head of the goat; Bhṛgu's moustache and beard be replaced by those of a goat; Adhvaryu and other priests who had lost their hands will use the hands of the Aśvins. Nārāyaṇa, to whom the sacrifice was offered, appeared on the sacrificial scene. All the gods requested Nārāyaṇa to protect the sacrifice. Dakṣa worshipped Nārāyaṇa through the sacrifice and then the other gods both through the principal and secondary types of sacrifices. With a concentrated mind he also waited upon Rudra with the share due to him. The sacrifice was concluded with the *avabhṛtha* bath.

### Destruction of the Sacrifice of Dakṣa According to the Kū. Pu (I. 15)

The *Kū. Pu* presents this myth differently. Dakṣa, the Prajāpati was cursed by Śiva. Therefore, he censured Śiva and started to perform a sacrifice at Gaṅgādvāra. All the gods were invited. On seeing this, a sage named Dadhīca questioned about the absence of Śiva in the sacrifice. The answer given by Dakṣa was that, in all the sacrifices the share to Śiva is not allotted. Dadhīca said that he is eulogized as one of a thousand rays by the singers of *sāman* hymns, the Hotṛ-s and Adhvaryu-s see him as Rudramūrti (one of the terrible form), of the creator of the universe and an embodiment of the three Veda-s. The haughty Dakṣa said that the twelve Āditya-s, who had come are known as suns and there is no other Sun. The sages who were present applauded Dakṣa. Lord Brahmā vanished from the sacrifice. Seeing this Dakṣa took refuge to Viṣṇu. Sage Dadhīca cursed the sages who had censured Śiva that they would attain hell after death. Śrīdevī implored Śiva to destroy the sacrifice of Dakṣa. Then Śiva created Rudra. He became the famous Vīrabhadra. Bhadrakālī was created by Umā. All the Gaṇa-s were very terrible. Weilding weapons, accompanied by their terrible wives they reached the sacrificial place riding on bulls. Vīrabhadra said to the sages that all the Gaṇa-s had come to the sacrificial place to receive their shares. The sages said that they did not know the mantra-s authorizing the shares of the Gaṇa-s. The *mantra*-s (personified)retaliated and left the gods. Vīrabhadra sportively plucked the eyes of Bhaga, knocked off the teeth of Pūṣan and kicked the moon god. He cut off the hands of the fire god and playfully pulled out his tongue. He had a combat with Viṣṇu, in which Garuḍa fled. Ultimately Lord Brahmā intervened and propitiated Vīrabhadra.

### Destruction of the Sacrifice of Dakṣa According to the Vām. Pu (Ch. II-VI)

Dakṣa, the Prajāpati, started performing a sacrifice after the end of autumn season. The reason given was that Viṣṇu woke up after this season. He invited twelve Āditya-s, chief gods such as Indra, along with Kaśyapa and appointed them as assistants of the sacrifice. The couples, namely Vasiṣṭha and Arundhatī, Atri and Anasūya, Viśvāmitra and Dhṛti, Gautama and Ahalyā, Bharadvāja and Amayā and the Sage Aṅgiras with his wife Candrā were invited in the sacrifice. They were the *sadasya*-s of the sacrifice. Dharma and Ahiṁsā were also invited. He became the Dvārapāla of the sacrifice. Ariṣṭanemī collected the fuel of the sacrifice and Bhṛgu was employed to recite appropriate *mantra*-s.

Dakṣa invited all his sons-in-law, daughters and grandchildren, except, Śiva and Satī. The reason why Śiva was not invited was that he had become a Kapālin (*Vam. Pu.* II. 17c-d). The background of Śiva becoming Kapālin is narrated by Pulastya. It has the strife between Lord Brahmā and Śiva at its roots. The enraged Śaṅkara severed with the tip of his nail, the head of Lord Brahmā. The head fell on the left palm of Śaṅkara and never dropped down from his hand. Since this was a *brahmahatyā,* where he went the rivers dried up. Inspite of having bath at various ponds in different forests, the sin was not washed off. He heard the sweet speech of Hari, who suggested that on visiting places like the hermitage of Lola Ravi, situated at Vārāṇasī and Daśāśvamedha and taking holy baths, the sins of Śiva would get washed off. The pond in which Śaṅkara took bath became known as Kapālamocana. The skull dropped down from the hand of Śiva after taking bath. This was the reason, why he was not invited in the sacrifice of Dakṣa.

Satī, the wife of Śiva, on realising that everyone except she and Śiva were invited in the sacrifice of her father, dropped down dead. This distressed Śiva and he created

Vīrabhadra, who went to the sacrifice of Dakṣa, to destroy it. Viṣṇu defeated Vīrabhadra, who informed about his discomfiture to Śiva. Śiva appeared on the scene. On seeing him Viṣṇu retired in Kubjāmra. On seeing the angry Śiva, the eight Vasu-s escaped. The track of their escape became the river Sarasvatī, The gods devoured the *puroḍāśa*, the moon and the stars leapt in the sky. The sages recited the Śatarudrīya hymn to appease Śiva. Śiva knocked off the teeth of Pūṣan, Bhaga's eyes were pulled out and the hands of Aṁśumat were broken. On the extinction of the sacrificial fire, the sacrifice assumed the form of the deer and flew in the sky taking Dakṣiṇā with him. Śiva followed him with a bow in his hand. The Purāṇa then narrates the formation of constellations and does not mention anything about the share of the sacrifice received by Śiva.

## The Destruction of the Sacrifice of Dakṣa According to the Pad. Pu (I. 5)

The King Dakṣa made the great altar for the sacrifice. He appointed four priests. Vasiṣṭha was the Hotṛ, Aṅgiras was the best Adhvaryu, Bṛhaspati was the Udgātṛ and Nārada was the Brahman. When the sacrifice commenced and oblations were offered into fires, all the Vasu-s and the twelve Āditya-s, the two Aśvins, Maruts and the fourteen Manu-s arrived there. Satī, the wife of Śiva, questioned the absence of her husband. The appearance of Śiva was so terrible that he would bring shame to Dakṣa, therefore Śiva was not invited in the sacrifice. This enraged Satī and she cast off her body at a place known as Śaunaka. Satī's death aggrieved Śiva and he sent orders for the destruction of the sacrifice of Dakṣa. The sacrifice flew to the heaven. Dakṣa tried to appease Śiva. Being pacified, Śiva gave Dakṣa the fruit of the sacrifice.

## Destruction of the Sacrifice of Dakṣa According to the Vāyu. Pu (Pūrva. Upo. 30. 94. ff.) and Brahmāṇḍa Pu. (I. 13).

Dakṣa, the Prajāpati, started the performance of a great Aśvamedha sacrifice. Āditya-s, Vasu-s, Sādhya-s, Marut-s, Indra and other gods arrived there for their share in the sacrifice. Śiva was not invited. When Dakṣa was questioned by Dadhīci for not inviting Śiva, he said that he had so many Rudra-s there armed with spears and having matted hair. They stayed in eleven forms. There was no need to invite Śiva. This sacrifice was in honour of Viṣṇu. The offerings sanctified by *mantra*-s would be offered in the Āhavanīya fire. The oblations would be held in a golden vessel. Dadhīca remarked that he, who has invited Śiva, has invited all deities, since no deity is superior to Śiva. Umā, the consort of Śiva, questioned him about his absence in the sacrifice. Śiva answered that his share in all sacrifices was not allotted to him. By following the traditional procedure, the gods do not give him due share in sacrifice (*Vāyu Pu.* 30. 112-113). Men of good qualities do eulogise him in sacrifices. They recite the Rathantarasāman. In the Brahmasattra, the *brāhmaṇa*-s worship Śiva and the Adhvaryu-s assign his share (*Ibid.* 30. 119). Then Śiva created a terrible form, i.e. Vīrabhadra and commanded him to destroy the sacrifice. Bhadrakālī also accompanied him in this task. Many Rudra-s were created for the destruction of the sacrifice. They broke the sacrificial vessels to pieces. The altar was completely shattered. Dakṣa began to flee through the sky in the form of a deer. Vīrabhadra cut off the head of Dakṣa. He commanded Dakṣa to seek refuge to Śiva. Dakṣa propitiated Śiva and by his grace derived the merit of a thousand Aśvamedha and a hundred Vājapeya sacrifices.

## Destruction of the Sacrifice of Dakṣa According to the Brahma Pu Ch. 32.

Satī, the daughter of Dakṣa had married Śiva. Dakṣa did not invite her to the sacrifice because Śiva did not bow down to him as he stood with his natural brilliance. The infuriated Satī performed the Āgneyī Dhāraṇa rite and reduced her body to ashes (Ch. 32. 24-25). The sages and Dakṣa were cursed by Śiva. He was cursed in return by Dakṣa that he will not be worshipped by *brāhmaṇa*-s. Dakṣa was reborn as Prācetasa Dakṣa in the Vaivasvata Manvantara and he performed the Aśvamedha. The Āditya-s, Rudra-s, Vasu-s, Sādhya-s, Marut-s and Viṣṇu came to take the share of the sacrifice. Dadhīci questioned as to why was Śiva not invited. Dakṣa answered that he had eleven Rudra-s and did not recognize any Maheśvara besides them. When Umā, the consort of Śiva questioned him for not attending the sacrifice, Śiva said that following the precedence, gods do not allot any share to him. There are people who praise him as the Lord of Sacrifices. They sing the Rathantarasāman for him and they worship him by means of sacrifices. The priests who perform sacrifices allot share unto him. On hearing this, the furious Umā created Bhadrakālī. (Bhadrakālī is a form of Pārvatī).

Śiva, on hearing about the self-immolation in the fire of his wife Satī, at the famous sacrifice conducted by Dakṣa, rushed in all anger to the spot and beat the earth with his matted hair and there ensued two forces called Vīrabhadra and Bhadrakālī. This Bhadrakālī was really Satī in another form[374]. Both Vīrabhadra and Bhadrakālī set out to destroy the sacrifice. From the pores of the hair of Vīrabhadra many followers of Rudra were created. The ritual vessels were broken into pieces and reduced to dust, the sacrificial chambers crumbled down. Foodstuffs and beverages were consumed by the goblins. They burnt the sacrifice. The head of the sacrifice was cut off. Sacrificial posts were pulled up and cast off here and there. The sacrifice took a form of deer and fled in the sky. Seeing the sacrifice flying in the sky, Vīrabhadra followed it with a bow and arrow. From the drop of sweat of Vīrabhadra, *jvara* was created. Being frightened of this, all the gods, including Lord Brahmā and Dakṣa, praised Śiva. Pleased by the eulogy of Dakṣa, Śiva said that he would beget the fruit of a thousand Aśvamedha and hundred Vājapeya sacrifices. Then the *jvara* was distributed among living beings.

## Destruction of the Sacrifice of Dakṣa According to the Varāha Pu Ch. 21.

Lord Brahmā, in order to create different beings, entered into deep thought, but could not create. He became angry and Rudra arose from his anger. Lord Brahmā gave his wife Gaurī to him. He persuaded Rudra to create. Rudra, finding himself to be incapable, entered into water to perform penance. Lord Brahmā lodged the beautiful Gaurī within his body and then, produced seven beings from his mind and also Dakṣa. Gaurī became Dākṣāyaṇī, i.e. the daughter of Dakṣa. Their children were Indra and other gods, eight Vasu-s, Rudra-s, Āditya-s and Marut-s.

Dakṣa started a sacrifice to propitiate Lord Brahmā. In that, the functions of the priests were taken upon themselves by the sons of Lord Brahmā. Marīci became Brahman, Atri the supervisor, Aṅgiras the Agnīdhra, Pulastya the Hotṛ, Pulaha the Udgātṛ, Kratu the Prastotṛ, Pracetas the Pratihatṛ, Vasiṣṭha the Subrahmaṇya. All the sons of Dākṣāyaṇī were to be honoured. Suddenly, Rudra arose from the depths of the water. He created the four kinds of mortals, celestials and five things. He saw the earth full of vegetation and big forests and peopled by human beings and beasts. He heard the recitation of the priests in Dakṣa's house. He became very angry. He roared aloud and from his roar emerged ghosts and goblins in crores. There was a fight between the gods and Rudra and his army. Bhaga was made eyeless and Pūṣan's teeth were pulled out. There was a dual combat between Rudra and Viṣṇu. Lord Brahmā calmed them down. Though the sacrifice was smashed the fruit of accomplishment was given to Dakṣa. Rudra was given a share in the sacrifices. Vināyaka was given the foremost position during sacrifices and ceremonies (23. 30).

### Destruction of the Sacrifice of Dakṣa According to the Nār. Pu (Utt. 66. 5 ff)

At Haridvāra, Dakṣa had performed a sacrifice to propitiate Lord Viṣṇu, who is the lord of the sacrifices. All gods except Śiva were invited. Sages, *gandharva*-s, *apsaras*-es, etc. participated in the sacrifice. Satī became eager to attend the sacrifice. Paying no heed to the advice of her husband that it was not conducive to go there, she went to attend the sacrifice. She was neither received nor honoured. She gave up her life at the sacrificial place. On hearing of her death, Lord sent Vīrabhadra to destroy the sacrifice. Śiva was propitiated and the disorganized sacrifice was complete.

### Destruction of the Sacrifice of Dakṣa According to the *Liṅga Pu.* (Ch. 99-100)

Dakṣa the Prajāpati, was cursed by Nārada that he would censure Śiva. Owing to his haughtiness Dakṣa dishonoured Śiva. When Satī came to know this she reduced her body into ashes by her Yogic power. The Gaṇa-s along with Vīrabhadra came on the sacrificial scene. The sacrificial place was near Gaṅgādvāra. The infuriated leaders of the

Gaṇa-s uprooted the sacrificial posts and hurled them about along with the Hotṛ and Prastotṛ. They burned everything. Vīrabhadra sportively uprooted the eyes of Bhaga with the tip of his finger. With his fist he hit the teeth of Pūṣan and made them fall. He kicked the moon with the toe of his foot. He cut off the head of Indra. After cutting off the hands of Agni and after uprooting his tongue, he kicked him on his head with his leg. The Āhavanīya fire fled in the sky in the form of a deer. Vīrabhadra beheaded it. He defeated Viṣṇu and also Sarasvatī. He was then pacified and pleased by Lord Brahmā. Vināyaka was assigned with the duty of creating impediment in the rituals of that person by whom the sacrifice had been performed without the monetary gifts on the surface of the earth (I. 105. 16).

## Destruction of the Sacrifice of Dakṣa According to the Satīkhaṇḍa of the Rudrasaṁhitā of the *Śiva Pu*

This section of the *Śiva Pu* describes the destruction of the sacrifice of Dakṣa in detail. Śiva was not given any share in the sacrifice performed by Dakṣa. Satī was insulted and she cast off her body. This enraged Śiva and he ordered Vīrabhadra to annihilate the sacrifice of Dakṣa. The sacrifice of Dakṣa was destroyed and he was beheaded and the head was thrown in the fire. Later on when Rudra was eulogised he resuscitated Dakṣa and the whole sacrifice was renewed. Due share was offered to Rudra, by all the gods (Rudrasaṁhitā Satīkhaṇḍa I. 24-40).

Formerly, a great sacrifice was performed by sages and noble souls who assembled at Prayāga. All the gods including Śiva gathered at the assembly. Dakṣa, the Prajāpati arrived there. Everyone bowed to him except Śiva. This annoyed Dakṣa and he expelled Śiva from sacrifices (Rudrasaṁhitā, Satīkhaṇḍa 17. 18). There were exchange of curses between Dakṣa and Nandin. Ultimately Śiva intervened by saying, "I am the sacrifice, the sacrificial rite, the ancillary adjuncts of the sacrifice, the Self of the sacrifice and one engrossed in sacrifice. I am out of the sacrifice too". Dakṣa started performing a great sacrifice. All the gods were invited and they arrived at the sacrificial scene at Kanakhala. It is to be noted that everything which was occurring was because of the Māyā of Śiva. Viṣṇu himself was the presiding authority along with the Marut-s. In that sacrifice which was being performed in that place Bhṛgu and other sages were made *ṛtvij*-s by Dakṣa. The sacrificial fire evinced its diverse forms in a thousand ways, during the sacrificial festivities, in order to receive the sacrificial offerings of Dakṣa. In that altar, sacrifice itself was present in its beautiful embodied form. There were 86,000 *ṛtvij*-s in the sacrifice, and 64,000 Udgātṛ-s. The seven sages severally repeated the *sāman* hymns. Śiva was not invited for that sacrifice because he was a Kapālin. Satī being his wife was not invited by Dakṣa. Dadhīci warned the assembly that the sacrifice cannot be perfect and complete without the noble-souled Śiva. Dakṣa being the father of Satī, she set out to meet her father. She could not bear the insult of her husband and therefore reduced her body to ashes. The furious Śiva created Virabhadra and ordered him to destroy the sacrifice of Dakṣa. He struck and smashed Bhṛgu, while Maṇibhadra kicked him on his chest and plucked off his moustaches. Nandin forcibly plucked out the eyes of Bhaga who was felled over the ground with anger because he winked at Dakṣa while cursing. Caṇḍa forcibly knocked off the teeth of Pūṣan, who had formerly laughed and showed his teeth while Śiva was being cursed. Vīrabhadra threw the head of Dakṣa in the fire and reduced it to ashes. Dakṣa regained his life by the grace of Śiva. Under his guidance the sacrifice was rearranged in which Śiva was duly honoured and worshipped. The entire account is covered in detail in Ch 27-Ch. 43 of the text.

## Destruction of the Sacrifice of Dakṣa According to the *Sk. Pu* (I. 1. 1-5)

Due to the request made by Lord Brahmā, Dakṣa gave his daughter Dākṣāyaṇī to Śaṅkara. Once, by chance he came to the Naimiṣa forest. On arrival, he was duly honoured by the sages as well as by the gods and the demons. All of them stood up on the arrival of Dakṣa, except Mahādeva. Dakṣa took it as an insult and cursed Śiva that he will be banned out of all sacrifices because he had gone beyond the castes and has transgressed the discipline of the castes.

Once Dakṣa performed a great sacrifice in which all the sages and gods were invited except Śiva. Dadhīca protested against Dakṣa and asked him to invite Śiva and his wife Dākṣāyaṇī for the sacrifice. On hearing this, Dakṣa said that the root cause of the existence of gods is Viṣṇu, in whom the eternal virtue is present. Veda-s and sacrifices are established in him. All those who have been invited in the sacrifice are worthy of being present over there. Dakṣa said that he did not consider Śiva worthy of being present in the sacrifice. Śiva is not of noble birth, he is doomed and he is always a favourite of the doomed. He is the sole Lord of goblins, ghosts and vampires. Therefore he is not invited in the sacrifice. At the abode of Śiva, Satī his wife decided to attend the sacrifice, though she was not invited. Śiva gave his consent and surrounded by Gaṇa-s, she arrived at the sacrificial place. She questioned those who were present there as why was her husband not invited. He is Yajña incarnate, the sacrificial offerings and everything related to the sacrifice. Satī could not tolerate her insult. Therefore she entered the fire and immolated herself. Seeing this the

Gaṇa-s also followed her immolation and gave up their lives. This made the sacrifice unclean. Śiva created Vīrabhadra and ordered him to destroy the sacrifice. Dakṣa requested Viṣṇu to protect the sacrifice. Viṣṇu reminded Dakṣa of the follies committed by him for offending Śiva. There was a tough fight between all the gods including Viṣṇu and Vīrabhadra and his Gaṇa-s. Vīrabhadra uprooted the beard and moustache of Bhṛgu and knocked off the teeth of Pūṣan. Dakṣa's head was chopped off and put in the sacrifical fire. A distorted head of an animal was placed on the headless body of Dakṣa and he was revived by Śiva. The destruction stopped when Dakṣa propitiated Śiva.

## The Source of the Myth can be Traced up to the Saṁhitā-s[375].

The *Tait. Sam,* refers to the gods excluding Rudra from sacrifice, which they were performing (II. 6. 8. 3ff). He, being angry, shot an arrow at the sacrifice. The gods felt uneasy at the incident and removed the wounded part of the sacrifice, which was equal to a barley-grain in measurement. They took it to Pūṣan, who having eaten it, had his teeth knocked out. Hence Pūṣan is toothless and is given only *karambha.* Then the piece was consumed by Bṛhaspati with great difficulty (details are avoided). The *Gop. Br* also refers to Rudra being denied any share in the sacrifice. He, being angry cut off a portion of the sacrifice. The *Śat. Br* associates the anger of Rudra with Prajāpati who was enamoured of his daughter. He united with her and this angered Rudra who shot a dart at Prajāpati.

The Puranic myths of the destruction of the sacrifice of Dakṣa appear to be embroidered around the Vedic motifs.

A) Rudra being excluded from getting any share in the sacrifices performed by gods.

B) His anger for Prajāpati for inculcating passion for his daughter. In the Puranic myths, Prajāpati became Dakṣa Prajāpati.

After enumerating the Epic and Puranic versions of the myth of the destruction of Dakṣa's sacrifice by Śiva, the following observations are made:

- Twelve out of the eighteen M. Pu-s have incorporated this myth. This myth has also been narrated in the two epics. This indicates that the myth was very popular for many centuries.
- Apart from the destruction of the sacrifice of Dakṣa, there is hardly anything common in all the versions of this myth.
- Each text adds its flavour to this myth and hence penning down all the variants was essential in this section. The Śaivite M. Pu-s mention the greatness and superiority of Śiva. The *Kū. Pu* makes Lord Brahmā solve this feud. The Vaiṣṇavaite M. Pu-s indirectly justify Dakṣa's neglect of Śiva to his crude and barbarous practices, nakedness, smearing ashes and even carrying the skull (*kapāla*). All these practices render the sacrifice unclean.
- In some variants, the cause of the feud between Dakṣa and Śiva was that Śiva did not stand up as a mark of reverence on the arrival of Dakṣa, which led to exchange of curses between them. The uncanny and terrible appearance of Śiva was another reason for which he was not invited by Dakṣa. Another reason was that no share in the sacrifice was devised for Śiva. Sages like Bhṛgu and others did not desire the presence of Śiva in the sacrifice.
- A noteworthy point is that the Rathantarasāman was attributed to Śiva and some *brāhmaṇa*-s did worship him. This indicates that the place of Śiva in the sacrifice

was not rejected; only certain sections disapproved the position of Śiva in the sacrifice.

- The different versions of this myth mention different sacrifices performed by Dakṣa.
- The self-immolation of Satī motivated the destruction of the sacrifice. In certain M. Pu-s, it was the consort of Śiva, whose fury caused the destruction of the sacrifice.
- The sacrifice was destroyed by Śiva himself or by Rudra or by Vīrabhadra, the attendant of Śiva. The texts project various names destroying the sacrifice.
- The sacrifice was either destroyed or it leapt in the sky taking the form of a deer.
- Most of the texts mention Bhaga, whose eyes were pulled out and Pūṣan, whose teeth were knocked off.
- The myth ends in the propitiation and pacification of Śiva by various gods and Dakṣa.

Gonda observes, "That certain circles continue to regard him (i.e. Śiva) as an outsider standing apart from the other gods may appear from the popular story of Dakṣa's sacrifice"[376]. To conclude, the myth of the destruction of the sacrifice of Dakṣa by Śiva represents the disregard displayed towards Śiva, initially by certain sections of the society practicising the Vedic sacrifices. The myth proceeds towards the end in assimilating and integrating Śiva in the Vedic sacrifice.

# 7

# Observations and Conclusions

A study of the nature of Vedic sacrifices and the rituals thereof, as reflected in the Sanskrit texts, has been done in the earlier chapters. By using a combination of two methodologies, viz. hermeneutics and historical textual criticism, an attempt has been undertaken to estimate the position of Vedic sacrifices in ancient India. Hermeneutics has not only assisted in bridging the historical gap but also the gap caused by laying the present century parameters to the ancient texts. Historical textual criticism has helped the stratification of various texts especially, the Epics and the M. Pu-s. Thus, by combining both the methodologies, the references to the Vedic sacrifice in Sanskrit texts have been discussed in the earlier chapters.

Based on this study some observations regarding the image of the Vedic sacrifice as reflected through these references is highlighted below:

## SACRIFICE AS A PRINCIPLE AND SACRIFICE AS A RITUAL

The early nature of the Vedic sacrifice was simple. It became developed into a complex structure incorporating tremendous resources. It was a time-consuming process. A probe into the references to Vedic sacrifices in the Sanskrit texts indicates that the importance of the sacrifice as a ritualistic endeavour has diminished over the ages. But its importance as an institution has remained uncontested. When the M. Pu-s attempted to substitute the sacrifice with the help of *tīrtha*-s, *vrata*-s, *pūjā*-s, etc. they tried to find a substitute equivalent to the greatness of sacrifice along with its capacity of yielding the desired fruit of the sacrificer. This indicates that sacrifice as a revered institution existed, even though as a practiced form of religion, it declined. The *vrata*-s followed the principles of sacrifice, viz. *dravyam devata tyagah* Some offerings were given to the deity, the deity was pleased and the desired object (if any) was achieved.

The Upaniṣad-s and the *Bhagavadgītā* had set some higher goals to be achieved other than achieving material gains and temporal position in the heaven, which were assured by the Vedic sacrifice. The speculations of the nature of Ātman or Brahman led to the emergence of the concept of Ātmayajña or Jñānayajña. (This term 'Jñānayajña' has also been popularized in the twentieth and the twenty-first century by the Chinmaya Mission by using this term for discourses on the *Bhagavadgītā*). This can be understood as the attempt of interiorizing the Vedic sacrifice. New dimensions of meanings were given to the old terms of Vedic sacrifice[377]. The thought depicted in the Upaniṣad-s throws light on the transition of ideas of the Vedic sacrifice for e.g.; *brahman* as sacred utterance, *karman* as careful ritual act and *tapas* as the sacrificial heat in fire and cooking; to supreme power or Ultimate Reality, action in general and interior heat respectively[378]. The allegorical references occurring in the Upaniṣad-s also indicate the importance enjoyed by the Vedic sacrifice. Same concepts of Ātmayajña and Jñānayajña have been stretched further by the *M. Pu*-s in the form of Japayajña and Tapoyajña. Inspite of procedural or ritualistic details suffering a decline, the Vedic sacrifice as a principle continued to enjoy a revered position in Ancient India. Even in the present times the sacrifices are not entirely obsolete. Some *soma*-sacrifices are still performed in different places in India. Moreover, the sacrificial terminology is still used in various vernaculars of India. Words like *yajamāna*, i.e. the head of a house or a husband, *sattra*, i.e. a long discussion session, *sadasya*, i.e. member of an institution, indicate the influence of this institution even in the present times. Moreover, laying down life for one's country is termed as *'āhuti'* of *'prāṇa'*-s for the country.

## COMPARISON BETWEEN THE SACRIFICES IN THE TWO EPICS

The two epics, viz. the *Rām* and the *Mbh* abound in sacrificial details. This leaves room for comparison of the nature of Vedic sacrifices between the two epics. Both the epics discuss the Aśvamedha with its ritualistic details, which agree to a great extent with the manuals of the Vedic sacrifice like the Brāhmaṇa-s and the Śrautasūtra-s. Among the two Aśvamedha-s performed in the *Rām*, one performed by Daśaratha was for the sake of progeny and the other performed by Rāma was as an expiation for deaths caused in the war. Yudhiṣṭhira in the *Mbh* also performed the Aśvamedha as an expiation for killing one's kinsmen in the great battle.

Being voluminous in size, the *Mbh* definitely has a larger number of sacrificial details than the *Rām*. It casts light on the different types of sacrifices right from the various *iṣṭi*-s like Sādyaskra and Darśapūrṇamāsa, *ahīna*-s like the Pauṇḍarīka and *sattra*-s like the Sarpasattra, Rākṣasasattra, etc. It also mentions about the various Somasaṁsthā-s like the Agniṣṭoma and the Vājapeya. It takes pride in describing the Rājasūya and Aśvamedha sacrifices performed by Yudhiṣṭhira and other kings. It gives a list of great kings who attained heaven due to the performance of great sacrifices. However, the *Mbh* voices dissent against the ritualistic details and violence occurring in the sacrifices. It also makes an attempt to substitute the institution of sacrifice by enumerating a list of *tīrtha*-s, which yield the fruit of various sacrifices, in which the Aśvamedha tops the list. The *Bhagavadgītā* which is the part of the *Mbh* relates maintenance of cosmic order to the institution of sacrifice, i.e. Yajñacakra. The Vedic sacrifice is also reflected through different allegorical expressions occurring in the text.

The *Rām* on the other hand considers the performance of sacrifices as a parameter of greatness for kings. The sacrificial details in the *Rām* indicate the position of sacrifice in different cultures. One interesting feature of the *Rām*, which is quite different from the *Mbh*, is that of the sacrificial names of the Rākṣasa-s which reflects their hostility towards the institution of sacrifice. *Rām* records certain customs like pacification of the site (*vāstuśamana*), offerings given by Kausalyā in the fire and Sītā assuring offerings to the rivers, namely Yamunā and Gaṅgā and certain customs of the Rākṣasa-s. The *Rām* does not record any dissent or protest against the sacrificial institution. Naturally there is no requirement of devising any substitute to the institution of sacrifice. This raises a question that if *Rām* is post-dated to the *Mbh* how is it that it does not record any dissent or change in the sacrificial institution? The *Rām* is called an Ādikāvya (first poetry) projecting the exploits of the great king Rāma, who upheld the institution of sacrifice. Since the text has projected only one hero and its expanse being not as vast as that of the *Mbh*, the *Rām* does not incorporate any statements reflecting change in the institution of sacrifice. The *Mbh* is a voluminous work having propagation of *dharma,* i.e. righteousness, as its purpose. It is regarded as Itihāsa, i.e. a work narrating the past occurrences. The development of the text is spread over centuries. Hence, it does track changes in the nature of religion occurring over these centuries. Sacrifice being an integral part of Vedic religion, the *Mbh* does record changing trends in the nature of Vedic sacrifice.

## THE NARRATOR AND THE ORNATE POET

The Ancient Sanskrit texts incorporated in this work can be classified into two:

a) Texts compiled by the *sūta*-narrators comprise of the epics and the *M. Pu*-s and

b) Texts composed by the poets patronized by some kings.

Since these two sets of texts have a structural and thematic difference it is essential to observe the reflections of the Vedic sacrifice in both the groups.

A common feature of the texts in 'group a)' is that they are embedded in a sacrificial background. This lent sanctity to the texts, which was essential to authenticate the religious principles propounded by them. The sacrificial scenario in which the texts were composed assisted in imbibing the religious principles preached by the texts on the audience which gathered on a large scale to listen to the narration of these texts.

From the study of the texts of 'group a)', it is observed that the narrators in the narration of the Epics and the *M. Pu*-s have reflected the changes undergone in the Vedic sacrifice. The purpose of narration was not merely entertainment but to inculcate and uphold values, faith, tradition and belief in Vedic religion. As far as descriptions of sacrificial performances are considered, the narrators of the epics have displayed thorough knowledge of the rituals, which indicates that they probably had an access to the texts documenting the rituals or they were a witness to many sacrifices performed. The *sūta*-narrators of the *M. Pu*-s have not gone into several ritualistic details of the Vedic sacrifice. They have given due place to the Vedic sacrifice in their cosmological descriptions regarding the creation of the universe and the place of sacrifice therein and how sacrifice was created by Lord Brahmā. Sacrifice finds due position in the genealogies of various royal dynasties. Kings, who were revered by the narrators were performers of sacrifices. The narrators sanctified the obscure births of some personalities by carving different myths of their sacrificial origin. This difference throws light on the upheavals faced by the Vedic sacrifice in specific and Vedic religion in general. However, in the effort of intermingling sacrifices and myths they have taken liberty and paid little or absolutely no attention to the ritualistic details. Understanding the changing approach of the society towards Vedic religion and the sacrifice, the narrators devised the *vrata*-s, *tīrtha*-s, *japa*, recitation of *stotra*-s, etc. as equivalent to Vedic sacrifice.

The ornate poets on the other hand composed poetry for the entertainment of the aristocratic class and only eulogized the pomp and fervour of the sacrifice with little or no attention to the authenticity of the rituals which they were describing. Apart from a dramatist like Bhavabhūti and poet like Bhaṭṭi, the ornate poets only used the Vedic sacrifice to add a tinge of religious flavour to their work. It is interesting to note that the dates of the compositions of the M. Pu-s and the compositions of classical works run parallel to each other, yet there is a great deal of temperamental difference in them. One can account this type of discrepancy to the purpose of the composition of classical works. Mammaṭa in his work *Kāvyaprakāśa* has well-defined the purpose of poetic compositions[379]. Besides, the purpose of the compositions of ornate poetry was for entertaining the scholastic audience of the royal court, eulogizing one's patron and displaying one's knowledge of 'polished' Sanskrit language. It cannot be denied that the ornate poets have set ideals of kings and commoners before the society, yet the purpose of propagating the sacrificial religion does not figure in this endeavour. Therefore the court-poetry does not abound in sacrificial details or at times has misquoted the ritualistic details of the Vedic sacrifice.

## BOND BETWEEN SACRIFICE AND KINGSHIP

As per the references occurring in the Sanskrit texts, when sacrificial rituals were performed by the priestly class, it was the king who was the sponsor/sacrificer. The *Mbh* and the M. Pu-s abound in exhaustive lists of kings who had performed and patronized sacrifices. The *Rām* also gives a list of kings who had performed the Aśvamedha sacrifice. Hence, the references to the Vedic sacrifice in the Sanskrit texts reveal royal support which this institution enjoyed during the period of the rise of Vedic religion. Gonda has analyzed the relation between sacrificial ritual and kingship:

> The king is an intermediary between the powers of nature and society. As such he is an essential factor for the well-being of the people... A good king should strive always to add to the prosperity of his people, bringing about a state of plenty and affluence. His first aim should be to seek his realm's happiness. Where the ideal king lives, the people are prosperous, cheerful and healthy, pure in conduct, expert in works; there the sacrifices are performed and the clouds always pour waters[380].

This indicates that the maintenance of cosmic order and the king performing sacrificial rituals were interlinked with each other. The texts stress that sacrifice is one of the essential duties of the king. Therefore Manu also says that the kings who are engaged in performing long sacrifices and religious observances are not liable to *aśauca,* i.e. impurity (*Manu Sm*.5. 93). The king stands for royal glory and might. In order to perform the kingly duties, which are in accordance to glory and might associated with kingship, he should be free from disability and disease. The king having any handicap was not eligible to take up the position of a king because he was disqualified as a sacrificer, says the *Mbh* (Udyoga P. 147, 149). Unless he can perform a sacrifice how can he maintain peace and prosperity in the kingdom? The equation that the king performed sacrifices and thereby ensured peace and prosperity in the kingdom was accepted by the ancient Sanskrit texts. Kings were associated with great sacrifices such as the Aśvamedha, Rājasūya and Vājapeya (statistically, the Aśvamedha has topped the list of sacrifices performed by kings). These sacrifices are associated with monarchical status and power, through which the king exercised his political authority. The religious performances in the form of sacrifices strengthened and legitimized the political authority of a king.

Just as the king personified royal glory and power, he was also regarded as a partial incarnation of Viṣṇu. Viṣṇu, the god, was equated with the sacrifice in the Vedic-Brahmanical and later Sanskrit texts. This equation was transferred to the king as he was Viṣṇu on the earth. Hence performance of sacrifices was mandatory for the king following Vedic religion.

Relationship between sacrifice and kingship can be better understood, if the political, social and economic upheavals faced by kingship in ancient India are taken into consideration. On the political sphere, in a span of eighth century BC to fifth century BC monarchy witnessed many changes. The powerful Paurava dynasty (lineage of king Janamejaya) declined, which gave rise to a number of small independent states. This was mostly in the form of republics. In the seventh and sixth centuries BC, there existed more or less powerful monarchies alongside the independent republics. There was a constant struggle between the monarchical and non-monarchical forms of governance, which led to the decline of republics and the rise of absolutism and imperialism of the Magadha Empire[381]. On the social sphere it was a transition from a pastoral society to urban culture, from the tribal ties to those of social responsibility in urban units[382]. On the economic front, land was brought under control of the king, to be used at his discretion. Since there was a decline in pastoralism, the form of *dāna* shifted from cattle to lands, especially given by kings to the priests for their performance of royal sacrifices[383]. Selvanayagam observes, 'Nevertheless Vedic ritualism and related beliefs held their sway. The leading kings were certainly not free from Vedic practices, mainly with a view to enhancing royal fame. They patronized grand sacrifices in times of war and victory, being constantly involved in petty warfare against tribes and other republics. Sacrifice also provided an occasion for the kings to receive tribute from defeated territories. The priests ensured the preservation of the rules and *mantra*-s of sacrificial performance, received royal gifts of land on a large scale. Both the priestly and princely classes had a natural right to enjoy public resources[384].

As long as kingship adhered to Vedic religion, the institution of Vedic sacrifice and the priestly class got an unquestioned support from kingship. As soon as monarchy started shifting from the Vedic religion to the *śramaṇa* religion, i.e. either Buddhism or Jainism, or even the Puranic religion, the sacrifice lost protection from kingship. The "Introduction" of this work gives a table of the list of kings who had performed the Aśvamedha sacrifices. The kings have performed in all thirty-three sacrifices. The loss of patronage from kings led to a successive decline in the performance of sacrifices. In this way the bond of Vedic sacrifice and kingship loosened in due course of time.

These observations indicate that over a period of time the institution of sacrifice has not remained static. The factors contributing to the changes are:

## IMPACT OF BUDDHISM AND JAINISM

Though Vedic religion along with its rituals was revered in Ancient India, its authoritarian nature was questioned by some thinkers in the society. The Ājīvika-s, Nirgrantha-s, Parivrājaka-s were the non-Vedic sects existing in the then society[385]. Dange opines that because of the different sects which propagated various ways of life and different ideologies, there was a confusion in the society. Based on the various ideologies, the then society can be clearly classified into two traditions, namely those following the Vedic tradition and *śramaṇa* tradition[386].

Etymologically, the term *śramaṇa* has the root √*śram*, i.e. to labour, to exert or to exhaust. This tradition came in conflict with the Vedic religion. It challenged the authority of the *Veda*-s and the performance of sacrifices. In the *śramaṇa* tradition, Jainism and Buddhism were prominent.

The Śvetāmbara sect of Jainism believed that Mahāvīra preached the principle of *ahimsā,* for the first time, to the gods for whom the sacrifices were performed. His first public discourse on *ahimsā* was in a sacrificial place, where the sacrifice was in progress. In this way the Jain *śramaṇa*-s visited houses where sacrifices were performed and preached the teachings of Mahāvīra. Initially they met opposition from the people, but later on won their hearts. The event narrated in the twenty-fifth lecture of the *Uttarādhyayana* has a dialogue between Jeyaghosa, a sage and Vijayakosa, a *brāhmaṇa* performing sacrifices. This dialogue is helpful in understanding the approach of Jainism to the Vedic religion in general and sacrifices in particular. The sage goes to the sacrificial hall for alms. But the *brāhmaṇa* says that the priests well versed in the *Veda*-s and sacrificial science can save themselves and others, are alone eligible to receive alms. The sage calmly replies that the most essential subject in the *Veda*-s is the sacrifice of virtues; the priests pretend to know the sacrifice; but the true *brāhmaṇa* is one who has no worldly attachment, who does not repent to having become a monk, who takes delight in noble words and in loving beings and not injuring them. The binding of animals for sacrifice cannot save the sinner because the binding of *karman* is very powerful. One does become a *brāhmaṇa* through chastity and virtues as one becomes a *śramaṇa* by equanimity, a *muni* by knowledge and a *tāpasa* by penance; by one's actions one becomes a *brāhmaṇa, kṣatriya, vaiśya* and *śūdra*. Vijayakosa was convinced and he gave alms to Jeyaghosa, who denied accepting them and requested the *brāhmaṇa* to accept their (Jain) order at once to save him from *samsāra*[387].

The opinion of the Buddha about the sacrificial institution can be understood through an event narrated in the *Kūṭadantasutta*. Once the Buddha and his disciples went to a village in Magadha where a Brāhmaṇa named Kūṭadanta was performing a great sacrifice in which hundreds of animals were being offered as victims. The

Buddha told him a story of a king who performed an excellent sacrifice with products like ghee, honey, oil and butter brought by using his wealth and not taxing people. Yet the subjects gave voluntary contributions since he did not commit any atrocities on them. The king was none else but the Buddha in his previous birth. The Buddha preached that instead of giving oblations in the fire, giving alms to the Buddhist monks or helping the Vihāra-s are more meritorious acts. Kūṭadanta stopped the sacrifice and gave a feast to the Buddha and his followers in the sacrificial place. He joined the order of monks of the Buddha[388].

Thus the two events narrated in the texts indicate anti-sacrifice approach of Jainism and Buddhism and their power to convince the sacrificing Brāhmaṇa-s of the futility of the sacrifice. Some members from the learned community got convinced and started accepting either of the two traditions. Kings like Aśoka and Harṣavardhana accepted Buddhism and banned animal sacrifices. The masses were convinced by Jain and Buddhist traditions owing to the public sermons delivered in their language, i.e. in the language of the masses.

Thus the popularization of Jainism and Buddhism is an important factor for the decline of Vedic sacrifice. It also brought about a change in the nature of Vedic sacrifice, which got reflected in the changing trends seen in the epics and the M. Pu-s.

## CHANGE IN THE APPROACH REGARDING ANIMAL SACRIFICE

The Vedic sacrifice which revived in second century BC witnessed some important changes in its structure. We have seen in the chapters on the *Mbh* and the M. Pu-s dissent towards the animal sacrifice. Sacrifice by giving offerings of food-grains, vegetables and milk products, was considered superior to the sacrifice in which animals were immolated. A fear is expressed in the M. Pu-s that violence performed in the sacrifices led the performers to bondage. The thoughts of non-violence were inherited by the revived sacrificial institution not only from the *śramaṇa* tradition but also from the Upanisadic school of thought. Sacrifice performed by those who accepted the Vānaprastha āśrama was also with the available forest products. The devotion propagated in the M. Pu-s had serious objections towards animal offerings in the sacrifice. Non-violence and vegetarianism attained prestige. The changed trend can be understood as an initiative taken by the composers of the *Mbh* and the M. Pu-s to popularize Vedic sacrifice in a new form by understanding that the sacrifices with animal offerings were no longer revered by the masses and the classes. Thus instead of rejecting the sacrifice, the composers of the *Mbh* and the M. Pu-s have presented it in a new form which appealed to the masses. This change is also followed in the sacrifices performed in the twentieth and the twenty-first centuries. The Vājapeya sacrifice performed in 1955 in Pune and Agnicayana ritual performed in 1975 in Kerala did not incorporate animal sacrifices. Goats used as offering in these sacrifices were released after the performance of the sacrifice.

## SIMPLIFICATION OF THE RITUAL

While understanding the nature of Vedic sacrifice, we have focused on the Śrauta tradition. The Epic and the Puranic tradition also gave importance to the sacrifices of the Gṛhya tradition. Gṛhya rituals as compared to the Śrauta rituals were simpler in nature and could be performed without the assistance of *ṛtvij*-s, etc. They were so designed to keep in view the society on the whole and not the upper classes. But the principles of the Śrauta tradition were embedded in the Gṛhya rituals. The Puranic tradition gives importance to Pākayajña-s. There are references to Brahmayajña and Devayajña in the M. Pu-s which indicate the attempt towards simplification of Vedic rituals. However, this process is not rejecting the Vedic tradition but retaining the ancient principles of sacrifice, in a modified form. Dange observes that:

> ... the Upanayana ceremony (thread-ceremony) follows the principle of Dīkṣā performed during a Vedic sacrifice. The importance of Agni has been retained in the Gṛhya tradition. The trees which were important in the Śrauta tradition are equally important in the Gṛhya tradition, for their faggots are used in the Gṛhya rituals. The Śrauta sacrifices like the Aśvamedha, Rājasūya and the Vājapeya could be performed only by kings (Vājapeya could be performed by *kṣatriya*-s and *brāhmaṇa*-s both). They were focused on the individual performer. On the contrary the Gṛhya rituals were pervading the society on the whole and the individual in particular[389].

The importance given to *iṣṭā-pūrta karman*-s, Pañcamahāyajña-s, Indramahotasava, etc. in the epics and the M. Pu-s indicates the increasing tendency towards simplification of Vedic rituals.

Sacrifices by using minimum ingredients were also admissible to the *Mbh* and the M. Pu-s. Sacrifices could be performed with mere sesamum seeds, ladles of ghee and Palāśa faggots. Sacrifices performed during the construction of water tanks or tree-plantations were also revered to yield fruit in the yonder world.

## OTHER ALTERNATIVES TO THE INSTITUTION OF SACRIFICE

The composers of the *Mbh* and the M. Pu-s did not merely restrict the society to rituals of some or other type. They also devised some other alternatives apart from the strict performance of rituals. These alternatives have been discussed in details in the last chapter. By deriving alternatives like, visits to holy places, performance of vows, hearing the narration of the *Purāṇa*-s, which are equivalent to the fruit obtained by the performance of many great sacrifices. This attempt of substitution of Vedic sacrifice should not be regarded as rejection of the sacrifice. Sacrifice as a 'revered principle' has remained intact in the minds of the composers. But the shortcomings of the same system were not neglected by texts. Therefore a new system of *tīrtha*, *vrata*, *japa*, etc. was devised by the *Mbh* and the *M. Pu*-s.

DEVELOPMENT OF PHILOSOPHICAL THOUGHTS:

The Upaniṣad-s and the *Bhagavadgītā* gave a new dimension to the Vedic sacrifice. They developed the spiritual aspect of the Vedic sacrifice. The concepts of Ātmayajña, Jñānayajña, Brahmayajña developed by the Upaniṣad-s and the *Bhagavadgītā* found due place in the *Mbh* and the M. Pu-s. This aspect of interiorization of the Vedic sacrifice, gave it a new dimension. The *Bhagavadgītā* gave stress on the performance of sacrifice, but without an eye on the fruit obtained from it. The sacrifice, which was performed for achieving material gains or attaining heaven, was modified to a sacrifice performed as an offering to god and not for petty individual gains. *'Idam na mama'* principle of the Vedic sacrifice was thus modified in the *Bhagavadgītā* as a selfless sacrifice. This approach gave birth to the *bhakti* cult where offerings were given to the deity but no fruit except the grace of that deity was desired.

Moreover, the development of the six systems of philosophy also posed a challenge to the institution of Vedic sacrifice. Apart from the Pūrvamīmamsā, which defines *dharma*, as that which has 'performance' as its characteristic; the other five systems do not highlight the importance of Vedic sacrifice.

This analysis of the Vedic sacrifice assists in understanding the change which the Vedic religion underwent for almost three millennia. Vedic religion which had sacrifice as its functional aspect evolved over a period of time. This evolution is natural as no religion is ever static. It needs to modify as per the social, economic and political conditions existing in the society.

We have observed changes in the sacrificial institution and have analysed the factors contributing to the change. But this change is not to be understood as a gulf between Vedism and Hinduism. As discussed in the introduction, some scholars regard these changes as the separation of Hinduism from Vedism. This type of understanding is like uprooting Hinduism from its roots[390]. Change in the functional aspect of Vedic religion, i.e. sacrifice; was essential and also inevitable. But this change has continuity in it[391]. This change and continuity of sacrifice in ancient India has been reflected in the Sanskrit texts. Here 'change' is signified by simplifications which the ritual has faced and the alternatives arisen in the place of sacrifice. Similarly, 'continuity' stands for the element of reverence expressed uniformly by all the texts for the VEDIC SACRIFICE.

# Notes and References


1. N.N. Bhattacharyya, *AIRSC*, (rev. & enl.) Manohar, New Delhi, 1996 (1975), Preface to the first edition, p. xiii.
2. Stephanie W. Jamison, *The Ravenous Hyenas and the Wounded Sun* (*Myth and Ritual in Ancient India*), Cornell University Press, Ithaca and London, 1991, Intro., p. 6.
3. *Encyclopaedia of Religion*, "Sacrifice", Macmillan Publishing Company, New York, 1987, Vol. XII, p. 544 ff.
4. Frederick M. Smith, *The Vedic Sacrifice in Transition (A translation and study of the Trikāṇḍamaṇḍana of Bhāskara Miśra)*, BORI, Pune, 1987, Intro., p. 9.
5. *The Oxford English Dictionary*, "Sacrifice", Second Edition, Vol. XIX, Clarendon Press, Oxford, 1989, pp. 340-341.
6. *Aṣṭadh.* III. 3. 90. *yaja-yāca- yata-viccha-praccha-rakṣo naṅ*||
7. *Kāt. Śr. Sū.* I. 2. 1-2. *yajñam vyākhyāsyāmaḥ dravyam devatā tyāgaḥ* |
8. P.V. Kane, *History of Dharmaśāstra,* Vol. II, Pt. 2, Second edn. BORI, Pune, 1974, p. 976.
9. *The Oxford English Dictionary*, Second edn., Vol. XVIII, Clarendon Press, Oxford, 1989, p. 1793.
10. *Encyclopaedia of Religion*, Vol. XII, 544. The typology of Vedic sacrifice is based on the typology illustrated in this Encyclopaedia.
11. *Kāt. Śr. Sū.* I. 1. 6.: *brāhmaṇarājanyavaiśyanām śruteḥ* |

12. *Tait. Sam.* VI. 6. 3.: *mekhalayā yajamānam dākṣayati yoktreṇa patnīm* |
13. *Kāt. Śr. Sū* I. 1. 9.: *rathakārasyā' dhāne* |
*Āp. Śr. Sū.* V. 3. 18.: *varṣāsu rathakāro ādadhīta* ||
14. *Āśv. Śr. Sū.* IV. 1. 6. *hotā –maitrāvaruṇo' cchāvāko grāvastudadhvaryuḥ pratiprasthātā- neṣṭonnetā brahmā brāhmaṇācchamsyagnīdhraḥ potodgātā prastotā pratihartā subrahmaṇya iti* |
15. P.V. Kane, *op. cit.*, Vol. II, Pt. 2, p. 981, fn. 2228.
16. *Ibid.*, p. 1069.
17. S.A. Dange, *VSEN*, Vol. I, Aryan Books International, New Delhi, 2000, pp. 22-23.
18. *Encyclopaedia of Religion*, p. 464.
19. P.V. Kane, *op. cit.*, Vol. II, Pt. 2, pp. 1106.
20. *Ibid.*, p. 1107.
21. S.A. Dange, *op. cit.*, Vol. I, Intro., pp. xlvi-xlvii.
22. *Kāt. Śr. Sū.*, I. 2. 6-7. *tiṣṭhadhhomā vaṣaṭkārapradānā yājyāpuronuvākyāvanto yajatayaḥ upaviṣṭahomā svāhākārapradānā juhotayaḥ* |
23. *Arthasaṅgraha: prayogasamavetārthasmārakāḥ mantrāḥ* |
24. *Śat. Br.*, III. 9. 2. 1-8.
25. *Ibid.*, III. 9. 3. 27.
26. *Ibid.*, III. 9. 3. 29; III. 9. 4. 14.
27. S.A. Dange, *op. cit.*, Vol. I, p. 1.
28. A *Sanskrit English Dictionary*, p. 87: *Aratni:* A cubit of the middle length from the elbow to the tip of the little finger, a fist.
29. S.A. Dange, *Sexual Symbolism from the Vedic Ritual*, Ajanta Publications, Delhi, 1979, pp. 51-70.
30. S.A. Dange, *VSEN*, Vol. I, p. 7.
31. P.V. Kane, *op. cit.*, Vol. II, Pt. 2, p. 988, fn. 2238.
32. *Ibid.*, pp. 988-989.
33. *Ibid.*, p. 1135.
34. C.V. Kashikar, *Shrauta Dharmachi Swarupacikitsa*, Poona University Press, Poona, 1977, p. 44.
35. *Śat. Br.* V. 2. 5. 1. ff.
36. *Kāt. Śr. Sū.* XXII. 10. 21-22. *udbhidbalabhidau cāharataḥ samyuktau. pūrveṇeṣṭvottareṇāvaśyam* |
37. *Āp. Śr. Sū.* XVIII. 8. 1. *rājā svārājyakāmo rājasūyena yajeta* |
XX. 20. 1. *rājā sārvabhaumo aśvamedhena yajeta. apyasārvabhaumaḥ* |

38. *Ibid.*, XVIII. 1.1. *śaradi vājapeyena yajeta brāhmaṇo rājanyo vṛddhikāmaḥ* |
39. P.V. Kane, *op. cit.*, Vol. II, Pt. 2, pp. 998-1008, fn. 2270-2271.
40. *Tait. Br. I. 6. 8.1,2. yadvaiśvadevena yajate praja eva tadyajamānaḥ | tā varuṇapraghāsairvaruṇapāśānmuñcati. sākamedhaiḥpratiṣṭhāpayati | traimbakai rudram niravadayate. pitṛyajñena suvargam lokam gamayati.*
41. P.V. Kane, *op. cit.*, Vol. II, Pt. 2, 1109-1132.
42. C.G. Kashikar, *op. cit.*, pp. 33-34.
43. P.V. Kane, *op. cit.*, Vol. II, Pt. 2, p. 1133.
44. *Āp. Śr. Sū.* X. 1. 14. *agnirme hotādityo me' dhvaryuscandramā me brahmā parjanyo ma udgātā........ ityupaṁśu devatādeśanam | asau mānuṣa ityuccaiḥ* |
45. P.V. Kane, *op. cit.*, Vol. II, Pt. 2, p. 1134.
46. C.G. Kashikar, *op. cit.*, pp. 35-42.
47. P.V. Kane, *op. cit.*, Vol. II, Pt. 2, p. 1204.
48. C.G. Kashikar, *op. cit.*, p. 43-44.
49. *Ibid.*, p. 44.
50. P.V. Kane, *op. cit.*, Vol. II, Pt. 2, p. 1205.
51. *Ibid.*, Vol. II, Pt. 2, p. 1206.
52. C.G. Kashikar, *op. cit.*, p. 44.
53. *Tait. Br.* I. 3. 4. 2. *vājapyo va eṣah | vājaṃ hyetena deva aipsan | somo vai vājapeyaḥ* |
    *Śān. Śr. Sū.* XV.1.4-6: *pāneyaḥ | annam vājaḥ | pānam vai pūrvamathānnam. tayorubhayorāptyai* |
54. C.G. Kashikar, *op. cit.*, pp. 45-47.
55. *DVR*, p. 132.
56. *Ibid.*, p. 161.
57. *Ibid.*, p. 161.
58. For details refer to P.V. Kane, *op. cit.*, Vol. II, Pt. 1, 821-824.
59. *Ibid.*, 826-829.
60. *Ibid.*, pp. 829-831.
61. *Ibid.*, p. 820.
62. S.A. Dange, *op. cit.*, Intro., pp. xiii-xiv.
63. S.A. Dange, *op. cit.*, Intro., p. xv.
64. K.R. Potdar, *Sacrifice in the Rgveda*, Bharatiya Vidya Bhavan, Mumbai, 1958, p. 96.
65. *Ibid.*, p. 99.

66. S.S. Dange, *Bharatiya Sahityacha Itihasa*, Mangala Prakashana for Maharashtra Vidyapeetha Grantha Nirmiti Mandal, Nagpur, 1975, pp. 79-85.
67. For details of the nature of sacrifice in the *YV*, C.G. Kashikar, *op. cit.*, pp. 72-82.
68. For more details of the subject matter of the *AV* to S.S. Dange, *op. cit.*, 86-97.
69. Stephanie Jamison, *op. cit.*, Intro., p. 13.
70. G.V. Devasthali, "Status of the Atharvaveda", *Indian Antiquary*, Third Series, Popular Prakashan, Jan. 1971, p. 14f.
71. For more details about the Brāhmaṇa literature, S.S. Dange, *op. cit.*, pp. 98-117.
    For more details about the Sacrifice in the Brahmana-s, G.U. Thite, *Sacrifice in the Brāhmaṇa –texts*, University of Poona, Pune, 1975.
72. S.S. Dange, "Concept of God according to the Āraṇyaka-s and the Upaniṣad-s", *Concept of God*, K.B. Archak and K. Pratap (eds.), Bharat Prakashan, Dharwad, 2003, pp. 44-63.
73. Stephanie Jamison, *op. cit.*, Intro., p.14.
74. S.S. Dange, "Ritual-setting of the Upanisadic Philosophy", *Journal of the Department of Sanskrit*, University of Calcutta, 1987, pp. 87-94.
75. *Kaṭha Upaniṣad*. I. 1. 13-19.
76. *Chāndogya Upaniṣad*. V. 11, V. 18.2.
77. S.S. Dange, *op. cit.*, pp. 90-91.
78. Ram Gopal, *India of Vedic Kalpasutras*, National Publishing House, Delhi, 1959, pp. 68-84.
79. As quoted by F. Smith, *op. cit.*, Intro., p. 11.
80. A.B. Keith, *The Religion and Philosophy of the Veda and Upanishads*, Pt. I, Harvard Oriental Series, Vol. 31, (Cambridge, 1925), Rep. by MLBD, Delhi, 1989, pp. 275-276.
81. Net edition: *A Critique of Evans-Pritchard: Luc de Heusch* It is to be noted that Hubert and Mauss have been criticized by the author of this edition.
82. A.B. Keith, *op. cit.*, p. 257.
83. *Ibid.*, p. 260.
84. *Ibid.*, p. 262.
85. G.U. Thite, *op. cit.*, Intro., p. 4.
86. As quoted by F. Smith, *op. cit.*, Intro., p. 10.

87. *Ibid.*, p. 11.
88. P.V. Kane, *op. cit.*, Vol. II, Pt. II, p. 978.
89. A.L. Basham (ed.), *A Cultural History of India*, Oxford, 1975, p. 14.
90. N.N. Bhattacharyya, *op. cit.*, p. 61 ff.
91. F. Staal, *Rituals and Mantras: Rules without meaning*. MLBD, Delhi, 1996, pp. 132-134.
92. J. Burde, Rituals, *Mantras and Science: An integral perspective*, MLBD, Delhi, 2004, Intro., p. 20.
93. J.C. Heesterman, *The Inner Conflict of Tradition*, Oxford University Press, Delhi, 1985, pp. 27-28.
94. I. Selvanayagam, *Vedic Sacrifice: Challenge and Response*, Manohar, New Delhi, 1996, Ch. 2, p. 55.
95. *Ibid.*, p. 55, fn. 14.
96. *Ibid.*, p. 56, fn. 21.
97. *Ibid.*, p. 56, fn. 22.
98. S.A. Dange, *VSEN*, Vol. I, Ādhāna (Intro.), pp. lii-liii.
99. J. Gonda, *Change and Continuity in Indian Religion*, Munshiram Manoharlal, New Delhi, 1985, p. 17 ff.
100. S.A. Dange, *Hindu Dharma ani Tattvajnana*, Shri Lekhana vacana Bhandar, for Maharashtra Vidyapeetha Granthanirmiti Manda, Nagpur, 1973, p. 6.
101. Oral discussion with S.S. Dange, on 10th April 2005.
102. T.N. Dharmadhikari, "The Philosophy of Vedic Sacrifice", *S. V. U. Oriental Journal*, Vol. XLII, Pts. I & II, Srivenkatesvara University, Tirupati, 1999, p. 124.
103. *Ibid.*, p. 124.
104. I. Selvanayagam, *op. cit.*, Intro., p. 39.
105. Gunnar Skirbekk, and Nils Gilje, *A History of Western Thought*, Routledge, London and New York, (English translation) 2001, p. 105.
106. J. Burde, *op. cit.*, p. 98.
107. *Ibid.*, p. 461.
108. *Ibid.*, p. 297.
109. As quoted by Selvanayagam, *op. cit.*, p. 46.
110. *Ibid.*, pp. 296-298.
111. M. Bairdeau, *Hinduism: The Anthropology of a Civilization*, Oxford University Press, New Delhi, 1997, (First Edition: 1989), Introduction, p. 9.

112. D.D. Kosambi, *The Culture and Civilization of Ancient India in Historical Outline*, New Delhi, 1976, p. 209.
113. I. Selvanayagam, *op. cit.*, p. 42.
114. N.N. Bhattacharyya, *op. cit.*, Intro., p. 25.
115. Y. Bentor, "Interiorized fire rituals in India and in Tibet", *JAOS*, Vol. 120, Michigan, 2000, p. 596.
116. F. Smith, *op. cit.*, Intro., pp. 32-33. He refers to a research paper presented by Harold Arnold entitled: "Hinduization of the Vedic sacrifice".
117. Brian Smith, *Reflections on Resemblance, Ritual and Religion*, OUP, New York, 1989, pp. 3-29.
118. S. Shastree: "Horse sacrifices in the Kali age". *VVRI.* Dr. Visva Bandhu Commemoration Vol. 1974, Vol. I, Pt. ii, pp. 351-360.
119. *Śat. Br.*, XIII. 4. 3. 1 ff.
Samiran Chandra. Chakrabarti, "A Study of the Pāriplava", *Indo-Iranian Journal*, Vol. XXXII, Netherlands, 1989, pp. 255-267.
120. S.S. Dange, "Sūta- The Paurāṇika", *Purāṇa*, All India Kashiraj Trust, Varanasi, Vol. XL, No. 2, p. 84.
121. *Rām*, Utt. 93. 1-2.
122. See note 2 *supra.*
123. M. Winternitz, *HIL*, Vol. I, (Introduction, Veda, National Epics, Puranas and Tantras) 2nd edn., MLBD, 1972, (University of Calcutta, 1927), pp. 314-315.
124. *Rām*, Bāl, Chaps. 8-18 & Utt. Chaps. 83-93.
125. Yardi, M.R., *The Rāmāyaṇa: Its origin and growth; A Statistical Study*, B.O.R.I., Pune, 1994, p. 17.
126. (Mrs.) Dange, S.S., *Bharatiya Sahityacha Itihasa*, pp. 206-210.
127. Yardi, M.R., *op. cit.*, p. 11.
128. *Vālmīki Rāmāyaṇa*, ed. Bhatt, G.H., (Critical Edition) Baroda, 1956, Preface, p. 31.
129. A. Guruge, *The Society of the Ramayana*, Abhinava Prakashana, New Delhi, 1989, (1953), Intro., p. 25.
130. P.V. Kane, *HDS*, Vol. II, Pt. 2, *op. cit.*, p. 1229.
131. *Tait. Br.* III. 8. 9. *rāṣṭram vā aśvamedhaḥ* |
132. c. f. *Kāt. Śr. Sū.* XX. 4. 17-20. *rajjudālo madhye abhitaḥpaitudāravau ṣaṭṣaṭ bilvakhadirapalāśāḥ trayastrayo' bhitaḥ* |
133. S.A. Dange, *VSEN*, Vol. I, pp. 22-23.
134. *Rām*, Bāl 12. 1. & 13. 1.

135. *The Rāmāyaṇa* (Cri.) Vol. I. Gaekwad Oriental Series, Baroda, 1956, p. 56.
136. *Rām* Bāl 14. 29. *sa cityo rājasimhasya sañchitaḥ kuśalairdvijaiḥ* | *garuḍo rukmapakṣo vai triguṇo' ṣṭadaśātmakaḥ* ||
137. Ramachandran, T.N. "Asvamedha site near Kalsi", *Journal of Oriental Research*, Madras, Vol. XXI, 1951-52, pp. 1-31.
138. *Ibid.*, Bāl 14.33. *kausalyā tam hayam tatra paricarya samantataḥ*| *kṛpāṇarviśaśāsainam tribhiḥ paramayā mudā* ||
139. *Ibid.*, Bāl 14. 33. commentary *Tilaka. patnyo' svasyāpi pathān kalpayati prāk kroḍāt pratyañcibhiḥ iti sūtrāt* |
140. *Āśv. Śr. Sū.* II. 4. 2. 1. *gaurabhijicca* |
II. 4. 2. 3. *paśukāmasya viśvajit* |
141. *Rām* Bāl 14. 43-44: *pracīm hotre dadau rājā diśam svakulavardhanaḥ* |
*adhvaryave pratīcīm tu brahmaṇe dakṣiṇām diśam* ||
*udgātre tu tathodīcīm dakṣiṇaiṣā vinirmita*
*aśvamedhe mahāyajñe svayambhūvihite purā* ||
142. S.A. Dange, *op. cit.*, Vol. II, p. 369.
143. N.N. Bhattacharya, *op. cit.*, pp. 3-4
144. A.B. Keith, *op. cit.*, Vol. I, Ch. 20, pp. 345-346.
145. Subhash Kak, *The Aśvamedha: The Rite and its Logic*, MLBD, New Delhi, 2002, p. 7.
146. *Kāt. Śr. Sū.* XX. 7. 7. *medo' syodharanti vapārthe* |
147. S.A. Dange, *Vedic Concept of 'Field' and Divine Fructification*, University of Bombay, 1971, p. 45.
148. *Rām* Bāl 15. 2: *iṣṭim te' ham kariṣyāmi putrīyām putrakāraṇāt* | *atharvaśirasi proktairmantraiḥ siddham vidhānataḥ* |
149. G.S. Altekar, *Studies on Vālmīki's Rāmāyaṇa*, BORI Research Unit Series No. 9, Pune, 1987, p. 194.
150. Rev. C. Bulcke, "The Genesis of the Bālakāṇḍa", *Journal of the Oriental Institute*, Baroda, Vol. II. No. 4. June 1953, p. 331.
151. G.S. Altekar, *op. cit.*, p. 197.
152. *Tait. S*am II. 2.1 ff.
153. P.V. Kane, *op. cit.*, Vol. II, Pt. 2, p. 1107 fn. 2478.
154. K. Upadhyaya, *Dharmasindhu*, Rajesh Prakashan, Pune, 1979, Third Paragraph, pp. 237-238
155. P.V. Kane, *op. cit.*, Vol. II, Pt. II, BORI, Poona, 1971, p. 1237.
156. *Rām* Utt 91.25. *kāñcanīm mama patnīm ca dikṣāyām jñānśca karmaṇi*| *agrato bharataḥ kṛtvā gacchatvagre mahāyaśāḥ* ||

157. *Ibid.*, Utt 83. 13-14. *yuvābhyām ātmabhūtābhyām rājasūyamanuttamam |*
*sahito yaṣṭumicchāmi tattra dharmastu śāśvataḥ ||*
*iṣṭvā tu rājasūyena mitraḥ śatrunibarhaṇaḥ |*
*suhutena suyajñena varuṇatvamupāgamat ||*
158. J.C. Heesterman, *The Ancient Indian Royal Consecration*, Houtox and Co; Gravenhage, 1957, Intro., p. 3.
159. S.A. Dange, *op. cit.*, Vol. II, pp. 285, 327.
160. G.U. Thite, "Antipathy to the Rajasuya: Why?", *Sambodhi*, Patan, 1972, Vol. I, No. 4, pp. 43-58.
161. M.R. Narsalay, "Vedic King Marutta in the Epics and the Purāṇa-s", *Purāṇa*, Vol. XLV, No. 1, All India Kashiraj Trust, Varanasi, 2003, pp. 75-84.
162. *Rām* Ayo 20. 15-16. *sā kṣaumavasanā hṛṣṭā nityam vrataparāyaṇā|*
*agnim juhoti sma tadā mantravatkṛtamaṅgalā ||*
*praviśya tu tadā rāmo maturataḥ puram śubham |*
*dadarśa mātaram tatra hāvayantīm hutāśanam ||*
163. *Ibid.* Ayo 56.22-23. *aiṇeyam maṁsamāhṛtya śālām yakṣyāmahe vayam |*
*kartavyam vāstuśamanam soumitre cirajīvibhiḥ ||*
*mṛgam hatvānaya kṣipram lakṣmaṇeha subhekṣaṇa |*
*kartavyaḥ śāstradṛṣṭo hi vidhirdharmamanusmara ||*
164. S.S. Dange, *Vedic Beliefs and Practices through Arthavāda*, Vol. I, Aryan Books International, New Delhi, 2004, pp. 186-187.
165. *Rām* Ayo 50. 12ff (Critical edition): *tam tu parvatamāsādya nānāpakṣigaṇāyutam |*
*ayam vāso bhavettāvadatra soumya ramemahi ||*
*lakṣmanānaya dāruṇi dṛḍhāni ca varāṇi ca ||*
*kuruṣvāvasatham soumya vāse me' bhiratam manaḥ |*
*tasya tadvacanam ṣrutvā soumitrirvividhāndrumān |*
*ājahāra tataścakre parṇaśālāmarindamaḥ |*
*aiṇeyam māṁsamāhṛtya śālām yakṣyāmahe vayam |*
*sa lakṣmaṇaḥ kṛṣṇamṛgam hatvā medhyam pratāpavān ||*
*atha cikṣepa saumitriḥ samiddhe jātavedasi |*
166. S.S. Dange, "Yajñapasuche Śira" (Marathi) *Vidarbha Samhodhana Mandal*, Annual No. Nagpur, 1997, p. 15.
167. S.S. Dange, "The Severed Head in Myth and Ritual", *Annals of BORI*, Amrta Mahotsava Vol. Poona, p. 464.

168. S.A. Dange, *op. cit.*, pp. 304-305.
169. *Rām* Bāl 30. 4. *adyaprabhṛti ṣaḍrātram rakṣatām rāghavau yuvām|*
*dīkṣām gato hyeṣa munirmaunitvam ca gamiṣyati ||*
*Ibid.*, Bāl 29. 18. *daśarātram hi yajñasya rāmam rājīvalocanam |*
*nātyeti kālo yajñasya yathāyam mama rāghava ||*
170. *Ibid.*, Bāl 30.9. *sadarbhacamasasrukkā sasamitkusumoccayā |*
*viśvāmitreṇa sahitā vedirjajvāla sartvijā ||*
171. *Ibid.*, Ayo. 116. 17. *avakṣipanti srugbhāṇḍānagnīnsiñcanti vāriṇā |*
*kalaśānśca pramardanti havane samupasthite ||*
172. Mrs. S.S. Dange, *Bharatiya Sahityacha Itihaasa*, p. 203.
173. *Ibid.*, Yuddha 32. 34. *agniṣṭomādibhiryajñairiṣṭavānāptadakṣiṇaiḥi |*
*agnihotreṇa samskāram kena tvam tu na lapsyase ||*
174. P.V. Kane, *op. cit.*, Vol. II, Pt. II, p. 984.
175. (Mrs.). S.S. Dange, *Hindu Domestic Rituals*; A Critical Glance, Ajanta Publications, Delhi, 1985, pp. 78-81.
176. All etymologies are discussed in *Bharatiya Samskritikosha*, Vol. III, Anamol Prakashan, Pune, 1993, pp. 450-451.
177. *Rām* Yuddha. 73. 16. comm.*sa samprāpya mahātejā yuddhabhūmimarindamaḥ |*
*sthāpayāmāsa rakṣāṁsi ratham prati samantataḥ |*
comm. *Tilaka* on the verse: *yuddhabhūmim yuddhajayasampādakahomasādhanabhūmim |*
*nikumbhilāsthānamityarthaḥ ||*
178. *Ibid.*: Sundara.24. 44cd-45ab.*surām cānīyatām kṣipram sarvaśokavināśinī |*
*mānuṣam māṁsamāsādhya nṛtyamo' tha nikumbhilām ||*
comm Tilaka on the above verses: *nikumbhilā nāma laṅkāyāḥ paścimadvārapradeśavāsinī bhadrakālī |*
179. E.W. Hopkins, *Epic Mythology*, MLBD, Delhi, 1986, (1915), p. 225.
180. V.R.R. Dikshitar, "*South India in the Rāmāyaṇa*", Proceedings of the All India Oriental Conference, 1933, p. 297.
181. *Rām*, Critical Edition, Sundarakanda, p. 708.
182. G. Subhramania. Pillai, *Tree-worship and Ophiliotry*, Anna Malai University, 1980, pp. 14-15.
183. *Rām* Yuddha 109. 23.*eṣo S S hitāgniśca mahātapaḥ vedāntagaḥ cāgryaśūraḥ |*
*etasya yatpretagatasya kṛtyam tatkartumicchami tava prasādāt ||*

184. S.A. Dange, *op. cit.*, Vol. II, p. 321.
185. P.V. Kane, *op. cit.*, Vol. II, pt. II, p. 1216.
186. S.A. Dange, *Myths from the Mahabharata, Probe in Early Dim History and Folklore*, Aryan Books International, New Delhi, 2002, pp. 57-60.
187. Bhagyashree Tarde, "Shunahshepache Akhyana: Kahi Samajika Sandarbha", (unpublished) presented at the Brihanmaharashtra Prachyavidya Parishad, Goa, 2004.
188. *Aṣṭādhyāyī:* IV. 2. 56. *saṅgrāme prayojanayoddhṛbhyaḥ* |
189. V.S. Suktankar, *On the meaning of the Mahabharata*, Lecture 1, the Asiatic Society of Bombay (Mumbai), Mumbai, 1957, p. 1.
190. M.R. Yardi, *The Mahabharata: Its genesis and growth (A Statistical Study)*, BORI, Pune, 1986, p. 18.
191. M. Winternitz, *History of Indian Literature*, MLBD, New Delhi, 1981, (first edn. Calcutta, 1927), Vol. I, p. 446 fn. 1.
192. C.V. Vaidya, *Mahābhārata: A Criticism*, Bombay (Mumbai), 1905, p. 21.
193. M.R. Yardi, *op. cit.*, pp. 128-129.
194. *Ibid.*, p. 131.
195. *Ibid.*, p. 133.
196. *Ibid.*, p. 133.
197. S.A. Dange, *VSEN*, Vol. I, pp. 117-118.
198. *Ibid.*, Vol. II, p. 285.
199. *Mbh.* Sabhā P 12. 36. *yasminsarve sambhavati vaśca sarvatra pūjyate*|
*yaśca sarveśvaro rājā rājasūyam sa vindati* ||
200. *Ibid.*, Sabhā P. 20. 10. *manuṣyānām samālambho na ca dṛṣṭaḥ kadācana* |
*sa katham mānuṣairdevam yaṣṭumicchaṣi śaṅkaram* ||
201. *Mbh* Sabhā P 32. 17. *iḍājyahomāhutibhirmantraśikṣāsamanvitaḥ* |
*tasminhi tatrapurdevāstate yajñe maharṣibhiḥ* ||
202. *Kāt. Śr. Sū* I. 6. 13-14, 16. *sattrāṇi brāhmaṇānāmṛtviksruteḥ* | *kalpānāmavaiguṇyāt* | *vaiāyarājanyayorgārhapateḥ* ||
203. *Tāṇ. Mbr* XXV. 6, 1, 4. *trayamtrivṛtaḥ samvatsarāstrayaḥ pañcadaśāstrayaḥ saptadaśastrayaḥ ekavimśaḥ prajapaterdvādaśasamvatsaram* | *etena vai naimiṣīyāḥ sarvvamṛdhnuvanti ya etadupayanti* ||
204. G.U. Thite, *op. cit.*, p. 56.
205. *Ibid.*, p. 57f.

206. *Mbh.* Ādi. P 109. 14-15. *agastyaḥ sattramāsīnaścacāra mṛgayāmṛṣi| āraṇyasarvadaivatyān mṛgānprokṣya mahāvane || pramāṇadṛṣṭadharmeṇa kathamasmān vigarhase | agastyasyābhicāreṇa yuṣmākam vai vapā hutā ||*
This particular passage has some variations. In verse 14d in the place of *mṛgān* the word is *paśūn*. In verse 15d in the place of *vapā hutā*, the variants are *vihito vadhaḥ* and *vadhaḥ coditaḥ*.
207. *Ibid.*, Ādi. P. 47. 17 c-d-18 a-b. *paryakrāmanśca vidhivatsve sve karmāṇi yājakāḥ | paridhāya kṛṣṇavāsāmsi dhūmasamraktalocanāḥ||*
208. S.S. Dange, "Sarpas and Vedic Ritual Tradition", *Journal of the Asiatic Society of Mumbai*, Vol. 79 for 2004, pub. In 2005, Mumbai, p. 38.
209. *Pañcavimśa Br.*, tr. Caland, W., Sri Satguru Publications, Delhi, 1982, (First edn. Calcutta 1931), p. 641, fn. 1.
210. Winternitz, M., "The Serpent Sacrifice mentioned in the Mahābhārata", *Journal of the Royal Asiatic Society*, tr. by N.B. Udgikar, London, 1925, p. 75.
211. Petteri Koskikallio, "Baka Dalbhya: a Complex Character in Vedic Ritual Texts, Epics and Purana-s".(Net edition) *Electronic Journal of Vedic Studies*, Dec. 1995, p. 6.
212. P.V. Kane, *op. cit.*, Vol. II, Pt. II, p. 1091.
213. *Ibid.*, p. 1093.
214. *Kāt. Śr. Sū.*, V. 2. 20. *prajākāmasyāpi vaiśvadevam |*
215. P.V. Kane, *op. cit.*, Vol. II, Pt. II, p. 1078.
216. *Ibid.*, p. 1009, 1133.
217. *Ibid.*, p. 1206.
218. Kāt. Śr. Sū XXIII. 5. 53. *pauṇḍarīkaḥ sarvārdhikāmasya |*
219. *Ibid.*, XXIII. 5. 33-37 (comm. Devayājñikapaddhati), the Chowkhambha Sanskrit Series, Benares, 1933, pp. 780-781.
220. *Mbh.* Sabhā. 5. 89. *kaccitkratūnekacitto vājapeyānśca sarvaśaḥ | puṇḍarīkānśca kārtsnena yatase kartumātmavān ||*
*Ibid.*, Van. 31. 16. *aśvamedho rājasūyaḥ puṇḍarīko' tha gosavaḥ | etairapi mahāyajñairiṣṭam te bhūridakṣiṇaiḥ ||*
221. *Ibid.*, Śal. P 49. 35. *yajante puṇḍarīkeṇa rājasūyena caiva ye | teṣām lokeṣvapasyācca jaigiṣavyam sa devalaḥ ||*
222. S.A. Dange, *op. cit.*, Vol. II, pp. 338-340.
223. *Śat. Br* XII. 7. 2. 10. *sautrāmaṇīṣṭiśca paśubandhaścobhayāddhyai |*
224. P.V. Kane, *op. cit.*, Vol. II, Pt. 2, p. 1224.

225. *Kāt. Śr. Sū.* XIX. 1.1. *brāhmaṇayajñaḥ sautrāmaāyṛddhikāmasya* |
226. *Ibid.*, XXI. 2. 1. *sarvamedhaḥ sarvakāmasya* |
227. *Ibid.*, XII. 1. 5. *dvādaśāhaḥ sattramahīnaśca* |
228. *RV.* X. 117. 6. *moghamannam vindante apracetāḥ satyam bravīmi vadha itsa tasya* |
*nāryamāṇam puṣyati no sakhāyam kevalāgha bhavati kevalādī* ||
cf. *Manu Sm.* 3. 118ab. *agham sa kevalam bhuṅkte yaḥ pacatyātmakāraṇāt* |
229. P.V. Kane, *op. cit.*, Vol. II, Pt. 2, p. 1109.
230. *Kāt. Śr. Sū* XXII. 11. 6-10. *ukthyo gosavo' yutadakṣiṇaḥ* || *vaiśyayajña ityeke* || *sa rājāno viśo yam puraskurvīrantsa etena yajeta* || *sthaṇḍile' bhiṣicyate pratiduha'' Shavanīyasya dakṣiṇataḥ*| *sthapatirityenam brūyuḥ* ||
231. *Ibid.*, XXI. 3. 1.*pitṛmedhaḥ samvatsara' smṛtau* ||
232. P.V. Kane, *op. cit.*, Vol. II, Pt. 2, p. 1121.
233. *Kāt. Śr. Sū.* IV. 1. 3. *paristīrya tam pūrvavatpātrāsādanamekaikaśaḥ*|
234. *Ait. Br* VIII. 16:*camasa udumbaraśākhā tasminetasminścamase' ṣṭhātayāni niṣutāni bhavanti, dadhi madhu sarpirātapavarṣya āpaḥ....* |
*Ait. Br.* VIII. 6:*vyāghracarmaṇatyuttaralomnā pracīnagrīveṇa kṣatram ca etadāraṇyanam paśunām yad vyāghraḥ kṣatram rājanyaḥ kṣatreṇaiva tatkṣatram samardhayati* |
235. *Nār. Pu* AITM. Vol. 15 Pt. 1 MLBD, New Delhi, 1980, p. 295 fn. 13.
236. *Śat. Br.* III. 2. 4. 7: *somaśca vāk ca sa yatsomam krīṇātyāgatyā' evāgatena yajā' ityanāgatena ha vai sa somena yajeta yo' krītena yajate* |
237. S.A. Dange, *op. cit.*, Vol. I, pp. 57, 60.
238. Oral discussion with Shri. Parashuram Paranjape of the Vaidika Samshodhana Mandal, Pune on 19th May 2004.
239. *Ibid.*, Śan. P 324. 4.*bījairyajñeṣu yaṣṭavyamiti vai vaidikī srutiḥ* |
*ajasamjñāni bījāni chāgam na ghnatumarhatha* ||
240. *Śat. Br* tr. Eggeling Julius, Pt. I. MLBD, Delhi, 1988 (1882), pp. 47-48 fn. 3.
241. *Mbh.* Śān. P Ch. 26.
242. The numbers are quoted from the Bhīṣma P of the *Mbh* and not the *Bhagavadgītā* as a separate independent text. 25. 9-15.

243. *Baudh. Śr. Sū* XVIII. 12. 15: *eṣa etena yajñakratūneṣṭvā śuciḥpūto medhyo bhavati sa yadi mukhena pāpakṛnmanyeta trivṛtam kurvītaiṣa ha vai mukhena pāpam karoti yoSnūcānasya ca munervā duravagatamāgacchati....*
244. *Ibid.*, Ud. P 13. 12-13. *teṣām tadvacanam śṛutvā devānām viṣṇurabravīt |*
*māmeva yajatām śakraḥ pāvayiṣyāmi vajriṇam ||*
*puṇyena hayamedhena māmiṣṭvā pākaśāsanaḥ |*
*punareṣyati devānāmindratvamakutobhayaḥ ||*
245. *Ibid.*, Śan. P 36. 6-7. *kratunā caśvamedhena pūyate nātra saṁśayaḥ|*
*ye cāsyāvabhṛthe snānanti kecidevamvidhā narāḥ ||*
*te sarve pūtapapmāno bhavantīti purā srutiḥ |*
*brāhmaṇārthe hato yuddhe mucyate brahmahatyayā ||*
246. S.A. Dange, *Myths from the Mahābhārata*, Vol. II, Aryan Books International, New Delhi, 2000, pp. 162-164.
247. *Mbh.* Ādi. P 57. 91. *tathaiva dhṛṣṭadyumno' pi sākṣādagnisamadyutiḥ |*
*vaitāne karmaṇi tate pāvakātsamajāyata |*
*vīro droṇavināśāya dhanuṣa saha vīryavān ||*
Ādi. P 155. 30. *tatastasya narendrasya upayājo mahātapāḥ |*
*ācakhyo karma vaitānam tadā putraphalāya vai ||*
248. S.A. Dange, *op. cit.*, p. 214.
249. *Ibid.*, pp. 156-157.
250. *Ibid.*, Ādi. P 69. 48. *śrīmāngovitatam nāma vājimedhamavāpa saḥ |*
*yasminsahasram padmānām kaṇvāya bharato dadau || ||*
251. *Śat. Br.* XIII. 5. 4. 19-23.
252. P.V. Kane, *op. cit.*, Vol. II, Pt. 2, p. 1211.
253. Dange, S.A., *op. cit.*, p. 200.
254. S.A. Dange, "Purūravas: A Research for Identity", *A Corpus of Indian Studies*, (Gaurinath Shastri Felicitation Vol.) Sanskrit Pustak Bhandar, Calcutta, 1980, p. 55.
255. *AV* XI. 7. 24.
256. *Bṛhadāraṇyaka Upaniṣad* II. 4. 10.
257. R.C. Hazra, *Studies in the Puranic records on Hindu rites and customs*, MLBD, Delhi, 1975 (1940), Ch. I, p. 1.
258. S.S. Dange, *Bharatiya Sahityacha Itihasa*, Pt. 1, pp. 272-273.

Pushpendra Shastri, *The Purana-s- the Light House of Indian Culture*, Rashtriya Sanskrit Samsthan, New Delhi, 1995, pp. 2-4.

259. *Ibid.*, p. 276
260. Pushpendra Shastri, *op. cit.*, p. 2.
261. *Śiva Purāṇa*, Pts. I-IV, Vols. 1-4, tr. J.L. Shastri, AITM, MLBD, New Delhi (first edn. 1970) 1990, Intro., p. 10
262. For details: S.S. Dange, *op. cit.*, pp. 282-305.
     Pushpendra Shastri, *op. cit.*, pp. 49-161.
263. Puspendra Shastri, *op. cit.*, p. 22.
264. *Ibid.*, p. 23.
265. C.V. Vaidya, *History of Sanskrit Literature*, Vol. I, Section IV, p. 6.
266. Puspendra Shastri, *op. cit.*, p. 23.
267. *Ibid.*, p. 23.
268. Hazra, *op. cit.*, p. 6.
269. P.V. Kane, *op. cit.*, Vol. I, Pt. I, p. 162.
270. Puspendra Shastri, *op. cit.*, p. 23.
271. *Ibid.*, p. 24.
272. R.C. Hazra, *op. cit.*, p. 8.
     Pushpendra Shastri, *op. cit.*, p. 24.
273. S.S. Dange, *op. cit.*, pp. 284-285.
274. *Manu. Sm* X. 71 & *Yājñavalkya Sm* I. 93-98.
275. *Kū. Pu*, Nag publishers, New Delhi, 1983, (reprinted from Srivenkateswara System Press, ed. Khemraja Srikrisnadasa). Notes on the Sūta: *Ku. Pu.* (Pt. I), AITM. MLBD, p. 3. fn. 1 & 2.
276. *Brahma Pu.* Nag Publishers, (reprint edn. from the Venkatesvara System Press), Delhi, 1985.
277. *Nār. Pu* Nag Publishers, (reprint from the Venkateshwara System Press), New Delhi, 1984.
278. *Liṅga Pu.*, J.L. Shastri (ed.), MLBD, Delhi, 1980.
     *Liṅga Pu.*, Pts. 1 & 2, tr. J.L. Shastri, AITM, No. 5-No. 6, MLBD, Delhi, 1973.
279. *Vāyu Pu* Purva. Prak. 1. 10-12.
280. *Baudh. Śr. Sū.* Vol. III, Caland (ed.), Munshiram Manoharlal Publishers Pvt. Ltd; New Delhi, 1982, Index of proper names, p. 15.
281. For details, see Intro.

282. *Encyclopaedia of Puranic Beliefs and Practices,* Navrang, New Delhi, 1989, Vol. IV, p. 1226, fn. 2.
283. *Śiva Pu.* Śiva Māhātmya. 1.39. *aśvamedhasahasrāṇi vājapeyaśatāni ca |*
*kalām śivapurāṇasya nārhanti khalu ṣoḍaśīm ||*
284. *Liṅga Pu.*I. 8. 20. *ahiṁsāpyevamevaiṣā dvijagurvagnipūjane |*
*vidhinā yādṛśī hiṁsā sātvahiṁsā iti smṛtā ||*
285. *Vāyu. Pu* Uttara. Anu. 29.45cd. *ekoSgniḥ pūrvamāsīdvai eilastrīṁstānakalpayat |*
286. The interpretation of this myth has been discussed in Chapter II.
287. *The Oxford English Dictionary,* Vol. III, Oxford University Press, Oxford, 1989, p. 282.
288. M. Winternitz, *HIL,* Vol. III, Pt. I, (reprint) MLBD, Delhi, 1985, pp. 178-179.
289. *Nāṭyaśāstra* I. 108, 111 *nānābhāvopasampannam nānāvasthāntarātmakam |*
*lokavṛttānukaraṇam nāṭyametanmayā kṛtam ||*
*duḥkhārtānām śramārtānām śokārtānām tapasvinām |*
*viśrāmajananam loke nāṭyametadbhaviṣyati ||*
290. *Mahākavibhāsa- A Comprehensive Criticism of the Dramas of Bhāsa,* Vol. I & II, ed. Baldeva Upadhyaya, Chowkhambha Sanskrit Series, Varanasi.
291. A.D. Pusalkar, *Bhasa-A Study,* Bharatiya Vidya Bhavan, Bombay, 1940, pp. 202-208.
292. *Tait. Br.* I. 1. 10. 1 ff.
For details refer to S.A. Dange, *VSEN,* Vol. I, p. 45.
293. S.A. Dange, *op. cit.,* p. 211.
294. *Pañcarātra* Act. I.25.
*ikṣvākuśāryātiyayātirāmamāndhātānābhāganṛgāmbarīṣāḥ |*
*ete sakośāḥ puruṣāḥ sarāṣṭrā naṣṭāḥ śarīraiḥ kṛtubhirdharante ||*
295. *Pratimānāṭaka* Act I. 29. *svairam hi paśyantu kalatrametad bāṣpākulakṣair- vadanairbhavantaḥ |*
*nirdoṣadṛśyā hi bhavanti nāryo yajñe vivāhe vyasane vane ca ||*
296. Winternitz, M., *op. cit.,* p. 47.
The present work has accepted the Gupta period theory of Kālidāsa's date.
297. *Mālavikāgnimitram* of Kālidāsa, M.R. Kale (ed.), A.R. Sheth & Co., Mumbai, 1959.

298. *Mālavikāgnimitram* of Kālidāsa, Sane and Godbole (eds.), A.R. Sheth & Co. Mumbai, 1959, has retained the same name.
299. N.N. Bhattacharyya, *op. cit.*, Ch. I, p. 1.
300. *Vikramorvaśīyam* of Kālidāsa, M.R. Kale (ed.), MLBD, Delhi, 1991, (1967 revised).
301. S.A. Dange, 'Purūravas-A research for identity', for details refer Chapter III.
302. *Abhijñānaśākuntalam* of Kālidāsa, M.R. Kale (ed.), MLBD, Delhi, 1969 (1898).
303. For details of *vedisamstaraṇa*, refer to Chapter III, p. 35, fn. 76.
304. *DVR*, p. 38.
305. S.S. Dange, *Aspects of Speech in Vedic Ritual*, Aryan Books International, Delhi, 1996, p. 37.
306. *Abhijñānaśākuntalam* Act VI. p. 244: *sānumatī- athavā śrutam mayā śakuntalām samāśvasantyā mahendrarājatananyā mukhādyajñabhāgotsukā devā eva tathānuṣṭhāsyanti yathā cireṇa dharmapatnīm bharatābhinandiṣyatīti* ||
307. Winternitz, *op. cit.*, p. 258.
308. Bhavabhūti, *Mālatimādhavam*, ed. & tr. Kale, M.R., MLBD, New Delhi, 1967 (1913).
309. P.V. Kane, *op. cit.*, Vol. II, Pt. 2, p. 1014.
310. *Kāt. Śr. Sū.* I. 3.35. *pālāśī jūhūḥ* |
*Ibid.*, I. 9. 10. *dviścābhighāraṇam* |
311. *Uttararāmacarita*, ed. and tr. M.R. Kale, MLBD, Delhi, 1982.
312. G.K. Bhat, *Sanskrit Natake ani Natakakara*, Srividya Prakashan, Pune, 1980, pp. 142-153.
313. M. Winternitz, *op. cit.*, pp. 233, 258.
314. *Ibid.*, pp. 36-37.
315. *Works of Kālidāsa*, Vol. 2, ed. and tr. by Deodhar, C.R., MLBD, Delhi, 1986 (1984).
316. *Kirātārjunīyam* of Bharavi, Chowkhambha Sanskrit Sansthan, Varanasi, 1987.
317. M. Winterniz, *op. cit.*, pp. 70-71.
318. *Śiśupālavadham* of Magha, Chowkhambha Vidya Bhavan Series, Varanasi, 1972 (3rd edition).
319. M. Winternitz, *op. cit.*, p. 72.
320. Baladeva Upadhyaya, *Bharavi aur Magha, Ek taulanik Adhyayana*, Sriprabha Prakashan, New Delhi, 1972, Intro., p. 13.

321. Mallinatha quoting *Amarakośa* in Sarvaṇkaṣā on XIV.6: *sapta tantavaḥ samsthā yasya tam saptatantum kratum| saptatanturmakhaḥ kratuḥ ityamaraḥ* |
322. P.V. Kane, *op. cit.*, Vol. II, Pt. 2, p. 1038.
323. *Naiṣadhīyacarita* by Śrīharṣa, ed. N.R. Acharya, Chowkhambha Vidya Bhavana, Varanasi, 1998.
324. M. Winternitz, *op. cit.*, p. 83.
325. For details refer to Chapter III on the *Mbh.* This myth occurs in the *Śat. Br* (IV. 1. 5. 1-19).
326. *Bhaṭṭikāvyam, Text and Translation*, ed. and tr. Karandikar M.A. and Karandikar S. MLBD, Delhi, 1982, intro. xii.
327. *Jānakīharaṇa* tr. Vyasa Brajmohan, Mitra Prakashan, Pvt. Ltd., Allahabad, 1967.
328. M. Winternitz, *op. cit.*, p. 70.
329. *Jānakīharaṇa*, Intro., p. 23
330. G.U. Thite, "Vedic Ritual: Kālidāsa and Bhavabhūti", *Three Mountains and Seven Rivers*, Prof. Musashi Tachikawa's Felicitation volume, Shoun Hino & Toshihiro Wada (eds.), MLBD, Delhi, 2004, pp. 503-507.
331. *Dūtaghaṭotkaca* Act I. 6b. *pañcānām pāṇḍavāgnīnāmātmā kenendhanīkṛtaḥ.*
332. *Mālavikāgnimitra* Act. I. v. 4ab. *devānāmidamāmananti munayaḥ kāntam kratum cākṣuṣam.*
333. *Oxford English Dictionary*, Vol. I, Oxford University Press, London, 1989, pp. 332-333.
334. Shanti Lal Nagar, *Varaha in Indian Culture and Literature*, Aryan Books International, New Delhi, 1993, p. 45.
335. *Ibid.*, p. 46.
336. *Mbh* Bhīṣma. P 63. 13. *madhusūdanamityāhurṛṣayaśca janārdanam| varāhascaiva simhaśca trivikramagatiḥprabhuḥ* ||
337. *Nirukta* V. 4. *,varāho megho bhavati varaharah | varamāhārmāharṣīr iti ca brāhmaṇam* |
338. The names and works of scholars are given in the notes on this topic.
339. Kalpana Desai, 'Varaha', *Journal of the Asiatic Society of Bombay*, 1970, Vol. 43-44, 1968-69, pp. 108-109.
340. *RV* X. 86.
341. As quoted by Kalpana Desai, *op. cit.*, fn. 19.

342. V.S. Agrawala, 'Yajña Varāha- An Interpretation', *Purāṇa*, Vol. V, No. 2, p. 225.
343. Haripriya Rangarangan, *Varaha Images in Madhya Pradesh* (An Iconographic Study), Somaiya Publications Pvt. Ltd., 1997, pp. 36-37.
344. *Ibid.*, pp. 36-37.
345. V.S. Agrawala, *op. cit.*, pp. 227.
346. *Vāyu. Pu* Ch. 6, 16-22.
347. T.A. Gopinatha Rao, *Elements of Hindu Iconography*, Vol. I, Pt. I, pp. 132 ff.
348. Rangarajan Haripriya, *op. cit.*, pp. 34-35.
349. *Ibid.*, p. 35.
350. *Ibid.*, p. 46. The figures have been illustrated in the same work
351. *Ibid.*, p. 114. also see V.S. Agrawala, *op. cit.*, p. 230.
352. *RV* X. 90.
353. O.P. Bharadwaj, "Vedic *tīrtha*-s in the *Mahābhārata*", *Mahābhārata: The end of an era (Yugānta)*, ed. Ajay Mitra Shastri, Aryan Books International, New Delhi, 2004, pp. 182-205, fn. 1.
354. *RV* X. 31. 3.
355. D.P. Dubey, "The concept and Practice of Pilgrimage in the *Mahābhārata*", *Mahābhārata: The end of an era (Yugānta)*, ed. Ajay Mitra Shastri, Aryan Books International, New Delhi, 2004, pp. 206-214. fn. 3.
356. As quoted by A.B. Bakre, *Religion in Social Flux*, Eastern Book Linkers, New Delhi, 1998, pp. 252-253, fn. 207.
357. *DVR*, p. 70.
358. P.V. Kane, *op. cit.*, Vol. IV, BORI, Pune, 1953, p. 984.
359. *Ibid.*, pp. 552-827.
360. *BSK*, p. 130.
361. Agehananda Bharati, 'Pilgrimage in the Indian tradition', *History of Religions*, Vol. 3, No. 1, Summer 1965, The University of Chicago Press, Chicago, USA, pp. 135-167.
362. Savitri Kumar, *The Puranic lore of water-places*, Munshiram Manoharlal Publishers Pvt. Ltd., 1983, Delhi, pp. 19-22.
363. *Kāt. Śr. Sū.* XXIV. 5. 36. *saḥ sthite' dhvaryurāhavanīyasamīpe sthibhyadhvam (?) śamyām prāsyati tadgārhapatyasthānam* || *Mān. Śr. Sū* quoted in the comm.. *Devayājñikapaddhati* on the *Kāt. Śr. Sū.* says

*tatra prajahito gārhapatyaḥ tataḥ sānnayye' ṣṭe samsthitāyāmadhvaryurāhavanīyasamīpe sthitvā' bhyadhvam ādhvānam pratiśamyām prāsyati | mārgam pratibalād dūram prakṣipati | evam preṣitā śamyā yatra patati tatra gārhapatyasthānam| tato yathoktamāhavanīyasthānam |*

364. *Pañ Br* (also known as *Tāṇ. Mbr*), tr. Caland, XXV. 13. 1. Sri Satguru Publications, Delhi, 1983 (Calcutta 1931), p. 639, fn. 1.
365. *Kāt. Śr. Sū.* XXII. 10. 21-22.*udbhidbalabhidau cāharataḥ samyuktau| purveṇeṣṭvottareṇāvaśyam ||*
366. A.B. Bakre, *op. cit.*, p. 256.
367. Savitri Kumar, *op. cit.*, p. 12
368. D.P. Dubey, *op. cit.*, p. 207.
369. Suryavanshi Bhagawan Singh, *Geography of the Mahabharata*, Ramanand Vidya Bhavan, New Delhi, 1986, pp. 202-203. This term has been used by him.
370. *Tait. Sam.* II. 5. 5. 6.*tasyaitad vratam nānṛtam vadennamāmsamaśnīyānna ||*
371. P.V. Kane, *op. cit.*, Vol. V, Pt. 1, BORI, Pune, 1958, p. 1.
372. *Ibid.*, p. 28.
373. Savitri Saxena, *Skanda Purana (A Study)*, Sanjay Prakashan, New Delhi, 2004, pp. 278, 284.
374. *Brahma. Pu.* (Pts. 1-3) ed. Prof. J.L. Shastri, AITM. No. 33, MLBD, New Delhi, 1985, p. 213, fn. 1.
375. For details of the myth see S.S. Dange, 'Prāśitra in Myth and Ritual', *PrabhakarNarayana Sriḥ Studies in Indology and Musicology, (Dr. Prabhakar Narayana Kawthekar Felicitation Vol.)* Pratibha Prakashana, Delhi, 1993, pp. 81-86.
376. J. Gonda, J., *Visnuism and Saivism-A comparison*, The Athelone Press, London, 1970, p. 13.
377. *Chāndogya Up* VIII. 5. 1.
378. Israel Selvanayagam, *op. cit.*, p. 129.
379. *Kāvyaprakāśa*I. 2. *kāvyam yaśase arthakṛtaye vyavahāravide śivetarakṣataye |*
*sadhyaḥ paranirvṛtaye kāntāsammitatayopadeśayuje ||*
380. Gonda, Jan., *Ancient Indian kingship from the religious point of view*, E.J. Brill, Leiden, 1969, p. 6f and fn. 53.
381. For details Pande, G.C., *Studies in the Origins of Buddhism*, MLBD, New Delhi, 1983, p. 312.

382. Romila Thapar, *Asoka and Decline of Mauryas*, OUP, Delhi, 1973, p. 149ff.
383. N.N. Bhattacharyya, *op. cit.*, p. 16.
384. Israel Selvanayagam, *op. cit.*, p. 142.
385. S.S. Dange, *Bauddha Dharma ani Tattvajnana*, Continental Prakashan, for Maharashtra Vidyapeetha Grantha Nirmiti Mandal, Pune, 1980, p. 14.
386. *Ibid.*, p. 18f.
387. Israel Selvanayagam, *op. cit.*, p. 148, fn. 45.
388. S.S. Dange, *op. cit.*, pp. 33-34.
389. S.A. Dange, *Hindu Dharma ani Tattvajnana*, Shri Lekhana Vacana Bhandar for Maharashtra Vidyapeetha Grantha Nirmiti Mandal, Pune, 1973, pp. 210, 260.
390. Dange has put forth this view that any change in Hinduism cannot take it away from Vedic religion but can be traced in the Vedic religion itself.
For details *Ibid.*, Intro., pp. 20-38.
391. This phrase has been used by Jan Gonda, *Change and Continuity in Indian Religion*, Mouton and Co, Hague, 1965.

# Appendix I

## LIST OF TĪRTHA-S OCCURRING IN VARIOUS TEXTS SUBSTITUTING VEDIC SACRIFICE

*Mbh.*

| *Tīrtha* | *Sacrifice* |
|---|---|
| Puṣkara<br>a) Performance of Abhiṣeka<br>b) Living in Puṣkara for twelve years<br>c) Living in Puṣkara for hundred years | <br>a) Aśvamedha (Van. P 80.47-48)<br>b) all sacrifices leading to Brahmaloka<br>c) Agnihotra (*Ibid.* 80.56-57) |
| Jambumārga | Aśvamedha leading to Viṣṇuloka (*Ibid.* 80.59-60) |
| Yayātipatana | Aśvamedha (*Ibid.* 80. 67) |
| Koṭitīrtha | Aśvamedha (*Ibid.* 80. 68) |
| Narmadā | Agniṣṭoma (*Ibid.* 80. 71) |
| Carmaṇvatī | Agniṣṭoma (*Ibid.* 80. 73) |

| | |
|---|---|
| Prabhāsa | Agniṣṭoma & Atirātra (*Ibid.* 80. 77) |
| Piṇḍāraka | Bahusuvarṇaka (*Ibid.* 80. 82) |
| Śaṅkukarṇa | Aśvamedha (*Ibid.* 80. 87) |
| Drumi | Aśvamedha (*Ibid.* 80. 90) |
| Vasordhārā | Aśvamedha (*Ibid.* 80. 92) |
| Pañcanada | Five sacrifices (*Ibid.* 80. 99) |
| Vimala | Vājapeya (*Ibid.* 80. 104) |
| Maladā (on offering *caru*) | Fruit higher than Rājasūya and Aśvamedha (*Ibid.* 80. 107) |
| Vastrāpada | Aśvamedha (*Ibid.* 80. 108) |
| Maṇimat | Agniṣṭoma (*Ibid.* 80. 109) |
| Devikā (on offering *caru*) | Sarvakāmasamṛddha (*Ibid.* P 80.112) |
| Dīrghasattra | Rājasūya and Aśvamedha (*Ibid.* 80. 117) |
| Camasodbheda | Agniṣṭoma (*Ibid.* 80. 119) |
| Rudrakoṭi | Aśvamedha (*Ibid.* 80. 129) |
| Kurukṣetra | Rājasūya and Aśvamedha (*Ibid.* 81. 6) |
| Satata | Aśvamedha (*Ibid.* 81. 9) |
| Pāriplava | Agniṣṭoma and Atirātra (*Ibid.* 81. 10) |
| Śālukini | Ten Aśvamedha-s (*Ibid.* 81. 11) |
| Sarpadarvī | Agniṣṭoma and Nāgaloka (*Ibid.*81. 12) |

| | |
|---|---|
| Varāhatīrtha | Agniṣṭoma (*Ibid.* 81. 15) |
| Somatīrtha | Rājasūya (*Ibid.* 81. 16) |
| Ekatīrtha | Puṇḍarīka(*Ibid.* 81. 17) |
| Śamita | Aśvamedha (*Ibid.* 81. 21) |
| Sūryatīrtha | Agniṣṭoma (*Ibid.* 81.39) |
| Sarasvatītīrtha | Agniṣṭoma (*Ibid.* 81. 42) |
| Sutīrthaka | Aśvamedha (*Ibid.* 81. 44-45) |
| Apagā | Agniṣṭoma (*Ibid.* 81. 57) |
| Ilaspada | Vājapeya (*Ibid.* 81. 64) |
| Kalaśī<br>Anajanmatīrtha<br>Dṛṣadvatī | Agniṣṭoma (*Ibid.* 81. 66)<br>Puṇḍarīka (*Ibid.* 81. 69)<br>Agniṣṭoma and Atirātra (*Ibid.* 81. 73) |
| Pāṇikhāta | Rājasūya (*Ibid.* 81. 75) |
| Mṛgadhūma | Aśvamedha (*Ibid.* 81. 85) |
| Śrīkuñja | Agniṣṭoma (*Ibid.* 81. 91) |
| Sarasvatī and Aruṇā | Agniṣṭoma and Atirātra (*Ibid.*81. 132) |
| Kanyātīrtha | Agniṣṭoma (*Ibid.* 81. 94) |
| Reṇukātīrtha | Agniṣṭoma (*Ibid.* 81. 139) |
| Sārasvata | Vājapeya (*Ibid.* 81. 164) |
| Kārāpatana | Agniṣṭoma (*Ibid.* 82. 2) |
| Plakṣa | Aśvamedha (*Ibid.* 82. 6) |
| Īśānādhyuṣita | Aśvamedha (*Ibid.* 82. 7-8) |
| Suvarṇākṣa | Aśvamedha (*Ibid.* 82. 19) |
| Gaṅgādvāra | Puṇḍarīka (*Ibid.* 82. 23) |
| Kanakhala | Aśvamedha (*Ibid.* 82. 26) |

| | |
|---|---|
| Gaṅgāsaṅgama | Aśvamedha (*Ibid.* 82.31) |
| Brahmāvarta | Aśvamedha (*Ibid.* 82. 38) |
| Source of Yamunā | Aśvamedha (*Ibid.* 82. 39) |
| Darvisaṅkramaṇa | Aśvamedha (*Ibid.* 82. 40) |
| Bhṛgutuṅga | Aśvamedha (*Ibid.* 82. 45) |
| Vetasika | Aśvamedha (*Ibid.* 82. 50) |
| Naimiṣa | Gavāmayana (*Ibid.* 82. 56) |
| Gaṅgodbheda | Vājapeya (*Ibid.* 82. 58) |
| Bāhudā | Devasattra (*Ibid.* 82. 60) |
| Cirāvatī | Vājapeya (*Ibid.* 82. 61) |
| Rāmatīrtha | Aśvamedha (*Ibid.* 82. 66) |
| Vārāṇasī | Rājasūya (*Ibid.* 82. 69) |
| Gomatī and Gaṅgā confluence | Agniṣṭoma (*Ibid.* 82. 70) |
| Gayā | Aśvamedha (*Ibid.* 82. 71) |
| Brahmasaras | Pauṇḍarīka (*Ibid.* 82. 74) |
| Brahmasarasyūpa | Vājapeya (*Ibid.* 82. 75) |
| Phalgu | Aśvamedha (*Ibid.* 82. 86) |
| Dharmapṛṣṭha | Aśvamedha (*Ibid.* 82. 87) |
| Brahmatīrtha | Rājasūya and Aśvamedha (*Ibid.* 82.88) |
| Udapāna | Aśvamedha (*Ibid.* 82. 94) |
| Vinaśana | Vājapeya (*Ibid.* 82. 96) |
| Gaṇḍakī | Vājapeya and Sūryaloka (*Ibid.* 82. 97) |
| Kampanā | Puṇḍarīka (*Ibid.* 82. 99) |
| Viśālā | Agniṣṭoma (*Ibid.* 82. 100) |

| | |
|---|---|
| Maheśvarī | Aśvamedha (*Ibid.* 82. 101) |
| Devahṛda | Vājapeya (*Ibid.* 82. 102) |
| Maheśvarapada | Aśvamedha (*Ibid.* 82. 103) |
| Tīrthakoṭi | Puṇḍarīka and Viṣṇuloka (*Ibid.* 82. 105) |
| Śālagrāma | Aśvamedha (*Ibid.* 82. 107) |
| Kauśikī | Rājasūya (*Ibid.* 82. 113) |
| Jyeṣṭhila | Agniṣṭoma (*Ibid.* 82. 115) |
| Niścīrā | Aśvamedha and Viṣṇuloka (*Ibid.* 82. 119) |
| Vasiṣṭhāśrama at Niścīrā | Vājapeya (*Ibid.* 82. 121) |
| Devakūṭa | Aśvamedha (*Ibid.* 82. 122) |
| Vīrāśrama | Aśvamedha (*Ibid.* 82. 126) |
| Agnidhārā | Agniṣṭoma (*Ibid.* 82. 127) |
| Pitāmahasaras | Agniṣṭoma (*Ibid.* 82. 128) |
| Gaurīśikhara | Aśvamedha (*Ibid.* 82. 132) |
| Tamrāruṇa | Aśvamedha (*Ibid.* 82. 133) |
| Nandinī | Puruṣamedha (*Ibid.* 82.134) |
| Dharmatīrtha | Vājapeya (*Ibid.* 82. 141) |
| Lohitya | Bahusuvarṇaka (*Ibid.* 83. 2) |
| Karatoyā | Aśvamedha (*Ibid.* 83.3) |
| Gaṅgā and ocean confluence | Aśvamedha (*Ibid.* 83. 4) |
| Śoṇa and Jyotirathyā confluence | Agniṣṭoma (*Ibid.* 83.8) |
| Vaṁśagulma | Aśvamedha (*Ibid.* 83. 9) |
| Vṛṣabhatīrtha | Vājapeya (*Ibid.* 83. 10) |

| Rāmatīrtha | Aśvamedha (*Ibid.* 83. 14) |
|---|---|
| Śrītīrtha | Aśvamedha (*Ibid.* 83. 16) |
| Godāvarī | Gavāmayana (*Ibid.* 83. 30) |
| Confluence of Veṇṇā | Vājapeya (*Ibid.* 83. 3) |
| Citrakūṭa | Aśvamedha (*Ibid.* 83. 56) |
| Śṛṅgaverapura | Vājapeya (*Ibid.* 83. 58) |
| Prayāga | Rājasūya and Aśvamedha (*Ibid.* 83. 76) |
| Bhogāvatī | Aśvamedha (*Ibid.* 83. 81) |
| Pṛthūdaka | Aśvamedha (Sal. P 39.7) |
| Śāṇḍilyāśrama | Aśvamedha (*Ibid.* 53.5ff.) |
| Naimiṣa | Puruṣamedha (Anu. P 26. 32) |
| Gaṅgāhṛda | Aśvamedha (*Ibid.* 26.33) |
| Kapotaka | Puruṣamedha (*Ibid.* 26. 39) |
| Aghamarṣaṇa | Aśvamedha (*Ibid.* 26. 53) |
| Piṇḍāraka | Agniṣṭoma (*Ibid.* 26. 54) |
| Brahmasaras | Puṇḍarīka (*Ibid.* 26. 55) |
| Maināka | Sarvamedha (*Ibid.* 26. 56) |

*Vām Pu.* (SM).

| *Tīrtha* | *Sacrifice* |
|---|---|
| Pāṇikhāta | Rājasūya and knowledge of Saṁkhya and Yoga (15. 51) |
| Pāriplava i.e. Daśakarṇa | Aśvamedha (13. 17) |
| Pauṇḍarīka | Puṇḍarīka (15. 39 cd) |
| River Dṛṣadvatī | Agniṣṭoma and Atirātra (15. 46) |
| Saptasārasvatatīrtha | Performance of all sacrifices. |
| Someśvara | Rājasūya (13. 34) |
| Sūryatīrtha | Agniṣṭoma (14. 26.cd) |
| Sutīrtha | Aśvamedha along with satisfaction of Pitṛ-s (14. 40) |
| Yāyāta | Aśvamedha (18. 37-38) |

*Pad. Pu* Section III

| *Tīrtha* | *Sacrifice* |
|---|---|
| Camasodbheda | Agniṣṭoma (25. 18) |
| Confluence of ocean and Sindhu | Aśvamedha (25. 20) |
| Dīrghasattra | Rājasūya and Aśvamedha |
| Dulikāśrama | Agniṣṭoma (12. 4-5) |
| Kanyāśrama | Sarvamedha(12. 6-7) |
| Koṭitīrtha | Aśvamedha (12. 10-11) |
| Kurukṣetra | Vājapeya and Atirātra (26. 6) |
| Malada | Rājasūya (25. 6) |

| | |
|---|---|
| Maṇimata | Agniṣṭoma (25. 7-8) |
| Prabhāsa | Agniṣṭoma and Atirātra (24. 9) |
| Rudrakoṭī | Aśvamedha (13. 25) |
| Southern end of the sea | Agniṣṭoma |
| Timi | Aśvamedha (24, 25) |
| Vasudhārā | Aśvamedha(24. 26-28) |
| Vitastā | Vājapeya (25. 1-3) |
| Yayātipatana | Aśvamedha (12. 8-9) |

*Mat. Pu* CLXXX. 70-75.
Importance of Avimuktatīrtha:

| *Karman performed* | *Sacrifice* |
|---|---|
| Bathing | Ten Aśvamedha-s |
| Fasting | Sautrāmaṇī |
| Worshipping Śiva | Ten Aśvamedha-s |
| Offering golden flowers | Agnihotra |

*Brahma Pu.* (66. 41 & 67. 69)
(Visiting *tīrtha* is superior to sacrifice)

| *Tīrtha* | *Sacrifice* |
|---|---|
| Ananta | Rājasūya & Aśvamedha |
| Puruṣottama | Aśvamedha |

*Varāha Pu.*

| *Tīrtha* | *Sacrifice* |
|---|---|
| Agniprabhā | Agniṣṭoma (145. 56-58) |
| Akrūratīrtha (bath during eclipse) | Rājasūya and Aśvamedha (155. 4) |
| Ariṣṭakuṇḍa and Rādhākuṇḍa | Rājasūya and Aśvamedha (164. 37) |
| Brahmapada in the month of Kaumuda on Dvādaśī day | Vājapeya (147. 42) |
| Cakrasvāmin (Giving up life) | Vājapeya (145. 41-44) |
| Devagiri | Vājapeya (164. 29) |
| Devahrada | Aśvamedha (145. 82) |
| Kālihrada (Forgoing six meals) | Naramedha (145. 48-49) |
| Koṭivaṭa (giving up life) | Crores of sacrifices (147. 46) |
| Mathurā (bath in river Yamuna) | Rājasūya and Aśvamedha (158. 6-7) |
| Prayāga (bathing and fasting for three nights) | Rājasūya (145. 100) |
| Siddhāśrama | Aśvamedha (145. 97) |
| Sudhana (bath on Dvādaśī in the month of Kaumuda | Rājasūya (155. 72-74) |
| Sūryatīrtha (bath on Sundays) | Rājasūya (152. 58) |
| Viṣṇupada | Atirātra (145. 45-47) |

*Varāha Pu* gives a combination of *tīrtha* and *vrata* at times.

*Nar. Pu* (Utt.)

| *Tīrtha* | *Sacrifice* |
|---|---|
| Bhadradeha (bath) | Aśvamedha (49. 4) |
| Candrapada (performing *srāddha*) | Aśvamedha (45. 23) |
| Dakṣiṇāgnipada (performing *śrāddha*) | Vājapeya (45. 22) |
| Gaṅgā (even one single bath) | Aśvamedha-s (39. 31) |
| Gaṅgādvāra and Kuśāvarta | Seven Rājasūya and two Aśvamedha-s (40. 29) |
| Gayā (*pradakṣiṇā* of the *yūpa*) | Vājapeya (45. 8) |
| Kuśāvarta & Kanakhala (holy dip) | Hundred Agnicit-s/two Jyotiṣṭoma-s/thousand Agniṣṭoma-s (40. 35) |
| Maṇikarṇikā (bath) | Ten thousand Aśvamedha-s (45. 24) |
| Mārkaṇḍeyahrada (worshipping Śiva) | Ten Aśvamedha-s (55. 20) |
| Pañcanada | Rājasūya & Aśvamedha (51. 29b-30a) |
| Pavitra | Two Viśvajit-s (40. 39) |
| Prayāga (ablution) | Rājasūya & Aśvamedha (63. 43) |
| Prayāga (bath) | Rājasūya (63. 41) |
| Prayāga (each step) | Aśvamedha (63.44) |

| Śarayu (worshipping Rudra & Śiva) | Two Viśvajit-s (40. 40) |
|---|---|
| Satyapada (performing *śrāddha*) | Jyotiṣṭoma (45. 23) |
| Sitāsita (dip in the month of Māgha) | Vājapeya (63. 45) |

# Appendix II

## VRATA-S AND DĀNA AND THE FRUIT OF SACRIFICES

*Pad. Pu.*

| *Vrata-s and dāna* | *Sacrifice* |
|---|---|
| Rasakalyāṇinī | Thousand Agniṣṭoma-s (I. 2. 134) |
| Wearing *rudrākṣa* for twelve months to please Āditya | Gomedha or Naramedha (I. 59. 187) |
| Serving Tulasī | Rājasūya (I. 60. 133b-134a) |
| Touching water flowing from Viṣṇu's feet | Crores of time greater than the fruit obtained from crores of sacrifices (IV. 17. 8) |
| *Homa* of Tulasī wood<br>One who offers incense of Tulasī to Viṣṇu | Agniṣṭoma<br>Hundred sacrifices or fruit of donating hundred cows (VI. 23. 25-26) |

| Trisparśa | Greater than all sacrifices |
|---|---|
| Fasting on the Trisparśa | Thousand Aśvamedha-s and hundreds of Vājapeya-s (VI. 34. 8. 38) |
| Mokṣadā Ekādaśī in the bright half of Mārgaśīrṣa | Vājapeya (VI. 39. 12) |
| Saphalā Ekādaśī in the dark half of Pauṣa. Hearing the account of this day | No sacrifice can equal to it One gets the fruit of Rājasūya (VI. 40. 19) |
| Listening and reciting the account of Putradā Ekādaśī in the bright half of Pauṣa | Agniṣṭoma (VI. 41. 53) |
| Śatatilā Ekādaśī falling in the dark half of Māgha | One should perform a sacrifice on this day. (VI. 42. 15a) |
| Listening and reciting to the account of Jayā Ekādaśī falling in the bright half of Māgha | Agniṣṭoma (VI. 43. 54) |
| Vijayā Ekādaśī falling in the dark half of the month of Phālguna | Vājapeya (VI. 44. 39) |
| Kāmadā Ekādaśi falling in the dark half of the month of Caitra | Vājapeya (VI. 47. 39) |
| Mohinī Ekādaśī falling in the month of Vaiśākha | All the sacrifices (VI. 49. 38) |
| Devaśayanī Ekādaśī falling in the bright half of the month of Śrāvaṇa | Vājapeya (VI. 53. 3) |
| Listening to the account of this day | Aśvamedha (VI. 53. 26) |

| | |
|---|---|
| Listening to the account of Kāmikā Ekādaśī falling in the dark half of the month of Śrāvaṇa | Vājapeya (VI. 54. 6) |
| Listening to the account of Ajā Ekādaśī falling in the bright half of the month of Śrāvaṇa | Aśvamedha (VI. 56. 23) |
| Listening and reciting the account of Indirā Ekādaśī falling in the dark half of the month of Āśvina | Vājapeya (VI. 58. 4) |
| Prabodhinī Ekādaśī | Thousand Aśvamedha-s and hundreds of Rājasūya-s (VI. 61. 18) |
| Worshipping Viṣṇu with Tulasī leaves in the month of Kārttika | Hundreds of sacrifices (VI. 64. 3-7) |
| Observing the vows of Cāturmāsa-s | Thousands of Aśvamedha-s (VI. 54. 3-7) |
| Ekādaśī fast | Superior than thousands of Aśvamedha-s and hundreds of Vājapeya-s (VI. 64. 117) |

*Vāyu Pu.*

| *Vrata-s and dāna* | *Sacrifice* |
|---|---|
| Offering incense, fragrant garlands to Pitṛ-s, gum-resins, along with honey and ghee | Aśvamedha (Utt. Anu. 13. 8) |
| Performance of *śrāddha* at Brahmatīrtha | Aśvamedha (Utt. Anu. 15. 54) |
| Offering milk and water to guest<br>By offering ghee to the guest<br>By offering honey to the guest<br>All possessions to the guest | Agniṣṭoma<br>Ṣoḍaśa-sattra(?)<br><br>Atirātra Sarvamedha (Utt. Anu.17.11-12) |
| Donations during *śrāddha* | Puṇḍarīka (Utt. Anu. 16.13) |
| Giving a beautiful residential place | Rājasūya (Utt. Anu. 16. 16) |
| Giving woollen and silk garments, excellent blankets, food, deer-skin to the *brāhmaṇa*-s | Vājapeya (Utt. Anu. 17. 20) |
| Different kinds of food | Agniṣṭoma (Utt. Anu. 18. 4) |

*Brahma Pu.*

| *Vrata-s and dāna* | *Sacrifice* |
|---|---|
| Utthānadvādaśī (first half of Kārttika) | Thousands of Aśvamedha-s and hundreds of Vājapeya-s (64. 52) |
| One with restrained sense-organs | Pañcamahāyajña-s (68. 15) |
| Avoiding consumption of meat | Performance of sacrifices (107. 66) |

*Brahmavai. Pu*

| *Vrata-s and dāna* | *Sacrifice* |
|---|---|
| One who pays obeisance to *brāhmaṇa*-s, having got up early in the morning | All the sacrifices (I. 11. 8) |
| One who drinks water from the feet of a *brāhmaṇa* and eats the Naivedya of a *brāhmaṇa* regularly | Rājasūya (I. 11. 32) |
| Recitation of Brahmeśadharmakavaca | Thousand Aśvamedha-s and hundred Vājapeya-s(I. 19. 59) |
| Recitation of Pṛthivīstotra | Hundred Aśvamedha-s (II. 8. 65) |
| Worships Nārāyaṇa by giving Tulasī leaf<br>Wears Tulasī beads necklace | One lakh Aśvamedha-s<br>Fruit of Aśvamedha at every step (II. 21. 44, 47) |

| | |
|---|---|
| Recitation of Dakṣiṇāstotra | Fruit of many sacrifices (II. 43. 84-87) |
| Recitation of Kṛṣṇakavaca | Rājasūya, Aśvamedha, Naramedha, Vājapeya (III. 31. 49-50) |
| Recitation of Veda | Superior to all sacrifices (IV. Utt. 97. 17) |

*Varāha Pu.*

| *Vrata-s and dāna* | *Sacrifice* |
|---|---|
| Rāmadvādaśīvrata falling in the month of Jyeṣṭha | Becomes a king performing sacrifices (45. 10) |
| Reciting ten chapters of the *Varāha Pu* | Agniṣṭoma and Atirātra sacrifices (217. 16) |

*Nār. Pu*

| *Vrata observed on Śukla Dvādaśī* | *Special form of Viṣṇu* | *Sacrifice (I. 17. 24ff.)* |
|---|---|---|
| Mārgaśīrṣa | Keśava | Pauṇḍarīka |
| Pauṣa | Nārāyaṇa | Eight Agniṣṭoma-s |
| Māgha | Mādhava | Vājapeya |
| Phālguna | Govinda | Gomedha |
| Caitra | Viṣṇu | Eight Atyagniṣṭoma-s |
| Vaiśākha | Madhusūdana | Eight Aśvamedha-s |

| | | |
|---|---|---|
| Jyeṣṭha | Trivikrama | Naramedha |
| Āṣāḍha | Vāmana | Hundred Agniṣṭoma-s |
| Bhādrapada | Hṛṣīkeśa | Brahmayajña |
| Aśvina | Padmanābha | Thousand Brahmayajña-s |
| Kārttika | Dāmodara | Thousand Aśvamedha-s |
| For performing these *vrata*-s | | Vājapeya |

*Nār. Pu.*

| *Vrata-s* | *Sacrifices* |
|---|---|
| Worshipping Kālikā with gifts and offerings | Aśvamedha (III. 84. 33) |
| Propitiating a *brāhmaṇa* on Caitra Śukla Dvitīyā | All sacrifices (IV. 111.2b-3a) |
| Śarkarāsaptamī | Aśvamedha (IV. 116. 23) |
| Worshipping Mahāmāyā by one meal a day | Vājapeya (IV. 118. 29a) |
| Single salutation to Kṛṣṇa | *avabhṛtha* of ten Aśvamedha-s (Utt. 6.1) |

*Bhav. Pu.*

| *Vrata-s* | *Sacrifices* |
|---|---|
| *Vrata* of Pratipadā drinking milk, Dvitīyā saltless diet and Pūrṇimā drinking | Ten-fold fruit of Kuśodaka Aśvamedha |
| If the above *vrata* is undertaken for three months | Hundred Rājasūya-s and Aśvamedha-s sacrifices |
| *Vrata* is undertaken for eight months | Thousand Rājasūya-s and Aśvamedha-s (I. 15. 18-23) |
| Bathing Lord Vibhu with cold water, hot milk and ghee | Thousand Aśvamedha-s (I. 17. 67-68) |
| Worship of Sūrya | Aśvamedha and Rājasūya (I. 96. 5-6) |
| Narrating the vow of worshipping Ravi | Aśvamedha sacrifice (I. 101. 25) |
| Worship of Āditya | Many sacrifices (I. 136, 44-45) |
| Seven Saptamī-s | Ten Aśvamedha-s (I. 195. 22) |
| Reading the Rāmacarita | Ten Aśvamedha-s |
| Reading it from one year | Many sacrifices (I. 216. 79-82) |

*Bhav. Pu. IV. 47. 1-14.*

| *Month (Saptamī)* | *Deity* | *Fruit* |
|---|---|---|
| Māgha | Varuṇa | Agniṣṭoma |
| Phālguna | Āditya | Vājapeya |
| Caitra | Vedāṁśu | Ukthya |
| Vaiśākha | Dhātṛ | Paśubandha |
| Jyeṣṭha | Indra | Vājapeya |
| Āsāḍha | Sun | Bahusuvarṇaka |
| Śrāvaṇa | Ravi | Sautrāmaṇī |
| Bhādrapada | Ravi | *tulādāna* |
| Aśvāyujī | Savitṛ | Giving thousand cows |
| Kārttika | Dineśa | Pauṇḍarīka |
| Mārgaśīrṣa | Bhānu | Rājasūya |
| Pauṣa | Bhāskara | Naramedha |

*Bhav. Pu. IV. 57. 1-57*

| *Kṛṣṇāṣṭamī* | *Worshipping Śiva* | *Fruit* |
|---|---|---|
| Mārgaśīrṣa | Śaṅkara | Atirātra |
| Puṣya | Śambhu | Vājapeya |
| Māgha | Maheśvara | Gomedha |
| Phālguna | Mahādeva | Rājasūya |
| Caitra | Sthāṇu | Aśvamedha |
| Vaiśākha | Śiva | Puruṣamedha |
| Jyeṣṭha | Paśupati | Giving lakh cows |
| Āṣāḍha | Ugra | Rudraloka |
| Śrāvaṇa | Śarva | Bahusuvarṇaka |
| Bhādrapada | Tryambaka | Annadīkṣā |
| Āśvina | Bhava | Pauṇḍarīka |
| Kārttika | Rudra | Agniṣṭoma |

# Bibliography


## SANSKRIT WORDS

### Saṁhitā-s

*Atharvaveda-saṁhitā*: Ed. by Satawalekar, S.D., Aundh, V. Samvat 1995.

*Kāṭhaka- saṁhitā*: Ed. by Satawalekar, S.D., Aundh, V. Samvat 1999.

*Maitrāyaṇī- saṁhitā*: Ed. by Satawalekar, S.D., Aundh, V. Samvat 1998.

*Ṛgveda- saṁhitā* (with Sāyaṇa's commentary): Ed. by Vaidika Samshodhana Mandal, Pune, 1933-51.

*Sāmaveda- saṁhitā*: Ed. by Satawalekar, S.D., with Marathi translation, Bharat Mudranalaya, Pardi, Valsad, 1970.

*Taittirīya- saṁhitā*: Ed. by Satawalekar, S.D., New Print, V. Samvat 2039, Anandashram, Pune, 1948.

*Vājasaneyi- saṁhitā*: Ed. by A. Weber, London, 1852.

### Brāhmaṇa-Texts

*Aitareya Brāhmaṇa*: Pt. I, 2nd ed., Anandashram, Pune, 1930; Pt. II, 3rd ed. Anandashram, Pune, 1977.

*Gopatha Brāhmaṇa*: Ed. by Jivananda Vidyasagar, Calcutta, 1891.

*Jaiminīya Brāhmaṇa*: Ed. by Raghuvira and Lokesh Chandra, MLBD, Delhi, 1986 (1954).

*Jaiminīya Upaniṣad Brāhmaṇa*: Ed. by Sharma, B.R., Kendriya Sanskrit Vidyapeeth, Tirupati, 1967.

Pañcaviṁśa Brāhmaṇa (=*Tāṇḍya Mahabrāhmaṇa*): Kashi Sanskrit Series, Chowkhambha, Benares, 1936.

*Śatapatha Brāhmaṇa*: Chowkhambha Sanskrit Samsthan, 2nd Ed., Varanasi, 1984.

*Taittirīya Brāhmaṇa*: Anandashram, 3rd Ed., Poona, 1979.

## TRANSLATIONS OF THE BRĀHMAṆA-TEXTS

*The Aitareya Brahmanam of the Rigveda*, Vol. I & II: Ed. tr. and explained by Haug, Martin, (Rep.) Bharatiya Publishing House, Delhi, 1977.

*Pañcaviṁśa Brāhmaṇa* (also known as Tāṇḍya Mahabrāhmaṇa): Tr. by Caland, W., Sri Satguru Publications, Delhi, 1983, (rep. Calcutta, 1931).

*The Śatapatha Brāhmaṇa* (According to the text of the Mādhyandina School)Pts. I-V Tr. Eggeling, Julius, Rep. MLBD, Delhi, SBE Vol. 12, 1988 (1882), SBE Vol. 26, 1988 (1885), SBE Vol. 41, 1989 (1894), SBE Vol. 43, 1978 (1885) SBE Vol. 44, 1978 (1900).

## UPANIṢAD-TEXTS

*Īśadi-Aṣṭottaraśatopaniṣad*: Ed. by Pansikar, V.L., Chowkhambha Vidyabhavan, Varanasi, 1991.

## SŪTRA-TEXTS

*Āpastamba Śrauta Sūtra*: Ed. by Richard Garbe in Bibliotheca Indica, Calcutta, 1882-1902.

*Āśvalāyana Gṛhya Sūtra*: Anandashram, Poona, 1936; also tr. and fully explained in Marathi by Pt. Shivaramashastri Shintre, Mumbai, 1938.

*Āśvalāyana Śrauta Sūtra:* Ed. by Ganesh Shastri in Anandashram Sanskrit Series, Poona 1917.

*Baudhāyana Śrauta Sūtra*: Ed. by Caland, W.C., Vol. I & II, Munshiram Manoharlal Publishers, Delhi, 1982, (Calcutta, 1904-13).

*Drāhyāyaṇa Śrauta Sūtra*: Ed. by Reuter, J.N., (part I only), London, 1904.

*Kātyāyana Śrauta Sūtra* along with Devayājñikapaddhati Ed. by Vedacharya Pandit Sri Vidyadhara Sarma, Benares, 1933.

*Lāṭyāyana Śrauta Sūtra*: Ed. by Ananda Chandra, in *Bibliotheca Indica*, Calcutta, 1872.

*Mānava Śrauta Sūtra*: Ed. by Knauer, St. Petersberg, 1900-1903.

*Śāṅkhāyana Śrauta Sūtra*: Ed. by A. Hillebrandt, in *Bibliotheca Indica*, Calcutta, 1886-89.

*Satyāṣāḍha Śrauta Sūtra (=Hiraṇyakeśi Śrauta Sūtra)*: Anandashrama Sanskrit Series, Poona, 1907-32.

*Vaitāna Śrauta Sūtra*: Ed. VVRI, Panjab University, Hoshiarpur, 1952.

## Translations of the Śrauta Sūtra-s

*Kātyāyana Śrauta Sūtra*-s -: (Rules for the Vedic Sacrifices) Tr. into English by Ranade, H.G., published by the author, Poona, 1978

*Śāṇkhāyana Śrauta Sūtra*: Tr. into English by Caland, W., edited with intro. by Lokesh Chandra, The International Academy of Indian Culture, 1953, Nagpur.

## Epics

*The Rāmāyaṇa of Vālmīki*: with the commentary 'Tilaka' Ed. by Panshikar, V.L., Indological Book House, Varanasi, 1983,(1930)

*The Vālmīkirāmāyaṇa*: (Critical Edition Vols. I-VII) Ed. G.K. Bhatt (Vol. I), P.L. Vaidya (Vol. II & VII), P.C. Diwanji (Vol. III), D.R. Mankad (Vol. IV), J.C. Jhala (Vol. V), U.P. Shah (Vol. VII) Gaikwad Oriental Series, Oriental Insitute, Maharaja Sayajirao University, Baroda, 1972-1975.

*The Mahābhārata*: (Text as constituted in the Critical Edition) Vols. I-IV Ed. by Sukthankar, V.S., and band of scholars, BORI, Pune, 1971-1975.

## The Mahāpurāṇa-s

*Agni Purāṇa*: Published by Apte, Hari Narayana, Anandashrama Sanskrit Series, Pune, 1900.

*Bhāgavata Purāṇa*: Gita Press, Gorakhpur, Samvat 2048.

*Bhaviṣya Purāṇa*: Nag Publishers, Delhi, 1984.
*Brahma Purāṇa*: Nag Publishers, Delhi, 1985.
*Brahmāṇḍa Purāṇa*: MLBD, Delhi, 1985.
*Brahmavaivarta Purāṇa*: Ed. by Marathe Vasudevashastri, Anandashrama Sanskrit Series, Pune, 1935.
*Garuḍa Purāṇa*: Nag Publishers, Delhi, 1984.
*Kūrma Purāṇa*: Nag Publishers, Delhi, 1983.
*Liṅga Purāṇa*: MLBD, Delhi, 1985.
*Mārkaṇḍeya Purāṇa*: Nag Publishers, Delhi, 1983.
*Matsya Purāṇa* (Vols. I & II): Nag Publishers, Delhi, 1984.
*Nārada Purāṇa:* Nag Publishers, Delhi, 1984.
*Padma Purāṇa* Vols. I, II, & III): Nag Publishers, Delhi, 1984.
*Śiva Purāṇa*: Nag Publishers, Delhi, 1984.
*Skanda Purāṇa*: Nag Publishers, Delhi, 1984.
*Vāmana Purāṇa*: All India Kashiraj Trust, Varanasi, 1973.
*Varāha Purāṇa*: Asiatic Society, Calcutta, 1893.
*Vāyu Purāṇa*: Nag Publishers, Delhi, 1983.
*Viṣṇu Purāṇa*: Gita Press, Gorakhpur, Saka 2045.

## Translations of the Mahāpurāṇa-s

*Agni Purāṇa* (Vol. Nos. 27-30): Tr. and annotated by Gangadharan, AITM, MLBD, Delhi, 1986.
*Brahma Purāṇa*: (Vol. Nos. 33-36) Tr. and annotated by Board of Scholars, AITM, MLBD, Delhi, 1985.
*Brahmavaivarta Purāṇa*: (Vol. Nos. 22-25) Tr. and annotated by Tagare, G.V., AITM, MLBD, Delhi, 1984.
*Garuḍa Purāṇa*: (Vol. Nos.12-14) Tr. and annotated by Shastri, J.L., AITM, MLBD, Delhi, 1978.
*Liṅga Purāṇa*: (Vol. Nos. 5-6) Tr. and annotated by Board of Scholars, AITM, MLBD, Delhi, 1973.
*Kūrma Purāṇa*: (Vol. Nos. 20-21) Tr. and annotated by Tagare, G.V., AITM, MLBD, Delhi, 1981.
*Mārkaṇḍeya Purāṇa*: Tr. and annotated by Pargiter, Baptist Mission Press, Asiatic Society, Calcutta, 1904.
*Nārada Purāṇa*: (Vol. Nos 15-19) Tr. and annotated by Shastri, J.L., AITM, MLBD, Delhi, 1980.
*Śiva Purāṇa*: (Vol. Nos. 1-4) Tr. and annotated by Board of Scholars, AITM, MLBD, Delhi, 1970.

*Skanda Purāṇa*: (Vol. Nos. 49-56) Tr. and annotated by Board of Scholars, AITM, MLBD, Delhi, 1995.

## Classical Sanskrit Dramas and Mahakavya-s

*Abhijñānaśākuntalam*: Ed. Kale M.R., MLBD, Delhi, 1969 (1898).

*Bhaṭṭikāvyam:* Text and Translation, ed. and tr. Karandikar, M.A. and S. Karandikar, MLBD, Delhi, 1982.

*Jānakīharaṇam:* Tr. Vyasa, Brajmohan,Mitra Prakashan, Pvt. Ltd., Allahabad, 1967.

*Kirātārjunīyam*: Chowkhambha Sanskrit Sansthan, Varanasi, 1987.

*Mahākavibhāsa-:* A Comprehensive Criticism of the Dramas of Bhāsa, Vol. I & II, Ed. Upadhyaya, Baldeva, Chowkhambha Sanskrit Series, Varanasi. (no year given)

*Mahāvīracaritam*: Ed. & tr. Ambardekar, R.R., Adreesh Prakashan, Mumbai,1968.

*Mālatīmādhavam*: Ed. & tr. Kale, M.R., MLBD, New Delhi, 1967 (1913).

*Mālavikāgnimitram*: Ed. Kale, M.R., A.R. Sheth & Co., Mumbai, 1959.

*Naiṣadhīyacaritam*: Ed. Acharya, N.R., Chowkhambha Vidyabhavana, Varanasi, 1998.

*Śiśupālavadham*: Chowkhambha Vidya Bhavan Series, Varanasi, 3rd edition, 1972.

*Uttararāmacaritam*: Ed. & tr. Kale, M.R., MLBD, Delhi, 1982.

*Veṇīsaṁhāram*: Gajendragadkar, A.B., Aryabhushana Press, Poona, 1941 (1922).

*Vikramorvaśīyam*: Ed. Kale, M.R., MLBD, Revised, Delhi, 1991 (1967).

*Works of Kālidāsa*, Vol. 2: Ed. and tr. by Deodhar, C.R., MLBD, Delhi, 1986 (1984).

## Other Texts

*Amarakośa*: Chowkhambha, Delhi, 1985.

*Arthasaṅgraha:* Ed. & tr. by Paranjape, S.M., Bombay, 1927.

*Aṣṭādhyāyī of Pāṇini*: Ed. & tr. by Vasu, S.C., MLBD, Delhi, 1962 (1891).

*Brahmasūtra-s of Bādarāyaṇa*: referred to in Works of Śaṅkarācārya in Original Sanskrit (Vol. III) MLBD, Delhi, 1998 (1985).

*Kāvyaprakāśa of Mammaṭa:* Ed. & tr. by Sir Ganganath Jha, (rev) Chowkhambha Publishers, Delhi, 1985 (1918).

*Manusmṛti*: (with the commentary of Kullūka) Nirnayasagar, Bombay, 1946.

*Mīmāṁsūsutra-s of Jaimini*: (Vol. I & II) Ed. & tr. by Sandal, Mohan Lal., MLBD, Delhi, 1980 (1923-1925).

*Nāṭyaśāstra:* Ed. by Sharma, Batuk Nath and Baladev Upadhyaya, The Kashi Sanskrit Series No. 60, Kashi, 1929.

*The Nighanṭu and the Niruta of Yāska*: Ed. & tr. by Sarup, L., MLBD, Delhi, 1967 (1926).

*Yājñavalkyasmṛti*: (with the commentary Mitākṣarā) Nirnayasagar, Bombay, 1935.

## OTHER TEXTS

Altekar, G.S.: *Studies on Vālmīki's Rāmāyaṇa*, BORI, Research Unit Series No. 9, Pune, 1987.

Bairdeau, Madeline: *Hinduism: The Anthropology of Civilization*, OUP, New Delhi, 1997 (1989).

Bakre, A.B.: *Religion in Social Flux*, Eastern Book Linkers, New Delhi, 1998.

Basham, A.L.: *A Cutural History of India*, Oxford, Clarendon Press, 1975.

Bhat, G.K.: *Sanskrit Natake ani Natakakara*, Srividya Prakashan, Pune, 1980.

Bhattacharyya, N.N.: *Ancient Indian Rituals and their Social Contents*, (rev. & enl.) Manohar, New Delhi, 1996 (1975).

Burde, J.: *Rituals, Mantras and Science: An integral perspective*, MLBD, Delhi, 2004.

Dange, S.A.: *Pastoral Symbolism from the Ṛgveda*, University of Poona, Poona, 1970.

——: *Vedic concept of "Field" and the Divine Fructification*, University of Bombay, Bombay, 1971.

——: *Hindu Dharma ani Tattvajnana*, (Marathi) Shrilekhan Vachan Bhandar, Pune, 1973.

——: *Sexual Symbolism from the Vedic Ritual*, Ajanta Publications, New Delhi, 1979.

——: *Vedic Sacrifices: Early Nature*, Vols. I & II, Aryan Books International, New Delhi, 2000.

——: *Myths from the Mahābhārata*, Vols. I-III, Aryan Books Interanational, New Delhi, 1997-2001.

Dange, (Mrs.) S.S.: *Bharatiya Sahityacha Itihasa*, Vol. I, Maharashtra Vidyapeetha Grantha Nirmiti Mandal, Nagpur, 1975.

——: *Bauddha Dharma ani Tattvajnana*, (Marathi) Continental Publications, Pune, 1980.

——: *Hindu Domestic Rituals—A Critical Glance*, Ajanta Publications, Delhi, 1985.

——: (Ed.) *Sacrifice in India—Concept and Evolution*, Viveka Publications, Aligarh, 1987.

——: *Aspects of Speech in Vedic Ritual*, Aryan Books International, New Delhi, 1996.

——: *Vedic Beliefs and Practices through Arthavāda*, Vols. I & II, Aryan Books International, New Delhi, 2004.

Gonda, Jan.: *Ancient Indian Kingship from the Religious Point of View*, E.J. Brill, Leiden, 1969.

——: *Viṣṇuism and Śaivism—A comparison*, The Athelone Press, London, 1970.

——: *Change and Continuity in Indian Religion*, Munshiram Manoharlal, New Delhi, 1985.

Guruge, Ananda: *The Society of the Rāmāyaṇa*, Abhinava Prakashana, New Delhi, 1989.

Hazra, R.C.: *Studies in the Puranic Records on Hindu Rites and Customs*, MLBD, Delhi, 1975.

Heesterman, J.C.: *The Ancient Indian Royal Consecration*, Houtox, and Co. Gravenhage, 1957.

——: *The Inner Conflict of Tradition*, Oxford University Press, Delhi, 1985.

Hopkins, E.W.: *Epic Mythology*, MLBD, Delhi, 1986 (Strassburg, 1915).

Jamison, Stephanie W.: *The Ravenous Hyenas and the Wounded Sun* (Myth and Ritual in Ancient India), Cornell University Press, Ithaca and London, 1991.

Kak, Subhash: *The Aśvamedha: The Rite and its Logic*, MLBD, New Delhi, 2002.

Kane, P.V.: *History of Dharmaśāstra*, Vol. II, Pts. 1 & 2, BORI, Pune, 1971 (1941), Vol. V, Pt. 1, BORI, Pune, 1962.

Kashikar, C.V.: *Srauta Dharmachi Swarupacikitsa*, Poona University Press, Poona, 1977.

Keith, A.B.: *The Veda of the Black Yajus School, Entitled Taittiriya Sanhita*, Pts. I & II, HOS. Vols. 18 & 19, 2nd Issue, MLBD, Delhi, 1967 (1914).

——: *The Religion and Philosophy of the Veda and Upanishads*, Pt. I, HOS, Vol. 31, Rep. by MLBD, Delhi, 1989(Cambridge, 1925).

Kosambi, D.D.: *The Culture and Civilization of Ancient India in Historical Outline*, Vikas Publishing House New Delhi, 1976.

Kumar, Savitri: *The Puranic Lore of Water-places*, Munshiram Manoharlal, Delhi, 1983.

Nagar, Shantilal: *Varāha in Indian Culture*, Aryan Books International, New Delhi, 1993.

Pande, G.C.: *Studies in the Origins of Buddhism*, MLBD, New Delhi, 1983.

Pillai, Subhramania: *Tree-worship and Ophiliotory*, Annamalai University, Madras, 1948.

Potdar, K.R.: *Sacrifice in the Ṛgveda*, Bharatiya Vidya Bhavan, Mumbai, 1958.

Pusalkar, A.D.: *Bhāsa-A Study*, Bharatiya Vidya Bhavan, Bombay, 1940.

Ram Gopal: *India of Vedic Kalpasutras*, National Publishing House, Delhi, 1959.

Rangarajan, Haripriya: *Varāha Images in Madhya Pradesh (An Iconographical Study)*, Somaiya Publications, Mumbai, 1997.

Saxena, Savitri: *Skanda Purāṇa (A Study)*, Sanjay Prakashan, New Delhi, 2004.

Selvanayagam, Israel: *Vedic Sacrifice: Challenge and Response*, Manohar, New Delhi, 1996.

Shastri, Pushpendra: *The Purāṇas: The Light House of Indian Culture*, Rashtriya Sanskrit Samsthana, New Delhi, 1995.

Skirbekk, Gunnar and Gilge: Nils *A History of Western Thought*, Routledge, London and New York, (English translation) 2001.

Smith, Brian: *Reflections on Resemblance, Ritual and Religion*, Oxford University Press, New York, 1989.

Smith Fredrick M.: *The Vedic Sacrifices in Transition (A Translation and Study of Trikāṇḍamaṇḍana of Bhāskara Miśra)* BORI, Pune, 1987.

Staal, Frits: *Rituals and Mantras: Rules without meaning*. MLBD, Delhi, 1996.

Sukthankar, V.S.: *On the Meaning of the Mahābhārata* (Lectures), The Asiatic Society of Bombay, Bombay,1957.

Suryavanshi, Bhagawan Singh: *Geography of the Mahābhārata*, Ramanand Vidya Bhavan, New Delhi, 1986.

Sutton, Nicolas: *Religious Doctrines in the Mahābhārata*, MLBD, Delhi, 2000.

Thapar Romila: *Aśoka and Decline of Mauryas*, OUP, Delhi, 1973.

Thite, G.U.: *Sacrifice in the Brāhmaṇa Texts,* University of Poona, Poona, 1975.

Upadhyaya, K.: *Dharmasindhu*, Rajesh Prakashana, Pune, 1979.

Vaidya, C.V.: *History of Sanskrit Literature,* Vols. I-III, Parimal, Delhi, 1986.

Winternitz, M.: *History of Indian Literature,* Vol. I & III, MLBD, New Delhi, 1981 & 1985, (Calcutta, 1927).

Yardi, M.R.: *The Mahābhārata: Its Genesis and Growth (A Statistical Study),* BORI, Poona, 1986.

——: *The Rāmāyaṇa: Its Origin and Growth (A Statistical Study),* BORI, Poona, 1994.

## PAPERS

Agrawala, V.S.: "Yajñavarāha: An interpretation", *Purāṇa*, All India Kashiraj Tr.ust, Varanasi, Vol. V, No. 2, 1957.

Bentor, Yale: "Interiorized fire rituals in India and Tibet", *JAOS*, Michigan, 2000, Vol. 120.

Bharadvaj, O.P.: "Vedic Tīrtha-s in the Mahābhārata", *Mahābhārata: The end of an era (Yugānta),* ed. Ajay Mitra Shastri, Aryan Books International, New Delhi, 2004.

Bharati, Agehananda: "Pilgrimage in the Indian Tradition", *History of Religions*, The University of Chicago Press, Chicago, Summer, 1965, Vol. 3, No. 1.

Chakrabarti, Samiran Chandra: "A Study of the Pāriplava", *Indo-Iranian Journal*, Vol. XXXII, Netherlands, 1989.

Dange, S.A.: "Purūravas: A Research for Identity", *A Corpus of Indian Studies*, (Gaurinath Shastri Felicitation Vol.) Sanskrit Pustak Bhandar, Calcutta, 1980.

Dange, (Mrs.) S.S.: "Ritual-setting of the Upanisadic Philosophy", *Journal of the Department of Sanskrit*, University of Calcutta, 1987. LXXII-LXXIII, Poona, 1991-92.

——: "The Severed Head in Myth and Ritual", *Annals of BORI*, Amṛta Mahotsava Vol. No. LXXII-LXXIII, Poona, 1991-92 pub. in 1993.

——: "Prāśitra in Myth and Ritual", *PrabhakarNarayanaSrī (Studies in Indology and Musicology),* Dr. Prabhakar Narayana Kawthekar Felicitation Vol. Pratibha Prakashana, Delhi, 1993.

——: "Yajñapaṇuche Śira" (Marathi) Vidarbha Samshodhana Mandal, *Annual No.* Nagpur, 1997.

——: "Sūta- The Paurāṇika", *Purāṇa,*, All India Kashiraj Trust, Varanasi, Vol. XL, No. 2, 1997.

——: "Concept of God according to the Āraṇyaka-s and the Upaniṣad-s"*Concept of God,* (eds.) K.B. Archak and K. Pratap, Bharat Prakashana, Dharwad, 2003.

——: "Sarpas and Vedic Ritual Tradition", *Journal of the Asiatic Society of Mumbai,* Mumbai, Vol. 79 for 2004, pub. in 2005.

Devasthali, G.V.: "Status of the Atharvaveda", *Indian Antiquary,* Third Series, Popular Prakashan, Jan. 1971.

Dharmadhikari, T.N.: "The Philosophy of Vedic Sacrifice", *Sri Venkatesvara University Oriental Journal,* Vol. XLII, Pts. I & II, Śrī Veṅkaṭeśvara University, Tirupati, 1999.

Dikshitar, V.R.R.: "*South India in the Rāmyaṇa*", Proceedings of the All India Oriental Conference, 1933.

Dubey, D.P.: "The Concept and Practice of Pilgrimage in the *Mahābhārata*", *Mahābhārata: The end of an era (Yugānta),* Ajay Mitra Shastri (ed.), Aryan Books International, New Delhi, 2004.

Luc de Heusch: A Critique of Evans-Pritchard, Net Edition, 1998.

Narsalay, M.: "Vedic King Marutta in the Epics and the Purāṇa-s", *Purāṇa,* Vol. XLV, No. 1, All India Kashiraj Trust, Varanasi, 2003.

Petteri Koskikallio: "Baka Dālbhya: A Complex Character in Vedic Ritual Texts, Epics and Purāṇa-s". (Net edition) *Electronic Journal of Vedic Studies,* Dec. 1995.

Ramachandran, T.N.: "Aśvamedha site near Kalsi", *Journal of Oriental Research,* Madras, Vol. XXI, 1951-152, pp. 1-31.

Rev. Bulcke, C.: "The Genesis of the Bālakāṇḍa", *Journal of the Oriental Institute,* Baroda, Vol. II, No. 4, June, 1953.

Shastree Siddhanta: "Horse sacrifices in the Kali age", *VVRI.* Dr. Visva Bandhu Commemoration Vol. I Hoshiarpur, 1974.

Thite, G.U.: "Antipathy to the Rājasūya: Why?", *Sambodhi,* Patan, Vol. I, No. 4, 1972.

Thite, G.U.: "Vedic Ritual: Kālidāsa and Bhavabhūti", *Three Mountains and Seven Rivers,* Prof. Musashi Tachikawa's Felicitation volume, ed. Shoun Hino & Toshihiro Wada, MLBD, Delhi, 2004.

Tarde, Bhagyashree: "Shunahshepache Akhyana: Kahi Samajika Sandarbha", (unpublished) presented at the Brihanmaharashtra Prachyavidya Parishad, Goa, 2004.

Winternitz, M.: "The Serpent Sacrifice mentioned in the Mahābhārata", *Journal of the Royal Asiatic Society*, tr. By N.B. Udgikar, London, 1925.

## ENCYCLOPEDIAS AND DICTIONARIES

*A Sanskrit English Dictionary*: M. Monier Williams, MLBD, 1995, (OUP, 1872).

*The Oxford English Dictionary*: Vol. III, XVIII, XIX Oxford University Press, Second Edition, 1989.

*A Dictionary of Vedic Rituals*: (Based on the Śrauta and Gṛhya Sūtra-s) Chitrabhanu Sen, Concept Publishing Company, Delhi, 1978.

*Encyclopedia of Puranic Beliefs and Practices*, Dange, S.A., Navrang Publications, Delhi, Vol. I – 1986, Vol. II – 1987, Vol. III – 1987, Vol. IV – 1989, Vol. V- 1990.

*Encyclopedia of Religion*, Vol. XII Ed. Mircea Eliade, Macmillan Publishing Company, New York, 1987.

*Bharatiya Samskritikosha*, Vol. III. (Marathi) Ed. Joshi, Mahadevashastri and Hodavar, Padmaja, Rep. Anamol Prakashan, Pune, 1993(Maharashtra Samskriti Mandal, Pune, 1967).

# Index